Twentieth-Century Oklahoma

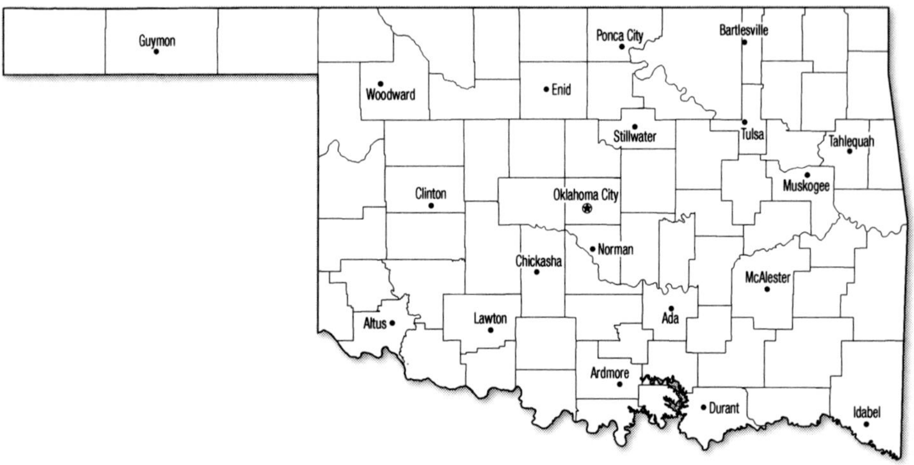

Guymon
Ponca City
Bartlesville
Woodward
Enid
Stillwater
Tulsa
Tahlequah
Muskogee
Clinton
Oklahoma City
Norman
Chickasha
McAlester
Ada
Altus
Lawton
Ardmore
Durant
Idabel

Twentieth-Century Oklahoma

Reflections on the Forty-Sixth State

by Richard Lowitt

University of Oklahoma Press : Norman

This book is published with the generous assistance of the Wallace C. Thompson Endowment Fund, University of Oklahoma Foundation.

Library of Congress Cataloging-in-Publication Data

Lowitt, Richard, 1922–
Twentieth-century Oklahoma : reflections on the forty-sixth state / by Richard Lowitt. — First edition.
pages cm
Includes bibliographical references and index.
ISBN 978-0-8061-4910-3 (pbk. : alk. paper)
1. Oklahoma—History—20th century. 2. Oklahoma—Politics and government—20th century. I. Title.
F701.L68 2015
976.6'053—dc23

2015022544

The paper in this book meets the guidelines for permanence and durability of the Committee on Production Guidelines for Book Longevity of the Council on Library Resources, Inc. ∞

For Kelly Brown and Carolyn Hanneman,
who made it happen,
and to the memory of
John Caldwell and Danney Goble,
who inspired it

Contents

Illustrations

Maps

Table

Text Acknowledgments

All articles and redactions thereof from the *Chronicles of Oklahoma* are published with permission of the Oklahoma Historical Society.

Chapter 1 originally appeared as "Regionalism at the University of Oklahoma," *Chronicles of Oklahoma* 73, no. 2 (1995): 150–71.

Chapter 2 originally appeared as "'Dear Miss Debo': The Correspondence of E. E. Dale and Angie Debo," *Chronicles of Oklahoma* 77, no. 4 (1999): 372–405.

Chapter 3, "Environmental and Cultural Ecology," copyright © Oklahoma Historical Society 2009. Reprinted, by permission of the Oklahoma Historical Society, from *The Encyclopedia of Oklahoma History* (Oklahoma City: Oklahoma Historical Society, 2009), vol. 1, pp. 453–57.

Chapter 4 originally appeared as "Fort Sill Enters the Missile Age," *Chronicles of Oklahoma* 83, no. 4 (2005–6): 389–402.

Chapter 5 is a redaction of "From Termination to Self-Determination: Indian Health in Oklahoma, 1954–1980, Part 1," *Chronicles of Oklahoma* 85, no. 4 (2007–8): 436–67; and "From Termination to Self-Determination: Indian Health in Oklahoma, 1954–1980, Part 2," *Chronicles of Oklahoma* 86, no. 1 (2008): 32–63.

Chapter 6 originally appeared as "Forty Feet Under: Kaw City and the Kaw Project on the Arkansas River, 1957–1976," *Chronicles of Oklahoma* 84, no. 4 (2006–7): 388–426.

Chapter 7 is a redaction of "Water and Power: Developing the Grand River Dam Authority, Part 1, 1935–1944," *Chronicles of Oklahoma* 87, no. 2 (2009): 132–65; and "Power for the People: Developing the Grand River Dam Authority, Part 2, 1945–1964," *Chronicles of Oklahoma* 87, no. 3 (2009): 260–93.

Chapter 8 originally appeared as "The 1969 Oklahoma City Garbage Strike," *Chronicles of Oklahoma* 88, no. 4 (2010–11): 462–91.

Chapter 9 is a redaction of "The Farm Crisis in Oklahoma, Part 1," *Chronicles of Oklahoma* 89, no. 3 (2011): 338–63; and "The Farm Crisis in Oklahoma, Part 2," *Chronicles of Oklahoma* 89, no. 4 (2011–12).

Chapter 10 originally appeared as "The Enigma of Mike Monroney," *Chronicles of Oklahoma* 91, no. 1 (2013): 4–39. 000

Chapter 11 originally appeared as "Oklahoma's Mike Synar Confronts the Western Grazing Question, 1987–2000," *Nevada History* 47, no. 2 (2004): 77–111.

Twentieth-Century Oklahoma

Introduction

When I joined the faculty at the University of Oklahoma more than twenty years ago, I was intrigued with the research opportunities on campus and in nearby Oklahoma City. Since then I have published seven books and prepared numerous articles, eleven of which appear in this volume. I was and still am fascinated with the state's colorful but complex history. The Indian Territory was initially a dumping ground for displaced eastern tribes and a land of opportunity for poverty-stricken blacks and whites fleeing oppression in the Deep South; the only leavening influence came with the early arrival of settlers from Kansas on the northern fringe who were largely Methodist and Presbyterian compared to the more evangelical outlook of the other settlers. Melding these groups to create the forty-sixth state produced a fascinating history similar to and yet markedly different from those of its neighboring states.

At the university, I began exploring the vast treasures of the Western History Collections and soon found myself probing the archives of the university press, whose first director, Joseph Brandt, had published several important books attracting both regional and national attention. *Deserts on the March*, by Paul Sears, is a notable example. At the same time, a small group of Kiowa artists nurtured their talents on campus and likewise gained widespread recognition. My research of these themes, as well as the fate of Angie Debo's manuscript "And Still the Waters Run," led to my first article published in the *Chronicles of Oklahoma*, "Regionalism at the University of Oklahoma" (1995).

It was followed in 2000 by an article examining the ties binding Edward Everett Dale and Angie Debo. While Dale and Debo hailed from similar backgrounds and were alike in many ways, they were locked in a close master-student relationship. Seeking to launch an academic career in the darkest days of the Great Depression, Debo received little help from her mentor until a fortuitous letter to Alfred A. Knopf turned her career around. As she gained in scholarly renown, her relationship with Dale also changed, though she always remained deferential.

It was the appearance of these articles in the *Chronicles* that led to an invitation to prepare an entry in the *Encyclopedia of Oklahoma History and Culture* examining the environment and cultural ecology of the state. This assignment prompted wide reading and much thought on my part. I envisioned Oklahoma as a land of transitions conflicted initially in outlook between Native Americans and the horde of settlers seeking land. Transition was also evident in land use predicated on varying soils. Timber and wildlife also fit into the picture, along with eastern and western, as well as urban and rural, transitions, among others. Like every other state, Oklahoma is continually changing, but outlines of the basic tensions and the various contours can still be discerned.

Preparing this entry stimulated my interest in land use, first in the Oklahoma Panhandle, which resulted in a brief book, *American Outback*, and then in southwestern Oklahoma. At the end of World War II, Fort Sill, home to the field artillery training center, was faced with oblivion as missile technology made caissons and cannons obsolete. Seeking to develop a viable use of missiles, officials at Fort Sill created a storm of controversy when their plans threatened the adjacent wildlife preserve and some of the best agricultural land in the state. The proposal affected politics from the local level to the nation's capital. It led to disputes within the military and embittered civilian-military relations. The matter was resolved in Washington, but it took a while for tensions to abate in southwestern Oklahoma.

While preparing the article on Fort Sill, I had the opportunity to tag along with a Choctaw colleague who was driving a student to the Indian Hospital in Lawton, the home of Fort Sill. The visit prompted an interest in Indian health that resulted in a two-part article. What unfolded was an abysmal tale of inadequate facilities, too many poorly trained doctors, and limited care that was unavailable to Indians in the state's two largest cities. Too many administrators were concerned more with their civil service status than with the health of their patients. It was a tale of woe. But change did occur. Indians gained control of the program. Attention was given to the needs of urban Indians. Efforts to improve facilities made some headway. But doctors who sought to understand their patients, their culture, and their history were still few and far between.

While Indian history hitherto had never commanded my attention, water power was a long-standing interest, as it was for Senator Robert S. Kerr. A key player in the development of the Arkansas River, the last major undeveloped river in the United States, Kerr became involved in what was known as the Kaw Project, the construction of a dam on the Arkansas, only after prominent business leaders in Ponca City asked that he integrate the proposal into the system already partially developed. I became interested when I learned that an entire community, Kaw City, was flooded to make way for this project. Taking down Kaw City, construction of the dam, clearing land titles, and numerous other chores became the responsibility of the Corps of Engineers, which generated controversy as it proceeded. The project brought class tensions within Kay County, where the dam was to be located, to the fore and led to conflict with other federal agencies. The article can serve as a case study of the factors involved in the construction of a major dam on a major waterway.

From the Kaw Project to the lone public power project in Oklahoma was an obvious next step. The Grand River Dam Authority (GRDA) involved projects constructed and paid for by the federal government and turned over to the state to administer. It was a long, arduous effort, and as would be expected, it aroused opposition and would not have happened but for the yeoman work of Congressman Wesley E. Disney during the New Deal. In the postwar years, Senator Robert S. Kerr continued the fight to its conclusion in the last year of his life. Power generated by the project stimulated the economy of eastern Oklahoma and turned a long-depressed area into the most prosperous part of the state. Today GRDA and the leading private utility work in harmony to meet power demands in the area. My article on the subject was published in 2009.

While I became aware of the 1969 garbage strike in Oklahoma City soon after I arrived on campus, I occasionally wondered why no scholar had deemed it worthy of study. It was not until I read Michael K. Honey's remarkable book *Going Down Jericho Road*, a study of "the Memphis strike, Martin Luther King's last campaign," that I decided to look into the minor but significant strike in Oklahoma City a year later. There were similarities: an intransigent and largely racist bureaucracy, poorly paid and overworked garbage workers, a restive black community and indifferent white power structure. The strike attracted the attention of both the National Association for the Advancement of Colored People and the Southern Christian Leadership Conference. Garbage collection was disrupted as workers and supporters practiced passive resistance. Every black official in the city spent some time in jail, as did several clerics. It brought to public attention Clara Luper, who had previously trained youth in the NAACP in passive resistance. She now practiced it, playing a large role in the remarkable standoff between strikers and police in front of the city hall. The dispute was finally resolved through the intervention of Chamber of Commerce leaders, with an assist from the governor. The strike unified the black community, strengthened its pride, and broadened the outlook of most urban residents.

The next article in this medley brought me back to agriculture, a longstanding interest. While I focus on the farm crisis in Oklahoma, the situation was replicated in varying degrees throughout the breadbasket of mid-America and involved many cattlemen as well. Government both caused and eventually resolved the crisis after much turmoil.

Its roots can be traced back to the war in Vietnam, when the U.S. government refused to raise taxes and thereby allowed inflation to make headway. The situation was further exacerbated when the Nixon administration reversed New Deal farm policy that sought to keep supply and demand somewhat in balance. Soon farmers and ranchers were caught in a cost-price squeeze of increasing intensity, with their fixed costs rising and their cattle and crops declining in value. Along with Earl Butz, Nixon's agriculture secretary, urging farmers to plant from fence post to fence post, there were embargoes curbing the sale of American grain while allowing foreign beef to enter the country without serious restrictions. In addition, every farm bill designed to assist beleaguered farmers was vetoed by the president, and no agriculture secretary echoed the farmers' concerns. Farm state members of Congress were not numerous and powerful enough to command the attention of their colleagues. To survive, farmers had to go deeper into debt and make other adjustments. And while a new organization, American Agriculture, championed their cause, protests received some attention but prompted no government response. Finally, with the complete collapse of the farm credit system, which accentuated the plight of rural Americans, government finally responded. How this crisis played out in Oklahoma is what I examined in this article.

Mike Monroney, long-serving congressman and senator, attracted my attention shortly after I arrived in Norman. His notable accomplishments, the Postal Training Center in Norman and the Aeronautical Center in Oklahoma City, added immeasurably to the welfare of the state and to his high regard among constituents. Certainly his career was worthy of scholarly attention. However, early on I learned that not only had Monroney burned most of his papers but the files on deposit in the Carl Albert Center are chiefly constituent mail and offer little insight. In 2002, after completing an earlier project, I decided to probe the enigma of Mike Monroney. Thanks to Allan Cromley, who covered Okies in Congress for the *Oklahoman* during Monroney's tenure in the Senate, and whose papers repose in the Carl Albert Center, I was able to get a handle on the problem. Fearful of being deeply entangled in the controversies provoked by Joseph McCarthy, Monroney sought "safe" topics and tempered his friendship with liberal colleagues and associates. The measures he endorsed called for legislative reform, promoting aviation, and other causes that would enhance his approval among voters who reelected him until 1968, when, owing to his vigorous support of the war in Vietnam as increasing numbers of Oklahomans were wearying of the conflict, he was defeated. Monroney retired comfortably in Washington, joining corporate boards and leading an active social life released from the tensions of public service.

The final chapter, the only one that does not have Oklahoma as its focus, examines a controversy launched and waged by Oklahoma congressman Mike Synar. Beginning in 1987, Synar, a rancher-lawyer, challenged western ranchers who grazed cattle on public lands at ridiculously low fees compared to the costs incurred by ranchers, like himself, who utilized privately owned lands. Synar wanted to raise those western ranchers' fees, and the furor that resulted divided the Congress, angered the Reagan administration, aroused the West, and ended with a Supreme Court decision. Synar, who served eight terms in Congress, died in 1996 before the issue was resolved.

I need to express my appreciatiion for the careful and critical reading of the manuscript by Linda Reese. She improved it by updating notes, correcting factual errors, and making suggestions, most of which I accepted. And to Charles Rankin and his staff at the University of Oklahoma Press, who redacted the articles cited in the text acknowledgments.

« 1 »

Regionalism at the University of Oklahoma

In the 1920s many American intellectuals exiled themselves in Europe to protest the new America that emerged following the First World War. The normalcy of Warren G. Harding's presidency, followed by that of his bland successor, Calvin Coolidge, appalled them. The mass-production, mass-consumption, and increasingly Catholic and urban America populated largely by recent Eastern and Central European immigrants added to their disenchantment. The new America, they believed, stifled creativity and limited their options. They sought a European haven, and many found Paris ideal.

At the same time, other American intellectuals reshaped old disciplines and developed new ones. New currents of thought opened all scholarly fields to gusts of fresh air and made clear the inadequacy of those approaches that considered only articulate elite groups and established frames of reference. Scholars in the humanities and the social sciences began to consider how people who lived in the past thought and behaved. People who found themselves out of the mainstream of American life normally received little recognition. Within that context there appeared in the 1920s, primarily on college campuses outside the Northeast and heavily urban areas, a nascent interest in regionalism devoted to the examination of all aspects of culture that had largely been ignored.[1]

Regionalists rejected the discontinuity they saw in the East with its smokestack factories and immigrants; they foresaw cultural disintegration in the wake of an industrialized urban society and sought to substitute a culture more reflective of regional roots. The University of Oklahoma witnessed many aspects of the regional approach.[2]

Central to the development of regionalism on the campus was William Bennett Bizzell, who became president of the university in 1925 following an eleven-year stint as president at Texas Agricultural and Mechanical College. Bizzell, a published scholar and a bibliophile of some repute, encouraged and supported scholarship. During his tenure (1925–1942), the regional impulse at the university reached its apogee before going into eclipse. It came to public attention in a most dramatic way. Near Anadarko in western Oklahoma several young Kiowas were tenaciously sketching and drawing, despite parental and Indian school disapproval. They drew from a cultural heritage gleaned from close association with their elders and with such intensity that their work eventually came to the attention of Oscar B. Jacobson, head of the School of Art at the university. Jacobson, a well-respected artist, had a long-standing interest in Indian art. Once he became aware of the Kiowa artists, Jacobson determined to encourage their endeavors. He invited them to Norman so he could be of immediate and direct assistance.

Early in 1927 six Kiowa artists, five men and one woman, accepted Jacobson's invitation and settled into a room in the art department, where they worked in relative privacy. Jacobson and a colleague, Edith Mahier, provided quality materials, concern, and interest without tampering in any way with the artists' highly individual style. Jacobson did, however, make them aware of art history in after-hours lectures conducted in his home. Thanks to the encouragement and knowledge they received, the Kiowa artists made a notable contribution to regional culture, a contribution Jacobson brought to public attention.

Before 1927 was out, the art of these artists had gained national recognition when displayed at the convention of the American Federation of Arts. Thereafter galleries throughout the United States exhibited their works to a wide and appreciative audience. In 1928 the Kiowas officially adopted Jacobson as a tribal member. Later that year the artists exhibited their work in Prague, Czechoslovakia, at an international art festival, and a folio of Kiowa paintings published in France soon followed. During the New Deal, the artists painted murals for buildings at the University of Oklahoma and on other campuses, for the Oklahoma Historical Society, and for hospitals, libraries, and post offices. Two of the Kiowa artists produced a set of magnificent murals in the recently constructed Department of the Interior building in Washington, D.C. All of this success was a result of the tremendous stimulus these southern plains Indians had received—thanks to the efforts of Jacobson and Mahier, who insisted that Indian painting be seriously examined as real art—on the campus of the University of Oklahoma.[3]

The work of a member of the English department, Walter S. Campbell, better known by his pen name, Stanley Vestal, also brought recognition to the university as a center of regional culture. His first book, *Fandango: Ballads of the Old West*, published in 1927 by Houghton-Mifflin Company, was followed in quick succession by an amazing number of books (twenty-seven by 1955), almost all of which focused on western, especially southwestern, themes.

Born on a claim in Kansas, Vestal came to western Oklahoma during territorial days. His stepfather served as the first president of the state normal school at Weatherford, from which Vestal graduated in 1908. The first Rhodes Scholar from the new state of Oklahoma, he came to the University of Oklahoma in 1915. Following military service, he resumed his teaching duties and soon began writing.

Feeling uncomfortable living in a region with a paucity of local literature but resonating with history and legend, he set out to create a regional literature, publishing biographies, novels, historical works, short stories, articles, poems, editions of documents, and edited books. Historical biography, however, became his chief occupation. From his boyhood days in western Oklahoma, he had developed an abiding interest in the history of the Southwest and particularly of the Indians of the Great Plains. He knew many "old-timers," and his stepfather had served as one of Hubert Howe Bancroft's researchers in western history. Throughout his career, Vestal traveled over the Great Plains and Rocky Mountains, diligently researching the subjects about which he wrote. He wanted to portray the American Indian, notably Sitting Bull, as a fully developed human being. Because the majority of his books were published outside of the region, Vestal brought the history of the American West to a large audience and called attention to the University of Oklahoma as a center of regional culture through his insistence, self-evident in his writings, that people have a right to claim their cultural inheritance.[4]

Another authentic native of the Southwest, with a background totally different from Vestal's, was Edward Everett Dale, who also brought the region, particularly Oklahoma, before a large audience. During the Bizzell years, Dale headed the Department of History. His great contribution lay in the acquisition of remarkable and invaluable western history collections that distinguished the university and attracted both scholars and the general public.

Born in Texas, Dale came to Oklahoma Territory at an early age. In his youth he worked for a time as a cowboy and later with one of his brothers as the owner of a ranch in southwestern Oklahoma, where he also taught in country schools. Already in his late twenties in 1906, he enrolled as a history major at Central State Normal School (University of Central Oklahoma) at Edmond and completed his undergraduate degree in 1911 at the University of Oklahoma. During his college years and immediately thereafter he served as superintendent of schools in several Oklahoma towns. In 1913 he entered Harvard, where he received a doctoral degree in 1922. He completed his dissertation, a study of the range cattle industry in Oklahoma, under the direction of Frederick Jackson Turner, the founding father of frontier history.

Turner captured Dale's imagination because he posed provocative and imaginative questions about the character of American society. Opposing the institutional slant of most historical studies, Turner stressed the connectedness of multiple forces shaping American history. By encouraging a regional approach, Turner and his students shifted historical inquiry away from the Northeast and began to examine the evolution of society. Dale's study of the range cattle industry brought attention to "common people" from backgrounds comparable to his own. Whether he recognized it or not, Dale wrote history "from the bottom up."

Dale came to the university as an instructor and by 1924 was head of the Department of History. Shortly thereafter he went to Washington to help prepare for the Bureau of Agricultural Economics a manuscript on the range cattle industry of the Great Plains, which, when published, established him as a major western historian. Invited to join a team surveying Indian affairs under the direction of Lewis Meriam, Dale spent the better part of a year visiting reservations and mission schools throughout the West.

As a scholar and teacher, Dale helped establish Oklahoma as part of a region with a fascinating and distinctive heritage. Meriam wrote Bizzell that the members of the survey staff well understood why Bizzell called Dale "one of the best loved men in Oklahoma." The staff found in him "that rare and happy combination of scholar, southern gentleman, breezy western cowpuncher, poet and story teller and kindly gentle human being." All his numerous publications in one way or another related to Oklahoma, as did his service as president of the State Folklore Association from 1915 to 1919 and briefly as associate editor of *The Chronicles of Oklahoma*.[5] Dale also collected documentary material pertaining to Oklahoma history, "including some twenty-five or thirty thick volumes of letters of Stand Watie, Boudinot, the Ridges, and other prominent Cherokees" plus a remarkably complete set of Choctaw papers. The Western History Collections, a major repository of both printed and manuscript materials focusing on Indians, Oklahoma, and the Southwest, got under way in 1927, when Frank Phillips, a prominent Oklahoma oilman, contributed $10,000—$2,000 annually for five years—to launch the collection. Phillips later renewed the grant for another five years. Dale supervised the growth of the collections, acquiring a notable donation of 625 volumes dealing with American Indians from the Brookings Institution and the *Indian-Pioneer Papers*, a set of 132 volumes of interviews of Indians and settlers conducted by members of a Works Project Administration team in the 1930s. More than his individual scholarship, Dale's contribution to the Western History Collections permanently established the university as an important center of regional culture.

In 1934 Dale received a grant of $1,500 from the Rockefeller Foundation that enabled him and two associates to tour eastern Oklahoma for five weeks, locating and logging historical materials that pertained to the various Indian tribes. What made collecting and researching Oklahoma history so fascinating to Dale was the compression of Turner's various stages of frontier development into a time frame that encompassed his own lifetime. Turner wrote about it; Dale lived it.[6]

In 1930 Dale tried unsuccessfully to shift his focus to more immediate concerns. With the active support of President Bizzell and the director of the university press, Joseph A. Brandt, Dale considered holding an annual Indian Institute at the university, "modeled somewhat upon the meetings devoted to politics and governmental affairs held each year at Williamstown and at Charlottesville." Because more than "one-third of all the Indians" of the United States lived in Oklahoma and the state had "a very considerable Indian problem," Dale believed an institute would lead to better cooperation between officials of the Indian Bureau, the commissioner of the Five Civilized Tribes, and superintendents in Oklahoma and a number of other states, plus others concerned with Indian rights and Indian welfare, as well as to a better understanding among the state's Indian leaders and government officials on issues of regional concern. In addition, the institute would help establish the University of Oklahoma as a center of Indian studies. Combined with the Western History Collections, it would also establish the university as the leading institution in the country concerned with Indian affairs, and Dale would be a key figure in its development.[7]

Money presented the biggest problem, and in 1930 funding simply could not be found. The proposal never got off the ground, but with the benefit of hindsight a lesson became evident in the effort: any attempt to discuss current issues that in any way discredited influential individuals in Oklahoma, their interests, and/or their political views would not be tolerated. As long as the university emphasized regional culture by examining the past, by encouraging arts and crafts, by being of service to the state, its industries, and its citizens, all would be well. Once regional concerns flowed outside those limitations, within the university or statewide, controversy arose.

At the time Dale made an effort to influence a broader public by giving a series of lectures "to the reporters and members of the editorial staff of the Times and Daily Oklahoman . . . on Oklahoma and Oklahoma History." He thought he had them "pretty well educated on a good many things," only to find they had "gone very far afield in regard to the Indian Bureau policy in Oklahoma." Even so, Dale did not believe the editorials and articles, feeling that they were "based upon complete misinformation and show complete ignorance in regard to the situation." The material Dale complained about concerned Indian education and the fact that rural counties containing large areas of nontaxable Indian lands could not adequately support public education by taxes on the property of each school district.[8] Challenging the status quo had never entered the minds of anyone participating in the developing regional movement on the Norman campus.

In 1928, with the establishment of the University of Oklahoma Press, Bizzell brought his promotion of culture to fruition and propelled the university to the forefront of regionalism. The appointment of Joseph A. Brandt as press director, responsible for maintaining scholarly standards and exercising publishing initiatives without the assistance of an advisory board or controlling committee, fit Bizzell's vision perfectly. Bizzell, a book lover and discriminating collector, had recently obtained funding for a handsome new library building. The need to overhaul the printing plant and a desire to publish a monthly alumni magazine provided the impetus for establishing the press.

Brandt, a graduate of the university and a Rhodes Scholar, came to Norman from the city room of the *Tulsa Tribune.* He brought with him a plan for the development of a pioneering regional press. "The year 1928," Brandt later recalled, was "more or less the Year 1 of regional book publishing." The Southwest had been explored by Spaniards and inhabited by Indians, and those were the topics the press emphasized (without, of course, ignoring other worthwhile manuscripts). The press came to national attention for its recognition of the Southwest as a distinct cultural region.[9]

The region with "the antiquities of Spanish Indian civilization" provided the background for a vivid consciousness that found expression in a regional miscellany entitled *Folk-Say*, the first volume published by Brandt and edited by Benjamin Albert Botkin. Botkin came to the university fresh from Harvard and Columbia in 1921. As a member of the English department, at the same time he was pursuing a doctoral degree at the University of Nebraska under folklorist Louise Pound. Botkin focused his attention on the Southwest, on the natural and social settings that both colored the thoughts and conditioned the behavior of its residents.

Folk-Say appeared in 1929 as a paperback publication of the Oklahoma Folklore Society, in an edition limited to 250 copies. Another 250 copies were printed, and the volume quickly became a collector's item. For the most part it was the work of Oklahoma writers, illustrated by Oklahoma artists, and printed by the newly established University of Oklahoma Press. Published in 1930 under the imprint of the press instead of the Folklore Society, the first volume cost one dollar. A second edition, running to 473 pages, sold for five dollars. That volume brought the University of Oklahoma Press to national attention, receiving a favorable notice on the front page of the *New York Times Book Review* section.

Two more volumes of *Folk-Say*, neither of which were best sellers, followed. Rather than focusing on the past, the later volumes concerned themselves with contemporary issues, reflected the crisis of the Great Depression, and examined cultural, racial, and class conflicts. The 1932 volume was temporarily suppressed and the series later suspended when, Botkin noted, "Oklahomans discovered that folklore and creative writing based on the folk are not always reading for children." While Botkin persevered to make the four volumes of *Folk-Say* "the organic focus of the folk and regional movement in America," he also began to question whether the development of regionalism flowed into "the whole problem of the contemporary economic system."[10]

While Brandt considered *Folk-Say* "a step in advance for University Press Publications," he followed those volumes with other significant regional publications. Another work, although one that failed to receive significant attention, was *Oklahoma Place Names* by Charles N. Gould, published in 1933. A professor of geology at the university, Gould had broad experience with both the Oklahoma Geological Survey and the United States Geological Survey. As a consulting geologist, he engaged chiefly in petroleum investigations. He arrived at the university in 1900, and in the course of his tenure he published numerous bulletins and scientific articles dealing with the minerals and geology of Oklahoma and other plains states. Traveling throughout Oklahoma, Gould always kept in mind the origin of place names. He divided his book into five chapters: "Linguistic Origins," "Physiographic Names," "Names of Counties and County Seals," "Names of Postoffices and Towns," and "Historic Names." "Oklahoma," wrote one delighted reader, "has more languages, more legends and more history than any state in the Union," all of which added to the romantic aura surrounding the state and its people.[11]

A year earlier, in 1932, Brandt had taken another step that projected the press and the university as a major center of southwestern regionalism. Brandt launched the Civilization of the American Indian Series, and by 1994 the press had published more than two hundred volumes devoted to aboriginal, historical, and contemporary Indian life. Oscar Jacobson prepared the press colophon, which featured an Indian peace pipe, but he brought the idea to Brandt too late for its use on the first books in the series, already on their way to the binder. The neglect of Indians, their language, and their civilization had long been a matter of concern to Brandt. Little effort, he believed, had been made to reconstruct Indian civilization in American universities. The Civilization of the American Indian series allowed the press to remedy that situation and make the university the logical center of Indian research in the United States.[12]

The third volume in the series, *Wah'Kon-Tah* by John Joseph Mathews, attracted national attention as part of a dual selection by the Book of the Month Club. A member of the Osage tribe and a graduate of the University of Oklahoma and Oxford, Mathews utilized the journal of Laban Miles, appointed in 1878 as agent for the Osage tribe, as the basis for his book. Before his death in 1931 Miles had asked Mathews to use the journal to keep alive his memories of the tribe. In *Wah'Kon-Tah*, Mathews reproduced a vanishing world of men and imagination, preserving through character sketches and interpolated roles the lives of dignified human beings before their culture declined as a result of the exploitation of oil reserves on their land.

Another volume that attracted attention was the first doctoral dissertation published in the series. Angie Debo submitted *The Rise and Fall of the Choctaw Republic* to her mentor, Edward Everett Dale. Published as the sixth volume in the Civilization of the American Indian Series, it received the Dunning Prize from the American Historical Association as the best contribution to American history in 1934. Thanks to the attention received by Mathews's and Debo's volumes, plus other solid studies, Brandt's vision of the University of Oklahoma as a center for the study of the American Indian took a long step forward.[13]

In 1930 Brandt considered publishing a "true account of Judge [Isaac] Parker's famous court at Fort Smith." Bizzell, however, was "rather inclined to think that we should not publish anything that might be questioned by the public." In 1935 the press published such a book, but instead of being criticized by the public, *Deserts on the March* by Paul B. Sears proved itself the most successful volume published during Brandt's tenure. Rather than glorify the rich cultural heritage of the region, Sears, like Botkin before him and Angie Debo later, raised questions and probed issues that touched current concerns and cast Oklahoma and some of its people in an unfavorable light.[14]

Sears, who headed the botany department, firmly believed that science could be an instrument of social good. His book appeared as dust storms turned day into night and wreaked havoc on the plains. Winner of a Book of the Month Club prize and discussed on the weekly radio show of the popular historian Hendrik Willem Van Loon, Sears's book examined the devastation of agricultural lands by flooding and soil erosion, as well as possible remedial action. Implicit in his discussion was the premise that farmers throughout the Great Plains, either through ignorance or greed or both, caused much of the suffering they experienced. It was not the railroads, eastern capital, or other outside interests that turned millions of acres into veritable deserts. The stewards of the land themselves, the ranchers and the homesteaders, who by overgrazing and overplanting, severed the topsoil from its anchor of matted grass roots and placed it at the mercy of wind and water. Millions of acres suffered topsoil depletion, forcing hundreds of families to abandon their lands, but many remaining farmers and ranchers continued their destructive practices.

Sears utilized prose both forceful and felicitous, but the social sins that he delineated did not produce a sense of guilt among those in the Southwest who read his book, or absorbed his message through the media, or choked in the dust-laden air in the spring of 1935. Soil erosion, Sears suggested, wiped out the productivity of land equivalent to all the cultivated acreage in Oklahoma every five years. His indictment, in effect a plea for state participation in a massive effort to stall and reverse the march of the desert, became a best seller, with Oklahoma newspapers giving it widespread attention. Not only did several large landowners seek advice from Sears, but he attracted no animosity for illustrating what residents in the Southwest had done to turn great agricultural areas into sand dunes.[15]

Deserts on the March revealed a sordid side to regionalism, despite the fact that it brought favorable attention to the author, the press, and the university. But the treatment of Angie Debo's manuscript, "As Long as the Waters Run," disclosed what could happen when an author challenged the power structure in Oklahoma.

In 1934, shortly after the publication of Debo's *The Rise and Fall of the Choctaw Republic*, Brandt received a letter asking, "Why don't you good people in Oklahoma write a history of what has happened to your Indians during the past thirty-five years?" Those were years in which the Five Civilized Tribes were dispossessed of nearly all their property while, as the letter pointed out, "your publications continually emphasize affairs relating to the tribes prior to 1900." Brandt thought the suggestion worthwhile and passed it along to historian Grant Foreman in Muskogee and to Edward Everett Dale. Both thought the topic important but felt it would divert them from their current research programs. Angie Debo pursued the suggestion by examining "the effect of allotment on the Five Civilized Tribes." She found it "a nauseating story."[16]

When Debo began her study, she had no preconceived views of Indian policy. The facts she unearthed in her research astonished her. She "had spent a lifetime in Oklahoma without knowing that these things were so." Debo noted that in 1900 "the Five Civilized Tribes owned half the soil of Oklahoma, an area greater in potential wealth than many an American state." Over a twenty-year period "they were almost stripped of their holdings, and thousands were rescued from starvation only through public charity." Through the policy of allotment, granting tribal lands to individual Indians and families, presumably to encourage farming and the awarding of citizenship, Indians "were despoiled individually" under laws about which they knew very little. Since the Indians were not treated in a tribal context, the parceling of the lands attracted little public attention. Lands were ruthlessly and efficiently taken from Indian ownership in a variety of ways involving unscrupulous use of the legal system.[17]

Brandt sent Debo's manuscript to readers on and off the campus. D'Arcy McNickle, a leading student of the American Indian, himself an Indian and an associate of John Collier, the commissioner of Indian affairs, in the Indian Service, responded enthusiastically. "Nothing quite so ambitious has been attempted" and "it is a real joy to come across a work of such competence" were typical of his remarks. To be sure, he felt it needed less detail and a more readable style, but, he concluded, "Publish it as it stands, if necessary."[18]

Another outside reader, Major Eugene M. Kerr, a member of the University of Oklahoma Board of Regents and a resident of Muskogee, thought the manuscript was "not a worthy contribution from an historical standpoint." It was not "a scholarly book" and he did not believe its publication "would be of service to the State of Oklahoma, either now or in the years to come." A similar conclusion came from the in-house reader. Professor Morris L. Wardell, a member of the history department and an assistant to President Bizzell, stated as his "candid opinion that the University of Oklahoma Press will come in for severe criticism." Too many of the people Debo mentioned were "friends of the University." He expressed concern that the state of Oklahoma and some of its prominent citizens would be maligned by its publication and that the university would become the focus of much criticism. His comments made no mention of Indians being maligned, though his own manuscript examining the political history of the Cherokee Nation would soon be published by the press.[19]

By June 1937 the fate of Debo's manuscript appeared resolved despite two negative reports, and the press scheduled it for fall publication. Floyd A. Wright, a member of the law school faculty, went "through the manuscript line by line to determine where there may be danger of libel." Brandt thought such a check should be made "in view of the reluctance of the administration in previous instances not to publish a book dealing with people still alive." But he made clear to Debo "the fact that the book deals with contemporaneous affairs will not prevent the contract being sent." If the careful reading of the manuscript indicated places of possible libel, they could be obviated with revisions, but the manuscript, Brandt assured Debo, "is practically ready for the printers."[20]

Wright's preliminary report proved less positive than Brandt thought it might be. He said that while the book contained no basis for criminal libel, Debo "must be prepared to stand a number of suits either from people who want to protect political reputations or from people who are particularly vindictive." Debo had known that she "was handling dynamite," something she tried to do carefully, in preparing the manuscript. Consequently Wright's report did not surprise her. The trouble arose from "the nature of the subject itself" and not from particular statements. If she reworked the manuscript to make it safe, she concluded, "there would be no book left." But since she had no money to hire a lawyer if litigation ensued from its publication, she did not know how to proceed.[21]

Wright gave the manuscript a careful second reading, deemed it "a masterpiece," and thought the "genuine scholarship" and slight revisions could keep libel suits to a minimum and possibly ensure none being filed. Brandt, following Wright's report, forwarded a contract to Debo, while recognizing that the book "held certain dangers for the Press," dangers that inhered "whenever one tells the unpleasant truth." Debo, in returning the signed contract, expressed amazement, because when she told people she was "making a study of the five Civilized Tribes," their response came in the form of bored expressions. Magazine articles she prepared on the subject "all came back." To be sure, Debo never discussed "the inflammable character of the material" she was handling, but the topic itself seemingly aroused no interest.[22]

However, Wardell discussed the topic with President Bizzell and urged that the manuscript not be published. Brandt countered by suggesting the entire problem be considered before deciding not to publish. The account Debo related was no worse than that told in Grant Foreman's 1932 book, *Indian Removal*, except that it dealt "with many people still living, some of whom today are the respected leaders of our state." If the Civilization of the American Indian series meant anything, Brandt insisted, "this manuscript has a definite, inescapable place in the series." If the series ignored the work of the Dawes Commission in Oklahoma, a major component would be missing. Brandt considered publication a moral obligation. The manuscript, he concluded, "is honest in intention and execution, it is history and not exposé, although its dealing with recent events sometimes gives it the appearance of exposé. It has all moral right on its side."[23]

Brandt said, however, that he would abide by Bizzell's decision. Bizzell thought the political pressure would be too great and accepted Wardell's view not to publish. Brandt then tried to market the manuscript with publishers outside of Oklahoma and suggested to Debo that she file the manuscript and wait until later to have it published. Debo returned the contract, and Brandt marked it "cancelled by mutual consent." He appreciated "the marvelous sportsmanship" Debo had shown. Not publishing the manuscript, Brandt said, "will always vitiate my enjoyment of my work here," though he recognized, as did Debo, that the press would not "be able to stand up very long without the full backing of the University." Bizzell regretted his decision and encouraged Brandt to do what he could to find another publisher.[24]

Several years later as director of Princeton University Press, Brandt published Debo's manuscript with a slightly altered title. And Wardell in 1941 published a favorable review, noting that Debo told "a vivid story of the devious ways by which the Indians were compelled to submit to almost unbelievable chicanery," in the *Annals of the American Academy*, a publication read by almost no one in Oklahoma.

Brandt's vision of the University of Oklahoma as a center of regional culture came to an abrupt halt in 1937 with the cancellation of the contract for Debo's manuscript. And Bizzell undoubtedly recognized that the university could continue to pose as a center for the study of regionalism only if the focus remained on the past. Reality caught up with regionalism at the University of Oklahoma, a point B. A. Botkin had realized earlier.

By 1935 Botkin became convinced that Oklahoma had no tradition, "no fixed procedures" in the sense that tradition provided an attitude as well as a way of living and pursuing the good life. With great insight, he perceived that Oklahoma "was settled on the run, just as its literature is being written and read on the run." In his "darker moments," Botkin feared that Oklahoma, including its writers, were continually "on the make," seeking success. And those who made it, as far as he could judge, usually left Oklahoma to pursue the good life elsewhere. In a sense, he believed, "Oklahoma is still pioneering, and a pioneering society is not a place for tradition or for literature," and by 1935 no longer a place for Botkin to pursue the study of regionalism.[25]

Botkin's shifting views received national attention in 1937 and created problems that pursued him for the remainder of his tenure at the university. In June he delivered a paper, "Regionalism and Culture," before the National Congress of American Writers meeting at Carnegie Hall in New York City. The League of American Writers, whose membership included many Communists, sponsored the meeting. All shades of liberal and left-wing views were represented among the 358 official delegates. In his remarks Botkin held that the culture of the American Southwest seemed largely "sentimental," and articulating his developing views, called for a "contemporary and realistic regional literature" that could portray people and their "living and working conditions." Such a literature, Botkin concluded, would be "truly social, not only in its sources but in its ends, for it promotes a sense of basic human relationships." When published, his remarks ran to seventeen pages. Quoting only a single paragraph in its story on the writers' congress, the *Saturday Review of Literature* reached the conclusion that by calling for the depiction of the class struggle, Botkin recommended that "regionalism be reconciled with Marxism."[26]

That one paragraph in a widely read periodical utilizing the words "Marxism" and "class struggle" in an article about a meeting where most of the delegates were Communists or left-leaning liberals branded Botkin as a Communist in the eyes of many in Oklahoma. Brandt, who had tried to argue with him about attending the conference, thought Botkin had "subscribed to the beliefs of the propagandist school" and believed the only way to fight fascism was to become a Communist. According to John Gould Fletcher, a prominent southern poet, the first to win a Pulitzer Prize, who attended the New York meeting, Botkin wished "to swallow up American literature in Communist propaganda." Brandt, who considered himself a liberal, agreed with Fletcher but said that as "a

University publisher I have to maintain a fairly objective point of view." Already embroiled in the crisis over Debo's manuscript, Brandt recognized any conflict regarding regionalism would further impair what he had striven to create as director of the University of Oklahoma Press. Brandt accepted Fletcher's evaluation and apparently did not consider that Botkin's mere presence at the congress brought home to many in the audience an awareness of regional participation in national culture.[27]

In 1938, as Brandt prepared to leave Norman for Princeton, Botkin wrote him what he already knew: "Personally, I think the regionalism movement is almost played out, and this might be a good time to take stock." Botkin had already taken stock, as had Paul Sears, who in 1938 also left the university. Botkin, on a leave of absence, wrote to Brandt from Washington, D.C. Despite the tempest over his New York speech, the Board of Regents gave him a promotion and granted a second and later a third leave of absence to continue his work with the Federal Writers' Project preparing a guide to American folklore. In 1939 the project moved to the Library of Congress, where Botkin supervised a staff engaged in folklore studies. But questions of his alleged radicalism arose once again at the university.[28]

In October 1939 the House Committee on Un-American Activities published a report on the American League for Peace and Democracy, an organization deemed a Communist front and listing Botkin as a member. Bizzell wrote Botkin claiming his name had appeared in the *Norman Transcript* and that an electric sign on the engineering building carried a strip citing his name as a Communist. Local newspaper editorials commented on the organization. According to Bizzell, a regent had raised the question of his loyalty, and his name had been sent to the governor on a list of disloyal faculty members. Nevertheless, the regents awarded him another leave of absence for the 1939–40 academic year to continue as director of folklore for the National Writers' Project under the sponsorship of the Library of Congress. The contretemps over the question of his loyalty abated at least temporarily, but Bizzell knew it would arise again when Botkin, who had spent the three previous academic years working in Washington, where he quickly established himself as the leading folklore specialist in the United States, asked for another leave in the spring of 1940. Bizzell considered the request impractical and doubted if the Board of Regents would approve it. They did not.[29]

Bizzell informed Botkin in May 1940 that his position would be declared vacant if he failed to return to campus for the fall semester, and that, given the controversy his activities had aroused, it might be the better part of valor if he resigned, which he did, on September 1, 1940. The University of Oklahoma as a major center for the development of a regional impulse thus came to an end. What Bizzell had encouraged during the previous decade, he then helped to dismantle. Bizzell made the final decision not to publish Debo's manuscript, and it was his awkward duty to suggest Botkin's resignation. By that time both Brandt and Sears had departed, leaving Dale to continue developing, on a much reduced scale, the Western History Collections and Vestal to publish on western themes. Jacobson still headed the art department and spearheaded creation of a campus museum. His interest in Indian art had to compete with other concerns. By 1940 Brandt's successor at the press recognized the inevitable and explained that "while the Press has devoted itself in the past to regional studies principally, an effort is being made to broaden its base of its publications, so that any publishable work of scholarship may be considered for its list."[30]

To a special issue of the *Saturday Review of Literature* devoted to a "cultural inventory" of the Southwest that appeared in 1942, both Joseph Brandt and John Joseph Mathews contributed articles. In Brandt's article, "Universities on the March," he expressed some of his bitterness about the reality of regionalism in Oklahoma. He observed that "the Oklahoma politician is acclaimed a statesman if he can return to his district and claim that he has reduced, to the lowest level in the United States, the appropriation for education." And he further noted that "the difficulty is not so much that the writers of the Southwest lack vision or courage as that they are living in a vast sociological laboratory which the universities have as yet scarcely touched." He expressed his own experience when he remarked that southwestern authors thus far were rarely "in a mood to turn their society into a clinic." Gone were the optimism and the ebullience Brandt had expressed when he launched the university press and published remarkable books attracting widespread attention.[31]

Mathews's article, a paean to the University of Oklahoma Press and Brandt as its first director, made no mention of the rejection of Debo's manuscript. Instead Mathews noted that Brandt and his successor, Savoie Lottinville, firmly believed Oklahomans "must be made aware of the culture of which they are a part." The press would better serve the society supporting it by promoting an understanding "of the eastern part by the western and the western by the eastern" portions of Oklahoma. Its publications, Mathews claimed, were bringing to the state's people "a consciousness of themselves."[32]

Several years later, when John Gould Fletcher, then busy compiling a massive collection of Ozark folklore, inquired about the situation in Oklahoma, Stanley Vestal responded that "when Botkin left our campus, a good deal of interest was lost."[33] So too by the end of the 1930s, with the departure of Sears and Brandt and the fiasco over Debo's manuscript, a good deal of the creative impulse for the surging interest in southwestern regionalism on the campus of the University of Oklahoma was lost. It all began and ended during the presidency of William Bennett Bizzell.

Notes

1. Harvard, where Frederick Jackson Turner conducted seminars in western history, is a marked exception.

2. I am indebted to Robert L. Dorman's splendid study, *Revolt of the Provinces: The Regionalist Movement in America, 1920–1945* (Chapel Hill: University of North Carolina Press, 1993). Dorman considers the University of Oklahoma along with numerous other regional developments; I have focused exclusively on the Norman scene, probing developments originating on the campus.

3. Arthur Silberman, "Early Kiowa Art," *Oklahoma Today* 23 (1972): 4–10; Oscar Brousse Jacobson, Introduction to 1929 Edition of *Kiowa Indian Ar*, (Santa Fe, New Mexico: Bell Editions, 1979). For Jacobson, see the translation of a 1955 article from UTLANDSSVENSKARNA Magazine in Oscar Brousse Jacobson Papers, Box 1, Western History Collections, University of Oklahoma, Norman (hereafter cited as WHC). In Box 1, there also are drafts of essays by Jacobson: "Art Exhibitions," "The Government in Art," and "Indians." The essay on Indians contains a listing of public buildings containing murals by Oklahoma Indian artists. See also an essay, "Indian Artists from Oklahoma" (Norman: University of Oklahoma Museum of Art, 1964).

4. Stanley Vestal's papers, a massive collection of correspondence, research notes, literary drafts of manuscripts, including articles, books, poems, and other material, are housed in the Western History Collections.

5. Lewis Meriam to William B. Bizzell, April 27, 1928, Edward Everett Dale Papers, Box 45, WHC. For a brief outline of Dale's early career, see Edward Everett Dale to Joseph A. Brandt, November 11, 1929, Dale Papers, Box 7, WHC. See also Dale's autobiography, *The West Wind Blows: The Autobiography of Edward Everett Dale*, ed. Arrell M. Gibson (Oklahoma City: Oklahoma Historical Society, 1984). Arrell Morgan Gibson edited the volume for publication after Dale's death in 1972 at the age of ninety-three. For an admiring essay on Dale by one of his top students, see Angie Debo, "Edward Everett Dale, Historian of Progress," n.d., Dale Papers, Box 77, WHC. For Dale's work as president of the State Folklore Association, see Dale to J. Frank Dobie, July 25, 1925, Dale Papers, Box 18, WHC.

6. For Dale's work in establishing the Western History Collections, see H. Glenn Jordan, 'Western History Collections at the University of Oklahoma," *Chronicles of Oklahoma* 54 (Fall 1976): 370–76; George Lynn Cross, *The Seeds of Excellence* (Norman, Oklahoma: Transcript Press, 1986), 30–36; Gibson, *West Wind Blows*, 340–351. Dale's account also discusses his 1934 tour throughout eastern Oklahoma logging materials the team examined in every school, library, Indian agency, and home they visited. See also Bizzell to David H. Stevens, Rockefeller Foundation, May 15, 1934, Dale Papers, Box 5, WHC. Dale submitted his resignation as head of the Western History Collections, initially called the Frank Phillips Collection, in a March 30, 1942, letter to Joseph Brandt, who followed Bizzell as president of the university, Dale Papers, Box 7, WHC. For Dale's initial efforts in collecting, see Dale to Grant Foreman, January 16, 1924, and Foreman to Frank Phillips, September 5, 1932, for an evaluation of the Western History Collection funded by Phillips, Dale Papers, Box 23, WHC.

7. Dale to W. Carson Ryan, November 12, 1930, Dale Papers, Box 59, WHC.

8. Dale to Ryan, September 15, 1931, Dale Papers, Box 59, WHC.

9. Joseph A. Brandt, "A Pioneering Regional Press," *Southwest Review* 26 (1940): 26–36. In this essay Brandt recounts high points of his decade as press director.

10. The best discussion of *Folk-Say* can be found in B. A. Botkin, "Folk-Say and Space," *Southwest Review* 20 (1935): 321–35. See also Brandt, "A Pioneering Regional Press," 30–31, and Brandt to Botkin, January 10, 1933, University Press Collection, Box 4, WHC, in which Brandt told Botkin that the series was being terminated (a decision mutually arrived at) because of financial considerations.

11. Gould's introduction relates his fascinating account of geological work in Oklahoma and his keen interest in its history and place names. See also

Fred Sutton to Charles N. Gould, October 14, 1933, University Press Collection, Box 9, WHC.

12. Brandt to Bizzell, September 7, 1929, University Press Collection, Box 1, WHC.

13. Arrell Morgan Gibson, "A History of the University of Oklahoma Press," *Journal of the West* 7 (1968): 553–61.

14. Bizzell to Brandt, October 3, 1930, University Press Collection, Box 1, WHC.

15. Brandt to Hendrik Willem Van Loon, December 17, 1935, University Press Collection, Box 20, WHC.

16. Warren King Moorehead to Brandt, June, 1934; Brandt to Moorehead, July 16, 1934, Box 3; Angie Debo to W. S. Campbell (Stanley Vestal), October 5, 1936, Box 25, University Press Collection, WHC; Suzanne H. Schrems and Cynthia J. Wolff, "Politics and Libel: Angie Debo and the Publication of And Still the Waters Run," *Western Historical Quarterly* 22 (1991): 185–203. Schrems and Wolff examine the controversy from a different perspective and in greater detail.

17. See the prefaces prepared by Debo in 1936, University Press Collection, Box 35, WHC. Indians became citizens when Oklahoma entered the Union in 1907.

18. Reader's Report of D'Arcy McNickle, September 3, 1936, University Press Collection, Box 65, WHC.

19. Readers' Reports by Major Eugene M. Kerr and Morris L. Wardell, n.d., University Press Collection, Box 65, WHC. While there is no direct evidence linking Dale to Wardell's report, there is much that is circumstantial. Dale and Wardell occupied offices next to one another in Monnet Hall, and Wardell could be considered a protégé of Dale. He brought Wardell to the university from a Tulsa secondary school. Once Wardell completed his PhD at the University of Chicago, Dale promoted him ahead of another faculty member already possessing a PhD. Moreover, Dale, like Wardell, did not want to offend prominent Oklahomans. In 1923, when the Agricultural History Society wished to publish his manuscript examining the range-cattle industry in Oklahoma, Dale balked. Too many of the cattlemen were still living, and their "curious intrigues and diplomatic struggles for grazing rights in the Indian Territory" involved "a certain amount of graft and corruption." The manuscript had to be revised and submitted "to one or two people concerned in the matter for their reading and criticism before it is offered for publication." In 1930 the press published his study of the range-cattle industry. Dale to Nils A. Olsen, November 17, 1923, Dale Papers, Box 50, WHC.

20. Brandt to Debo, June 1, 1937, University Press Collection, Box 35, WHC.

21. Brandt to Debo, June 11, 1937, Angie Debo Papers, Oklahoma State University, Stillwater (hereafter cited as OSU); Debo to Brandt, June 14, 1937, University Press Collection, Box 35, WHC.

22. Brandt to Debo, June 15, 1937, Debo to Brandt, July 16, 1931, University Press Collection, Box 35, WHC.

23. Brandt to Bizzell, July 20, 1937, University Press Collection, Box 32, WHC.

24. Brandt to Debo, July 21, 1937, Debo Papers, OSU, Brandt to Bizzell, July 23, 1937, Brandt to Debo, July 26, 1937, University Press Collection, Box 35, WHC.

25. Botkin, "Folk-Say and Space," 331–35. For a partial rebuttal of Botkin see the remarks of Stanley Vestal in "What Price Tradition?" *Southwest Review* 21 (1935): 83–88.

26. B. A. Botkin, "Regionalism and Culture," in *The Writer in a Changing World*, ed. Henry Hart (New York: Equinox Cooperative Press, 1937), 140–57; Eugene Armfield, "The Second Writers' Congress," *Saturday Review of Literature* 16 (June 12, 1937), 7.

27. Brandt to John Gould Fletcher, October 27, November 4, 1937; Fletcher to Brandt, October 30, 1937, Joseph Brandt Papers, Box 1, WHC.

28. Botkin to Brandt, March 1, 1938, University Press Collection, Box 49, WHC.

29. See Dorman, *Revolt of the Provinces*, 303–304, for the account of Botkin's difficulties with the university. It is interesting to note that neither the campus newspaper, the *Oklahoma Daily*, the *Norman* (Okla.) *Transcript*, the *Daily Oklahoman* (Oklahoma City), nor *Harlow's Weekly* in late October and early November made mention of Botkin, nor was there any account of an electric sign on the engineering building in the campus newspaper. On October 24, 1939, the *Transcript* printed a picture of Botkin with a caption stating that he was leaving the university to return to the Federal Writers' Project. The *Oklahoma Daily* noted on October 25, 1939, that Botkin was returning to Washington and that President Bizzell would recommend that Botkin be granted a further leave of absence. The *Daily Oklahoman* in an October 28, 1939, editorial said, "It is difficult to get excited over this roster [of the League for Peace and Democracy]. The people on the list aren't sinister red plotters against the government. They are just gullible idealists who are giving unconscious moral support to schemers whose motives are questionable." There were 563 names on the roster. In a feature story appearing on the same day, President Franklin Roosevelt was quoted as saying that publication of the roster employed "a sordid procedure," a point reflected in the remarks of others, including members of the Dies committee. On October 29 the *Transcript* carried a story with pictures of two government officials who were members of the league, but there was no mention of Botkin.

For an evaluation of Botkin's work with the Federal Writers' Project, see Jerre Mangione, *The Dream and the Deal: The Federal Writers' Project, 1935–1943* (Boston: Little, Brown, 1972), 269–72, 275–78. Mangione remarked that "Botkin performed a singular cultural service for the nation."

30. Savoie Lottinville to Debo, August 24, 1940, University Press Collection, Box 65, WHC.

31. Joseph A. Brandt, "Universities on the March," *Saturday Review of Literature* 25 (May 16, 1942): 19.

32. John Joseph Mathews, "Scholarship Comes to Life," ibid., 20–21; Brandt to Mathews, May 23, July 5, 1939, Brandt Papers, Box 5, WHC.

33. W. S. Campbell (Stanley Vestal) to Fletcher, May 23, 1949, John Gould Fletcher Papers, Special Collections Division, University of Arkansas Libraries, Fayetteville. A carbon copy can be found in Vestal Papers, Box 27, WHC.

« 2 »

"Dear Miss Debo"

The Correspondence of E. E. Dale and Angie Debo

For almost fifty years, Oklahoma historians Edward Everett Dale and Angie Debo produced a voluminous correspondence that began in 1925 when Dale was a full professor and head of the Department of History at the University of Oklahoma (OU). Debo was teaching in Canyon, Texas, not yet a matriculated doctoral candidate. The correspondence continued into the 1970s, shortly before Dale's death in 1972, though it had tapered off considerably by the 1950s. The correspondence is informative on several levels. First, it provides insight into graduate education in history at a new state university. It also provides insight into the character and talents of both individuals.

Edward Everett Dale was essentially a storyteller, a raconteur, who recycled his previous experiences into his endeavors as a historian. Angie Debo was a serious scholar, highly motivated, even driven, to succeed in her professional labors despite the handicap of being older than most beginning PhDs and a woman. For Debo that meant seeking an academic post in a depression-ridden economy when openings were few and far between. Women like Debo were usually the first to be dropped from faculties so that married male colleagues could provide for their families. The correspondence reveals the hardships Debo endured, her persistence, and her eventual triumph over adversity despite the fact that she never held a permanent academic post. Throughout, she remained deferential to her mentor, who always proclaimed his desire to help in furthering her career. Implicit in the correspondence, however, is the recognition on both their parts that she became a far better historian than he, and that what success came to her was based entirely on her own merits, with little real assistance from Dale in easing her way—with one lone exception.[1] Throughout the correspondence, Debo never wavered in addressing her mentor as "Dear Dr. Dale." In turn, until the last letters he always wrote his salutation as "Dear Miss Debo."

Dale and Debo were similar in many ways. Both came from pioneer backgrounds and were late in launching their careers as historians. Dale was born in 1879 in a log cabin on a North Texas farm and had a varied career as a cowboy and ranchman before seeking a formal education. He graduated from OU in 1911 and earned a PhD at Harvard eleven years later with Frederick Jackson Turner as his major professor. He was an instructor when Debo entered the university in 1915. When she graduated in 1918, having shifted her major from science to history, Dale was an assistant professor. Debo was born in 1890 on a homestead in Marshall County, Kansas. At age nine she traveled to Oklahoma Territory in her parents' covered wagon, settling in the town of Marshall in Logan County, which became her permanent home. Like Dale, she taught in rural schools and at age twenty-eight received her college degree. Dale was four years older, aged thirty-two, when he received his degree. Debo began formal work for the PhD in 1930, having earned a master's degree from the University of Chicago in 1924. J. Fred Rippy, her thesis director, helped in securing her a teaching position in Canyon, Texas.

On January 16, 1925, writing to Dale from Canyon as a member of the Department of History at West Texas State Teachers College, Debo explained why she held him in such high regard: "You took the time to supervise our undertaking and organization of material when you asked us to write a term paper." No other teacher in her undergraduate years "showed us anything about procedure," and while at the University of Chicago she claimed that among her fellow graduate students she seemed to be the only one "who had been taught how to conduct research." That was the great lesson learned from Dale, and she reiterated it at times throughout their correspondence.

Dale responded graciously and asked Debo if she "would be willing to make some inquiries as to material on the range cattle industry . . . any old letters, brand books, account books, or other material." He was engaged in contract research for a bulletin for the United States Department of Agriculture, on the topic "A History of the Range Cattle Industry on the Great Plains," out of which came his first scholarly monograph, *The Range Cattle Industry* (1930). Thus the correspondence was launched. Dale's letters were typewritten, Debo's written in longhand. She assisted Dale in obtaining photographs for his manuscript, which he completed and filed with the Department of Agriculture in June.[2]

Debo continued to send Dale photographs she thought might interest him; in turn she inquired about several poems he'd written for the 1924 *Sooner*, the senior yearbook at OU. She claimed that, having lived through most stages of Oklahoma's development, "the romance of the frontier is in my blood." Dale's lines read to her "like an epic," though she admitted she was unable to judge their literary merit.[3]

In late 1927 Debo applied for a fellowship from the American Association of University Women to pursue a line of research relating to her master's thesis. She asked Dale if he "would be kind enough" to write on her behalf and if Oklahoma offered fellowships for which she might apply. Dale responded, "It is a real pleasure to us to write you a letter of recommendation," but he noted there were no fellowships at Oklahoma "of interest to you." Debo was not optimistic about her chances and indicated that if she did not win an award she would spend the upcoming year "in study," some of it at OU.[4]

At the time, plans were under way for establishing a PhD program in the OU Department of History. Already, Dale wrote, four students had begun to work toward that degree. If Debo's plans failed to materialize and if she wished to come to the university, he wrote, "we shall be very glad to welcome you back." And that is what happened. Debo failed to receive any appointment "except one so small that I did not care to accept." Early in the following year, 1929, Debo wrote that she planned to attend the university in the fall, provided she could secure a leave of absence and that Dale would be offering his Oklahoma history course.[5]

Debo started course work in the 1929 fall semester and concluded taking courses two years later, at the end of the 1931 fall semester. Thereafter she engaged in dissertation research examining the post–Civil War history of the Choctaw Nation and resumed her teaching career at West Texas State Teachers College. Her relationship with Dale then assumed a new status, that of mentor and student. Dale supervised the preparation of her dissertation, and it was that topic that prompted correspondence when Debo was not on campus. In March 1931 she explained her absence from Norman; her brother in Richmond, Kansas, was ill, and she had to abandon research and temporarily assume new responsibilities. If unable to return to campus, she assured Dale, "I shall return my fellowship to the university." However, she believed that "as things are going now" she would be back at her research within a week. Dale was happy to know her brother was recovering and assured Debo he would be glad to discuss her future plans and missed seeing her in "the Seminary room very much."[6]

In the summer of 1931 Debo researched newspapers at the Oklahoma Historical Society in Oklahoma City and inquired if Dale could secure permission for her to use the law library, which closed during the summer. Before departing for Muskogee to examine records in the office of the superintendent for the Five Civilized Tribes and for Washington to research files in the Department of the Interior and the Library of Congress, she hoped Dale could provide her with information about rooms in Muskogee and with instructions about doing research in Washington. For his part, Dale wished to see her in Norman if possible before she went to Muskogee and certainly before she went to Washington. He wanted to provide her with "some letters that I think will be useful."[7]

On her research trip, Debo found time to write only one letter to inform Dale that "everybody here and at Muskogee has been kind in giving me every facility for study," including the Choctaw attorney and Grant Foreman. She found little of value at the Library of Congress but "a great deal at the Indian Office." Most of what she found in Washington only confirmed what she had already learned. Unless she discovered something very important, she would "stay only a few days longer. . . . I am about ready to begin writing."[8]

By mid-August she was in Marshall drafting her dissertation. She had completed one chapter but hesitated to send it during the vacation period, though Dale said he wanted to see each chapter as soon as it was completed. She next wrote at the end of September from Canyon, Texas. Her brother was "failing very rapidly." She had spent several weeks with him "night and day" and had had no opportunity to work on her dissertation. But she soon mailed the two chapters already completed.[9]

Several days later she received a detailed letter from Dale commenting on the first draft of her chapters. He had read them with "a good deal of care" and then passed the copies along to Morris Wardell and Ralph Records, departmental colleagues. All agreed that her introductory chapter was too long, "especially in view of the fact that much of your material seems to be taken almost entirely from secondary sources." It needed to be shortened and should not rely heavily on secondary accounts and various articles in the *Chronicles of Oklahoma.* Contemporary documents should be cited whenever possible. Dale also questioned her presentation of life sketches of some individuals and the leaving out of others whose names were mentioned "and whose part in your story may be equally important." Unless she was prepared to present a brief life sketch of every important character mentioned, it would be better to leave them out entirely. That was the extent of Dale's criticism. He suggested she finish drafting her chapters before making "too many corrections." She needed time "to think a little more fully on the subject" before putting her draft into final form. And he was not sure she could do that "without more work at Washington," as he knew "there must be many thousands of pieces of manuscript there on the Choctaws that you could not examine in the brief stay you had there."[10]

Debo responded almost immediately. She apologized for the typographical errors and said she would hire a typist to prepare the final copy. But she was troubled by the criticism that she "had used too much secondary material." She said, "I do not think I am guilty," noting that in the chapter in question there were "128 footnotes and only six are secondary." In addition, she explained that "there were about ten other numbered citations where one secondary reference was given along with one to six source references," reinforcing her premise that almost every bit of evidence was derived from original sources.[11]

For the period before June 19, 1865, the date of the surrender of the Choctaw forces and the launching date for her dissertation, she read widely from secondary works, "but even here the most of it was either from source material or from contemporary secondary accounts such as the reports of travellers." She thought she was "justified in doing that with regard to a period which does not come into the scope of my investigation." But she concluded it would probably be best "to leave the problem of the introduction unsettled" until the dissertation was written. As she saw it, the succeeding chapters would be more easily understood with the background material.[12]

As for the brief biographies, she believed they could be omitted. She thought that because Choctaw statesmen were almost entirely unknown, it would have been interesting to include biographical information about the principal chiefs "and those who figured very prominently in the diplomatic or political life of the tribe." She would abide by Dale's decision, including or omitting the biographies, "according to whether or not you think they add to the value of the book." Then, as if to assure Dale of the value of his efforts, she concluded, "I think the wording of some of my sentences is very greatly improved by some of the changes suggested," and out of fear of offending him she added, "Please do not think the vigor with which I am defending myself indicates any lack of appreciation for the kindly criticisms which I have received." She had the whole study in mind, while he was basing his judgment upon the material submitted.[13]

Dale accepted her comments, noting that protracted arguments usually ended with each party feeling exactly as they did before. Because he could not imagine himself "arguing very much" with Frederick Jackson Turner, the director of his thesis, "in regard to his suggestions and criticisms," he had concluded after lengthy discussion with a previous graduate student "never to argue again with a student over something in a dissertation." He related that information to explain "why I do not offer any counter defense and so that you may not expect it in the future." While he would continue to offer criticisms and suggestions, he would never attempt to defend them. She could do as she pleased, bearing in mind that her dissertation "must at least be acceptable to your committee, but of this I am only one member." He admitted that "by this time you know a great deal more about the subject than I do." He wanted her to push her writing along as fast as possible, "for I am eager to see you finish and take your degree as soon as possible."[14]

That exchange between Debo and Dale clarified and defined their relationship and indicated much about each of them. Dale revealed himself as a professor who above all wished to avoid controversy. Genial, easygoing, informal, and an effective classroom teacher, he was well liked, but he rarely if ever willingly stated and defended in a public setting the courage of his convictions. Debo was free to accept or to disregard his suggestions. As for Debo, the exchange reinforced her independence as a scholar. She would come to her own conclusions in her own way. There would be little fruitful interchange to help her sharpen, modify, change, or reject perceptions emanating from her research and writing. They remained both polite and cordial in their correspondence. It was "Dear Dr. Dale" and "Dear Miss Debo." But by the end of 1931 each more clearly understood the other and each needed the other, Debo more so than Dale.

Thereafter their correspondence tapered off, as Debo was reading, researching, and writing. Dale wrote in April 1932, congratulating her on "Southern Refugees in the Cherokee Nation," which appeared in the *Southwestern Historical Quarterly*. He asked for a reprint. She had written it as a seminar paper for Dale "that semester when we interpreted Southwestern History to mean Oklahoma History." In June she asked Dale to return "the chapter of my dissertation that I sent you a little while ago." She needed it to finish the chapter she was working on; she wanted to reorganize her material. Dale obliged after hurriedly reading it. She quickly revised and sent it off, saying "I am afraid you will be as sorry to see all this as I am glad to be rid of it."[15]

This time around she accepted some of Dale's suggestions, moving, for example, the section about citizenship into another chapter. She explained her problems and how she was trying to resolve them. But she made no reference to Dale's suggestions as to how she might proceed. She asked advice about citing books in the Office of the Commissioner of Indian Affairs, and she accepted his suggestion with regard to using small letters instead of capitals. She also said she would make the changes he suggested about agriculture, but she would do it later.[16]

Soon chapters were pouring in to Dale, two in July. As soon as her committee finished reading them, she planned to travel to Norman to check references and to make "whatever changes are necessary." She also thought Dale might be interested to know that the *Mississippi Valley Historical Review* had accepted her chapter on Reconstruction. She believed if part of her dissertation was published, "it might serve to establish my right to work on it." But she did "not know whether it was the best policy or not."[17]

At the end of the month Dale returned four chapters and reported he was "quite well pleased." With the summer session corning to an end, he doubted if the other members of her committee would have the time to read the chapters critically. He asked if she would prepare a table of contents giving a half- or a full-page outline of a chapter under the chapter title. He had had to read the chapters piecemeal and wanted, when the dissertation was fully completed, to read it again. He asked if she could more precisely separate the footnotes from the text so they would "stand out and would save time and the danger of confusion in reading." Sometime in September he would ask her committee (Carl Coke Rister and Cortez Ewing) to read it carefully and critically. If it was as good as he thought it would be, Dale did not anticipate there would be "a great deal of revision to do."[18]

Dale also offered her sound advice. Her degree under the best of circumstances could not be confirmed until the following June. There would be plenty of time to get the dissertation "exactly right without hurrying yourself or anybody else." If the committee offered suggestions with which she disagreed, she should explain why she wrote as she did. But if they insisted on changes, she should make them "promptly and cheerfully," remembering that "it never pays to argue with a traffic cop." Her readers were judging *her* work, not "the other way around."[19]

At that point Debo was inclined to accept Dale's suggestions because she knew he liked her chapters. But she also had another concern. She was interested in securing another teaching position, though she had "the opportunity to return to Canyon next fall." She was "dissatisfied by the increase of Peabody and Columbia Teachers College graduates with what seems to me an underestimate of purely academic work." For several years, she explained, "I have been increasingly desirous of a change." She asked Dale to keep her in mind "in case something did turn up." What she did not tell Dale was that during the 1920s there had been four or five members in her department; by 1932 there were three. While finishing her degree was her primary concern now, the goal of attaining a secure teaching job would soon replace that.[20]

In September Dale cleared with the graduate office the scheduling details for the written examinations Debo would have to take satisfy various requirements. And once her committee read her dissertation, he would "[explain] everything that needs to be explained." Dale remained impressed with her chapters and did not believe much revision would be necessary. He noted a few points, "some of them mechanical and other matters that I think could be better if slightly restated." But he assured her his suggestions were "very few and comparatively unimportant."[21]

For her part, Debo anticipated problems. Besides being inconvenient, owing to a six-day teaching schedule, there was the expense involved in making a special trip to Norman for her written examinations. A one-way ticket from Canyon to Oklahoma City would cost more than fifteen dollars, the entire trip around forty dollars. She suggested that she "be relieved of the written examination." Her course work indicated that there was no danger of her failing it. And, more important, there had been no such requirement when she first enrolled in the fall of 1929. If that was not feasible, she asked to take the written examinations on her own campus or during the Christmas holidays. All of those options failing, she wondered if she could take the written examinations on the morning "before I take the orals."[22]

Dale was sympathetic to her plight and said he would discuss the matter with the dean of the graduate school. More important, he shortly thereafter informed her that the committee had read and discussed her manuscript, which he was returning "by express, collect." The committee had little to object to "as far as the larger aspects of the work are concerned." Their criticisms involved "questions of punctuation, capitalization, citations and occasionally sentence structure." Their criticisms dealt "largely with mechanics and not with the content at all." In effect, they copyedited her manuscript. Rister suggested she use "op. cit. instead of repeating the title of sources frequently used." But Dale and Ewing thought "a repetition of a title is perfectly clear and is in fact, somewhat less confusing to the reader." Therefore, Dale informed her she could "disregard entirely marginal requests to use *op. cit* and *ibid.*" The committee quibbled over their criticisms of Rister. Where Dale disagreed with them, Debo was free to ignore them. Matters of punctuation and style were the essence of the criticisms, nothing of substance pertaining to content or sources. But what pleased Debo most was Dale's conclusion that every member of the committee was "much pleased" with her dissertation. She had "done an excellent piece of work," and it "ought to be published."[23]

Debo meanwhile did have something published. A fragment of her dissertation appeared in the *Chronicles of Oklahoma.* She received her dissertation and the report of her committee. Thanks to the cancellation of classes in honor of a homecoming football game, she promptly began revising it and did not dissent from the comments and criticisms she received. She claimed to be "shocked at the errors in grammar and sentence structure unearthed by the vigilance" of her committee and was "very grateful" for all their suggestions. Where Dale suggested she might want to shift the place of a chapter, she decided to leave it in place because he left the decision with her. And she went further, saying if she found instances where she still preferred her own version, she would seek the approval of her committee before disregarding their suggestions. She had learned her lesson and would follow all of Dale's suggestions as she sought to complete all the degree requirements. For his part, Dale made suggestions and was willing to allow her to use her own judgment in resolving them.[24]

Before the Thanksgiving break Debo sent Dale a copy of her bibliography and worked over the dissertation during the holiday, "trying to put it in the exact form I want." She also was thinking of another book. She recalled an earlier suggestion by Dale about "a study of the process by which the land embraced in the old Indian Territory passed out of the possession of members of the Five Civilized Tribes to whom it was allotted, and came into the possession [of] the whites." At the time she said she did not understand the significance of the topic; now she thought she did and believed she knew how to undertake it. Consequently, she applied to the American Association of University Women for a fellowship and asked Dale to write on her behalf. And early in 1933 she sent Dale a telegram asking if he would recommend her for a vacancy at Western Reserve University. Later in the month she applied for a Social Science Research Council grant to pursue the study of the alienation of Indian land. While working on her dissertation, she had collected a great deal of material that would make a good beginning for the project. Meanwhile, her dissertation was being typed by a student who was doing "an excellent piece of work."[25]

As she completed her bibliography, prepared an abstract of her dissertation, and attended to other necessary chores, Debo asked Dale once again to keep her in mind if he heard of any teaching vacancy. She said she liked her work in Canyon very much when she first arrived because she saw the possibility of building up the educational system of a pioneer community, but she no longer saw "much prospect of its realization." Teachers' colleges were "under strong fire" in Texas. She liked "the professional spirit" she found on the campus but did not think "a fine professional spirit can be made to substitute for academic thoroughness." And shortly thereafter she introduced a foreboding note: "I am finding it necessary to be rather stingy this year because the future looks rather dark for me right now." Dale, of course, said he would keep her in mind if he learned of any job opening, but he added, "I almost never learn of anything anymore."[26]

Finally, after much discussion, April 29 and May 1 were deemed satisfactory dates for Debo to take her examinations, the written on Saturday and the oral the following Monday afternoon. The written examination would cover American history since 1789 and American government. The oral would involve Debo suggesting the "important points developed or the important questions raised and answered" in her dissertation. Thereafter, various members of the committee would question her first on her written examination and then on aspects of their fields of specialization. The committee had been expanded to include Asa K. Christian (constitutional history) and Alfred Bundy Thomas (Hispanic America). The final examinations, Dale informed her, would be "far more technical and explicit than was the general examination." She should prepare "with the utmost care" until she left Canyon and "then forget it" until she entered the examination room. She did just that, and Dale later informed her that "I have heard nothing but the most favorable comments on your examination." He also forwarded a carbon copy of a letter he wrote to the president of West Texas State Teachers College so he would know "what this Department thinks of you.[27]

Debo was delighted. Dr. J. A. Hill, president of the college, showed Dale's letter to her and to others "and seemed very much pleased about it." But in a letter to Dale he explained that, while her associates were proud of her record, "it now looks as though we shall lose Miss Debo due to an unfortunate complication of circumstances." He would try to find some place for her, "be it ever so small," as the college made adjustments in coping with "legislative hostility." Debo suspected her days as a member of the department were numbered. She was grateful for the letter Dale wrote, but she added, "I do not know that Mr. Hill or anybody can do anything for me now."[28]

In June 1933 Angie Debo was awarded the second PhD in history at OU. She had completed all the degree requirements and had submitted her dissertation to the university press, but instead of being exhilarated, Debo faced the dismal prospect of finding another teaching position. The publication of her manuscript would be, she told Dale, "a sort of compensation for all I have lost." She followed "every lead I could possibly think of" and in mid-July went to Lubbock to talk with Dr. Bradford Knapp, president of Texas Technological College, about a possible job opening. The interview, she believed, "was highly satisfactory." She hoped she could "impress a few presidents enough" so they would remember her when schools started "growing again." Her "greatest fear," she explained to Dale, "is that if I once drop out of the profession, it will be impossible for me to establish the necessary contacts." Meanwhile, she would try to do some writing while she was still in touch "with libraries and historical documents." The *Panhandle Plains Historical Review* accepted "some very interesting letters" she edited, thereby enabling her to keep in touch with the profession. If she ever got "out of the woods," she would let Dale "know at once. . . . I am so grateful for your interest."[29]

At that point the relationship between Dale and Debo began take a new turn. She no longer was a student with Dale as her mentor. Though she had shown some independence as a graduate student, she had nevertheless depended on Dale to guide her through the maze of chores she had to complete to receive her degree. Moreover, though Dale no doubt was affronted when she disagreed with some of his suggestions, he nevertheless recognized her great ability and was sympathetic to her plight. If she heard of a vacancy that he might be able to help her secure, she should not hesitate to write and "tell me just what you want me to do." By the summer of 1933, in the midst of the Depression and as the New Deal was getting under way, Debo had returned to the family homestead in Marshall, Oklahoma. Her outlook improved when President Hill in Canyon offered her "employment of a sort" at the newly completed Panhandle Plains Historical Museum at a salary of fifty dollars a month. There she could keep in touch with the academic world, have an opportunity to engage in research and writing, and be so happy to have a job that she would not worry about its inadequacy. And she credited Dale with her good fortune, believing it was his "tactful letters to Mr. Hill that first caused him to feel some responsibility in my case.[30]

Her spirits soared several weeks later when Joseph Brandt, director of the University of Oklahoma Press, wrote that her dissertation had been approved for publication. She knew Dale was one of the readers and that his favorable report had assisted in the decision to publish. It pleased her that Dale thought the work worthy of publication. But she was not satisfied. She thought the manuscript "all right for a dissertation," but as a book for the general reader it could be improved by adding a couple of chapters on the period before the Civil War, by expanding that brief introductory chapter to three. When Dale suggested she cite primary and not secondary sources in those chapters, Debo objected and Dale deferred to her. So she decided to send the student who had typed her dissertation to take notes on the additional material in the Phillips Collection at OU.[31]

While she appreciated the courtesies Dale extended to her student, she was able to reciprocate and helped Dale secure a complete set, six volumes, of the *Panhandle Plains Historical Review* for $7.50. She also reported that her researcher and another former student who had recently completed course work for a master's degree at OU both spoke glowingly of him. Debo thought it would be necessary "to establish quarantine lines to keep too many of our Texas young people from falling under your influence." But she was still under his influence when she wired him requesting that he contact Professor Robert Binkley at Western Reserve University at her expense. There was a history vacancy, and they wanted a woman. In addition, J. Fred Rippy, who had directed her master's thesis at the University of Chicago and who then was at Duke University, wrote on her behalf. As it turned out, the opening was in Modern and Latin-American or Far Eastern and Russian. She did not qualify.[32]

Debo, of course, was grateful for Dale's telegram to Binkley. In turn, she invited Dale to serve as a judge in an essay contest dealing with some phase of Panhandle history, sponsored by the women's clubs of the district and with prizes offered by the Panhandle Plains Historical Society. Indeed, evaluating her situation, though she still did not have anything in the way of prospects, she was optimistic that something would develop for her. She was "eating regularly," and she "was not even assured of that a year ago." Moreover, she asserted, "I have made a conspicuous success in my profession." She expressed those views in a letter written on her forty-fourth birthday, a difficult age for any person, let alone a woman, seeking an entry-level academic position in the 1930s.[33]

If she was hopeful about her prospects, that mood quickly evaporated and gave way to one approaching despair. A letter from the director of the press informed her that the free distribution of one hundred copies of her dissertation "required by the graduate school" would "reduce our market too much." Debo wrote to the dean of the graduate school asking if a summary would not satisfy the requirement. In relating the development to Dale, she discussed her situation in marked contrast to what she had written earlier. "Aside from the salary," she wrote, "conditions here are about as nearly intolerable as it is possible for anybody's life to be." She had saved a little money, which she intended to spend in starting another book. "If I do not arrange to get into the writing field," she informed Dale, "it seems to me that I am stuck here forever." If the dean accepted her suggestion, her manuscript would be published and a new project could be launched. She explained her predicament to Dale, because "it is a habit I have." Dale, a member of the graduate council, would advise the dean regarding her request. She knew he would do all for her that he thought it right to do, "and you would not do more than that even if I were to ask you to."[34]

That crisis was soon resolved, but another embarrassing situation arose. Nowhere in the preface of her manuscript was the "proper acknowledgment" of Dale and the support he had rendered. She admitted she should have made such an acknowledgment, but she did not know why "I have such an unreasonable and illogical prejudice against putting things of that sort into print." She dedicated the book to the memory of her brother and said if she had to supply one hundred copies of her dissertation to the university for free distribution "that would have been an acknowledgment of my obligation to the history and government departments, which would put me under everlasting gratitude, and to the school that furnished me the fellowship." To further rationalize her not mentioning Dale, she explained, "I think Mr. Brandt feels, and I think he is right about it, that any identification of that book with the dissertation will spoil its chance of sale." She claimed to be ashamed of the absence of acknowledgments, stating, "I seem to have a positive genius for doing things wrong."[35]

Dale responded graciously in writing, "I think you are troubling yourself quite unnecessarily with respect to the acknowledgments which you did not make in your preface." He resolved the situation with the dean. She could submit an abstract, the cost of which would be no more than ten dollars. The way was then cleared for the prompt publication of her manuscript, and Debo was delighted. While she regretted not mentioning any of her mentors, she asked Dale if he considered it meaningful to send a copy of her book to Frank Phillips, whose funds secured the manuscript collections Dale supervised. She wished to express appreciation to Phillips for what he had done in furthering the cause of scholarship in western history.[36] In a convoluted way, Debo's plight at that time indicates a strong disinclination to be beholden to anyone. While she might have harbored doubts about Dale's scholarly abilities, she found herself unable to thank him publicly for his support and assistance. At the time Debo was a very vulnerable woman, revealing her liability to Dale as she sought to rationalize her behavior. Because she could no longer be a professor, she was determined to establish herself as a writer dependent on as few people as possible for advice and support. Thereafter, once her manuscript was published in the summer of 1934, the nature and tone of their correspondence slowly changed to reflect Debo's new status as a published historian.

With the publication of *The Rise and Fall of the Choctaw Republic*, Debo searched for a new topic. She considered a study of another of the civilized tribes but concluded there would be so much similarity in "land holding, regulation of non citizens, and autonomous government" that the material would "fall rather flat" to tell it again. She recalled Dale suggesting she write about the Kiowas. She began to research the topic but concluded there was not enough material for a book. Dale said he mentioned it only because it would be interesting; he had not investigated available source material. But he did congratulate her on the success of her book, about which he heard "many excellent comments." Debo, without a topic in hand, was determined to start research on another book. To make ends meet, she taught summer school. While she was happy "to be back at real work," she knew there was no permanent place for her in the department and she wanted to devote her time to a new project. She quit her position at the museum to devote full time to writing and making "every possible effort to secure a position." Buoyed by the favorable reception of her book, optimism once again pervaded her outlook. She informed Dale, "If I do not succeed, it will be just too bad, but I shall have written the book."[37]

Debo's new project brought her back to Oklahoma. Correspondence between the two tapered off as they then could visit with one another. She was researching the disposal of lands assigned to members of the Five Civilized Tribes by Congress in the late nineteenth century. In 1936 she applied "for a literary fellowship from the Houghton Mifflin people" to enable her to write a history of the Creek Indians when the "allotment book" was completed. She submitted as part of her application the Choctaw book and a plan of her current project. She hoped a letter from Dale would indicate to Houghton Mifflin "the seriousness and the integrity" of her candidacy, and in the fall she applied for a Guggenheim Fellowship. She received neither fellowship.[38]

In late summer of 1936 Debo followed a lead about a government project "to collect and edit Indian material." She wanted to apply for the position as director. She assured Dale she had ample experience as a project director. As curator of the museum in Canyon, Texas, she believed she inspired greater enthusiasm in Federal Emergency Relief Administration workers and got more work out of them "than anybody else in the Panhandle." She said, "I do my work quietly, but it gets done." She could pursue the job opening because her completed manuscript was then at the press. She titled it *And Still the Waters Run.* Joseph Brandt, the director of the press, however, thought the manuscript was too long, and she faced the "painful process" of throwing away "some pretty good pages.[39]

By year's end none of her grant proposals had been accepted. She applied to the American Council of Learned Societies and to the Social Science Research Council to complete a history of the Creeks. Brandt agreed to write about her current manuscript, which he liked, but it proved too controversial for some of its in-house readers because it indicated that several prominent citizens of Oklahoma, some of them friends of the university, had bilked Indians of the allotted lands. It remained unpublished, and Debo spent her time on the Creek project. And she still pursued a teaching post. Dr. William Bizzell, president of the university, in a gracious interview gave her names of people in Texas to write and permission to use his name. She also talked with people on campus about possible junior college and state college openings in Oklahoma. Depressed with the fate of her manuscript, she again sought a teaching post.[40]

None of those leads developed, but Debo did secure a job with the Works Progress Administration (WPA) in Oklahoma as the editor of an Indian-pioneer history project. Grant Foreman, the leading scholar on Oklahoma Indians, directed the project. At the outset, Debo followed leads suggested by the material that field workers collected and from the interviews they conducted. She informed Dale, "I am happier than I have been for—can't possibly be that long?—six years." He assisted her by providing a list of pioneers in southwestern Oklahoma and was delighted to learn of her good fortune in receiving a grant of $1,000 from the Social Science Research Council, the first recognition emanating from the numerous applications and letters she and Dale had been writing. The award would enable her to continue her history of the Creeks. Her work with Foreman was giving her "the best possible background." She told Dale that "as long as I can learn history and get paid for it, I shall not need to start drawing on the Council's funds." She was happy in her work and enthusiastic over the material they were securing. Her attitude and outlook, despite the rejection of her manuscript, had markedly improved.[41]

When she learned of the resignation of a member of the Department of History at OU, she immediately asked Dale if they planned to recruit another faculty member and if he had thought of her as a possible applicant. She recognized that few women were employed on history faculties, but she hoped her other qualifications "might serve to balance this defect." She reminded Dale of her remarkable academic record, only one B on her undergraduate record, and that was in mineralogy. At the University of Chicago she had compiled a straight A record, and her master's thesis had been published in the *Smith College Studies.* Dale, of course, knew of her record at OU, and that she had written another book since receiving her degree. She added that there were not many students who had won national recognition with their doctoral dissertation. She regretted that Dale had not heard her speak to an audience, but she assured him she could win a "responsive interest" from any group. While she had never taught graduate students, she had "initiated a large number of undergraduates into the technique of historical writing," a skill she had learned as a sophomore from Dale at the outset of his career "as a great teacher of history." She further explained she had left Canyon "only because it was a little school without standards," and because she was working "directly under a man who had an unfounded distrust of his own ability and a corresponding fear of people with advanced degrees." If Dale would offer only a temporary appointment, the future, she was confident, "would take care of itself." But no matter how Dale responded, it was to his "interest and encouragement" that she owed whatever success she had achieved as a historian.[42]

Neither her qualifications nor her flattery succeeded. The professor who resigned had for ten years developed the "Hispanic American field," and Dale deemed it "absolutely necessary" to recruit someone whose primary training and interest was in the same field. While he "deeply appreciated" her kind remarks and would continue to help her at any time he possibly could, she in no way qualified for the vacancy. Debo had no choice but to "understand the situation" and get on with her own work. That involved leaving her post with the Indian-pioneer history project and pursuing "the Creek Study." Her work with the project had given her "new insight into the inner life of the people" who made Oklahoma, and she deemed it "a privilege to be associated with the Foremans." She considered them great scholars, "people of almost unbelievable fineness and considerateness." It would come as no surprise that she dedicated *The Road to Disappearance: A History of the Creek Indians*, when it was published in 1941, to Grant and Carolyn Thomas Foreman.[43]

Almost a year later, writing from Washington, Debo again inquired if Dale would write for her to an old associate from earlier in his career, W. Carson Ryan. He was with the Carnegie Institution for the Advancement of Teaching in New York and possibly could use her in a research capacity. She also soon asked Dale to write on her behalf for an opening at the Texas State College for Women. That opening appeared to Debo to be the only chance she had "at an adequate position since she lost her job at Canyon" six years earlier. On a more positive note she informed Dale how another of his students, Gaston Litton, had assisted her as she started researching in the new National Archives Building.[44]

Two years later Debo, by then state supervisor of the Oklahoma Writers' Project helping to prepare the state guidebook, asked Dale to recommend graduate students and others who could assist in writing sections of the guide. She also asked Dale to prepare an introduction, interpreting the "Oklahoma Spirit" comparable to things he said to his Oklahoma history classes. "Nobody," she wrote, "can express the distinctive character of Oklahoma as you can." Dale complied with an essay he hoped was along the lines she wanted; if not, he told her, "feel free to chuck the whole thing in the waste basket." She would not hurt his feelings by doing so. Debo, delighted with his fine characterization of the "Oklahoma Spirit," nevertheless condensed the essay to meet space requirements without doing violence to his literary style. If he disapproved, Debo said, "We will change them back." Dale returned the manuscript with "a couple of minor suggestions," gratefully accepting the editorial revisions that improved "The Spirit of Oklahoma" so much that he wondered why he "couldn't have thought of those things in the first place." Clearly the relationship between Dale and Debo had moved to a different level. They were functioning as equals, professional historians working together to ready the state guide for publication. But that would soon change, and Angie Debo, then in her fifties, would once again be adrift and asking Dale to be on the lookout for a teaching position for her.[45]

In March 1941 she asked to be relieved of her position as soon as the state guide was finished. She explained to Dale that her experience with the Writers' Project convinced her it was based "upon an economic fallacy." She had forty people assigned to her project, "most of them intelligent and conscientious, and capable of performing acceptable research under supervision"; but, she explained, only one among them "was able to write." The "responsibility of planning, correcting, and supervising the research of forty people" left her with no time for writing. Moreover, "the piling up of research which could not be used was completely repugnant" to her "standards of thrift in the use of public funds." She concluded she could not continue at work she considered "socially indefensible," and she soon left to seek private employment. Debo worried that perhaps southwestern history, her field of specialization, was a handicap. She had done work in other history fields, but because her books about Indians "have been so outstanding," she feared people would assume she was "ignorant of all other subjects." She hoped Dale could help her; "there should be a place where my talents could be used." She was not "desperate or discouraged"; she could "always find things to do," but she was not satisfied to waste her talents as one who could "hold the attention of a college class and inspire students to enter into research and writing." Dale said that he "fully understood" why she had left the Writers' Project and would let her know if he learned of anything. In the meantime, he suggested, she too should "write around a bit" and make inquiries.[46]

Debo returned to the family home in Marshall when she completed her Creek history. She asked if Dale could track a rare United States Senate document she believed might have been in the Phillips Collection. Fortunately, the document was available, "the only copy in the state, with the exception of Grant Foreman's personal copy." In relaying the information, Dale departed from his hitherto formal salutation and for the first time in their correspondence addressed her as "Dear Angie." She was so pleased she considered framing the letter. She said, 'You used to call me by my given name . . . since I was a freshman taking Government I." She hoped he would continue to do so. And he did for the most part, but she always addressed him as Dr. Dale. He admitted that he considered himself her "academic Godfather, I have always taken myself some crumbs of credit for your rise to fame as a writer and historical scholar."[47]

During a break in her research and writing, Debo read the "History" chapter in *Oklahoma: A Guide to the Sooner State.* She was shocked, telling Dale, "I hope you will never read it, but if you do, I want you to know that I never saw it until a few days ago." He would be distressed to think his students could "turn out that kind of work." While she rode herd on the other writers, she wrote the "History" chapter herself. It was satisfactory to the woman in Washington overseeing the state guides. The book, she said, was complete when she left except for some revision in the section examining the principal cities.[48]

After she left the project, someone in the Washington office decided to discard her article and substitute another in its place. While she claimed she "had no particular yen" to see her words in print, she was "distressed beyond measure to think such an illiterate article should go out over my signature." She knew the book had been favorably reviewed and recognized that it would be "very useful," but she regretted that she allowed her signature to be used. She wanted Dale to know the book was changed without her knowledge. He thought she took the matter "a bit too seriously." Most people would "never notice the difference," and the few who would note the errors probably understood the situation. He did not think she needed "to worry too much."[49]

Debo followed his suggestion and, rather than worry, launched a new project. As a graduate student in Dale's Oklahoma history class, she had prepared a term paper examining the history of her hometown, Marshall. It received an A and a "Good" in Dale's handwriting. It seemed to her then, as well as in 1942, that while one small Oklahoma community of itself was not important, "its development spans in time and space most of the life of the American people." From early settlement on through the impact of the Great Depression and the reaction to outside events such as Pearl Harbor, Debo knew people who had played a part in all of it, and she could remember much of it as well. She wanted "to use reminiscences of old timers for color and detail" and validate them with substantive research, "dry but necessary information." She asked Dale, if he believed she could do it, to write to Alfred A. Knopf in her support as a candidate for a fellowship to enable her to write it. She intended to make the book "more popular" than her previous books, but she assured Dale she aimed "to be as thorough in scholarship" as always. She forwarded with her application 10,000 words of the proposed study. While waiting to hear of the fate of her application, she informed Dale that the Social Science Research Council had awarded her $500, a smaller sum than she requested, for a study of Indian policy.[50]

Alfred A. Knopf shortly thereafter wrote Dale explaining that "we are very much taken by Dr. Debo's project." He wanted assurance, however, that her project could properly be classified as history. Uncertainty arose because Debo chose to treat her subject compositely; "Prairie City," like "Middletown," was a fictitious name, and because she made no claim that real persons were represented, Knopf wanted assurance that the history fellowship went to a work that professional historians would accept as such. Dale said that in taking "a small town as a type of thousands of other small towns throughout the Great Plains, she would in effect be presenting a history of an entire great region." Such a procedure and such a study constituted sound history "so recognized by virtually all historians." Knopf was satisfied. He informed Dale in strictest confidence that she would be awarded the fellowship in history.[51]

As soon as she learned of the award, Debo started collecting experiences "from the Old Timers" as they were "falling off pretty fast." She recognized that Dale's letter "had a great deal of influence," and she was "very grateful." She had experienced hard times since she lost her teaching position at Canyon, but she claimed it was "the best thing" that ever happened to her. The award of $100 a month for twelve months meant that Knopf would be devoting the skills of his publishing house to marketing her manuscript. Because she was the only one of Dale's PhDs not placed satisfactorily, the time had come, she told him, when "you can take me off your worrying list." If she did not succeed with the new venture, it would be her own fault. And, she added, "I will burst a blood vessel rather than to let that happen."[52]

The fellowship and all that went with it marked Angie Debo's coming of age as a scholar able to function without depending for assistance on her mentor. Then in her early fifties, she was confident she could earn her livelihood publishing significant historical studies. The fellowship would secure her national recognition and could bring her books to the attention of a broad audience. She told Dale, "Bustin' is the only word that expresses it."

In October of the following year, 1943, she wrote Dale, "The last word of the preface is written." Prairie City, the story of a "composite Oklahoma town, which is the history of the United States in Microcosm," was the only one of her books, she explained, "that I felt belonged to you in its content." She asked Dale if she could dedicate it to him. Dale, of course, was delighted, regarding it as "a very high honor . . . one of those things that come to a man only about once his life." He wanted her to know how proud he was of her and her accomplishments. In dedicating *Prairie City*, published in 1944, to Dale, Debo made amends for not previously publicly thanking him and literally declared her independence of him. For the first time they truly could relate to one another as equals, something she had tried unsuccessfully to do as far back as her days as a graduate student challenging Dale's criticism of the introductory chapter of her dissertation.[53]

In 1945 Debo began teaching a summer school class at Oklahoma Agricultural and Mechanical College (Oklahoma A&M), but that was the last class she ever taught. Dale visited with her in Stillwater and spoke to her class. Though offered a permanent position in the department, she turned it down "in favor of some work in the library" that would interfere less with her writing. The following spring she applied for a fellowship awarded by the University of Oklahoma Press. She proposed to write a general history of the state. Dale thought she could launch her project once summer school was over and that she could complete it within a year.[54]

In 1947, while preparing her study of Oklahoma, she sought information from Dale about the number of cattle in Oklahoma during the "cow country" period so she could make a comparison between the earlier period and the present. She believed there were more cattle in the state at the time she was writing. Dale said her guess of 1.5 million in 1885 "may not be far off." In addition, she asked Dale's permission to include a sketch of his life in a section of her script that would introduce the reader "to some typical Oklahomans." Most of the information she needed was available "from a term paper I wrote about your life and work long ago." She wished to add "a little human detail" and wanted to know if he camped in a chuck wagon "out by the creek" when he started college. He did not, Dale replied. The closest he came was while attending a "Summer Normal" at Cloud Chief in Washita County; he slept on the prairie and paid two dollars a week for meals at a nearby home. Dale provided further details of his early life, all of which helped round out her portrait of him.[55]

As one of the readers of her manuscript, Dale trusted she would not be offended by his comments and criticisms, because he thought the manuscript needed "quite a good deal of revision." He said that it was at his suggestion the subject she wrote about was chosen and that she was selected as the proper person to do it. He had hoped to tackle the topic himself but was quite willing to turn it over to her, because "there is so much to do and so little time left me to do it." The director of the press and five readers, including Dale, had read her manuscript and concluded that revisions were necessary. Debo, however, "manifested a lack of confidence in their judgment," and a reader of her own choosing agreed with her. But Dale noted that six to one "is a pretty large majority." She had been paid for the work through a fellowship, and the director of the press was faced with having to expend thousands of dollars more to publish a manuscript "which his readers and his judgment tell him should not be published in its present form." Dale asked, "Can a fair-minded person like yourself justify asking him to do this?"[56]

Dale disagreed with her suggestion that the manuscript be released elsewhere for publication. The book was written by an Oklahoman about Oklahoma, and the grant she received came from OU. Moreover, the awards committee, Dale insisted, "should not be forced to assume responsibility for a book over which it had no control, either to its content or format." Frankly, he thought she had taken the criticisms and suggestions of the six readers "far too seriously." The outstanding characteristic of every scholar, he said, should be "humility." No one expected her to agree with all the criticism. This time, unlike the time Debo had confronted Dale as a graduate student, Dale, buttressed by the support of the press committee, indicated he would not yield to her. He noted that the readers offered little objection to the first hundred pages. Only the last two-thirds seemed to require considerable revision. Dale said, "Surely that should not prove an insurmountable task." Then he admitted that he had time only for "a hasty survey" of her manuscript, but he would be glad to set aside his own work and go over it, "chapter by chapter and page by page . . . praising where praise seems due and not 'pulling any punches' if such seems necessary." Certainly, she had had confidence in his judgment in the past, and he knew she did not question his sincerity, friendship, or eager desire to promote her best interests.[57]

Dale asked permission to let him review her manuscript and to submit his comments to the press director, Savoie Lottinville, so she could revise with "considerable assurance" that her final revision would be acceptable to the publisher. However, if she still adhered to her original position "to change a word now and then but not many," Dale said there was no need for him to go over her manuscript. He urged her to reconsider and allow him and the press committee to help her produce "an outstanding contribution" that would add to her reputation. That lengthy letter, the longest he had ever sent to her, posed a real dilemma for Debo. She had challenged the comments and criticisms of the press committee only to learn in the letter that, while Dale urged her to make revisions and not reject their remarks, he had not carefully read her manuscript.[58]

Debo thanked Dale for his "fine letter" and indicated she would be grateful for his advice and criticism. While she did not blame Lottinville "for accepting the opinion of five readers" (she had the good grace not to mention that Dale was one of them), she insisted the reports forwarded to her did not represent "honest criticism." She considered them "a bitter, hostile attack" in which her statements were "twisted and tortured." She said she was not sensitive to criticism, and while she knew authors were sometimes asked to revise manuscripts, she had "not had much experience of this in the seven books" she had written for three different publishers. Alfred Knopf had read the Prairie City manuscript himself. He questioned only two sentences. *And Still the Waters Run*, she said, had received a favorable reader's report recommending publication but suggesting the manuscript be "shortened greatly." She saw the wisdom of those remarks and considerably improved the manuscript.[59]

She could respond to intelligent criticism, but to a sweeping condemnation, her options, she believed, were "to surrender and quit writing, or rise above it." And she intended to rise above it, drawing on the self-confidence generated by the reception accorded her previous publications. She wanted to make some revisions before she sent the manuscript to Dale. She was grateful for his interest and "for all the years in which you have been my adviser." However, she indicated her vulnerability and her reliance on Dale by the phrase she used in signing the letter, "With all the old affection."[60]

Dale went over her manuscript with great care. Though he had perused her manuscript for only one evening when she first returned it to the press, he noted that she had made considerable revisions, which he believed markedly improved it. However, he objected to her dedicating the book to former university press director Joseph Brandt, who had stood by her in the controversy over *And Still the Waters Run.* Brandt had later returned to Oklahoma as president of the university. When Dale threatened to leave for a post at Oklahoma A&M, Brandt appointed him research professor of history, thereby effectively removing him from running the department. As president, Brandt had objected to the governor of the state interfering in university affairs and in 1944 resigned to become director of the University of Chicago Press. Dale, always sensitive to public opinion, argued that her dedication to Brandt, followed by "whom Oklahoma lost," would revive "ancient controversies" and could do her book real harm. Following Dale's suggestion, she changed her dedication to "Joseph A. Brandt, Ex-Oklahoman."[61]

Dale said he devoted much time and effort to his criticisms, some of which might seem sharp, "but we are old friends." In a sense, Debo was invading Dale's turf. Oklahoma history was his field of specialization, and he had published numerous books examining state history as well. His entire career was involved in almost every way with Oklahoma history, and his "favorite PhD," who already had a national reputation rivaling and even surpassing his, appeared to be challenging him directly with an Oklahoma history of her own.[62]

In August 1948 Lottinville sent Dale a copy of Debo's revised manuscript, together with her report on his memorandum of critique. Dale said he was pleased; she had accepted "far more of my criticisms and suggestions than I had any right to expect." He thought the manuscript was greatly improved and that her troubles with respect to it were "about over." Where she disagreed with his criticisms, they would elicit no response from him, the same reaction he had had when Debo was a graduate student who disagreed with his criticism of portions of her dissertation. Dale claimed he provided her with a frank and honest appraisal. And then gracious almost to a fault, he remarked how deeply touched and embarrassed he was by the evidences of "friendship and admiration" appearing in her report and by her "almost childlike faith" in his judgment and ability as a historian. He said he never professed to be an "expert in the field of Oklahoma history," let alone a "great historian," and claimed that others, including Debo, knew as much about Oklahoma history as he did.[63]

Dale's lengthy memorandum did not pull any punches and suggested otherwise. It was divided into two parts, one presenting general comments and the second consisting of notes with respect to each chapter. Among the general comments, he thought she would benefit greatly by examining John Gould Fletcher's *Arkansas* and George Sessions Perry's *Texas*, interpretive studies by master craftsmen of states abutting Oklahoma. He also thought she mentioned too many living persons and smaller towns. Neglected individuals and chambers of commerce of omitted towns could complain. He thought she devoted too much attention to "shameful operations" of Oklahoma's past and too openly indicated her preferences without "saying so in so many words." And at times Dale believed some of her material "might have been written by the secretary of the most enthusiastic of booster clubs." In short, Debo let her passions and prejudices come to the fore and they needed to be tempered. He thought she should "steer clear" as far as possible of "the Negro question." She did not cover topics he thought needed discussion, the liquor problem for one. Churches and religion needed further amplification. And he went on.[64]

But in doing so, Dale revealed more about himself and his fear of controversy, of offending prominent individuals, as well as his focus on the smiling aspects of Oklahoma life and history and toning down, if not ignoring, the darker aspects. Her object should be both to please and to inform readers. Debo in her previous works had been concerned with writing history, relating the unvarnished truth as she saw it. She tried to follow the same approach with the new manuscript, a general popular history that would appeal more to a wider audience than had her previous monographs. Whereas Dale had written more popular studies than monographs, their views were bound to clash. Debo once again had to give the appearance of yielding to his superior wisdom, while maintaining as much of her draft as she considered valid.

Debo prepared and sent to Lottinville a fourteen-page "Report on Dr. Dale's Memorandum," in which she dealt with specific criticisms before addressing his general comments. She said she would have liked to express appreciation to Dale in the preface but refrained because of his biographical sketch in the body of the book. She accepted, albeit reluctantly, some of Dale's objections, telling Lottinville in one instance, "I will willingly make the deletions if you say so." At another point, despite Dale's comments, she insisted "it will have to stand as it is." She revised when she believed Dale's comments were valid; when not, she held firm by stating why she held firm and where she had secured her information. Occasionally she told Lottinville, "Here is a place you will have to decide." She hoped the specific changes she made would remove the general objections to her manuscript; if not, she said, "There is nothing I can do about it." Despite Dale's hard work on the manuscript, for which she was grateful, the book, she said, "is an expression of my own personality and not of Dr. Dale's." She would not rewrite it "on radically different lines," but, she concluded, "Somehow I have a feeling that our troubles are over."[65]

Dale considered his work with the manuscript at an end when he sent it back to the press. Thereafter, he told Lottinville, "It is yours and her problem." He read her comments on his memorandum and checked the changes she made. He appreciated her confidence in him, treasured her friendship, and wished her well. He told her to "drop me a line when you can find the time." Several months later she found time to drop him a line requesting prints from photographs in the Phillips Collection. Thus their relationship returned to a more placid level, and their correspondence tapered off.[66]

A year later, in belatedly returning a photograph to the Phillips Collection, she told Dale about her summer. The Indian Rights Association had asked her to prepare a survey of the social and economic conditions of "the Five Tribes Indians." She was pleased with the contacts she had made and with her interesting experiences. Dale told her of his lecture tour and how it was interrupted owing to the critical illness and death of his brother. While they again had a relationship of equals, they were drifting apart. Moreover, their correspondence usually covered subjects other than history.[67]

In November 1949, at a dinner honoring Angie Debo and the publication of *Oklahoma: Foot-loose and Fancy-free*, her sixth book, given under the auspices of the library staff at Oklahoma A&M, Dale delivered what must have been a standard speech, "The Spirit of Oklahoma." Debo talked about some of her experiences while collecting material for her books. Dale said it was a grand party. He swelled with pride, believing he could take a little credit for her success. Most revealing on both their parts was Dale's thanking her for a copy of the book with its "lovely inscription," which he said "adds so much to its value." He paid compliments to Debo's mother, whom he had met for the first time, and signed his letter for the first time as "Sincerely, your friend." Dale at the time was seventy years old, and Debo was fifty-nine.[68]

When it appeared in 1951, Debo sent Dale a copy of her survey of the Five Civilized Tribes. While engaged in the research for the book, she told Dale of individuals she met who had spoken fondly of him, and she also mentioned her experience at a meeting of the Oklahoma

Historical Society, where she learned that most people attending did not know what a "cattle guard" was. She queried, "Can it be that Oklahomans are getting too civilized?" Dale responded that it was not a matter of civilization but of "profound ignorance." Their relationship was easygoing and becoming a close and valued one, evident when Dale acknowledged "the beautiful tribute" she paid him in a letter included among a file of tributes accorded him at Oklahoma A&M during his summer lecture. Debo drove from Marshall to be on hand for the occasion.[69]

But Dale had not quite forgotten or forgiven. In 1955, when J. Fred Rippy considered sending a manuscript to the University of Oklahoma Press, he wanted to ask Debo to put in a good word for him with Savoie Lottinville. Dale's response was, "For Heaven's sake . . . do not call on Angie Debo to use her influence with Savoie! . . . She ain't got none." He related the controversy over *Oklahoma: Foot-loose and Fancy-free.* He claimed to be "quite fond" of her but noted that "she nearly drove Savoie crazy" in the course of publishing the volume. It seemed to Dale, as he explained it to Rippy, that she had developed a complex that her words were sacred and that changes suggested by "the editorial staff were bound to be wrong." Lottinville swore, according to Dale, that he would never again go through such an experience. Fearing that perhaps he had given the wrong impression, Dale told Rippy of his high regard for Debo, that her first book was awarded the Dunning Prize of the American Historical Association, that she had dedicated one of her later books to him. But he admitted that she was "a little peculiar" and that Lottinville was "much discouraged with her."[70]

Even that impression changed after Debo complimented Lottinville in a *New York Times* review of *Oklahoma: A Guide to the Sooner State*, a revised edition of the WPA volume she helped prepare. Lottinville wrote Debo, "That was just about the nicest thing anybody ever said to me." In her review Debo said that Lottinville's essay, "The Spirit of Oklahoma," was "a penetrating interpretation, perhaps the best ever written, of the qualities that give the state its distinctive character." For the earlier edition of the guide, Debo had solicited a similar essay from Dale. Debo's remarks about Lottinville's essay could be read as an indication of her doubts about the depths of Dale's historical insight. Each had doubts about the other's abilities, which cropped up in different places but never directly between themselves.[71]

Dale died in his early nineties in 1972, Debo in her late nineties in 1988. In their twilight years their correspondence, though infrequent, was even more gracious and cordial. In 1958 Dale wrote a letter to be read at a celebration honoring Debo in her hometown. In another letter Dale remarked that it would be fun to talk over "all the events we shared in days gone by." In the summer of 1967 she had a good visit with the Dales and a chance to teach a course in Indian history at OU, at an institute for teachers of Indian children. The course brought an opportunity for her to visit tribal areas in New Mexico and Arizona, but Dale was not instrumental in either instance.[72]

In 1969, in a handwritten letter, Dale complained that it seemed like a long time since he had heard from her. He sent a picture of the new social science building that was named for him and hoped she could attend the dedication of Dale Hall the following year. He wanted to know what she was doing and said she was "by far" the most distinguished author "among the some twenty scholars whose dissertations he directed." He also informed Debo he was completing his memoirs. It is interesting to note that in his posthumously published autobiography, *The West Wind Blows*, Dale mentioned Angie Debo only once, as a recipient of a grant "for a book called *Oklahoma: Foot-Loose and Fancy-Free*," adding that Debo was not a member of the university faculty. But he signed a 1970 letter, "Sincerely and with much love, Your oldest friend."[73]

In December 1970 Debo appeared in Norman to autograph copies of her new book, *A History of the Indians of the United States*. Dale, owing to illness, was unable to attend. He had hoped she would stop by or telephone. He wanted to purchase a copy of the book, which he wanted her to autograph, and again expressed a yearning to go over old times, times when he was the dominant figure in her tempestuous unfolding career. Debo was disappointed that she did not see Dale in Norman. In writing her book she said she thought often of the course he offered in Indian history, the only such course in the United States at the time. She had followed in his footsteps and brought the topic up to date. She sent Dale an autographed copy as an indication of how much she owed him, mentioning especially that she had learned how to do research as an undergraduate in his history courses. She signed her letter, "Love to Both of you."[74]

In 1972, at age eighty-two, Debo wrote Dale that she was to present a paper, "Major Indian Record Collections in Oklahoma," at a conference at the National Archives. She inquired about the gift from Frank Phillips and the way in which Dale had obtained the material he used in the collection. Dale was too ill to respond, and he died several weeks later. As a final tribute to Dale, Debo told his widow that she had the privilege of preparing an essay on Dale for the memorial volume Arrell M. Gibson was editing. It was published in 1975. In Dale's final publication he barely mentioned Debo. In the memorial volume she honored his memory with a sparkling essay, "Edward Everett Dale: The Teacher."[75]

Notes

1. The Dale-Debo correspondence is largely located in Box 17 of the Edward Everett Dale Papers in the Western History Collections, University of Oklahoma Library, Norman (hereafter cited as Dale Papers and WHC). Unless otherwise noted, all citations are from this source. Oklahoma State University houses the Angie Debo Collection, which contains a few Dale-Debo letters not available at the University of Oklahoma. Both institutions now have a full selection of the correspondence, each library having secured copies of the letters not originally in its files.

2. Dale to Debo, January 21, June 27, June 30, 1925; Debo to Dale, June 4, July 14, 1925.

3. Debo to Dale, November 30, 1925, February 10, 1926; Dale to Debo, January 23, 1926; *Sooner: Yearbook of the University of Oklahoma*, 1924, 26.

4. Debo to Dale, November 17, December 18, 1927; Dale to Debo, November 21, 1927.

5. Dale to Debo, January 8, 1928; Debo to Dale, May 21, 1928, August 15, 1929.

6. Debo to Dale, March 18, 1931; Dale to Debo, March 23, 1931. The seminary room would be the equivalent today of the graduate bullpen.

7. Debo to Dale, June 30, 1931; Dale to Debo, July 2, 1931.

8. Debo to Dale, July 26, 1934.

9. Debo to Dale, September 29, 1931. This is the first typewritten letter she sent to Dale.

10. Dale to Debo, October 7, 1931.

11. Debo to Dale, October 9, 1931.

12. Ibid.

13. Ibid.

14. Dale to Debo, October 14, 1931.

15. Dale to Debo, April 6, July 1, 1932; Debo to Dale, April 14, June 29, July 5, 1932.

16. Debo to Dale, July 5, 1932.

17. Debo to Dale, July 23, 1932. The article never appeared. A review of her book appeared in *Mississippi Valley Historical Review* 21 (1934–35): 409–10.

18. Dale to Debo, July 28, 1932.

19. Ibid.

20. Debo to Dale, August 4, 1932.

21. Dale to Debo, September 20, October 8, 1932.

22. Debo to Dale, October 19, 1935.

23. Dale to Debo, October 24, November 2, 1932.

24. Debo to Dale, November 3, November 5, 1932; Dale to Debo, November 7, 1932. Debo's article, "Education in the Choctaw Country After the Civil War," appeared in *Chronicles of Oklahoma* 10 (September, 1932): 383–91.

25. Debo to Dale, November 23, November 28, December 6, 1932, January 5, January 24, 1933. She failed to secure the American Association of University Women fellowship. See Debo to Dale, February 11, 1933.

26. Debo to Dale, February 21, February 28, 1933; Dale to Debo, February 24, 1933.

27. Dale to Debo, April 21, May 3, 1933.

28. Debo to Dale, May 4, May 15, 1933; J. A. Hill to Dale, May 8, 1933, Dale Papers, Box 30, Folder 19, WHC.

29. Debo to Dale, May 18, July 16, 1933. "An English View of the Wild West" appeared in *Panhandle Plains Historical Review* 6 (1933): 24–44.

30. Dale to Debo, July 19, 1933; Debo to Dale, September 1, 1933.

31. Debo to Dale, October 5, 1933. Thanks to a generous gift from oilman Frank Phillips, Dale organized and administered the Western History Collections, initially called the Frank Phillips Collections.

32. Debo to Dale, November 11, 1933, January 4 (telegram), January 11, 1934. See also J. Fred Rippy to Debo, January 4, 1934. She sent the letter to Dale, who filed it with his Debo correspondence.

33. Debo to Dale, January 30, 1934. Dale explained that his colleague, Carl Coke Rister, knew more about Panhandle history than he did and would be better qualified to judge the essays. She then invited Rister. See Debo to Dale, February 13, 1934.

34. Debo to Dale, April 17, 1934. Debo would have had to pay the cost of printing the hundred copies available for free distribution.

35. Dale to Debo, April 18, 1934; Debo to Dale, April 30, 1934.

36. Debo to Dale, May 7, 1934; Dale to Debo, May 9, 1934. Dale further suggested Debo send an autographed copy of her book to Patrick J. Hurley, whose papers he would secure for the Western History Collections.

37. Debo to Dale, July 3, August 14, 1934; Dale to Debo, August 8, 1934. Her book was awarded the John A. Dunning Prize by the American Historical Association.

38. Debo to Dale, March 18, September 29, 1936; Dale to Debo, March 23, 1936.

39. Debo to Dale, August 26, September 2, 1936; Dale to Debo, September 8, 1936.

40. Debo to Dale, December 26, 1936, and n.d. [1937?]; Dale to Debo, January 4, 1937.

41. Debo to Dale, February 13, February 17, April 2, April 6, 1937; Dale to Debo, April 3, April 6, 1937.

42. Debo to Dale, June 19, 1937.

43. Debo to Dale, June 26, 1937.

44. Debo to Dale, May 5, May 8, May 2, 1938; Dale to Debo, May 14, May 24, 1938.

45. Dale to Debo, September 13, September 19, September 28, November 19, 1940, January 15, January 20, 1941; Debo to Dale, September 26, 1940, January 17, 1941.

46. Debo to Dale, March 24, 1941. By 1941 Debo had published two more books, *And Still the Waters Run* (Princeton, N.J.: Princeton University Press, 1940) and *The Road to Disappearance* (Norman: University of Oklahoma Press, 1941). Dale to Debo, March 26, 1941.

47. Debo to Dale, November 25, December 4, 1941; Dale to Debo, December 2, December 5, 1941.

48. Debo to Dale, January 11, 1942.

49. Dale to Debo, January 13, 1942.

50. Debo to Dale, February 6, February 14, March 29, 1942; Dale to Debo, February 10, March 31, 1942.

51. Alfred A. Knopf to Dale, April 24, May 5, 1942; Dale to Knopf, April 29, 1942, Box 38, Dale Papers, WHC.

52. Debo to Dale, May 22, May 27, 1942; Dale to Debo, May 22, June 5, 1942. Dale sent her his correspondence with Alfred Knopf and asked that she return the letters. He also recommended her for a special award of $2,500 from the American Association of University Women. See Dale to Laura A. White, January 5, 1943, Box 72, Dale Papers WHC.

53. Debo to Dale, October 12, 1943; Dale to Debo, October 14, 1943. Earlier in 1943 the University of Oklahoma Press published her study, *Tulsa: From Creek Town to Oil Capital.*

54. Dale to Debo, June 14, 1945, May 2, May 8, June 10, 1946, April 12, 1947; Debo to Dale, May 4, 1946, March 28, 1947.

55. Debo to Dale, March 28, April 9, May 30, June 5, 1947; Dale to Debo, April 1, June 3, June 9, 1947. For her discussion of Dale, see *Oklahoma: Foot-loose and Fancy-free* (Norman: University of Oklahoma Press, 1949), 137–40.

56. Dale to Debo, March 22, 1948, Angie Debo Papers, Oklahoma State University (hereafter cited as Debo Papers, OSU). None of the letters pertaining to this controversy are in the Dale Papers.

57. Ibid.

58. Ibid.

59. Debo to Dale, March 27, 1948, Debo Papers, OSU.

60. Ibid.

61. Dale to Debo, June 5, 1948, Debo Papers, OSU.

62. Ibid.

63. Dale to Debo, August 19, 1948, Debo Papers, OSU.

64. Dale to Savoie Lottinville, August 19, 1948, University of Oklahoma Press Collection, Box 256, WHC (hereafter cited as Press Collection). Appended to this letter is Dale's five-page memorandum critiquing her manuscript. He also included a three-page memorandum for Lottinville citing specific disagreements. He did not think it would do any good to send a copy of it to her. It was dictated, he explained, "soley [*sic*] for you and your staff."

65. Report on Dr. Dale's Memorandum, Box 256, Press Collection, WHC.

66. Dale to Debo, August 23, 1948, Debo Papers, OSU; Dale to Debo, November 8, November 13, 1948; Debo to Dale, November 6, November 18, 1948.

67. Debo to Dale, August 13, September 5, 1949; Dale to Debo, August 22, September 19, 1949.

68. *Stillwater* (Okla.) *NewsPress*, November 4, 1949; Dale to Debo, November 10, 1949.

69. Debo to Dale, May 14, 1951; Dale to Debo, May 15, 1951, June 24, 1952.

70. Dale to J. Fred Rippy, January 27, February 10, 1955, Box 58, Folder 2, Dale Papers, WHC.

71. *New York Times Book Review*, September 8, 1957; Lottinville to Debo, September 16, 1957, Box 36, File 14, Press Collection, WHC.

72. Debo to Dale, n.d. [April, 1958?], Christmas, 1967; Dale to Debo, April 14, 1958, September 20, 1967, Debo Papers, OSU.

73. Dale to Debo, March 30, 1969, July 16, 1970, Debo Papers, OSU. See also Edward Everett Dale, *The West Wind Blows: The Autobiography of Edward Everett*

Dale, ed. Arrell M. Gibson (Oklahoma City: Oklahoma Historical Society, 1984), 352.

74. Dale to Debo, December 3, 1970, Debo Papers, OSU; Debo to Dale, December 7, 1970.

75. Debo to Dale, March 24, 1972; Debo to Rosalie Dale, December 26, 1972. See also Arrell M. Gibson, ed., *Frontier Historian: The Life and Work of Edward Everett Dale* (Norman: University of Oklahoma Press, 1975), 21–37.

« 3 »

Environmental and Cultural Ecology

Before the advent of non-Indian people in the lands that became Oklahoma, Native inhabitants generally believed that trees, hills, rocks, lakes, and other objects of nature contained guardian spirits. Indians accepted the premise that they were, whenever possible, to live in harmony with nature. Their function was to enjoy and protect what they had been bequeathed. The land gave them their livelihood and identity.

The pioneers, with their Christian religion and capitalist ethos, brought with them a markedly different outlook. Rather than being caretakers of the earth, their relationship with nature was to be its master, to "tame" their environment, to bring the technology of the nineteenth-century Industrial Revolution and its scientific achievements, to the extent that their means allowed, into an area that advanced quickly from a territorial status to statehood. Following the biblical injunction to "be fruitful and multiply and replenish the earth and subdue it," the faithful were challenged to convert their newly acquired lands into a veritable garden. Their conception of work involved mining, logging, and especially farming.

Because viewpoints differed at the outset within the boundaries of Oklahoma, which by 2000 was a state with a very large population of American Indians, seeds of culture conflict were sown. Indian beliefs and values persisted, though their supporting economic and political structures vanished, were adapted, or were absorbed into the dominant white culture. What holds for Indians holds as well for white and African American Oklahomans: the values they attached to pioneering persist in cheerful defiance of contrary evidence. The values, however, were not monolithic, as different environments produced different cultures. Nor was it surprising that a society spread thinly across the land exhibited, in most instances, a privatized culture.

Oklahoma was admitted into the union as the forty-sixth state on November 16, 1907, but there was no consensus as to whether it was a southern state, a plains state, or a southwestern state. It all depended on the settler's perception. Noting a farm enclosure for livestock, for example, a southern settler probably would signify it as a cow pen, a settler from Kansas or further north and east would call it a barnyard, and a Texan most likely would designate it as a corral.

Located largely between the 33rd and 37th parallels north and the 94th and 103rd meridians west, Oklahoma, with seventy-seven counties, ranks eighteenth in size among the states and occupies almost 70,000 square miles. With the exception of Minnesota, it is larger than any state east of it and smaller than any other western state, except Washington and Hawaii. Oklahoma is unusual in that it was cobbled out of territory other states did not want as part of their domain and out of land set aside by the federal government to be "forever a home for the Indians." Oklahoma then was created as a dumping ground for Indians and as a meeting ground for peoples from other countries and sections of the nation.

By the 2010 census, Oklahoma had reached a population of 3,751,357. Many of the more than 337,000 Indians in the state are descendants of the original sixty-seven tribes forcibly located in Indian Territory. They comprise 9 percent of the population, and African Americans comprise 7.6 percent (285,103). People of Asian descent comprise 1.9 percent (71,276) of the state's inhabitants. In addition, by 2010 more than 348,000 people of Hispanic origin lived in Oklahoma, chiefly part of the 81.5 percent (3,057,978) that forms the white population. In the late nineteenth and early twentieth centuries, concentrations of Italian, German, Pole, Czech, Slovak, and Mennonite (chiefly Russian and German) immigrants brought their own traditions to eventually merge with those of the other white population. In general, eastern Oklahoma is more densely populated than western Oklahoma, with the metropolitan areas of Oklahoma City and Tulsa containing between them about 1.8 million people. The remaining major cities, all under 100,000 people, with the exception of Enid, either border Interstate 35 or are east of the highway. Counties along the western border of the state, including the Panhandle, have the fewest inhabitants and the lowest population density.

Like its variations in peoples, Oklahoma is characterized by variations in climate, landforms, soils, and vegetation. Mountainous lands give way to extensive areas of almost level plains. The atmosphere above is a meeting space for polar continental and tropical maritime air masses. Heavy rainfalls and violent storms are caused by the mixing of cold, dry polar fronts and warm, moist tropical fronts. Tornadoes occur quite commonly, with April and May being the most active months. Between 1875 and 1970 more than 1,600 tornados struck Oklahoma. In 1997 the state experienced 57. But the most devastating by far occurred on May 3, 1999, and on May 20, 2013. Oklahoma's climate then reflects the nature of its geography. Average annual precipitation varies from more than 50 inches in the pine forests of the Ouachita Mountains in the southeast to approximately 15 inches on the High Plains of the western Panhandle. The dimensions of the state, coupled with its geographic diversity, create situations in which one area suffers drought while another enjoys surplus water.

Similarly, there is a wide variety of soils, some highly productive and others of little or no value for yielding crops. Vegetation ranges from forest, which covers about 23 percent of the state's land area, especially in eastern Oklahoma, to prairies in the central areas to steppe grasslands of the western portions of the state. But even these lands are snaked by strands of trees along the watercourses. As the historian Angie Debo noted, the state "probably has more kinds of country, more kinds of weather, and more kinds of flora and fauna than any other area of similar size in the United States." Oklahoma then is a transition land. The eastern and western halves of the state differ physically in landforms, vegetation, and climate. They differ culturally from the contrasting development of Indian Territory, Oklahoma Territory, and the Panhandle, areas consolidated in 1907 into the state of Oklahoma. In addition, the northern and southern halves differ in length of growing season, in crops (cotton, initially in the southern half, and wheat in the northern half as the chief crops), in roughness of local topography, and in culture, because of settlement by people from the northern and southern sections of the nation.

In a transition land such as Oklahoma, different ideas, traditions, and viewpoints come together and mingle. At times this was done successfully, leading to profitable agricultural, mining, and industrial activities. Where people and nature have not worked well together, there are areas of severely eroded farmlands, denuded forests, polluted waterways, mining spills, decaying towns, and villages accompanied by human poverty.

Oklahoma lies on a northwest-to-southeast drainage plain with such a scramble of landforms that some streams flow north and west before entering the drainage pattern. The land rises from 300 feet above sea level near Idabel in the southeastern portion of the state to 4,973 feet in the Black Mesa region of the Panhandle. The state is a patchwork of plains, hills, and mountains and, moreover, is drained by two great river systems, the Arkansas and the Red. The Arkansas, born in the Colorado Rockies, enters Oklahoma in the north, gathering the Salt Fork, Chickaskia, Cimarron, Verdigris, Grand, and Illinois Rivers. The Canadian River is its principal southern feeder. The North Canadian, formed at the junction of the Beaver River and Wolf Creek in the Panhandle, enters the Canadian near Eufaula. The Red River, forming on the High Plains of the Texas Panhandle, delineates Oklahoma's southern border, gathering in its course the waters of the North Fork, the Washita, the Boggy, the Blue, and the Kiamichi.

Until the 1870s, rivers were main arteries of transportation. Keelboats plied the upper waters of the Arkansas and Red and some of their tributaries into the 1920s. A century earlier, in the 1820s and 1830s, steamboats had plied the Arkansas and Red and had traversed the navigable portions of some of their tributaries. The Missouri, Kansas and Texas Railway (MK&T or Katy), the first railroad to operate in Oklahoma, ran trains to Muskogee in the Creek Nation, Indian Territory. Late in 1872 the MK&T crossed the Red River into Texas at Colbert's Ferry. At statehood in 1907 more than 5,000 miles of track crisscrossed Oklahoma.

Indian governments were not enthused about railroads, fearing the trains would bring droves of white settlers. And the settlers, like the Populists before and Progressives after statehood, were suspicious of railroads and of other out-of-state corporations. The railroads in turn, besides encouraging settlement, sought to develop natural-resource tonnage. Seeking to recruit coal miners, the railroads sent agents to Europe to hire men to work in the mines in the Choctaw Nation. Because Indians in general were not interested in becoming miners, immigrants from several European countries were brought to eastern Oklahoma.

Another extractive industry active before statehood was zinc and lead mining in the Tri-State Mining District in northeastern Oklahoma. This industry developed when prospectors entered Indian Territory in 1891. By the 1980s, when mining activities were no longer significant, the Environmental Protection Agency ranked the area among the nation's most hazardous waste sites and assisted a campaign to eradicate 70 million gallons of acid mine waters that over decades had formed as groundwater and now spilled to the surface.

In other parts of the Indian nations, springs and streams with green slicks of oil were valued for their therapeutic qualities. In the Chickasaw Nation natural gas spewed to the surface, allowing Indians to light their council fires with torches fueled by it. Both oil and natural gas would become gigantic industries in the twentieth century, with discoveries occurring in almost every county in the state.

In eastern Oklahoma, oak and hickory forests dominate the Ozark Plateau in the northeast and the northern and western sections of the Ouachitas. In the southeastern corner, pine forests dominate. First water-powered and then steam-driven sawmills yielded huge cargoes of hardwoods and pine that were shipped by rail to eastern markets. At the end of the twentieth century, the industry still thrived on a sustained yield basis.

As one proceeds from east to west, the land and its use changes from woodlands to semiarid grasslands. In between, there are gently rolling farmland, wooded hills, meadows that provide pasture for livestock, broad basins, scenic mountains, deciduous forests, grasslands, a major salt plain containing a wildlife refuge, sand dunes, and vast expanses of winter wheat and other crops. The Cross Timbers, a large, wooded area, extends through central portions of the state, separating eastern forests from the largely treeless western plains. Oklahoma flora runs the gamut from cypress trees in the warm southeast to pinions in the windswept Panhandle.

Western Oklahoma contains several ranges of sandstone and gypsum hills. The granite peaks of the Wichita Mountains rise abruptly from the plains of southwestern Oklahoma. The High Plains of northwestern Oklahoma have an elevation in excess of 2,000 feet above sea level and rise to more than 4,500 feet in Cimarron County in the western portion of the Panhandle. Cimarron County is the only county in the nation that borders four states: Kansas, Colorado, New Mexico, and Texas.

On the western plains, before Oklahoma was organized as a territory in 1890, bison (buffalo) were slaughtered for their hides, tongues, and hindquarters. While cattle raising was evident before the Civil War in the Indian nations, the cattle industry expanded enormously in the late nineteenth century and today is a major economic activity in western Oklahoma. Tensions that arose in the post–Civil War years united cattlemen and the Indian tribes in opposition to further development, while bankers, businessmen, and railroad executives seeking additional homesteaders encouraged it. Tensions continued in the years following the opening of the Unassigned Lands to settlement in 1889. Thereafter, agriculture became the dominant industry.

By the 1930s, during the Depression years, thoughtless farming practices, the one-way plow, and one-crop farms sacrificed one-third of the topsoil to wind and water erosion. These factors, combined with drought and whipped by black "dusters" chiefly in the western counties, created an ecological disaster of huge proportions, one that drove many Oklahomans from the land to the cities and led others to leave the state. Indeed, the population of some counties at the end of the twentieth century had not exceeded that of 1930.

In response to this disaster, the State Planning and Resources Board was created in 1935 to assume jurisdiction over parks, forestry, and water resources. Thereafter, with federal assistance, particularly from the U.S. Army Corps of Engineers, numerous man-made lakes and dams were constructed. Conservationists, flood control advocates, navigation interests, and others worked to control flooding, promote irrigation, and make Oklahoma verdant and productive once again. In 1946 Congress authorized a comprehensive plan of development for the Arkansas River, the last major undeveloped river in the nation. In 1971, some sixty-five years after the last of the river steamers coursed the waterway from Fort Smith to Muskogee, the McClellan-Kerr Arkansas River Navigation System's 440-mile water stairway allowed barges to leave the Port of Catoosa on the Verdigris River. Tulsa and Muskogee also developed port facilities, enabling them to ship and receive, via barges, goods destined for or received from New Orleans and ports either before or beyond the Crescent City.

In eastern Oklahoma, dams created seven upstream reservoirs that play a major role in the Arkansas River Navigation System. In all, twenty-nine major federal reservoirs are located in Oklahoma, and Lake Texoma and Lake Eufaula are among the largest man-made reservoirs in the nation. Oklahoma's man-made lakes—virtually all lakes within the state—provide recreational facilities, encourage tourism, and in some instances provide water for irrigation in the western portions of the state. Some dams also generate electricity, which in turn encourages industry.

The total surface area of the water bodies in Oklahoma exceeds 1,200 square miles. Today, the Water Resources Board plans for the orderly control, protection, conservation, development, and utilization of the state's water resources.

In addition to conservation storage in major reservoirs, by the 1980s Oklahoma had some 3 million acre-feet of flood control storage in almost 2,000 lakes completed by the Soil Conservation Service of the U.S. Department of Agriculture. Land treatment practices to curb flooding were evident by the 1950s. Not to be overlooked is the development of groundwater. Vast amounts of groundwater, buried in geologic formations, are yielded to thousands of wells and springs. Most important is the Ogallala Aquifer, a vast underground water resource that extends from Nebraska to Texas and underlies two-thirds of the Panhandle. Its waters irrigate corn and other feed crops, allowing for the development of feedlots and packing plants. However, the reserve is being diminished at a rate that alarms many observers, and tensions were created when petroleum producers in the Panhandle exploited the aquifer to flush oil from depleted fields (large portions of the Hugoton-Guymon field, the nation's largest natural gas field and the world's second largest, underlies much of Beaver and Texas Counties in the Panhandle). While most users of the Ogallala are conservation conscious, some authorities believe that the Oklahoma portion of the resource will be depleted before the twenty-first century ends.

As already indicated, agriculture is a major component of the environment and the economy. About 34 million acres of land are included in more than 70,000 farms and ranches operating in the 1990s. The cattle industry is the major agricultural enterprise in terms of the value of total production, but more than 14 million acres are designated as cropland. Winter wheat is the leading crop in terms of acreage planted and total crop value. Other important crops include peanuts, cotton, hay, soybeans, and grain sorghum. Important noncrop agricultural products include poultry/eggs and hogs/pigs. Agricultural products significant on a local basis include corn, oats, peaches, barley, rye, sheep, goats, and catfish. Virtually every community in Oklahoma is related one way or another to the agricultural economy. This endeavor dominates the state's land use and affects perceptions of space and place. It is a major factor in defining Oklahoma's identity. Looming above a flat horizon, grain elevators identify market points and agricultural and commercial centers. These structures provide verticality on an otherwise flat landscape: they range from small country elevators to massive terminal elevators with towering concrete bins in long parallel lines that store millions of bushels of wheat and dispatch huge shipments to distant markets. The railroad provides the link, bridging space to bring the wheat from small rural elevators to terminals from whence it is shipped to markets near and far. In addition, local and regional processing elevators mill grain into flour sold to bakeries. Although only four flour mills were operating in the state as of 1992, milling remains an important manufacturing industry. These elevators provide a fine example of form following function, an engineering solution to a critical agricultural concern.

At one time cotton was grown throughout eastern Oklahoma. It is now cultivated chiefly in the southern half of the state. But the growing season proved too short in some areas and water too scarce in others. Producers soon found other crops or more suitable land uses. Nevertheless, cotton, following the westward migration of the crop in the twentieth century, is still an important cash crop in the southwestern quarter of the state, where much of it is irrigated.

The size of Oklahoma farms increases from east to west. But on most farms, preharvest operations, such as clearing land, planting, and cultivating, have been increasingly performed by tractors and new farm implements. Landowners therefore required fewer tenants and sharecroppers as resident laborers. They relied instead on nonresident, seasonal laborers, a situation that helped to depopulate rural areas. Tractors also reduced the need for horses and mules. Indeed, mechanization displaced more farmers than did drought and dust storms.

Technology in the form of the automobile altered the social geography of rural counties by shrinking the cultural distance between town and countryside. The telephone, radio, motion picture, and all the accouterments of the electronic age almost destroyed this distance. But the cultural distance in rural counties remained evident in three types of towns: county-seat towns, market towns, and elevator towns. County-seat towns contain government offices, sometimes a hospital, possibly a college, and other public and professional facilities. They are the population centers, housing professional people who provide the varied services available in the county. Market towns usually have the second largest concentrations of population. In grain-farming areas there are grain elevators, and these towns are a hub of transportation activity. But their sphere of influence is not county wide. Elevator towns are rural villages, usually with a very small business strip along a main highway. Their most prominent feature is a grain elevator adjacent to a railroad track.

In rural Oklahoma human activity has always been fashioned by the natural landscape: sky, land, weather, soil, water. Pastoral landscapes predominated, though forested areas in the eastern regions produced a different set of human activities. However, early in the history of the state mineral fuels replaced land as the new frontier of opportunity. Oklahoma emerged as a leading mineral-producing state, especially in the production of energy resources. Even before 1907 statehood, income from minerals was greater than income from agricultural production. As oil and natural gas pools were found in all but six of the state's seventy-seven counties, derricks soon dotted the landscape, along with wellheads, pipelines, tank farms, and some refineries. A huge petrochemical industry emerged in Tulsa, Bartlesville, Ponca City, and elsewhere. The industry grew first with oil and more recently with natural gas. It quickly assumed an urban dimension; beginning in 1897 pools were discovered in both urban and rural areas. At one time, for example, the Oklahoma City oil field comprised about two hundred active wells. By the 1920s, Oklahoma was the largest producer of oil in the United States.

The industry developed a culture of its own, dominated by colorful individuals who emerged from a series of rushes that overshadowed all previous quests for hidden wealth in the American West. It also took on a boom-and-bust aspect from 1912 to 1929, as fortunes were quickly gained or lost. Individuals involved in the industry came from all backgrounds, adding a cultural dimension markedly different from that of individuals engaged in pastoral pursuits. Although more wells were drilled in 1949 than in any other year to that point, the rate of depletion by the 1960s exceeded discoveries. Nevertheless, in 1975 Oklahoma had five oil fields ranked among the top one hundred producing pools in the nation. Although production in the Panhandle atop three giant gas fields continued unabated, the boom years were over, despite the fact that much crude oil remained to be brought to the surface. The landscape was no longer sprouting hordes of derricks. What remained were environmental hazards with unsealed wells polluting the soil and water, eyesores that are slowly being returned to a more verdant state. But some refineries continue to pollute the atmosphere and pose a threat to people and the environment.

The petrochemical industry was headquartered in urban areas, as were the refineries and other operations. Displaced and retired farm families, who generally settled in an urban environment, were joined in the years after World War II by returning veterans and the "baby boom" generation. All helped to change the complexion of Oklahoma cities. Urban sprawl and the growth of suburbs made for marked changes in land use, as did the development of three major interstate highways and newly constructed turnpikes. Crosstown expressways, interchanges, and loops made it possible to live in "bedroom communities" and commute to work.

The growth of urban centers further accentuated the decline of rural towns as residents found greater opportunities for employment and recreation in the metropolitan areas. Tulsa and Oklahoma City are the main commercial, industrial, cultural, and health centers of the state. Initially, industry was related to developing natural resources and land use; however, it now provides the basis for urban development. In the cases of Tulsa and Oklahoma City, growth also fed upon itself, as business and services catered to the needs of an expanding and diversified population. Manufacturers and processors today can choose between railroads, barges, trucks, airfreight, and pipelines when shipping finished products to market or receiving materials necessary for their production strategies.

Although their state possesses virtually no leisure class, Oklahomans romanticize a past with which they have minimal connections. At no time could farming compete with ranching as an ideal way of life, yet most residents were descended from transplanted southerners and midwestern homesteaders with no connection to ranchers and cowboys. More southern than western is the state's approach to most political and social questions, yet more western than southern are the manners of most of its people. Meanwhile, the largest number of Indians in the nation live in a state that regards them as neither black nor white, although both American Indians and African Americans remain largely at the bottom of the social and economic ladder. They continue in part to lead segregated lives, despite the fact that the cultural attainments of Indians are largely recognized. Moreover, in reducing all whites of European descent into one category, the term "Anglo" fails completely to identify any single ethnic group. The cultural landscape, like the natural landscape, is exceedingly complex, fascinating, and ever changing.

The Oklahoma environment, as already suggested, is still in transition. And the tension between the traditional concern of Indians for the land and the developmental ethos of white residents continues, with the scales heavily weighted on the side of the Christian-capitalist approach to land use. Yet even here the balance is slowly shifting. There is growing concern that Oklahoma is a significant part of the planet, with natural resources and human potential that need wise use and preservation in harmony with the natural environment. As it was at the outset, so it remained at the centennial of statehood in 2007: Oklahoma's primary source of wealth still comes from the land. However, ranching, farming, forests, mineral products, and water provide opportunities that allow manufacturing to loom larger than any other factor. Manufacturing makes the eastern half of the state the more metropolitan portion, even though the physical environment is not undergoing marked change. As diverse as its geography are Oklahoma's people, who will add new dimensions to the cultural environment of the state in its second century.

Bibliography

Franks, Kenny A. *The Oklahoma Petroleum Industry.* Norman: University of Oklahoma Press, 1980.

Gibson, Arrell M. *Wilderness Bonanza: The Tri-State District of Missouri, Kansas, and Oklahoma.* Norman: University of Oklahoma Press, 1972.

Green, Donald E., ed. *Rural Oklahoma.* Oklahoma City: Oklahoma Historical Society, 1977.

Johnson, Kenneth S. *Mountains, Streams, and Lakes of Oklahoma.* Oklahoma Geological Survey Informational Series No. 1. Norman: Oklahoma Geological Survey, 1998.

Meredith, Howard L., and Mary Ellen Meredith, eds. *Of the Earth: Oklahoma Architectural History.* Oklahoma City: Oklahoma Historical Society, 1980.

Morris, John W., ed. *Drill Bits, Picks, and Shovels: A History of Mineral Resources in Oklahoma.* Oklahoma City: Oklahoma Historical Society, 1982.

———. *Geography of Oklahoma.* Oklahoma City: Oklahoma Historical Society, 1977.

Morris, John W., Charles R. Goins, and Edwin C. McReynolds. *Historical Atlas of Oklahoma.* Norman: University of Oklahoma Press, 1986.

Oklahoma Comprehensive Water Plan. Oklahoma Water Resources Board Publication 94. Oklahoma City: Oklahoma Water Resources Board, 1980.

Oklahoma Comprehensive Water Plan. Oklahoma Water Resources Board Publication 139. Oklahoma City: Oklahoma Water Resources Board, 1997.

Oklahoma Water Atlas. Oklahoma Water Resources Board Publication 120. Oklahoma City: Oklahoma Water Resources Board, 1980.

Oklahoma Water Atlas. Oklahoma Resources Board Publication 135. Oklahoma City: Oklahoma Water Resources Board, 1990.

Reese, Linda W., and Patricia Loughlin, eds. *Main Street Oklahoma: Stories of Twentieth-Century America.* Norman: University of Oklahoma Press, 2013.

Skaggs, Jimmy, ed. *Ranch and Range in Oklahoma.* Oklahoma City: Oklahoma Historical Society, 1978.

Stein, Howard F., and Robert F. Hill, eds. *The Culture of Oklahoma.* Norman: University of Oklahoma Press, 1993.

« 4 »

Fort Sill Enters the Missile Age

Once a powerful fort responsible for maintaining peace in an area that was home to hostile Comanche and Kiowa raiders and to the more sedentary Wichitas and Caddos, Fort Sill emerged in the early twentieth century as the nation's main field artillery center. During World War II, Fort Sill graduated more than 110,000 officers and men to keep the caissons rolling and make the field artillery a major part of the U.S. Army. However, in the postwar years, as the United States entered the missile age and the Cold War became a dominant factor in military thinking, the field artillery, Fort Sill, and the army underwent massive changes. In 1955 Fort Sill was designated the nation's Artillery and Guided Missile Center, a title that promised more than it delivered.

By the end of 1955 the army had missiles with a range of well over fifty miles that were capable of carrying nuclear warheads for delivery of devastating power to close and distant targets. In addition, a new family of artillery weapons, all designed for increased range accuracy and lethality, was being developed. More directly, Fort Sill, as a federally owned military reservation, had a responsibility for managing approximately 74,000 acres of land in southwestern Oklahoma, not enough range if it were to play an active role as a major guided-missile center with a responsibility for testing Corporal, a surface-to-surface guided missile, and Honest John, a free-flight rocket fired from launchers like a cannon. Both could carry either a conventional or a nuclear warhead.[1] In addition, Fort Sill had to meet its responsibility for the development of tactical and organizational doctrines for weapons in the surface-to-surface category. While basic instruction on more potent missiles—Sergeant and LACROSSE—would be offered, none would be fired.[2]

Abutting the northern edge of Fort Sill was the Wichita Mountains Wildlife Refuge, the nation's first such refuge, set aside by Theodore Roosevelt in 1905. To carry out its mission, in 1955 Fort Sill sought an additional 31,020 acres, 10,700 acres from the refuge managed by the Department of the Interior and 20,320 acres in Comanche County under private ownership. The acquisition was deemed necessary because the range of modern artillery by the 1950s was measured in miles compared to weapons in use before World War II, which usually fired from 2,000 to 5,000 yards. Moreover, some weapons, such as the 280 mm cannon, the Honest John rocket, and other newly developed electronic projectiles, were extremely long-ranged and beyond the capabilities of the reservation in providing for maximum safety zones. Acquisition of the proposed 31,020 acres would assure adequate areas for training and maneuvering "not only for the present but the foreseeable future," according to a fact sheet prepared at Fort Sill.[3]

Opposition, of course, was expected from the affected landowners as well as from wildlife and sportsmen's groups, who were categorized in the fact sheet as "wholly unfamiliar with and generally misinformed on the vital defense issues involved." The response to that opposition, predicated on "a cleverly conducted campaign based on half truths," was that "the defense of the nation must be rated far above the value of a few picnic spots and the dedicated principles of a few bird lovers."[4]

The Wichita Mountains Wildlife Refuge occupied land set aside when the Kiowa, Comanche, and Kiowa-Apache Indian Reservations were declared open to homesteading by President William McKinley in 1901. In 1905 Theodore Roosevelt established, by executive order, the Wichita Mountains Forest Preserve, also a national game preserve. In 1907 the New York Zoological Society donated fifteen buffalo to start a herd, and in 1911 elk were introduced from St. Anthony, Idaho, and from Jackson Hole, Wyoming. In 1927 Texas longhorn cattle, captured and corralled in the Brazos, Rio Grande, and Gulf Coast regions of Texas, were brought to the refuge. In addition, antelope, wild turkeys, white-tailed deer, prairie dogs, and numerous other animals found a home in its

60,000 acres. A peculiar uniqueness marked it as a place where eastern and western tree species met but advanced no further. That demarcation also applied to the grasslands range and to many of the 185 kinds of birds found in the Wichitas. By the 1950s the refuge was attracting more than 700,000 visitors annually. It comprised one of the most unique places in the southern plains and was administered by the Fish and Wildlife Service of the Department of the Interior.[5]

While Fort Sill had sought additional land in 1952, it did not seek to enter the wildlife refuge, and the effort, which had the enthusiastic support of the Lawton Chamber of Commerce, came to naught. The third largest city in Oklahoma, Lawton bordered on Fort Sill and was economically dependent on it. The chamber's Military Affairs Committee was acutely aware that Fort Sill spent more money in Oklahoma than most any other entity, and that its growth and expansion were directly responsible for the economic well-being of Lawton and other nearby communities. The Lawton newspaper endorsed those views, and Victor Wickersham and his successor in Congress from the Sixth Congressional District agreed. The Department of the Army also considered the proposals favorably.[6]

As expected, Fort Sill's effort to secure additional land in 1955 aroused controversy. Both Oklahoma senators, along with Congressman Wickersham, endorsed the proposal. On April 19 Wickersham told his constituents that "the White House informed us today that the President had requested the Bureau of Budget to clear the request and it has cleared today." It was submitted the following day.[7]

Despite such impressive support, concerned visitors to the refuge and its recreational areas expressed their views in letters to the editor, in editorials, in congressional testimony, and through lobbyists for conservation organizations. In June, John Taylor of Elk City voiced his opposition to members of the Senate Armed Services Committee. His remarks were trumped by those of Senator Robert S. Kerr, who supported the army request. Those of Charles H. Callison, conservation director for the National Wildlife Federation, and representatives of the Wilderness Society and the National Parks Association made no significant impression on the senators. Earlier, the House Armed Services Committee approved $2,216,000 to purchase the private land, ignoring the pleas of threatened landowners.[8]

Despite that action, members of the Oklahoma delegation were deluged with letters and petitions opposing further expansion of the Fort Sill Military Reservation, claiming there were vast federal lands unsuitable for agricultural purposes that could be utilized for weapons testing. Because Wickersham, a member of the House Armed Services Committee, was considered by growing numbers of his constituents as favorable to expanding the reservation, he stood to pay a heavy political price for his stand; rural residents throughout his district were increasingly hostile.[9]

Meanwhile, Lovie Whitaker, a housewife in Norman, and her friends were alerting members of Oklahoma garden clubs, the Oklahoma Outdoor Council, Audubon societies, and other conservation groups and organizations of the threat the military posed to the refuge. The opposition the ladies engendered reenforced the opposition of the Wichita Landowners Association, which in turn garnered support from the Oklahoma Farm Bureau, the Oklahoma Cattlemen's Association, and their national counterparts. Indians also were involved. Quanah Parker, the last chief of the Comanches, and more than six hundred other Indians were buried in an area slated to be absorbed into the reservation. Every chamber of commerce, except that of Lawton, opposed the takeover.[10]

Gene Torbett, president of the 62,000-member Oklahoma Outdoor Council, in a widely distributed letter spelled out the urgency of the situation and its broader implications. In 1952, he recalled, an army proposal to obtain 38,000 acres abutting the refuge's eastern and southern boundaries was defeated. He also mentioned another tract of more than 90,000 acres that would be coveted if the current acquisition was successful. Torbett recognized that the land hunger of Fort Sill would not easily be abated unless the wildlife refuge, adjacent farm and pasture lands, and the historic Post Oak Monument, which included the graves of Quanah Parker, his white mother, and his home, the Star House, were maintained in their present sites.[11]

If Wickersham was deluged with critical correspondence, so too were Oklahoma's senators. One correspondent observed, "There is no other place in the Southwest where both animal and plant life are to be found in one geographic area in such abundance." But all the letters, petitions, editorials, and statements were of no avail. Senators Kerr and Mike Monroney saw no reason to change their decision to support the extension of the Fort Sill Military Reservation at the expense of part of the Wichita Mountains Wildlife Refuge as well as the acquisition of private property.[12]

In June the discussion shifted to the nation's capital, where the House Armed Services Committee was considering military funding requests. Secretary of the Army Robert Stevens endorsed "the acquisition of 31,000 acres at Fort Sill, Oklahoma, at a cost of $2,200,000 'to accommodate' new and long range artillery weapons such as the 280 millimeter gun with a range of 31,000 yards and the Honest John rocket, with a range of 25,100 yards which add so greatly to the firepower of our Army." However, when the committee discussed the matter, chair Carl Vinson remarked, "Before we buy any more land, we certainly ought to exhaust and make a thorough study and see if we have some other facility. It is not going to hurt anything to move a little training from one base to another base." In further comments he noted that "if they enlarge the facilities, then they enlarge the training." Jack Brooks of Texas added "that we are taking too much land away from our people." Camp Polk in Louisiana, he asserted, could easily accommodate the firing of heavy artillery with its 600,000-plus acres of land not being effectively utilized.[13]

The discussion was extensive, with General Edward Thomas Williams from Fort Sill and Lieutenant Colonel W. P. Knowles from the office of the assistant chief of staff on hand to answer questions. They argued that the public would not be inconvenienced, "except probably on the highway which might be closed for certain periods." Vinson further demanded assurance that firing would not go over communities and roads. General Williams responded, "That is correct, sir." Colonel Knowles admitted under questioning that there were a number of other installations where the new weapons could be fired; some were already being fired at Fort Bragg.[14]

The committee also allowed opponents of the proposal to comment. Frank Ikard, a Texas congressman whose district was about fifty miles away from the wildlife refuge, lauded the terrain as the finest recreation area in his part of the world, one that his constituents enjoyed and used. Other opponents expressed their views in person or in prepared statements, to make sure that the members of the committee were fully aware of the dimensions of the controversy. However, at the conclusion, the committee, reassured by the response of the military officers, approved the request.[15]

The Senate Subcommittee on Real Estate and Military Construction concluded its discussion in late June. It consisted of three senators and some of their staff, with Senator Henry Jackson asking questions similar to those posed in the House hearing. Resolutions in opposition as well as statements by national conservation leaders and area residents were also presented. Howard Zahniser of the Wilderness Society and Devereaux Butcher of the National Parks Association, along with individuals representing affected landowners, asked questions. One pervasive point suggested by people from the region was that the proposal represented merely the first step in acquiring more land, despite a statement by Colonel Knowles to the contrary. The subcommittee approved the proposal. The military budget would next be debated by the Congress. In the House the entire Armed Services Committee participated; in the Senate Henry Jackson alone conducted the hearing for the subcommittee.[16]

So concerned was the mayor of Lawton about the land transfer that at almost midnight on June 9 he phoned Wickersham at home to impress on him that the expansion of Fort Sill was "one of the most vital issues, in our opinion, that has come our way in a long time." Though the mayor was assured that "the situation was well in hand," Carl Vinson, the chair of the House Armed Services Committee, on that very morning announced his opposition to the expansion of Fort Sill into the Wichita Mountains Wildlife Refuge. Vinson said expansion into the refuge would create "a terrific fire hazard" and very quickly "it won't even be a safe place for a rattle-snake." He suggested that the army, after giving students at Fort Sill general instruction on all weapons, take them elsewhere to fire the big guns.[17] But his committee, with only three members joining him in opposition, approved the expansion.

As a result, the business community in Lawton heaped praise on Wickersham. In the full Senate, several weeks later, Henry Jackson led the discussion, saying that "this matter has been reviewed and rereviewed by all those in the executive branch." However, after extended discussion, those present "had to admit there was no alternative." While Jackson agreed with that conclusion, he also posed a hypothetical question about land acquisition: "Where are we going to end?"[18]

Other senators, however, questioned the conclusion reached in the executive branch. That was precisely what Hubert Humphrey did in arguing for maintaining the integrity of the wildlife refuge. To reinforce his views he introduced documents, some of which had previously been presented to the House Committee on Merchant Marine and Fisheries. Richard Neuberger, who shared "the feeling of alarm" expressed by his colleague, secured permission to interrupt and place in the record additional supporting documents.[19]

In a later debate Humphrey expressed his concern that the transfer measure cleared the Senate so rapidly "that there was little opportunity to correct some understandings." He hoped it would receive more consideration by the Appropriations Committee. He then inserted in the record statements by spokesmen for organizations opposing the transfer. Humphrey called attention to excerpts from the House debate in which Robert Sikes of Florida spoke strongly against appropriating $2 million "for acquiring an additional 20,320 acres of private land" for Fort Sill to round out the proposed transfer from the Department of the Interior of 10,700 acres from the Wichita Mountains Wildlife Refuge. Initially Sikes had come to approve the transfer, but, he explained, "After the committee had completed its deliberations and reported to the full committee," a request came from the Wildlife Management Institute and others asking to be heard. The requests came after both houses of Congress had approved the authorization, which was then at the White House. Nevertheless, Sikes's subcommittee called a "special hearing." To his great surprise he found that "some of the statements made by those who oppose the transfer of this land are almost exactly opposite to the statements that have been made by the Army," which asserted that the land was of little value. Sikes heard testimony that the transfer land "was some of the most valuable land in the refuge," heavily used by tourists who valued its recreational opportunities. Sikes wanted to be fair and protect "our wildlife resources."

His views were endorsed by Lee Metcalf of Montana, who hoped that further investigation could balance the needs of the refuge with those of the military without impairing "the operation of Fort Sill and its magnificent artillery school."[20]

Richard Neuberger expressed concern that the proposed "invasion" of the refuge came at a time "when there has been a new succession of attacks upon the various public land realms which belong to the United States." His colleague from Oregon, Wayne Morse, lent his support, claiming to be "somewhat amazed to discover that the witnesses on behalf of the Department of the Army would resort to the age-old tactic of attempting to discredit an opposition witness in an effort to gain their objective." The criticisms and inferences that many witnesses hurled at some conservationists in the hearings, according to Morse, "were simply uncalled for."[21]

Several days later, as the Senate resumed consideration of supplemental appropriations, Neuberger proposed an amendment to let the legislative record show that "Congress is opposed to the transfer of any part of the Wichita National Wildlife Refuge to Fort Sill." Both Oklahoma senators vigorously endorsed the land transfer, insisting it was "absolutely necessary" to preserve what Mike Monroney called "the nation's oldest and most famous artillery post." Military necessity required it, and he did not believe it was "asking too much to take from the southernmost boundary a strip about 1½ miles across and about 6 miles wide." The Armed Services and Military Appropriations Committees approved the action, although the Wichita Mountains Wildlife Refuge came under the jurisdiction of the Department of the Interior and committees other than the Armed Services Committees.[22]

Monroney's colleague Robert S. Kerr followed with withering remarks about credentials, claiming he doubted if the Oregon senator had ever visited the refuge and therefore was limited in his knowledge of it. Wayne Morse more effectively presented the conservation position and called for more consideration of the views of the opponents of the land transfer. But Neuberger's amendment was defeated, and the Senate approved the supplemental appropriation measure that quickly worked its way through Congress and was signed into law before the session ended on August 2,

1955. The land transfer of 10,700 acres and the purchase of 20,320 acres of private land to allow Fort Sill to expand its firing range could then, seemingly, get under way.[23]

But there were questions. Senator Arthur Watkins of Utah asked, "Are you Oklahomans and the Army combining to ruin one of the best and most popular wildlife ranges in the country, as some people are charging?" That charge was reflected in a story in the *Daily Oklahoman* entitled "State Groups Band Together to Fight Fort Sill Expansion." Kerr explained the situation to Watkins, claiming that "it is much cheaper for the government to acquire the lands for the expansion of the artillery school at Fort Sill than it would be to move the entire school to some other location."[24]

The land to be purchased was located in Comanche County, about two miles north of Lawton. It was predominantly agricultural, a major portion being grazing lands. Included in the area were Craterville Park, a privately owned recreational facility, and the Post Oak Mission, an old Indian establishment consisting of a school, church, cemetery, and four dwellings. The graves would be relocated to a site outside of the military reservation. In addition, roads and telephone and power lines would be removed or relocated. While the private landowners opposed land expansion, most came to regard continued opposition as futile, but there was growing concern throughout the neighboring rural areas as to where the expansion would stop.[25]

A snag occurred on October 20, two days after the army formally requested the land transfer, when Secretary of the Interior Douglas McKay, whose department was responsible for the Wichita Mountains Wildlife Refuge, announced his unalterable opposition and recommended that "an exclusive use permit should not be granted." At best he offered to create a buffer zone in which the public would be barred only during firing periods. As a result, the army and the Department of the Interior reached a tentative settlement over the proposed acquisition of 10,700 acres of the Wichita Mountains Wildlife Refuge. Charles Finucane, undersecretary of the army, hammered out the compromise with Wesley D'Ewart, assistant secretary of the interior. Finucane explained that "all we want is use of the land" so artillerymen could fire into a new impact area comprising the privately owned land to be purchased by the army.[26]

Wickersham and Oklahoma's senators, all of whom had worked hard to achieve the land transfer, were keenly disappointed. Wickersham informed the secretary of the interior that "he was placing himself in the position of flouting the will of Congress, the Bureau of the Budget, the Department of Defense and the President of the United States." It was McKay's duty "to immediately take action" and transfer jurisdiction of 10,700 acres of the wildlife refuge to the army. He assured the secretary that both senators Kerr and Monroney were working with him in the matter. Desperate to reverse McKay's stance, Wickersham contacted members of the Senate Subcommittee on Real Estate, the chamber's final authority on establishing the military budget. From them he learned that John Stennis, who chaired the committee, had concluded that approval of the land transfer must be withheld until Interior and the army formally ratified the compromise and resolved the question whether the army could use the privately owned land without owning the government land.[27]

McKay remained firm in the soundness of his position. While ready and willing to work out a solution, the Department of the Interior was "not authorized to transfer jurisdiction over the area to the Department of the Army." The primary purpose for which the lands were used could not be changed "without specific action on the part of Congress." The recent debate in Congress, McKay noted, "did not enact any law or provision of law which authorized the transfer," a position "concurred in by attorneys for the Department of the Army." Moreover, he believed the military's requirements could be met "without transferring primary jurisdiction over the area." Resolving the refuge matter in no way affected the army's acquisition of privately owned lands. Thus, Wickersham informed correspondents, the army planned "to take a long-term lease on 10,500 acres of this land for use in connection with Fort Sill, not bothering the other acreage in the Refuge."[28]

McKay's decision was reinforced by a report from Harry Donohue, who, as a special assistant in the department, had made a thorough inspection of the area, accompanied by the superintendent, Ernest Greenwalt.

Donohue considered the refuge a unique national asset, teeming with wildlife in a rugged natural setting that, in addition, was the most heavily visited wildlife refuge. There was very little acreage, Donohue concluded, that was not important for wildlife management.[29]

He further remarked that officers at Fort Sill "emphasized the need for having the 10,700 acres for maneuver purposes in order to set up firing positions which would fire directly south into what is now private land." In developing the positions it would be necessary, Donohue insisted, for the army to install equipment on a permanent basis, thereby destroying the usefulness of the area for wildlife purposes. Donohue's report led Secretary McKay early in January 1956 to reaffirm his stand against granting an exclusive-use permit. Unless Congress specifically authorized a transfer of the acreage to the Department of the Army, the secretary would not make the transfer.[30]

The army, having no choice, entered into discussions with the Department of the Interior, seeking an arrangement for the joint use of 10,700 acres of refuge lands. That development spurred conservation groups in Oklahoma to bring their fight to increased national attention. Anything sent to the Oklahoma congressional delegation in effect was "water down the drain," explained Bess Smith from Arcadia, Oklahoma. "Kerr and Monroney, his yes man," she said, "are aching and aching about why nobody in Oklahoma is protesting the use of the wildlife refuge by the army, just outside organizations." Meanwhile, Dewey Short, a member of the House Armed Services Committee, claimed that the members had received "the biggest flood of mail from people new to the corresponding field that they had ever had on anything."[31]

In February, when the House Armed Services Committee considered the military budget, Wickersham inquired about the delay in the land transfer. The spokesman for the army could not provide an answer but noted that "in the meantime we are proceeding with the purchase of the land which was authorized." That process would take some time. To speed the process, Wickersham and the Oklahoma senators introduced bills to force the transfer of land from the wildlife refuge to the secretary of the army for use as part of the Fort Sill Military Reservation. Wickersham then wrote the chair of the House Committee on Merchant

Marine and Fisheries, requesting a report on his bill "as quickly as possible," given the army's dire need to fire guided missiles, "which is very important to our National Defense." To add to the urgency of the matter, Wickersham informed correspondents that "officials of the Department of the Army advised Congress that it was necessary to have this additional land, else the post would have to be moved." Thus, despite McKay's effort to work out a satisfactory arrangement, the army seemingly would not agree to anything other than exclusive use of the land, and the fear that the base would be moved could build momentum for the enactment of the bills.[32]

In the House of Representatives the transfer measure (House Resolution [HR] 9665) was considered by the Committee on Merchant Marine and Fisheries. The secretary of the army, Wilber M. Brucker, wrote the committee chair, Herbert Bonner, endorsing the transfer of approximately 10,700 acres of the refuge to the Department of the Army. Previously the Congress, in approving the military construction bill, provided for the acquisition of the lands only to learn that because the refuge had been established in 1905 by a presidential proclamation the transfer could not be administratively accomplished." Passage of HR 9665 would provide the authority necessary to accomplish the transfer.[33]

Several days later, Assistant Secretary of the Interior D'Ewart wrote Bonner opposing the transfer and recommending that HR 9665 "be not enacted." While Brucker stressed military necessity, D'Ewart called attention to "Interior's great system of wildlife refuges" and the fact that it was "Oklahoma's last great primitive area, as well as its greatest recreational area." He also made clear that "we are prepared to work cooperatively with the Army authorities in solving Fort Sill's firing problems by mutual conference and agreement." Military considerations, he asserted, "should be evaluated in their true perspective along with nonmilitary considerations relating to public use and the national importance of the National Wildlife Refuge."[34]

The transfer of refuge lands was then discussed in extended hearings before the House Committee on Merchant Marine and Fisheries. Among the witnesses were Undersecretary of the Army Finucane and the new commandant at Fort Sill, Major General T. E. DeShazo. One person representing local conservation organizations testified, along with representatives of other conservation groups. The military was well represented, as was the Lawton Chamber of Commerce. D'Ewart was the only person representing the Department of the Interior. The hearings covered two days, May 23 and May 24. In his remarks D'Ewart noted that "we have had no less than five or six conferences with Army representatives during the last year in an effort to work out this problem." He was convinced that the Department of the Interior could accommodate the army and at the same time save the refuge "from the proposed reduction of its boundaries and the permanent despoliation that an impact area would irretrievably cause." With the exception of firing more guns, the army was already using the area "under our cooperative permit with respect to all the other types of training that they originally contemplated here." In conclusion, D'Ewart quoted from a 1953 special message of President Dwight Eisenhower to the Congress wherein he stated that "the federal government has a responsibility to manage wisely those public lands and forests under its jurisdiction in the interests of the public as a whole" and added that "public lands should be made available for their best use under conditions that promote stability for communities and individuals and encourage full development of the resources involved."[35]

The hearings ended on June 26 with a letter from Finucane that was read by Lieutenant Colonel W. P. Knowles. Finucane noted that on June 19 the secretary of the interior informed Secretary Brucker that, after carefully evaluating the situation, he concluded that granting the army a permit for use of the land was not in the best interests of his department. The secretary proposed to grant the army a narrow buffer zone from which the public would be excluded only when scheduled firing made the zone a danger area. The proposal, Finucane asserted, was unsatisfactory because the zone was not large enough and access to the area should be denied at all times. Accordingly, Finucane urged prompt committee consideration of HR 9665.[36]

Although Congress did not resolve the issue of wildlife refuge land acquisition, it approved the acquisition of 20,320 acres of privately owned land. By June assessors found many landowners distressed at the sums offered for their lands. With private landowners disturbed and with no resolution of the refuge matter, the second session of the Eighty-fourth Congress adjourned on July 27, 1956, allowing members to campaign for reelection and for the presidential race to get fully under way. Before Congress adjourned, the entire Oklahoma delegation sent the president a resolution asking that as commander in chief he take action to insure "that the absolute minimum training requirements of the Army at Fort Sill will be satisfied at an early date." The earliest date, of course, would be sometime in 1957, after the new Congress was in place and the Eisenhower administration determined how to proceed. Earlier, in May 1956, Fred Seaton had replaced Douglas McKay as secretary of the interior, and it remained to be seen what his role would be.[37]

When Congress convened in January 1957, there was one noticeable change in the Oklahoma delegation. Victor Wickersham had been handily defeated in the Sixth Congressional District primary runoff by Toby Morris, who had held the post for the three terms previous to Wickersham. Morris won by more than 5,000 votes and in the November election defeated his Republican opponent by more than 47,000 votes. Wickersham had invited the hostility of ranchers, farmers, and other private landowners threatened with the loss of their land. But in Toby Morris, a resident of Lawton, the chamber of commerce and its supporters favoring land acquisition found another strong ally. Morris, like Wickersham, would be a member of the Armed Services Committee and strive to represent the best interests of Fort Sill.[38]

Early in the new session, Morris had "a very favorable conference" with Secretary Finucane and Assistant Secretary of the Interior Ross Leffler. Both assured Morris that a "satisfactory solution" to the proposed wildlife refuge acquisition could be reached "within the very near future." He could therefore inform his correspondents he was working on their behalf. At the same time he made sure that Milton Keating, the secretary-manager of the Lawton Chamber of Commerce, saw all the right people when he was in Washington. Keating reported that members of the chamber were well satisfied, as was General DeShazo, commandant of Fort Sill, who was "very proud of you."[39]

From being well satisfied the Lawton Chamber of Commerce soon became "deeply concerned" over a press report regarding an agreement in which the amount of land granted the army in the wildlife refuge was much less than requested and much less than "the absolute minimum required for safety." The chamber's concern was presented to the secretary of the army because of its vital interest in the future of Fort Sill and its collaboration "during the past two years" to secure the 10,700 acres the army sought from the interior department. The chamber hoped the secretary would "not think us presumptuous" in opposing such an agreement.[40]

Senator Kerr, also concerned, learned from the army chief of legislative liaison that a final resolution of the matter had not been achieved, though private conversations had been held between Secretary Finucane, Secretary of the Interior Fred Seaton, and Assistant Secretary Leffler. Shortly thereafter, on February 27, 1957, Finucane, Leffler, and representatives of various conservation organizations worked out a proposal that offered the army a ten-year permit establishing a buffer zone along the south boundary of the refuge, approximately one-third of the 10,700-acre tract originally requested. Other items specified how the army would care for the range. Finucane and Leffler agreed in principle to the proposal, which "would serve as a basis for implementation by the respective departmental staffs." Kerr was informed that the Department of the Army had released nothing to the press about the proposal.[41]

There the matter stood until September 6, 1957, when the compromise agreement was approved. In final form it authorized military maneuvers and training activities under restrictions and stipulations preserving the recreational and wildlife values of the area. The Department of the Interior, well satisfied with the agreement, was assured by Finucane that no further expansion of the Fort Sill Military Reservation was contemplated that would jeopardize the integrity of the refuge. From the 10,700 acres the army initially requested, the agreement provided for the use of 3,600 acres as a buffer zone, with firing only along its outer perimeter.[42]

While the controversy over the wildlife refuge was resolved, officers at Fort Sill were not enthused. Earlier, in July, addressing the Rotary Club in Oklahoma City, General DeShazo reiterated the contention that Fort Sill needed at least 10,700 acres of refuge lands to keep its long-range guided missile program in operation. He insisted that "you can't let a $250 million plant go to pot for lack of $10 million worth of additional land." Senator Monroney agreed, saying the expansion of the Fort Sill Artillery and Guided Missile Range was vital to national defense and Oklahoma's future. Monroney articulated what many in Lawton were saying, namely, that expansion of the firing range was necessary though it might cause hardship in the affected areas.[43]

Expansion was deemed necessary because of the sense of urgency prompted by the Soviet launching, on October 4, 1957, of the first man-made satellite, Sputnik, followed a month later with a second satellite carrying a live dog. Monroney's remarks reflected the frustration, alarm, and anger felt by many in Congress and throughout the nation that the United States had suffered a severe setback in the Cold War. Moreover, after Eisenhower suffered a stroke on November 25, Monroney's assertion two weeks later merely heightened anxiety that Fort Sill officials would seek to expand its guided-missile range by claiming thousands of acres in Kiowa and Caddo Counties. Though no specific proposal had been presented, residents of fifteen communities began organizing the Southwest Oklahoma Survival Association (SOS) to prevent what they feared would be the eviction of hundreds of ranchers and farmers. Representative Morris told a meeting in Hobart, the Kiowa County seat, that he would favor the expansion if he deemed it vital to national defense. His remarks, greeted with derision, firmly polarized the Sixth Congressional District, with Morris backed by the Lawton Chamber of Commerce and its supporters aligned against the rural residents threatened with the possible loss of thousands of acres of some of the more productive ranch, oil, mineral, and farmland in Oklahoma.[44]

The first announcement of the new proposal was presented by Secretary Finucane, who in September had proclaimed the resolution of the wildlife refuge controversy. He launched a new struggle that was made more explicit on November 27, 1957, when General DeShazo spoke to mayors from several of the affected communities at a Rotary luncheon in Snyder. His remarks indicated that the expanded range would take in at least half of Kiowa County. His luncheon speech prompted the meeting at Hobart on December 6, when Congressman Morris spoke for the expansion and where a map indicating the proposed Fort Sill Impact Range was prominently displayed. The expansion would take nearly half of Kiowa and Caddo Counties and an additional section of Comanche County.[45]

The proposal launched a campaign that made the fight over the expansion of the wildlife refuge pale in comparison. At the outset, the mayor of Hobart sent a letter to every member of the state's congressional delegation explaining the expansion program based on information provided by General DeShazo. He claimed that the economy of the communities around the perimeter of the proposed expansion had "already been adversely affected from the rumors and the statements made by Senator Monroney, Congressman Toby Morris and the commanding officers at Fort Sill." Moreover, he insisted, it would be more economical if classroom instruction at Fort Sill was followed by moving troops to less populated areas for the "actual firing of rockets and other weapons," a practice followed by "the other military services of the United States." Those views were reiterated in various ways and in greater detail as opponents became fully aware of the proposal.[46]

Retired major general James C. Styron, who had commanded the Forty-fifth Infantry Division in Korea and in 1957 was a cotton buyer and resident of Hobart, emerged as a leader in the fight to keep the army from expanding the Lawton facility. He told the Mangum Rotary Club that "we're not fighting national security, we're trying to preserve the rights of man—the sanctity of a man's home and his property." Styron countered the views of the congressional delegation that they could not afford to lose the benefits of the Fort Sill payroll to Lawton and the state of Oklahoma. He claimed that cotton, wheat, cattle, and oil in the disputed counties would yield much more than the payroll at Lawton. Styron concluded, "We can't win this without some outside sympathy and aid."[47]

The army also sought outside assistance. General John C. Hayden, commander of troops at Fort Sill, for example, spoke in Altus. He stressed Fort Sill's responsibility to train soldiers in firing the expanding range of missiles already available to the army. While manpower was available and new missiles were coming online, Fort Sill's most immediate concern was more land. While training in the use of various missiles—Corporal, Honest John, and more recently Little John—was constant, Hayden explained that units had to travel to White Sands Missile Range in New Mexico to further train and then practice firing missiles. To accomplish their mission at Fort Sill, army officials had circulated a proposal through military channels to provide an additional training and testing area. With the new territory, missiles could be launched without their traveling over private land. For longer ranges the plan was to fire from post to post—to and from Fort Sill and Fort Bliss, five hundred miles away. To be sure, a few towns would be directly affected, but General Hayden estimated that no more than two hundred families, fewer than a thousand people, would be displaced over a period of years. The general was confident that over time the displaced individuals would secure jobs created by the expansion of Fort Sill's facilities. Hayden's address clearly articulated the essence of the proposal. It was reiterated throughout the Lawton area, and it aroused tremendous opposition in the targeted rural counties and elsewhere. However, until a measure would be considered and approved by Congress, specifics could not be precisely defined, though the debate intensified with the emotions it aroused.[48]

General Hayden's remarks were quickly disputed by people in southwestern Oklahoma, with Hobart, the largest community abutting the affected area, as the center of the opposition. There people talked about the homes of 30,000 people, including a town of 6,000, being declared expendable. Although the army had not released precise details, opposition leaders estimated that in Kiowa County alone 321,000 acres of the best farming and grazing land could be taken. Both General Styron and Hobart mayor William A. Trawick insisted it was not a matter of fighting Fort Sill; rather, it was a matter of protecting their rights as citizens, a matter of human rights. As would be expected, concerned residents bombarded their congressman with mail, many not recognizing that he was firmly in the camp of the army in endorsing the expansion of Fort Sill.[49]

Opposition quickly led to organization. The Southwest Oklahoma Survival Association, or SOS, as it was quickly known, was headquartered at the Hovaka Hotel in Hobart, with a state office in the Biltmore Hotel in Oklahoma City. Its director, John Causten Currey, was a prominent figure in Republican circles in Oklahoma City, with a wide range of experience as an air force intelligence officer in public relations. He quickly spread the word to his numerous contacts in Oklahoma and Washington, D.C., as well as through conferences, correspondence, and phone conversations. SOS made much of one point in its publicity: the potential conflict between Fort Sill and the nearby air force base at Altus, which was responsible for that area's booming economy. Despite the fact that the state's congressional delegation endorsed the Fort Sill proposal, that was a dispute that potentially pitted one branch of the services against another. SOS was wise in playing it up; it would be considered in the corridors of power in the nation's capital.[50]

In conveying their message, Currey and others in SOS asked their correspondents to further spread the word by contacting members of Congress and having their associations, service clubs, and other groups pass resolutions against the proposed land grab and encourage their national organizations to do likewise. In response to the deluge of mail pouring into his congressional office, Morris promised to do his best to see that people adversely affected would be fully compensated for any loss. He also said, "If the need for this extra land is justified, from a defense standpoint, I will be compelled by my conscience, to be for it." SOS countered that the 426 square miles of land sought contained productive oil fields, some of the best farmland in the state, excellent grazing lands, and quarries of great value. Taking that valuable acreage, an SOS leaflet noted, "would kill the towns on the perimeter by taking their supporting trade territory." To SOS and the people in the threatened territory the fight signified a battle of "dollars vs. people," saving dollars by not utilizing firing ranges on government-owned lands in more remote areas of the West.[51]

The proposal was endorsed late in 1957 when Secretary Finucane visited Fort Sill and declared additional range expansion "absolutely necessary." Army Chief of Staff Maxwell Taylor, a few days later after visiting the post, called the plan "sound and reasonable with a minimum of dislocation." Outside the Lawton area, those views did not resonate well. Earlier in the year the House Armed Services Committee had learned that the White Sands Proving Ground in New Mexico was the only guided-missile proving ground in the nation offering a land range of ninety miles and that Fort Bliss had an artillery range covering more than a million acres so that "with guided missiles coming in so fast . . . we can't hesitate to have complete tests." During the 1957 hearings, Fort Sill never entered the conversation as expanded firing ranges for missiles were favorably reviewed.[52]

Moreover, there was no suggestion of it in "Our Future Security," the major address that President Eisenhower delivered in Oklahoma City on November 13, shortly after the Soviets launched their two satellites. In outlining the nation's overall military policy, Eisenhower stressed "the retaliatory nuclear power of our Strategic Air Command and our Navy." When he discussed missiles, it was in terms of furthering long-range missile development for the air force and the navy to counter Soviet intercontinental and intermediate-range ballistic missiles. The army was not specifically mentioned as he outlined the steps he deemed necessary to further "our national security activities for the coming year." From the president's remarks, and the mounting fear that the United States was falling behind in the outer-space race, it was becoming apparent that expanding Fort Sill's missile range would not command a high priority when the proposal came to the attention of Congress.[53]

None of those developments affected the burgeoning controversy in southwestern Oklahoma. Officials at Fort Sill continued their case, and SOS's campaign to prevent the removal of more than four hundred square miles from the tax rolls, let alone abandoning small towns, gained intensity in 1958. The National Cattlemen's Association and the Oklahoma State Farmers Union sponsored a day-long talkathon on a local radio station in January featuring statements from SOS directors and others from the area. The press also reported that Currey had sought the support of the Reserve Officers' Association in the establishment of a single joint-use missile range in wasteland areas "before inter-service rivalry [takes] tens of thousands of people from their homes and livelihood." Meanwhile, a group of Cooperton businessmen went to Fort Sill to confer with General DeShazo, who told them that "unless we can have all we are asking for, we do not want any."[54]

The Fullingim family, however, gained far more attention. In front of their ranch home near Mountain Park, W. A. Fullingim, 102 years old, Mrs. Fullingim, 98 years old, two sons in their seventies, and their daughter in her sixties made it clear that they would not be moved: "They'll have to come and take us away if they want this place," a 1,720-acre cattle spread. The human interest aroused by that possibility was trumped by the forceful stance of Senator Monroney in supporting the expansion of Fort Sill. Surprisingly, he indicated no recognition of the administration's views on strategic defense, arguing that if the army deemed the land acquisition necessary he would do all in his power to see that the process was fairly and humanely conducted. However, Monroney recognized that the proposed expansion was not immediate.[55]

The people in the affected area quickly went to work. A form letter from Carnegie, Oklahoma, set the tone in proclaiming that "we in the Southwest part of Oklahoma are in serious peril because of the Army's and Fort Sill's proposed expansion of the reservation into a missile impact area and we are calling upon our friends, relatives and Congress to assist us in this, our time of peril, in fact, our very existence." Those efforts paid off. Lyndon Johnson agreed to ask his Senate Preparedness Subcommittee to look at the proposal, especially because there was adequate space for an expanded missile range at Fort Bliss near El Paso. In addition, Oklahoma Governor Raymond Gary, over a statewide network originating from Hobart, expressed grave doubts about the necessity of the proposed expansion. Others speaking in opposition included the state presidents of the Farmers Union and the Farm Bureau, as well as legislators from the threatened counties. A Kiowa spokesman in his native tongue, assisted by an interpreter, expressed tribal opposition.[56]

Yet to be heard from as the controversy increased in intensity was the state's senior United States senator. Previously, Kerr had led the state delegation in endorsing the expansion of Fort Sill into the wildlife refuge. By 1958, however, he had begun to have doubts about an expansion that could affect thousands of families, their farms, their homes, and their businesses, explaining, "I have not seen what I regard as an adequate justification for overriding the opposition of these people in the affected area." Kerr's position buoyed the members of SOS and others in the threatened region. Attracting much less enthusiasm was the fact that former representative Victor Wickersham had now jumped into the fight, blasting his successor for favoring the position he had formerly endorsed.[57]

The proposal, of course, found aroused supporters in Lawton: the chamber of commerce, the business community, residents who found employment at Fort Sill, and newspapers, all of whom argued that the expansion of Fort Sill was a vital cog in national defense that generated the second largest payroll in the state. General DeShazo, the commandant at Fort Sill, soon entered the fray. Addressing students at the University of Oklahoma, he explained that, while the plans still had to go through the army chain of command and be approved by the Bureau of the Budget and by Congress, approval would lead to the spending of millions of dollars and new jobs for displaced people. Farmers would be able to lease back much of their land at a nominal fee and be allowed to enter the area for two weeks in the spring to plant and another two weeks in the fall to harvest their crops, but, he made clear, if the army needed to go through the crops it would do so. Soon thereafter the general invited local officials throughout the affected area to a stag party and briefing at his headquarters.[58]

Meanwhile, Currey stalked the corridors of power in Washington. He told presidential assistant Bryce Harlow, a native Oklahoman, at a lengthy White House conference that the proposal put nineteen communities "in a state of suspended animation," that no real estate loans were being made in the 426-square-mile area "staked out" for a missile firing range. In other meetings Currey learned that the Fort Sill expansion plan had reached the Pentagon. He received assurance that the Senate Preparedness Committee planned to investigate the matter, but the first formal indication that the expansion plan had reached the Pentagon came when President Eisenhower wired Governor Gary, explaining the controversial issue. Shortly thereafter Senator Henry Jackson, on an inspection at Fort Sill, said there was "no chance" of Congress appropriating funds because there was no request for an appropriation and it was not in the budget. However, he endorsed the missile program at Fort Sill, explaining that "we simply can't haul the men out to the Pacific or New Mexico to fire the missiles." If that were done, the training program could not be integrated and the men would not be fully prepared for missile warfare. For the present, as Gary commented after receiving the president's telegram, "It has a long road to travel."[59]

The fact that Fort Sill's proposal would not be acted upon in 1958 did not resolve the matter. Retired general Styron expressed the sentiments of many when he remarked, "We don't feel we can live in this situation too much longer," but he made clear the fight sparked by SOS would continue to disclose the detrimental effects on local communities. The letter-writing campaign continued unabated, as did Currey's efforts in Washington. How the controversy related to the nation's accelerated effort to rapidly expand the production of long-range missiles was not clarified in any way. In 1958 the fight over the expansion of Fort Sill's range was not considered within the context of the thirty-eight missile programs already under way as the nation struggled to maintain its deterrent power both on Earth and in space. Local issues would not decide the matter. National concerns would determine how many missile ranges were needed, where they would be located, and if they must be exclusive to each branch of the armed services.[60]

Adding to the intensity of the local controversy was the fact that Morris's seat in Congress was up for renewal in 1958. When the Kiowa County Democratic Central Committee met in late January, it approved resolutions condemning Morris for supporting "the Lawton Land grab" and for his failure to consider "the human rights" of people whose personal and property rights were being threatened "to satisfy the greed of the city of Lawton." Senator Monroney was also criticized, while the aims of SOS were endorsed. What was evident, as the campaign season got under way, was the animosity evident throughout the threatened section of southwestern Oklahoma toward the city of Lawton and Morris. The only official complimented was Senator Kerr, who continued to express doubts about the proposal.[61]

Supporters of expansion gained additional support when an organization headed by a former Chickasha publisher appeared to combat the efforts of SOS. The new organization, the Oklahoma Defense League, feared that SOS's opposition might force the removal of basic functions from the training center. Dave Vandiver, who headed the organization, had been Oklahoma war manpower director in World War II. He argued that "displacement of this kind has been going on since the dawn of civilization and will continue." He reminded Oklahomans that Fort Sill was the only artillery training post and surface-to-surface missile center in the country and was training North Atlantic Treaty Organization and allied officers from forty-one nations.[62]

By that time, however, Currey and SOS had done their work well and achieved some of their goals. Numerous organizations already opposed range expansion. Through the efforts of both the White House and the governor of Oklahoma, the Pentagon released statements on the status of the proposal: it had been received but not yet reviewed, it was not included in the 1959 budget, and information about the proposal would emanate from the Pentagon and not from Lawton. Moreover, with missile technology developing at a rapid rate, it was becoming evident that newer long-range missiles could not be safely fired from Fort Sill. The situation in the area was beginning to receive national attention, most notably in a story by Russell Baker entitled "Oklahomans Put Army on Defense" that appeared in the *New York Times.* Baker's story examined the plight of embattled Oklahomans and suggested "what the missile age means when taken off the cosmic plane in Washington and translated into human terms." In the end, the impact of the Oklahoma Defense League would be minimal, a conclusion that was reinforced when the secretary of the army suggested that staff officers "cool down on the thing and not excite the people down there." He was responding to a statement by Texas congressman George Mahon that "there is a little revolution going on down in Oklahoma by reason of so-called extension of Fort Sill."[63]

In Washington, Currey learned that there was "a serious question of how much the Army eventually expects at Ft. Sill." He was informed that the Redstone missile, which traveled two hundred miles to impact, would never be fired there. Other missiles—Pershing, Sergeant, Corporal—were simply too long-range. That left several missiles, such as Honest John and Little John, Dart, and LACROSSE, that could be fired within the present range. However, with advances in missile development those weapons could become too long-range even for Fort Sill's proposed expanded range, all of which led Currey to believe there was a real possibility that "this proposal will never leave the Pentagon."[64]

The inability to fire missiles at Fort Sill was made clear in a meeting in Hobart of citizens from most southwestern Oklahoma towns. It was the first mass meeting since SOS had been launched the previous December. Fort Sill's inability was the message SOS conveyed, not only to those in attendance but also to a larger radio audience. At the meeting Byron Bolar, the chair of SOS, noted that the group had already raised $30,000 of its $50,000 fund goal. At another meeting on the same day, February 7, at Clinton, the Sixth District Democratic Convention, comprising twenty-three counties, went on record with a resolution opposing the proposed expansion.[65]

To ease the rising tensions evident throughout the congressional district, tensions that threatened to disrupt the Democratic Party, Fred Harris, the state senator representing Cotton and Comanche Counties, wrote the secretary of the army expressing his belief that "the great majority of the people of Southwestern Oklahoma are greatly interested in the installation at Fort Sill and its continued strength." He called "the notion" that the expansion plan originated in the Lawton Chamber of Commerce "ridiculous" and expressed the hope that his letter would be of some value to Brucker "in assessing and appraising the situation in regard to this expansion." On the copy he sent to Morris, Harris scribbled, "Here is a letter I wrote at the request of the C. of C. committee. I believe things are beginning to simmer down a little here at home."[66]

Such a perception, however, was hardly the case. Currey was an effective public relations expert, indefatigable in getting the message of SOS out to individuals and organizations both near and far. On February 19 he secured a major coup when a public hearing on the proposed Fort Sill land expansion was conducted at the state capitol. General DeShazo and four members of his "key staff" presented in detail the general outline of the proposal and its current status. The officers explained the organization, operation, and requirements of the artillery and missile school and the tactical units training there. Members of SOS, including Currey, also presented their views. In some detail, Jack Haley, an archivist at the University of Oklahoma whose home was in Kiowa County, presented a history of the controversy, concluding that if all the facts were examined it would be "clearly observed that the Army's and Lawton's tactics have not changed and perhaps are even more misrepresented and confusing than ever before." Senator Harris, who disputed Haley's sharp criticism of the Lawton Chamber of Commerce and business community, peppered Haley with questions. While Haley discussed the background of the controversy, Currey examined its current dimensions, noting the injury it would inflict upon vast portions of southwestern Oklahoma. The crisis was, he argued "economic and social, as well as emotional." While it could rapidly be resolved, "recovery," he claimed, "could take some time." Before the hearing concluded, DeShazo offered further observations on missile development and the need for an expanded range. The general insisted that while great strides were being made in long-range missile technology, missiles could be fired "with perfect safety within the area we have proposed," and DeShazo declared, "We don't want to move away to some place else." When all was said and done, he made clear, the decision would come from Washington. Despite the general's firm conclusion, an editorial in the *Daily Oklahoman* trumped his remarks by asserting that "one great weakness in the case for enlarging Fort Sill is the Army's inability to show convincingly that its present request will be the last."[67]

Supporting the general, the Oklahoma Defense League agreed that "more than 60 percent of the 273,000 acres on the proposed Fort Sill expansion area consists of sub-marginal land—either eroded, rocky or on one of three mountain ranges encompassing the area." As evidence, it cited a 1931 Department of Agriculture map and several Soil Conservation Service studies to indicate that only "spotty acreages" in the area were highly productive. Citing data from the Bureau of Business Research at the University of Oklahoma, the release noted that population in the affected counties was declining, more people having left the land than would be displaced by an expanded missile range. In addition, it provided data to show that the Lawton area "experienced a great growth and an expanding economy." The figures were promptly refuted by SOS, which charged that the data overlooked thousands of people, tenant farmers and others residing in the acreage staked out by the army. But the Oklahoma Defense League's integrity was impaired by the resignation of three members of its executive committee.[68]

By March, as the *Daily Oklahoman* observed, the Fort Sill fantasy was beginning to fade. It was abundantly clear that the proposal would not be forthcoming from the Pentagon, which had not evaluated it for inclusion in its 1958–1959 budget being readied for submission to Congress. The Pentagon had not indicated just when the proposal would be evaluated. Nevertheless, the proposal's promoters nearly paralyzed business in several communities. Farmers and ranchers stopped purchasing needed equipment. Bankers and others hesitated before purchasing municipal bonds or risking money on possible ghost towns. Most residents were already aware that the army utilized huge areas for ranges, as did the navy and air force, which trained missile crews and then took them to isolated areas for actual firing. Though the proposal seemed to be fading, SOS and the people in the affected area did not let up in their efforts to call attention to their plight.[69]

To ease strained relations between communities, SOS released a form letter letting friends and neighbors know that its members did not "bear any ill feelings toward the people of Lawton." They remained proud of Fort Sill, had no desire to see it moved, and recognized its importance "to your livelihood as our farms and ranches are to ours." It was a feeble gesture; tensions remained. SOS did not let up in its effort, and one member of the legislature announced that the issue was "snowballing into one of the biggest political issues of all time in western Oklahoma." The residents of the territory considered for confiscation were so upset that they were "about ready to attack anything or anybody who supports the military land grab."[70]

Another person who had reason to be upset was the Sixth District representative, who in the upcoming election would face the opposition of thousands of residents. Though he could count on the support of the Lawton Chamber of Commerce and of voters in that city, the largest in the twenty-three-county district, Toby Morris's reelection would be sharply contested. Already the District Democratic Convention and the Oklahoma Democratic Central Committee opposed the proposal, all indications that he would face a rough reelection campaign. That became evident when Grady County attorney Wilson Smithen announced he would enter the race in opposition to the expansion of the missile range. A week later Victor Wickersham indicated that he would seek to regain the seat as an opponent of the proposed expansion. A three-person primary race offered Morris some hope. Because neither Smithen nor

Wickersham resided in Kiowa County, the primary center of the opposition, issues other than Fort Sill's expansion could emerge, and opposition voters, by having two choices, could benefit Morris. Nevertheless, SOS had reason to believe that its fight was beginning to strike a responsive chord and that the matter would be settled "through capitulation or compromise in their favor."[71]

That view was reenforced in early April when the Special Study Committee on the Fort Sill Land Expansion Question presented its recommendations to the executive committee of the Oklahoma Legislative Council. They were accepted with only one dissenting vote. The committee opposed the proposal and recommended that Governor Gary submit their views with the findings and information they assembled to the president, the Department of Defense, and the Congress. That favorable report was enthusiastically received by people in the affected area, as was the news of two new discoveries in the oil field within the proposed missile range.[72]

SOS and its director achieved their greatest victory several weeks later, when a group of women went to Washington to discuss the proposed expansion. Senator Kerr's office arranged for a meeting to which the entire Oklahoma delegation was invited, as were members of the Senate Real Estate Subcommittee that reviewed the military budget. In addition, the women intended to lobby members of Congress and several organizations, and six of the women had a White House appointment. Their appearance was the first formal protest to be presented to Congress from residents of southwestern Oklahoma.[73]

On April 22 Senator Kerr called the meeting to order. In attendance was a forty-five-woman delegation. Six well-prepared ladies reviewed the proposal and its impact. Merle Watkins of Hobart, a member of the Democratic National Committee, spoke first and introduced the other speakers, each of whom focused on different aspects of the situation. Tully Morrison, a Native American, expressed the concern of "some 350 Indian families involved in this expansion." Members of the Oklahoma delegation either asked questions or offered brief comments. Undersecretary of the Army Dewey Short spoke in general terms about the necessity for impact missile ranges but assured the ladies that, if the expanded range for Fort Sill survived the lengthy approval process, residents losing land would be fairly and justly treated. He was followed by Brigadier General Theodore Francis Bogart and Colonel Ken Belieu, who further assured the audience that if the missile range was expanded no atomic weapons would be fired. They also responded to questions, and Bogart asserted that no post-to-post firing of missiles, from Fort Bliss to Fort Sill, was contemplated, despite a story in a recent issue of *Newsweek*.[74]

More significant were the remarks of Senator Henry Jackson, who reiterated that no decision had been made and that "this is not the only range under consideration to do the type of training that we have been talking about." He also informed his audience that his subcommittee would have to approve the proposal and that it had not yet come to their attention. He added, "If it does come before our committee, it will be one of the largest land acquisitions that I believe we have ever considered." Like other speakers, Jackson complimented the ladies for the "fine and fresh and sincere presentation of the problems that you have experienced and should experience should this happen." Before adjourning the meeting, Kerr asked Colonel Belieu if he had any final observation. Belieu remarked "that judging from this pile of letters, you have only begun to fight. For this is just about 1% of all the mail we have gotten. . . . So your problems are not unknown to our committee." The delegation, SOS, and all opposed to the proposal then understood that decision makers in Washington were aware of what they were going through and were sympathetic, and that the lengthy process of arriving at a decision was not yet under way.[75]

Chairing the meeting further convinced Kerr of the validity of his opposition to what, following the point made by Senator Jackson, he now called "one of the largest acquisition proposals that has been made by the military." He expressed concern about the adverse effects such a large acquisition of land would have on the area and its inhabitants. Later he joined with Monroney and conferred with the army assistant secretary. They learned that the proposal was pending in the office of General Maxwell Taylor and asked that General Styron of Hobart be invited to discuss the matter with Taylor and his staff prior to forwarding their decision to the secretary of the army. Above all, they urged that "a final decision be speeded up so that the communities affected will not suffer economic paralysis with the issue left in doubt for several years."[76]

In May, when the senators issued a press release about their meeting, the House Armed Services Committee began its consideration of construction proposals. In general remarks delivered before the committee began discussions, Dewey Short, assistant secretary of the army, briefly mentioned the Fort Sill proposal and concluded, "We have $250 million invested at Sill. You can't walk off and leave it." The committee authorized for fiscal year 1959 almost $8 million for improving the White Sands Proving Ground in New Mexico and almost $14 million for Fort Bliss in Texas. Both installations included missile ranges. The request of Fort Sill for an authorization of $3,227,000 was discussed after all the army proposals had been considered. But there were no requests for land acquisition, and none had been approved by the secretary of the army. The plight of the people in southwestern Oklahoma remained in limbo.[77]

While they remained in limbo about the fate of the proposal, residents of the Sixth Congressional District had an opportunity to vent their views as Toby Morris, a friend of the proposal, sought reelection. His chief opponent in the upcoming July primary would be Victor Wickersham, by then a firm opponent of expansion. A record turnout was expected, one that would pit populous Lawton and Comanche County against the remaining twenty-two counties in the district. Helping ensure a record turnout was a story appearing in the July issue of *Reader's Digest* that represented another major coup for SOS. In "Do the Armed Forces need a 35-million acre empire?" Charles Stevenson informed readers of the "alarming rate" at which the armed services were "gobbling up our land." Attention at the end of the article was devoted to Fort Sill "as the nucleus of a vast new missile training center in the heart of America's farm belt and oil fields." Stevenson said the problem was worrying Congress and that "it had better the public, too." It certainly worried Sixth District voters as they flocked to the polls on primary election day.[78]

With five candidates in the race, no one received a majority, thereby forcing a runoff. Morris was the top vote getter with 34,226, or 40 percent of the votes. Victor Wickersham polled 33,743, or 39.4 percent. The elimination of three other candidates, none of whom garnered 10,000 votes, guaranteed that a tight race between the two contenders would be even tighter on July 22, when the winner secured the Democratic nomination and an assurance of victory in November. By the closest of margins, Morris edged out a victory, receiving 45,513 votes to Wickersham's 45,432. A margin of 81 votes sent Morris back to Washington to champion the cause of Fort Sill. SOS lost more than a chance to change the congressional seat; it also lost the services of its executive director, John Causten Currey, who had resigned to run as a Republican to represent the Fifth Congressional District. He was badly defeated in his primary race, as was his opponent in the November election.[79]

By the end of the year the Fort Sill expansion project had gone into abeyance, collecting dust somewhere in the Pentagon. General Taylor said there was no indication of any action "in the immediate future." With no specific time frame suggested, citizens of the affected communities, and of the farming and mineral regions in between—some 30,000 people—remained stymied in most of their activities because of uncertainty. The bitter election contest indicated that the political process would not yield any pressure toward resolving the matter. Previously, in May, a House Appropriations Subcommittee had examined the controversy in a closed session. The transcript made public in January 1959 indicated a desire to have the controversy settled but offered no precise recommendation.[80]

Residents of southwestern Oklahoma certainly wished the controversy settled. They continued to bombard the secretary of the army with letters calling upon him to renounce the proposed plan. Despite 75 of the 116 state representatives endorsing a motion that questioned DeShazo's proposal, and with Morris and Monroney calling for a prompt decision by Secretary Brucker, still no decision was forthcoming. Kerr noted that there was nothing in the 1960 fiscal year authorization or appropriations bills granting the army authority to acquire additional land in the vicinity of Fort Sill.[81]

While the squabble continued, though lacking in the intensity of previous years, a brief examination of the Eisenhower administration's military and strategic policy in the years following the end of the Korean conflict suggests that the Fort Sill proposal would never be realized. As the United States entered the missile age, the nation faced an increasing threat from the Soviet Union. Massive retaliation, predicated on nuclear weapons, became the framework of the administration's national security policy. To better achieve its goals, the armed forces reorganized to maintain a carefully controlled level of defense expenditures, while at the same time expanding the effort to contain the Soviet Union by maximizing the production of intermediate and long-range ballistic missiles. That policy meant that the air force and the navy became of vital significance in combating the threat of missiles launched from bases within the Soviet Union as well as from ships and submarines. That the army was not destined to play a major role in that strategy is best illustrated by a glance at the military budget. By the mid-1950s the air force was already receiving about 50 percent of the military budget, the navy 27 percent, and the army 23 percent. Previously the army had always drawn the highest portion of the budget. After Sputnik (October 1957), with the growing fear of a missile gap, the call for increasing funds for the air force and the speedy development of improved long- and intermediate-range missiles increased.

Army Chief of Staff Maxwell Taylor did not agree that the administration's policy of massive retaliation predicated on a nuclear response was the best approach. Taylor advocated what he called Flexible Response, an army capable of fighting brush-fire and guerrilla wars. His was a lone voice. Like Taylor, the field artillery during those years was having difficulty in finding a place for itself in the new missile age. New technology made it imperative that Fort Sill, the nation's premier artillery post, redefine itself. Expanding its firing range to include missiles offered an obvious solution, and the increasing intensity of the Cold War seemed to make it a patriotic mandate. However, given the urgent concerns of the Eisenhower administration, the proposal emanating from Fort Sill had a very low priority, but people in southwestern Oklahoma and the Oklahoma delegation in Washington had no option but to take the proposal seriously. Only Senator Kerr began to express doubts, and Representative Morris, who served on the Military Affairs Committee and should have known better, never informed the Lawton Chamber of Commerce and other supporters of range expansion of the dubious chances of its success.[82]

In January, 1958, retiring General James Gavin, referring to President Eisenhower's defense emergency fund request, said, "[T]here is not one red penny in that budget for the Army and I have been begging for money—money for the anti-missile, money for a space program." Later in 1958 the defense appropriations bill gave the secretary of defense control of the missile weapons program and authorized him to transfer lands between the army and air force in determining which type of missile system to employ in various defense areas. Gavin's frustration and Taylor's concerns were all cast aside in Eisenhower's insistence on minimizing the vulnerability of the nation's strategic forces to Soviet ballistic missiles. That matter overshadowed all other security concerns. By early 1959 there were indications in Washington that finally the imperial desire of General DeShazo and his staff would receive the attention of the Armed Services Committee.[83]

In a closed hearing before the House Armed Services Committee in March when appropriations for Fort Sill were considered, Major General Lyle Edward Seeman was pointedly asked if there were any plans in reference to acquisition of real estate at Fort Sill. He responded, "There are no present approved plans for acquiring any real estate at Fort Sill." While there were further off-the-record remarks, no recorded mention of the matter was made. In May the three members reviewing military construction for the Senate Armed Services Committee probed the matter in more detail. Responding to a question by John Stennis, General Seeman responded that no land had been acquired at Fort Sill, "although as time goes on, the missiles get further and faster and it is going to be a continuous problem." Another member, Henry Jackson, observed that "there is a limit to land acquisitions" and that "they better do a little research in using the oceans or something." There was no limit to expanding the range, "because technology, science, moving so fast can take all of the United States." Seeman indicated that the army's dilemma was that with its heavy investment in Fort Sill it was "the most efficient place to stay," though much of its property would either have to be replaced or overhauled and new construction undertaken. Moreover, the annual report of the secretary of the army for 1959 made no mention of land acquisition at Fort Sill, while noting that two LACROSSE surface-to-surface missile battalions were activated and training there. The post's responsibility would be "for the tactical and technical training of artillery and missile units," and it would continue as "the home of the U.S. Army Artillery and Missile School," the Army Artillery Board, and the Aviation Unit Training Command. Fort Sill's construction budget would continue to request large sums, but there was never a line calling for land acquisition.[84]

Later, in hearings before a House Subcommittee of Appropriations, Seeman admitted that at "Fort Sill they can just barely fire the LACROSSE missile at its minimum range." While there were three national research and development missile ranges, only one, the White Sands Missile Range, had an area suitable for troop training and firing schedules "along with their research and development training schedule." The Appropriations Committee members, like their counterparts on the Armed Services Committees, were concerned about spending funds "for a potentially obsolescent operation" at Fort Sill. The best response Seeman could offer was that "there is not going to be a tremendous number of firings," as the missiles "are going to cost too much." In response to further questioning he said that the Department of Defense had approved the army's request to extend the White Sands Research and Development Range for forty miles.[85]

Despite mounting evidence that the expansion of Fort Sill was not looked upon with favor by members of key congressional committees and that the administration had a set of priorities in which Fort Sill had no place, the army still supported the proposal. Retiring as army chief of staff, Taylor envisioned no early resolution of the issue. And SOS, almost moribund following Currey's departure, expressed its appreciation to members of the House subcommittee for their questioning of General Seeman on the Fort Sill proposal. Members were gaining confidence that the encroachment would be stopped. As it became clear that opposition to expansion was becoming more evident in Washington, so too did SOS renew its enthusiasm in battling the expansion plan, which had been "hanging fire" for three years.[86]

The issue briefly bubbled to the surface in the House of Representatives in August, when an influential member of the Appropriations Committee urged the expansion of Fort Sill as members considered funding military construction. His view was seconded by Morris, who protested the slash that had stripped Fort Sill of funds for new missile activities. The fund cut served to verify speculation that the army's failure to make a decision on the expansion issue indicated its demise.[87]

In September the army finally yielded to the inevitable. It announced that while training in the use of missiles would continue at Fort Sill, the actual firing would be conducted "in the Fort Bliss–White Sands Missile Range area or at other existing ranges." The army, according to its chief of legislative liaison, "has not programmed for the expansion of Fort Sill in Fiscal Year 1960 or in the foreseeable future." Paraphrasing the renowned lines in T. S. Eliot's poem *The Wasteland*, the controversy ended "not with a bang but a whimper." In a press release following the official announcement, Morris, while disappointed with the outcome, claimed that he was happy to have "assurances that the proposed land acquisition at Fort Sill is not a necessity."[88]

Ecstatic with the outcome and that its efforts were at an end, SOS expressed its satisfaction that Fort Sill's mission in national defense would continue. All residents of the area could begin to work together to make southwestern Oklahoma a better place in which to live and earn a livelihood. Members went to church the next Sunday and gave thanks for a prayer answered. Some even tried to heal their differences with their congressman. In a Christmas letter SOS president M. A. Callen expressed "a special thank you to our friends for help when we needed it most." In accord with the spirit of the season, SOS sent a copy to its antagonistic member of Congress.[89]

There was, however, a residue of bitterness. In the 1960 primary election Morris lost to the man he defeated in 1956, Victor Wickersham, by 402 votes (40,304 to 40,706). In turn Wickersham defeated his Republican opponent by a mere 76 votes (68,192 to 68,116). In 1960 Wickersham won reelection in another tight race by less than 1,400 votes. In 1964 he lost the seat to his Republican opponent; in 1966 and again in 1968 he was defeated by his Democratic primary opponents. With Wickersham's fading fortune, the antipathy toward the representatives who had endorsed the views of the Lawton Chamber of Commerce and business establishment abated.[90]

The irony of the situation is that it should never have occurred. Given the urgency of the Cold War and the Eisenhower administration's strategic policy of massive retaliation, which placed great emphasis on air force and naval capacity to both launch and counter intercontinental ballistic missiles, the army had a lesser role to play. That was reflected in the reversed allocation of the military budget, from the top allocation during the Korean War to the minimal allocation during Eisenhower's second term. Fort Sill and the field artillery, seeking to redefine their role, never seriously gained the attention of the joint chiefs of staff, top Pentagon officials including the secretary of defense, or members of the Senate and House Armed Services Committees, with the exception of Wickersham and Morris, who carried no weight in the committee deliberations. While Senator Kerr changed his mind and came out in support of the fight SOS was making, he was not a member of the Military Affairs Committee but did his best to get the views of SOS before key officials in Washington. In a crucial sense, then, residents in southwestern Oklahoma on both sides of the issue, as well as the generals in command at Fort Sill from 1955 through 1959, were all casualties of the Cold War.

Notes

1. Department of Defense, *Semiannual Report of the Secretary of Defense and the Semiannual Reports of the Secretary of the Army, Secretary of the Navy, Secretary of the Air Force, January 1 to June 30, 1955* (Washington, D.C.: Government Printing Office [GPO], 1956), 85–86, 123 (hereafter all Department of Defense reports cited as DOD with appropriate year). For general information on the army missile program in the 1950s, see Boyd L. Dastrup, *The Field Artillery* (Westport, Conn.: Greenwood Press, 1944), 64–65, and DOD 1954, 117–18.

2. Victor Wickersham, *Fort Sill*, Box 10, Folder 12, Victor Wickersham Papers, Carl Albert Center, University of Oklahoma, Norman (hereafter cited as CAC).

3. Salient Facts in Proposed Fort Sill Range Expansion, n.d., copy in Box 10, Folder 13, Wickersham Papers, CAC.

4. Ibid.

5. I have relied for my remarks on the Wichita Mountains Wildlife Preserve on Jack Dan Haley, "A History of the Establishment of the Wichita National Forest and Game Preserve, 1901–1908" (MA thesis, University of Oklahoma, 1973), and several leaflets on the refuge available to visitors.

6. Hobart Chamber of Commerce, Resolutions Adopted October 28, 1952, Protesting Fort Sill Expansion Program, Box 42, Folder 4, Wickersham Papers, CAC; *Kiowa County Star-Review* (Hobart, Okla.), October 30, 1952; John Jarman to Wayne Rowe and Fred Ferrell, Jr., November 6, 1952, Box 10, Folder 9, Wickersham Papers, CAC. Rowe and Ferrell were protesting on behalf of the Wichita Landowners Association. See also the newsletter of the Oklahoma Outdoor Council, February 3, 1953, wherein a letter from Senator Mike Monroney is quoted defining the position of the army, Box 42, Folder 2, Lovie Whitaker Papers, Western History Collections, University of Oklahoma, Norman (hereafter cited as WHC). For the views of the Lawton Chamber of Commerce, see undated clippings in Box 10, Folder I, Wickersham Papers, CAC.

7. Robert S. Kerr, draft letter to opponents, n.d., Topical Box 10, Folder 29, Robert S. Kerr Papers, CAC; Mike Monroney, draft letter, n.d., Box 10, Folder 11, Wickersham Papers, CAC. See also Wickersham to Dear Friend, April 19, 1955, and General C. F. Hauk, Jr., to Wickersham, April 20, 1955, Box 10, Folder 4, Wickersham Papers, CAC; J. Teague Self to Kerr, April 7, 1955, Topical Box 10, Folder 29, Kerr Papers, CAC, for a letter opposing the takeover of land in the wildlife refuge. Mike Monroney to Mrs. John Whitaker, May 4, 1955, Box 42, Folder 1, Whitaker Papers, WHC.

8. See, for example, "More Comments on Fort Sill," *Big Pasture News* (Grandfield, Okla.), April 21, 1955, and "Fort Sill vs. Recreational Growth," *Big Pasture News*, April 28, 1955; "Friday Forum" letter, *Oklahoma City Times*, June 17, 1955; "Senators Hear Foes of Fort's Expansion Talk," *Oklahoma City Times*, June 15, 1955; Wickersham to Carl Vinson, April 26, 1955, Box 10, Folder 9, Wickersham Papers, CAC. Vinson chaired the House Armed Services Committee.

9. Mrs. Endee Wilson, Secretary and Treasurer, Snyder Chamber of Commerce, to Wickersham, April 26, 1955, Box 10, Folder 9, Wickersham Papers, CAC. Petitions to members of the Oklahoma's congressional delegation can be found in Box 10, Folder 10, Wickersham Papers, CAC, and in Topical Box 10, Folder 28, Kerr Papers, CAC. Of interest was a letter from Oklahoma Agricultural and Mechanical College students, "a handful of country boys from the dusty prairies of western Oklahoma," who considered the wildlife refuge "one of the very few places in western Oklahoma where we can see clear water, tall native grasses, and wildlife in abundance." Paul Keith and others to Wickersham, May 2, 1955, Box 10, Folder 5, Wickersham Papers, CAC. See also the critical letter of Lucius W. Long, Jr., to Wickersham, May 16, 1955, Box 10, Folder 6, Wickersham Papers, CAC. Long owned and leased about 5,000 acres of ranch land and produced about 175,000 pounds of beef each year.

10. Bess Smith to Dr. Harriet Barclay, May 5, 1955, Smith, Memorandum, May 13, 1955, Smith to Melvin Price, May 7, 1955, Box 42, Folder 1, Whitaker Papers, WHC. Smith said she wrote forty one-page letters to members of the House Armed Services Committee with a copy to each National Wildlife Federation president in that representative's state. See letters prompted by Whitaker in the *Norman* (Okla.) *Transcript*, May 9, 12, 1955; Gene Torbett to Dear Fellow Citizen, May 13, 1955, Box 42, Folder 2, Whitaker Papers, WHC.

11. Torbett to Dear Fellow Citizen, May 13, 1955, Box 42, Folder 2, Whitaker Papers, WHC; *Norman Transcript*, May 15, 1955.

12. M. L. Wardell to Kerr, May 20, 1955, Charles V. Collins to Kerr, May 23, 1955, Topical Box 10, Folder 32, Kerr Papers, CAC. Wardell was a history professor at the University of Oklahoma; Collins was a Grady County judge.

13. Military Public Works: Hearings Before the Full Committee of the Committee on Armed Services, House of Representatives [no. 201 on HR 5700], 84th Cong., 1st sess., 3635–47, 3869–3927. The hearings were conducted over several days from June 3 through June 9, 1955.

14. Ibid.

15. Ibid.

16. Hearings Before the Subcommittee on Real Estate and Military Construction of the Committee on Armed Services, United States Senate, 84th Cong., 1st sess., 13–315, 681–711. The hearing got under way on May 22, 1955, but the bulk of the discussion occurred on June 23, 1955.

17. C. R. Ellsworth to Wickersham, June 10, 1955, Box 10, Folder 2, Wickersham Papers, CAC; Allan Cromley, "Vinson Opposes Fort Sill Move," (Oklahoma City) *Daily Oklahoman*, June 10, 1955; Smith to Whitaker, June 15, 1955, Box 42, Folder 1, Whitaker Papers, WHC; *Kiowa County Star-Review*, June 16, 1955. Though not permitted to appear before the Armed Services Committee, conservationists nationwide learned about the threat to the refuge in Margaret Morse Nice, "Wichita Mountains Wildlife Refuge in Peril," *Nature Magazine*, June–July 1955. Nice was associated with Lovie Whitaker and her group battling against the land transfer.

18. Exall English to Wickersham, June 21, 1955, A. B. Hambrick to Wickersham, June 25, 1955, Wickersham to William Keating, June 28, 1955, Box 10, Folders 2, 3, 5 respectively, Wickersham Papers, CAC; *Congressional Record*, 84th Cong., 1st sess., July 1, 1955, 9708.

19. *Congressional Record*, 84th Cong., 1st sess., July 1, 1955, 9709–11.

20. Ibid., July 20, 1955, 1040–45. Sikes's full remarks and those of Lee Metcalf can be found in the House debate on July 14, 1955, 10591–93.

21. Ibid., 1042–43, and July 22, 1955, 11306.

22. Ibid., July 26, 1955, 11497–98.

23. Ibid., 11497–11505. See also "Sill Expansion Law Doesn't Cool Debate," *Daily Oklahoman*, August 8, 1955, which discusses the debate between Kerr and Neuberger.

24. Arthur Watkins to Kerr "and members of the Oklahoma Congressional Delegation," July 29, 1955, Kerr to Watkins, August 4, 1955, Box 10, Folder 9, 5 respectively, Wickersham Papers, CAC; *Daily Oklahoman*, July 25, 1955.

25. *Kiowa County Star-Review*, August 11, 1955; Paul McClung, *Papa Jack: Cowman from the Wichitas* (Norman: University of Oklahoma Press, 1976). Chapter 18, "The Land Grab," discusses Jack Howenstine's losing fight to avoid being dispossessed. Lieutenant Colonel B. W. Legare to Wickersham, August 23, 1955, Box 2, Folder 34, Wickersham Papers, CAC. Legare assured Wickersham that the Post Oak Mission cemetery would be relocated at government expense and that the land and improvements owned by the church would be purchased. If desired by the church, the buildings and improvements could be retained by the owner and removed to a new location.

26. Allen Cromley, "Fort Sill Land Fight Is Settled by Compromise," *Daily Oklahoman*, October 27, 1955.

27. Wickersham to Douglas McKay, November 2, 1955, Box 10, Folder 6, Wickersham Papers, CAC; John Stennis to Wickersham, November 10, 1955, Francis Case to Wickersham, November 14, 1955, Henry Jackson to Wickersham, November 18, 1955, Box 10, Folders 8, 1, 4 respectively, Wickersham Papers, CAC. The three senators comprised the Subcommittee on Real Estate and Military Construction.

28. McKay to Wickersham, November 18, 1957, Wickersham to L. A. Collier, December 22, 1955, Box 10, Folders 6, 2 respectively, Wickersham Papers, CAC.

29. Military Public Works, Hearings Before the Full Committee of the Committee on Armed Services, House of Representatives [no. 61] on HR 8625 and HR 9893, 84th Cong., 2nd sess., February 22, 1956, 6167–68, 6246–47.

30. Ibid.

31. *Congressional Record*, 84th Cong., 2nd sess., January 9, 1956, 248–49; Hauk to Wickersham, January 11, 1956, Box 10, Folder 4, Wickersham Papers, CAC; Smith, Memorandum, January 28, 1956, Box 42, Folder 1, Whitaker Papers, WHC. For a discussion of the military efforts to downplay the value of the lands it sought, see *Conservation News*, January 15, 1956, 6–7.

32. Wickersham to Herbert Bonner, Chairman of the Merchant Marine and Fisheries Committee, March 1, 1956, Wickersham to Elise Owings, March 17, 1956, Box 10, Folders 1, 6 respectively, Wickersham Papers, CAC; "New Threat to Wichita Mountains National Wildlife Refuge," *Citizens Committee On National Resources*, March 20, 1956, 1, Box 42, Folder 1, Whitaker Papers, WHC; Smith, Memorandum, March 28, 1956, Box 42, Folder 1, Whitaker Papers, WHC.

33. Wilber M. Brucker to Bonner, April 30, 1956, copy in Box 10, Folder 1, Wickersham Papers, CAC; Brucker to Richard B. Russell, Chairman of the Senate Committee on Armed Services, May 15, 1956, copy in Topical Box 10, Folder 37, Kerr Papers, CAC.

34. Wesley A. D'Ewart to Bonner, May 14, 1956, copy in Box 10, Folder 13, Wickersham Papers, CAC. No action was scheduled at that time on S 3360, an identical measure introduced by Senators Monroney and Kerr. *Citizens Committee on Natural Resources*, May 14, 1956, copy in Box 42, Folder 1, Whitaker Papers, WHC. The newsletter claimed that although "the Army admits that it has at least five installations in other states that easily could accommodate the Fort Sill activities, it was threatening to move the Artillery and Guided Missile School from the state."

35. The unpublished hearings before the Committee on Merchant Marine and Fisheries are available on LexisNexis Congressional, CIS-No. 84 HME-T.38 and T.48 and refer to HR 9665 discussed during the second session of the Eighty-fourth Congress. Assistant Secretary D'Ewart, statement, May 23, 1956, copy in Box 10, Folder 13, Wickersham Papers, CAC.

36. Charles C. Finucane to Bonner, June 20, 1956, copy in Topical Box 10, Folder 37, Kerr Papers, CAC. The pertinent discussion can be followed on pages 113–36 of the Unpublished House Committee Hearings available on LexisNexis. Earlier, General Hauk, chief of legislative liaison, sent Bonner a letter indicating the type of weapons to be tested at the Artillery and Guided Missile School at Fort Sill. Hauck to Bonner, June 5, 1956, copy in Box 10, Folder 9, Wickersham Papers, CAC.

37. Oklahoma Delegation to the President, June 27, 1956, Topical Box 10, Folder 37, Kerr Papers, CAC; Gregory Fewell to Wickersham, June 23, 1956, Box 2, Folder 34, Wickersham Papers, CAC; District Engineer, Tulsa District, Corps of Engineers, U.S. Army, *Questions and Answers Concerning the Acquisition of Your Land by the Government*, pamphlet, n.d., copy in Box 10, Folder 4, Wickersham Papers, CAC.

38. Oklahoma State Election Board, *Oklahoma Elections: Statehood to Present*, 2 vols. (Oklahoma City: Oklahoma State Election Board, July, 1988), 1: D-400, D-408.

39. Statement of Honorable Toby Morris, February 16, 1957, Milton Keating to Morris, February 19, 1957, General Box 2, Folder 7, Toby Morris Papers, CAC.

40. Lawton Chamber of Commerce to Secretary of Army Brucker, February 28, 1957, General Box 2, Folder 7, Morris Papers, CAC.

41. J. S. Kimmitt to Kerr, March 6, 1957, Topical Box 11, Folder 5, Kerr Papers, CAC.

42. *Lawton* (Okla.) *Constitution*, September 10, 1957; *Conservation News*, October 1, 1957, 6–7. The terms of the agreement were substantially the same as those announced in February which aroused the Lawton Chamber of Commerce.

43. "Army at Wichita," *National Parks Magazine*, October–December, 1957, 176, 189; *Guthrie* (Okla.) *Daily Leader*, December 8, 1957.

44. *Guthrie Daily Leader*, December 8, 1957; Joy Ganoung to Dean Earl, December 3, 1957, General Box 2, Folder 7, Morris Papers, CAC. Ganoung, a

resident of Cooperton (population 125), would lose her land if the missile range was developed.

45. "Proposed Fort Sill Impact Range in Southwest Oklahoma," leaflet, n.d., copy in General Box 2, Folder 15, Morris Papers, CAC.

46. W. A. Trawick, Jr., to Monroney et al., December 11, 1957, General Box 2, Folder 7, Morris Papers, CAC.

47. *Mangum* (Okla.) *Star*, December 12, 1957.

48. For a story on General Hayden's talk, see *Altus* (Okla.) *Times Democrat*, December 17, 1957; *Daily Oklahoman*, December 22, 1957.

49. Ibid.

50. *Daily Oklahoman*, December 22, 1957; Mrs. J. B. Skeen to Morris, December 13, 1957, R. Place Montgomery to Morris, December 17, 1957, General Box 2, Folders 7, 9 respectively, Morris Papers, CAC. On December 23 General DeShazo informed Morris that the proposed expansion constituted the Artillery and Missile Center recommendations and were not an approved Department of the Army plan. See DeShazo to Morris, General Box 2, Folder 7, Morris Papers, CAC. *Tulsa* (Okla.) *Tribune*, January 11, 1958. This story by Ned Curran detailed the creation of SOS and the unfolding controversy. The papers of Morris and Kerr each contain extensive SOS files. Letters from Currey and other SOS officers appear in the files.

51. Morris to Don and Georgia Gish, December 23, 1957, General Box 2, Folder 7, Morris Papers, CAC, is a typical letter. *S-O-S from the Shortgrass*, "Calling All America!," copy in General Box 2, Folder 7, Morris Papers, CAC.

52. *Lawton* (Okla.) *Constitution and Morning Press*, December 29, 1957; Military and Naval Construction Hearing Before the Committee on Armed Services [no. 36], 85th Cong., 1st sess., May 16, 1957, 1533–34.

53. *Public Papers of the Presidents of the United States: Dwight D. Eisenhower . . . 1953– [1960–61]*, vol. 5 (1957) (Washington. D.C.: GPO, 1953–61): 810–13. Department of Defense, Semiannual Report, January 1 to June 30, 1957 (Washington, D.C.: GPO, 1958), 49, noted that "guided missile and training sites are measured in millions of acres, while 50,000 acres were ample for artillery ranges. While some existing installations can be expanded to meet new requirements, in other areas the disposal of an outmoded facility and the building of a modern one will be more economical."

54. Undated and untitled clippings, General Box 2, passim, Morris Papers, CAC; *Oklahoma Farm Bureau Farmer*, January 3, 1958, copy in General Box 2, Folder 15, Morris Papers, CAC; *Hobart* (Okla.) *Democrat-Chief*, January 5, 1958. The articles noted the role of women in organizing a letter-writing campaign. Another story discussed Currey's letter to the president of the National Reserve Officers' Association.

55. *Hobart Democrat-Chief*, January 9, 1958; Monroney to Trawick, January 6, 1958, copy in General Box 2, Folder 20, Morris Papers, CAC.

56. *Hobart Democrat-Chief*, January 15, 1958; Form letter, Carnegie, Oklahoma, January 14, 1958, copy in General Box 2, Folder 20, Morris Papers, CAC; *Clinton* (Okla.) *Daily News*, January 15, 1958.

57. Kerr to Zeke Mullen, January 14, 1958, Topical Box 11, Folder 13, Kerr Papers, CAC; *Clinton Daily News*, January 15, 1958; "Victor Makes Hay on Fort Sill Range," untitled clipping, n.d., in General Box 2, Folder 15, Morris Papers, CAC. For Morris's response see *Daily Oklahoman*, January 18, 1958.

58. See *Lawton Constitution*, January 15, 1958, for a series of stories on Fort Sill; Wichita Mountains Chapter Oklahoma Society of Professional Engineers, resolution, n.d., copy in General Box 2, Folder 15, Morris Papers, CAC; *Norman Transcript*, January 15, 1958; *Clinton Daily News*, January 17, 1958. Letters from Lawton endorsing the stance of Morris and Monroney were balanced by letters in opposition.

59. *Clinton Daily News*, January 17, 24, 1958; *Norman Transcript*, January 19, 24, 1958; *Daily Oklahoman*, January 19, 1958.

60. *Daily Oklahoman*, January 19, 1958; "The U.S. Missile Program," *Time*, January 20, 1958, 19–20.

61. *Kiowa County Democrat* (Snyder, Okla.), January 23, 1958; Kerr to George W. Barber, January 23, 1958, Topical Box 11, Folder 13, Kerr Papers, CAC.

62. *Daily Oklahoman*, January 30, 1958.

63. *New York Times*, February 3, 4, 1958. Baker's story appeared on February 3, an editorial, "Kiowa County Asks Help," on the following day. "League Claims Sill Expansion Would Aid Area," untitled clipping, n.d., in Box W-42, Folder 16, Whitaker Papers, WHC. The *Norman Transcript*, on February 9, 1958, published an Associated Press story paralleling that of Baker in the *New York Times*.

64. Currey to Morris, February 1, 1958, General Box 2, Folder 15, Morris Papers, CAC. For missiles see *Time*, January 20, 1958, 19–20.

65. *Hobart Democrat-Chief*, February 11, 1958; Resolution of the Sixth District Democratic Convention, February 7, 1958, copy in General Box 2, Folder 15, Morris Papers, CAC; State Democratic Central Committee, resolution, February, 1958, copy in General Box 2, Folder 16, Morris Papers, CAC; Republican State Convention, resolution in opposition, 1958, copy in General Box 2, Folder 18, Morris Papers, CAC.

66. Fred Harris to Brucker, February 13, 1958, General Box 2, Folder 11, Morris Papers, CAC.

67. Examples of Currey's work in arousing opposition are among the press clippings in General Box 2, Folder 17, Morris Papers, CAC, and in Matt Triggs, Assistant Legislative Director of the American Farm Bureau Federation, to Department of the Army, February 20, 1958, copy in Box 2, Folder 18, Morris Papers, CAC; State Legislative Council, Special Study Committee, Public Hearing on the Proposed Fort Sill Land Expansion, February 19, 1958, 4–6, 36–39, 84–93, passim, copy in Topical Box 11, Folder 13, Kerr Papers, CAC; *Daily Oklahoman*, February 13, 1958.

68. Oklahoma Defense League, press release, March 1, 1958, copy in Topical Box 11, Folder 14, Kerr Papers, CAC; *Hobart Democrat-Chief*, March 2, 1958; *Purcell* (Okla.) *Register*, March 6, 1958. SOS hired a statistician to refute in detail the Oklahoma Defense League's charges.

69. "Editorial," *Daily Oklahoman*, March 2, 1958; "Brucker States Ft. Sill Expansion Not Yet Decided," *Daily Oklahoman*, March 6, 1958.

70. Charles B. Bolar to Dear Friend and Neighbor, March 4, 1958, copy in General Box 2, Folder 18, Morris Papers, CAC; *Purcell Register*, March 6, 1958; see also Ira Nash to Sam Rayburn, n.d., wherein a disgruntled resident asked for help, and "Ft. Bliss retains its Missile Center," copy in General Box 2, Folder 12, Morris Papers, CAC.

71. *Purcell Register*, March 6, 1958; "Victor to Take Plunge Thursday," untitled clipping, and Mr. and Mrs. Luther Roberts to Morris, March 7, 1958, General Box 2, Folders 18, 13 respectively, Morris Papers, CAC; *Lawton Morning Press*, March 6, 1958.

72. Committee Recommendations, April 4, 1958, copy in Topical Box 11, Folder 15, Kerr Papers, CAC; *Kiowa County Star-Review*, April 10, 17, 1958.

73. *Lawton Morning Press*, April 18, 1958.

74. Washington Hearing, April 22, 1958, transcript, General Box 2, Folder 11, Morris Papers, CAC; "Where We're Firing Our Missiles," map, *Newsweek*, March 10, 1958, 73. It noted that Pershing missiles would be fired from Fort Bliss to Fort Sill, a distance of five hundred miles. General Bogart, responding to a question, said, "No such firing is contemplated," and "You surely do not believe everything you read."

75. Washington Hearing, April 22, 1958, transcript, General Box 2, Folder 11, Morris Papers, CAC.

76. Kerr to Arthur Watkins, April 24, 1958, Topical Box 11, Folder 14, Kerr Papers, CAC. Watkins was a senator from Utah. Senators Kerr and Monroney, press release, May 20, 1958, copy in General Box 2, Folder 13, Morris Papers, CAC; *Oklahoma City Times*, May 21, 1958. General Styron and Byron Bolar, the president of SOS, expressed their views in Pentagon conferences on June 24 arranged by Senator Kerr. See *Kiowa County Star-Review*, June 25, 1958. A copy of Styron's statement is available in General Box 2, Folder 20, Morris Papers, CAC.

77. Military and Naval Construction: Hearings Committee on Armed Services, House [no. 86], 85th Cong., 2nd sess., 7089–90 (Dewey Short), 7121–23 (White Sands Proving Ground), 7171–81 (Fort Bliss), 653 (Fort Sill). Fort Sill was considered on May 28, 1958. The testimony appeared in a supplementary volume.

78. *Elk City* (Okla.) *Daily News*, June 20, 1958; *Reader's Digest*, July 1958, 73–77. Reprints were widely circulated throughout the congressional district.

79. *Oklahoma Elections: Statehood to Present*, 1: D-414, D-415, D-417.

80. "Eventually, Maybe," *Oklahoma City Times*, November 21, 1958; Allan Cromley, "Army Ponders Fort Sill Fate," *Oklahoma City Times*, June 22, 1959.

81. Topical Box 11, Folder 17, Kerr Papers, CAC, contains copies of letters sent to the secretary of the army, as well as copies of editorials noting that the ruckus had died down but was still not resolved. Morris to Mrs. C. C. Clark, February 11, 1959, General Box 2, Folder 21, Morris Papers, CAC; William Metcalf to Clifford McIntyre, July 2, 1959, copy in General Box 2, Folder 22, Morris Papers, CAC. Metcalf was a state representative from Kiowa County and McIntyre a congressman from Maine. Kerr to Jack Haley, July 2, 1959, Topical Box 11, Folder 17, Kerr Papers, CAC.

82. There is an extensive literature that examines Eisenhower's military policy. I have relied on Douglas Kinnard, *President Eisenhower and Strategy Management: A Study in Defense Policies* (1977; reprint, Washington, [D.C.]: Pergamon-Brassey, 1989). See also Ernest J. Yanarella, *Missile Defense Controversy* (Lexington: University Press of Kentucky, 2002); Peter Roman, *Eisenhower and the Missile Gap* (Ithaca, N.Y.: Cornell University Press, 1995). I have also perused the annual reports of the secretary of defense for the late 1950s. See also Maxwell Taylor, *The Uncertain Trumpet* (New York: Harper, 1960).

83. *Congressional Quarterly Almanac* 14 (1958): 237–38, 670; Roman, *Eisenhower and the Missile Gap*, 166.

84. Military and Naval Construction: Hearings Before the Committee on Armed Services, House of Representatives [no. 17] 86th Cong., 1st sess., March 10, 1959, 1346; Hearings Before the Subcommittee on Military Construction of the Committee on Armed Services, United States Senate, 86th Cong., 1st sess., May 17, 1959, 288–91; *Annual Report of the Secretary of the Army*, July 1, 1958–June 30, 1959, 171. The Military Construction Authorization Bills for 1960 contained no mention of land acquisition for Fort Sill.

85. Subcommittee on Military Construction Appropriation: Committee on Appropriations, House of Representatives, 86th Cong., 1st sess., June 3, 1959, 205–207.

86. *Lawton Constitution*, June 17, 1959; *Oklahoma City Times*, June 23, August 10, 1959; *Daily Oklahoman*, June 25, 1959; Jack Haley to Morris, June 30, 1959, General Box 2, Folder 21, Morris Papers, CAC.

87. *Congressional Record*, 86th Cong., 1st sess., August 10, 1959, 15367–68; *Daily Oklahoman*, August 11, 1959.

88. R. L. Vittrup to Morris, September 11, 1959, General Box 2, Folder 21, Morris Papers, CAC; Vittrup to Kerr, September 11, 1959, Topical Box 11, Folder 17, Kerr Papers, CAC. Vittrup, a major general, was army chief of legislative liaison.

89. Press release, September 13, 1959, General Box 2, Folder 21, Morris Papers, CAC; *Hobart Democrat-Chief*, September 16, 1959; C. A. Smelser to Morris, September 25, 1959, and Dear Friend, n.d., in General Box 2, Folder 21, Morris Papers, CAC.

90. For the election results, see *Oklahoma Elections: Statehood to Present*, vol. 1.

« 5 »

From Termination to Self-Determination

Indian Health in Oklahoma, 1954–1980

In the long history of relations between the United States and the Indian nations, the mid-twentieth-century policy of "termination" of tribes was one of the saddest episodes. Termination, a goal promoted during the pre– and post–World War II years and accepted by the administration of President Dwight D. Eisenhower in the 1950s, called for federal withdrawal from Indian affairs. This new approach was intended, as rapidly as possible, to make Indians subject to the same laws and entitled to the same rights and responsibilities as all other American citizens. Termination was expected to promote the assimilation of Indians into the general population, and relocation of Indian individuals and families from rural to urban centers was a corollary. The process, begun in 1953, resulted in the disbanding of numerous tribes, mostly in the East but including the Ottawa, Peoria, and Wyandotte tribes in Oklahoma, and it continued until reversed by President Richard M. Nixon in 1970. In a message to Congress, Nixon called for "self-determination without termination" and launched a new approach that envisioned the fulfillment of the government's responsibility to Indian peoples. Within this seventeen-year span, Indian health programs helped to promote and establish the concept of self-determination.

From 1849 to 1955, federal responsibility for Indian health care fell to the Bureau of Indian Affairs (BIA). Despite funding specifically earmarked for health services, the level of care and Indian health deteriorated during the first half of the twentieth century. Studies documenting deterioration by the Bureau of the Budget (1948), the Hoover Commission (1949), and the American Medical Association (1949) led to calls for a new approach. Health services provided by the BIA were terminated in 1954, and in 1955 the newly organized Indian Health Service (IHS), a division of the Public Health Service (PHS) in the Health Services Administration of the Department of Health, Education, and Welfare (HEW), became a key agency to assure comprehensive health services for American and Alaskan Indians. The experience of Oklahoma Indians indicates that it was a long and rocky road, but by the late 1970s a path toward self-determination had begun.[1]

The goal of the Indian Health Service was to assure accessibility to a high-quality delivery system, as well as to all health programs to which Indians were entitled as American citizens. To achieve this lofty goal, in the 1970s the IHS was servicing a tribal membership whose average annual income was 75 percent below the national average, while unemployment among Indians was about 40 percent, more than ten times the national average. Such depressed economic circumstances, which usually manifested themselves in Indian communities earlier than elsewhere, caused high disease rates among Indians, higher than any other racial group in the nation. In all diseases, except venereal, Oklahoma's Indians tallied higher rates than the rest of the American population. The life expectancy of Indian people was ten years less than that of other Americans.[2]

The provision of health services was complicated by the heterogeneous cultural background, language barriers, social isolation, and varying health and sanitation customs and practices among Indian groups. In many instances, in Oklahoma and elsewhere, Indians had no alternative to the Indian Health Service because they lived in isolated places with few medical facilities. Another variable involved cultural assimilation. Particularly, but not exclusively, in remote rural areas some Indians spoke no English, followed traditional ways, and did not accept modern health practices. Providing them with meaningful health care was problematic at best. Even urban Indians living chiefly in Oklahoma City and Tulsa had no direct access to health care, and low economic status contributed to alcoholism, which led indirectly to child neglect and to conditions conducive to high morbidity and mortality.[3]

But there were other, non-Indian problems related to administering better-quality health care. For one, Indian health services were enmeshed in a huge bureaucracy. Delivery of care was divided among eight IHS Service Units, each with its own director. An individual serving as a Service Unit director was most likely a clinical physician, fresh from medical training, with a maximum of one year's experience in Indian health issues and an eagerness to cure patients. Service Unit directors first received a briefing from the Indian Health Area director (IHAD) at the IHS Area Office in Oklahoma City. Rather than a review of medical procedures, this scant training included a discussion of tribal customs, along with explanations of the workings of the Bureau of Indian Affairs and other government agencies. "Branch chiefs," specialists in different fields of Indian health, such as purchasing experts, construction engineers, and health consultants, worked to develop the program approved by the IHAD. Service Unit directors assumed responsibility for carrying out this program and directing employees, administering sanitation programs, managing financial appropriations that could reach $1 million, and maintaining the buildings and grounds of the hospital itself.

Service Unit directors also determined their patients' eligibility to receive care. They made these decisions "that go to the very heart of the complex legal and social problems of the Indian Health Program" without the understanding and training necessary to render them reasonably. Their desire to heal was now confronted "with legal rights to grant such services." By this convoluted methodology, a staggeringly bureaucratic complex impeded the mission of Indian Health Service doctors. Patients grew critical of and hostile to white man's medicine.[4]

What the Service Unit directors and other Public Health Service doctors learned to recognize, despite improvement in preventive and curative medicine, was that their patients were a people in transition. About half retained strong ties to their respective cultures and had their own beliefs concerning the causes and cures for illnesses. In 1959, with the passage of the Indian Sanitation Facilities Act, Congress took a step that, if adequately funded, would enhance Indian health more effectively than direct patient care. The program could be crucial to improving living conditions and reducing water- and waste-borne communicable diseases. In Oklahoma, unfortunately, the law was applied primarily to new housing, and then only sporadically. It thus penetrated more slowly the older and more debilitated housing occupied by underemployed and marginally educated Indians living in deprivation and frequently in squalor. Many Indians nurtured a deep-seated reluctance, often reinforced by their contact with the IHS, to trust the white man and his medicine.[5]

Initially, the entire Oklahoma congressional delegation opposed legislation that would transfer Indian hospitals to the Public Health Service. The members feared that four of Oklahoma's six Indian hospitals—at Clinton, Lawton, Pawnee, and Claremore—would be shut down.[6] Once the transfer occurred, however, opposition quickly dissipated. Within the eight Oklahoma Service Units no major changes were foreseen, although most facilities needed more beds and suffered an endemic shortage of doctors and nurses.[7]

As the basic organizational framework in the Indian Health Service program, the Service Unit comprised a defined geographical area within which there were three types of delivery venues for health care. Six of the areas had a hospital, while Shawnee and Tishomingo relied on health centers. The latter furnished outpatient clinics and public health services to Indians in outlying locations. They had full-time physician services and more sophisticated facilities and equipment. Field stations, the lowest level of delivery, differed from health centers in that they did not provide continuous medical coverage, although they might have a full-time dentist, a public health nurse, and a sanitation or other general worker, but not a physician or staff. All three types of facilities were plagued by turnover and staff vacancies, heavy patient loads, isolation from other members of the profession, lack of modern medical equipment, inadequate living quarters, and no prospects for career advancement, all of which worked to the detriment of Indian health.

Eight Service Units should have been adequate to provide for the health needs of Oklahoma Indians, but such was not the case. Precise statistics are not available, but perhaps as many as 20 percent of the total Indian population resided within the Oklahoma City and Tulsa areas. Their numbers were increasing as rural families moved into the state's two largest metropolitan areas in search of employment. Having moved, they discovered that the previously available health services now were unavail-

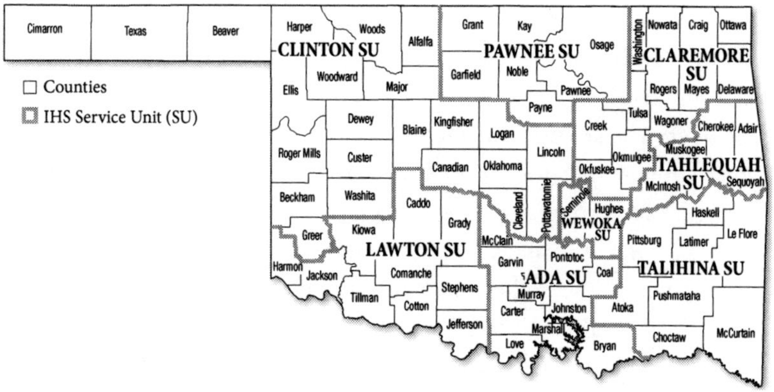

Indian Health Districts. Source: Health Care Information, Center for Health Statistics, Oklahoma State Department of Health.

able, unless they were willing to travel forty miles to the Shawnee Health Center or ninety miles to the Lawton Indian Hospital. From Tulsa it was forty miles to the Indian Hospital in Claremore.

Oklahoma Indians were caught in a dysfunctional political loop that involved distant bureaucrats with little need to hear them and officials on hand who did not represent them. Indians registering their health concerns used the time-honored means of requesting something: petition. Tribal leaders employed that method continually, using respectful, ritual language. By their very nature, petitions reaffirmed Indians' exclusion from everyday American political life and their dependence upon others to make decisions for them. Part of the heritage of a conquered people, petitions were effectively utilized from the mid-1950s through 1980, decades that witnessed increasing Indian control of health services.[8]

One individual, Sula Saltsman Goodman, Area Indian Health public information specialist, tried to bring some coherence to the health program during the early years following the transfer of responsibility from the BIA to the Public Health Service. She planned the area information program by initiating a newsletter, "Talking Leaves," for tribal leaders and numerous others involved with or interested in the transfer of responsibility. At the onset PHS had closed an outmoded, but venerated, tuberculosis sanatorium at Shawnee, a move that aroused considerable controversy. The newsletter covered this story for readers throughout Indian country.

Goodman also used the media to keep state officials as well as professional groups informed about Indian health programs. She further developed a supplementary mimeographed newsletter to allow the various program chiefs to explain their operations to one another in order to achieve better cooperation. The newsletter helped people who transferred into, or voluntarily entered, the Public Health Service to better understand their new positions. In explaining the use of contract arrangements in shifting from federal to state Indian health programs, Goodman dramatically introduced the notion of Indians assuming more responsibility for health planning with non-Indians in their communities.[9]

The experience of Talihina Hospital located near the Arkansas border was typical. In the 1960s Talihina served the health needs of nearly eleven thousand Indians residing in sixteen counties of southeastern and south-central Oklahoma. From the Talihina Indian Hospital's establishment in 1914 as a tuberculosis hospital, the Choctaws and Chickasaws, the dominant tribes in the area, looked upon it as their source of health care. In 1938, with a decline in the need for tuberculosis beds, the hospital became a medical center with a tuberculosis unit. By 1963, with a continuing decline in the number of Indians needing those beds, tuberculosis patients were moved to a state-operated sanatorium. The hospital then functioned as a general medical center. Talihina Service Unit's constituency was large, but in 1963 the Talihina Indian Hospital was considered accessible to only 40 percent of the population in the service area.

Behavioral and social attitudes were beginning to change, however. In the Talihina Service Unit, for example, most Choctaws dressed like their non-Indian neighbors, indicating acceptance of the non-Indian material culture. They spoke English. Still, ideas strongly held by older residents in more isolated settlements in Indian country, including belief in spells, the evil eye, and hexing as causes for illness and hard luck, persisted. Staff at the Talihina Service Unit said in earlier years patients' relatives had actually taken them out of the hospital so that they could see a medicine man. Now the local pharmacist had replaced the herbalist. Nevertheless, reliable observers insisted that an Indian beneficiary would often try all sorts of patent and folk medicines rather than admit to a non-Indian that he or she was ill. While patients visited the Service Unit for visible ailments such as cuts, bruises, swelling, and infections, nondramatic illnesses such as gastroenteritis, colds, influenza, and pneumonia were tolerated at home unless they involved considerable pain and discomfort. Abuse, delays in treatment, and staff incompetency also prompted complaints and deterred Indians from seeking health care at Talihina.[10] Expanding contract services—white man's medicine—offered at Indian hospitals would not resolve, and most likely could only exacerbate, the challenging problems confronting the area medical officer in charge of the IHS's Division of Indian Health (DIH) in Oklahoma. In many ways, the problems and concerns of the Talihina Service Unit were reflected and reiterated in other Service Units.[11]

Other problems prevented effectiveness in Indian health care in Oklahoma as well. For example, health care was basically rationed because of the criteria that had to be met to qualify for it. Three criteria prioritized the applicants' needs. The first was medical need. The second was the applicant's Indian blood (someone with a higher degree of blood quantum gained priority over one with a lesser degree). A third criterion was economic status. Being eligible for veterans' benefits, having access to crippled children's facilities, having health insurance, and the like were also considered in the decision. While hospital employees would be provided with emergency care, they were expected to go elsewhere, even if they lived on hospital grounds, to meet their less significant medical needs. Also, Indian federal employees and their dependents were not considered eligible for medical services.[12]

Marriages of Indians to non-Indians complicated the delivery of health care. There were regulations to follow. The IHAD Area Office in Oklahoma City made decisions on eligibility based on regulations that were reviewed in the Division of Indian Health. The situations varied. If an Indian woman married a non-Indian, for example, her husband was expected to provide for her medical care. If he could not, and there were no other accessible facilities, then, if otherwise eligible, she might be cared for by the DIH. In the event an Indian woman divorced a non-Indian husband, she then became the head of her family and could receive medical services through the Indian health program. However, if she failed to provide the Public Health Service with proof of her divorce, or if she had money, she and her children would be denied care. In one instance a nurse at the clinic in Anadarko told one such woman "not to come crying on my shoulders if your kid gets sick, because we won't treat him."[13] Another instance involved a non-Indian woman who had received treatment for herself and her children while her Indian husband lived. According to regulations, after he died, she could receive care only if she was raising the children of the marriage. If the children were no longer at home, she was no longer eligible.[14]

By the 1960s concerns about the care received from the Indian Health Service prompted tribal leaders and others to demand melioration. Besides better coordination with the Bureau of Indian Affairs to resolve management problems, the Public Health Service needed to confer directly with Indians "instead of some 'white-collared' dude, that has a title of some description, installing rules and before putting them into effect," in the words of Lewis Zadoka of the Wichita Executive Committee. Indian leaders' correspondence and petitions to officials, including members of Oklahoma's congressional delegation, showed increasing demands for a greater voice in matters affecting their health.[15]

The staggering problems besetting Indian health were evident in a report on the Choctaw County Health Clinic in 1964. Open only twice a week, the clinic restricted the services offered to adults in order to concentrate "on child health, prenatal and other public health activities." No home care was offered. A depressed area, the county had a population of about 750 Indians and 3,000 African Americans. When work was available, wages ranged from fifty cents to a dollar an hour. There were five practicing doctors in a county that was on the decline. Contract physicians helped out at clinics in Choctaw and neighboring counties, but the problem of providing medical and sanitation services for Indians was unending. Thus, limitations of facilities, staff, and funds ensured that delivery had to be prioritized. For this reason, Indian patients were asked to complete an application so that physicians could determine who should be treated.[16]

Eligibility for service was also affected by an Oklahoma Area Office policy stating that "in order to be considered a beneficiary of the Division of Indian Health an individual of the Five Civilized Tribes must be one-half or more Indian blood, except minor children of one-fourth or more degree Indian blood who are being educated at government expense." A 1906 law provided that property allotted to members of the Five Tribes who were of one-half or more Indian blood would be held in trust by the federal government, which would then extend to them health care, among other community services. The 1955 transfer of responsibility from the Bureau of Indian Affairs to the Indian Health Service brought about health care delivery by the Division of Indian Health. The blood requirement continued as a major criterion identifying which members of the Five Tribes were to be considered legitimate candidates for federal health services.[17]

Until the 1960s Indians could do little more than express their concerns through petitions and resolutions. A first step toward amending the situation came in 1965, with the creation of the Community Health Representative (CHR) Program, which gave Indians a small voice in the programs of the Indian Health Service. The CHR was a tribal employee, funded by the IHS, who advised on the delivery of tribal health services. The program was a significant step in cracking dependency, subordination, and exploitation in the delivery of health care to Oklahoma Indians. At the same time, President Lyndon B. Johnson's War on Poverty called for the inclusion of Indians in its multiplicity of programs. Members of Oklahoma's congressional delegation, instead of seeking to assist Indians in resolving their individual and tribal concerns with the Indian Health Service, now sought to broaden the facilities and services available to them. In January 1966 a cornerstone was laid for a new Public Health Service Indian hospital northeast of Lawton. And in March, Representative Ed Edmondson urged the House Appropriations Interior Subcommittee to provide funds for programs vital to eastern Oklahoma Indians, including the replacement of the Claremore Indian Hospital, which had been built in 1928, with surgical facilities added in 1935.[18]

In a Senate speech, Fred Harris went further and insisted that "if the Indians are to succeed in their self-help efforts there must be changes of attitudes, and not just by the Indians." He cited statistics to show that many Oklahoma Indians were worse off than the average citizen by any standard of measurement. The basic problem, as Harris saw it, "was isolation of the Indians from the non-Indian community, partly self-imposed as a defensive mechanism and because of cumulative disappointments." Unless changes occurred on the part of all concerned, Harris insisted, "we will be treating symptoms and not causes."[19]

Further progress became evident in 1966 when the Indian Health Office in Oklahoma City agreed to pay 95 percent of billed charges for care of eligible Indians at Mission Hill Memorial Hospital in Shawnee. Hospital officials credited their congressman with the success of the proposal, which represented a significant, albeit small, step forward.[20]

Meanwhile, the problem of health care for urban Indians persisted, affecting an ever-larger number of Oklahoma Indians, particularly those of Oklahoma City and Oklahoma County. There the Division of Indian Health did not provide services to Indian residents because they presumably were eligible for the health and welfare resources available to all other citizens, such as the county Department of Public Welfare. In less populous counties, officials worried that Indians in their locales could impose burdensome costs upon the local United Fund agencies if they tried to provide help.[21]

For all other Oklahoma Indians, income became a criterion. According to Indian Health Services director Dr. Benjamin McBrayer, "The figures of $2,000 (take home pay) for a single person and $4,500 for a family unit shall be the level of income after which the applicant will be interviewed by the medical officer." The figures were the "minimum below which there is no question." For those qualified who needed hospitalization, if the Indian hospital was not equipped or staffed to provide the necessary measures, one of the Indian Health Service contract hospitals would be authorized to do so. McBrayer informed the Inter-tribal Health Council in December 1966 that the Indian really had a choice: "He can utilize our services if he falls within our priorities, he can go to the county and state which provide health services, or he can go on his own to a private practitioner." And in the latter instance, he could not expect the Indian Health Service to help defray the costs. In addition, McBrayer made it abundantly clear that "we have neither the funds nor the personnel to provide transportation to clinics." He recognized that most rural Indians who qualified for health care lived in remote places some distance from available facilities, but only in emergency situations could the Service Unit director authorize ambulance service. One mitigating factor was Medicare, recently made available to all Indians over age sixty-five. They would be provided hospital care if their ailments fell within the priorities of the Indian Health Service. McBrayer insisted that while his personnel operated under tremendous budgetary restrictions, they were doing their best to serve eligible patients.[22]

Indians' dissatisfaction with McBrayer's handling of his office became so intense that he was moved out of Oklahoma in 1967. Before he left, however, he arranged for a public health official in Alaska to succeed him. This led to a further outcry from Oklahoma Indian leaders, prompting DIH director Dr. Erwin S. Rabeau to reopen the search. Instead of selecting John Spaan, who worked in the Division of Indian Health out of the Oklahoma City Area Office and who was the candidate favored by tribal leaders and members of the Oklahoma delegation, Rabeau selected an Oklahoma native, Dr. Calvin Beames, as McBrayer's successor.[23]

In the mid-1960s Indian health was brought to the attention of the general public when Iola Taylor, executive director of Oklahomans for Indians Opportunity (OIO), sharply criticized health care before a group of federal officials. Calling some conditions inexcusable and others "terrible human tragedies," she cited the case of a Comanche woman who broke her leg and was taken to a hospital. She "lay suffering in the hallway until verification of her eligibility was obtained." As another example, Taylor mentioned that "a 14-year-old girl had her teeth pulled in an Indian Hospital on November 17 and still had been unable to secure dentures on February 16." The story appeared in an April 1967 edition of the *Oklahoman* under the bold headline "Indians' Medical Situation Criticized." In April and May 1967 the *Oklahoma Health Bulletin* informed its readers that Indians residing in the state followed the national trend of a greater death rate from infectious diseases than other races. The article also noted that the tuberculosis death rate in most years had been four to six times higher than in all other races, in spite of the successful effort of the Indian

Health Service in markedly lowering the incidence of the disease among their patients.[24]

Joining the fray, seasoned advocate Sula Goodman brought Representative Carl Albert up to date with a long, rambling account of the Indian Health Service. One perennial problem, thus far not resolved, was that of transportation to Indian health facilities: "It seems to be no organization's responsibility, and the Indian cannot solve it individually," she explained. She mentioned other objections as well: "No services for the Indian wife of a white man and his children; Chickasaws having to be half blood; and proof of indigency before care." But Goodman, as did one or two Indian leaders, felt that behind mounting concern over these and other issues was the premise that the "Indian Health setup" was moving ever closer to the goal "they visualize for the Nation as a whole, with the underlying purpose that of power over people." While Oklahoma Indians were calling for a greater voice in matters affecting their health, Goodman remarked about the tone of a talk the IHS director, Rabeau, had recently given to the staff of the Oklahoma City Indian Health Area Office. The only way Goodman could express his meaning was to put it in different words: "O.K. you sons-of-bitches you are to treat the Indian as if he were human. That's the PHS policy." To Goodman it was "characters" like Rabeau among the staff, in the field, and at the hospitals "that lets us all down." She believed that as long as the Public Health Service had men like Rabeau in charge, the majority of fine professionals in the service were in a sad way.[25]

Nevertheless, Indians continued, and even accelerated, their calls for improved health care. Aware that Indian Health Service officials in the Washington office had agreed to open some outpatient clinics in areas where the services could be carried to the people, Indian activists launched an effort to open a clinic in Oklahoma City. At the same time, Indians in northeastern Oklahoma's Ottawa County called attention to their acute medical needs, owing to the absence of physicians, clinics, and hospitals. Increasing numbers of Indians in Oklahoma City, in Tulsa, and even in remote rural areas were becoming keenly aware that they were not full participants in the benefits emanating from Lyndon Johnson's

Great Society, and their petitions and calls for federal funds became more persistent by the late 1960s. By the same token, DIH officials called for greater emphasis on getting Indian people to identify their own health needs and to suggest solutions. Indian leaders were ready and willing to assume more responsibility, to the extent that the DIH provided them opportunities.[26]

The Inter-Tribal Council of the Five Civilized Tribes were so encouraged by a visit of Rabeau and others from his office that they forwarded to him a series of resolutions, nineteen in all covering hospital admissions and medical care, copies of which were sent to the congressional delegation and others in Washington and Oklahoma. Indians from other tribes joined in calling attention to their needs, even criticizing tribal leaders for their lack of attention. In the case of the Pawnees, leaders called for a new hospital that would serve tribal members and other residents of the community.[27]

Meanwhile, Senator Harris was beginning to play a more direct role by familiarizing himself with immediate Indian concerns. In spring 1967 he visited eastern Oklahoma as part of a task force to evaluate poverty. He quickly became aware of the shortage of physicians and health care facilities in the region. In Cherokee County there were only four physicians for approximately twenty thousand persons. Muskogee County had a ratio of one per seven hundred. Harris also listened as Indians testified about being neglected at the Indian Health Service Hospital in Tahlequah. In addition, Carl Albert learned that the IHS planned to reduce its presence in Antlers and Pushmataha County.[28]

More positive was news that the DIH, as a result of meetings by Director Rabeau and other Public Health Service officials with Indian leaders, was beginning to relax policies relating to eligibility for health care. Most notable were the reduction of the blood quantum requirement for the Five Tribes from one-half to one-fourth, and the abandonment of the means test for establishing eligibility for treatment in Indian hospitals. But the Division of Indian Health in 1967 was not interested in integrating its services and fully cooperating with community hospitals throughout the state. Until Indians were granted equal rights with the elderly (medical), the indigent (welfare), the deprived young (Aid to Families with Dependent Children, AFDC), and the military, they would continue being second-class citizens.[29]

To be sure, not all Indians were unhappy about the health care offered them. Chickasaw tribal leaders, "fully aware of the great distance of travel from the Chickasaw Nation to the Indian Hospital at Talihina," were delighted in May 1967 when health clinics were established within the nation at Tishomingo and Coalgate. In January 1968 tribal leaders expressed their thanks to the Indian Health Service doctors and others responsible for this development. Other tribes were pleased as well. The area director in Oklahoma City asserted that the number of field clinics had been markedly increased since the onset of the 1968 fiscal year. In January 1968 there were twenty-eight clinics, not counting outpatient activities at the base facility or at the Indian Health centers.[30]

Central to the problems of Indian health, as already noted, was a lack of funds. Insufficient funding, however, did not prevent the Oklahoma City Community Relations Commission from calling on the Oklahoma delegation to assist in making possible an Indian health clinic in Oklahoma City. Such a facility, it claimed, was "greatly needed and eagerly anticipated by the 8,000 to 12,000 Indians throughout the metropolitan area of Oklahoma City." Besides offering better care, the clinic would eliminate the necessity and great inconvenience of traveling long distances to facilities outside the metropolitan area. Moreover, conversations were already under way to coordinate Indian health services in the metropolitan area with the Oklahoma County Medical Association and the Medical Center of the University of Oklahoma. There was now a distinct possibility that urban Indians could go from receiving virtually no medical care to getting the best medical attention offered to Indians in Oklahoma.[31]

Indians living outside urban areas now more openly sought to meliorate their lot. After calling for Representative Albert's support for a new Indian hospital, one woman explained to him, "I felt we ought to do something for ourselves [*sic*] all of us Indians." Her call was reiterated in resolutions calling on Congress for funds to allow the Public Health Service to fulfill its mission to provide comprehensive health service and to encourage and increase Indian participation in program planning. By the late 1960s, Lyndon Johnson's Great Society and its programs calling for recipient participation were becoming familiar to many Indian residents of the state.[32]

Oklahoma Indians were on the road to self-determination. The Community Health Representative Program was a prominent example of a "new and unique concept for augmenting the provision of health services to Indian people." Tribes would select members to work on health problems in their own communities. The Indian Health Service would contract with tribes for the services of Community Health Representatives and then provide them with suitable training, thereby helping to expand the participation of the Indian community in managing its health affairs. In Oklahoma, the Kiowa and the Cheyenne-Arapaho tribes were among the earliest recipients of grants to seek the services of a Community Health Representative.[33]

Change was occurring. By the end of the 1960s the Indian Health Service was beginning to shift from saying "this is good for you" to cutting "the pattern to fit the person." With this new approach, Calvin Beames, health service executive officer, said "the Indians are our Board of Directors. We are here to meet the needs of the people." As a result of these steps toward self-determination, Oklahoma Indians began utilizing health services at a rate that overwhelmed staff, facilities, and medical supplies. Now health officials had to contemplate the difficult task of turning away people who needed care. A brief chart in a 1969 status report dramatically illustrates the point (see table 1).[34] In addition to the need for personnel in all areas, preventive health programs could not achieve desirable levels.

Growth in number of patients served by Indian Health Service in Oklahoma, 1967–1969

	FY 1967	FY 1969	% INCREASE
Hospital admissions	8,400	12,000+	43
Outpatient visits	114,480	160,000+	40
Field clinic visits	59,747	125,000	109

Source: *Comparative Trends and Operation Problems, Oklahoma City Area, Spring 1969.*

The deterioration of physical facilities still remained an issue, but this increasingly became another target of reform. With the exception of the hospital in Lawton (built in 1967), every other Indian hospital was considered obsolete and in need of replacement. All had been constructed in the 1930s and had been designed to serve only a small fraction of the current clientele. Patients overflowed into corridors and lined the halls, standing for hours or waiting in cars on the hospital grounds. Every available space was being used to capacity. The Indian Health Service in the Oklahoma City area had exhausted its capacities for further extension of its services, and it was "actually overtaxed to even continue at the present utilization rates, according to a 1969 report."[35] The deplorable conditions led members of the Oklahoma delegation to call for further assistance. Representatives Ed Edmondson and John "Happy" Camp called for a special committee of the Indian Affairs Subcommittee to make a field inspection and share their observations. Such a report, they hoped, would encourage Congress to take constructive steps toward bringing Indian Health Services up to "modern standards." Thus a seed was planted to the effect that federal legislation would be required if Indian health care delivery was to be manifestly improved.[36]

More change came in 1969 when, for the first time in their history, all of the Indians under the Public Health Service agreed to cooperate for a common cause. They established a national advisory board to the Indian Health Service. Indians now could bring greater pressure on Congress to recognize and act on their health care needs. By the end of 1969 officials in Washington were, with increasing frequency, receiving petitions and letters from Oklahoma Indians calling for increased funding to improve their health care. Fred Harris responded by offering an amendment to an appropriation bill increasing funds for Indian Health Services by $2 million. The Senate promptly accepted it.[37]

At the same time, all eight Area Indian Health Advisory Boards petitioned the secretary of the Department of Health, Education and Welfare to allocate funds appropriated by the Congress "for immediate use by the Indian Health Service." Representatives of 178 tribes plus the Alaska Federation of Natives, signing for 53,000 natives, along with the Navajo areas of Arizona, New Mexico, and Utah, representing

120,000 Navajo people, signed the petition, assuring it national attention. In Oklahoma, the plight of urban Indians was exposed publicly when the Inter-Tribal Council of the Five Civilized Tribes asked Congress for $1.5 million in additional funds "to relieve the disgraceful health situation of urban Indians," who now comprised about 20 percent of the state's Indian population.[38]

Early in February 1970 almost a hundred members of Congress united in urging President Nixon to stop freezing funds that were urgently needed for Indian health care. The previous autumn Indian leaders had visited Washington to warn of deteriorating conditions; hospitals were curtailing services, refusing admissions, postponing medical care, and discontinuing immunization shots for children. Suitably swayed, Nixon released almost two-thirds of the needed health care money.[39] While Indian leaders appreciated the effort, the Oklahoma delegation still received letters about services received or denied. Even the Lawton Indian Hospital, the state's newest and most modern, was constantly plagued with shortages of staff and funds, prompting a long list of complaints.[40]

Also during the summer, on July 8, 1970, President Nixon sent a special Indian affairs message to Congress. The text prompted Congress to consider the plight of American Indians and changed the outlook in Indian country. In Oklahoma, among other matters, changes for improved health care accelerated. By calling for self-determination without termination, Nixon rejected paternalism and vowed to encourage new policies "to strengthen the Indian's sense of autonomy without threatening his sense of community." Among his recommendations to the Congress were to call for more money for Indian health and to help urban Indians. Tribal self-determination in health care now became an issue of increasing intensity.[41]

Thanks to the president's message, BIA area offices were to be converted from management to service agencies, thereby shifting greater power to tribal governments. Indian tribes began to organize to better effect change and take advantage of this dramatic policy shift.[42] Cultural issues nonetheless complicated the search for solutions. For example, the Sac and Fox Nation of Oklahoma, adding its voice to the outcry about Indian health, called for the rigorous enforcement of one-fourth degree

Indian blood quantum for services at Indian health facilities. Tribal leaders insisted that if the rule would be diligently enforced, despite opposition from those possessing less than that degree, many of the problems confronting health care delivery would be eased.[43]

The neglect of urban Indians, which bothered Harris and others, also concerned local authorities. The Tulsa City-County Health Department in 1966 created the Tulsa Indian Center. Its goal was to help Indians achieve a satisfactory adjustment to urban living by cooperating with all private and public agencies in the Tulsa Metropolitan Area and beyond. The center played a key role by helping Indians enter the system through serving as their spokesperson. By organizing transportation, the center helped overcome a major obstacle in getting patients to the Claremore hospital, to doctors' offices, and to clinics. Because health problems often were tied to employment and housing, these issues also came within the purview of the center.[44] The number of urban Indians in Oklahoma was growing, but it was increasing more slowly than the general urban population.[45]

Rural Indian health also drew considerable attention. Letters of complaint poured into congressional offices, telling horrific tales of people who refused to go to an Indian hospital because they had been there before and had suffered indignities of all kinds. The complaints were matched by IHS explanations that blamed the dearth of services on lack of funds and rationalized the ill treatment. As health care was the only thing many Oklahoma Indians needed from the government, clearly Washington needed to act, and quickly. Especially among Indian youth, patience was wearing thin. If nothing was done, soft-spoken and patient Oklahoma Indians, if not becoming militant, would join those already rejecting the IHS and reverting to traditional folk medicine or merely suffering in silence and even dying.[46]

Child health care, a topic that had never attracted much attention, now became the primary concern of the Inter-Tribal Health Committee representatives of the Lawton Indian Hospital. Health among Indian children, the representatives insisted, was "at least as bad or worse" than that of adults. Children aged twelve years and younger outnumbered their elders. The Lawton committee called for the reopening of the hospital's pediatric ward with an adequate nursing staff. While the eighty-bed facility served approximately fifteen thousand Indians in southwestern Oklahoma, there were only enough nurses to staff sixty beds. That inequity had provided the basic reason for closing the pediatric ward and, as the committee members noted, thereby risking the health of "the future generation of our Indian people."[47]

In early 1972 disgruntled health care providers decided to try to effect change on their own. Twenty Oklahoma Area Indian Health Service physicians met to expand the discussion about health care at the Lawton Indian Hospital. The doctors agreed that as most Indian people did not have a choice of facilities, they should be offered health care in a dignified and humane way. Substandard medical care was a direct result of shortage of physicians and nurses, the twenty physicians insisted, adding that unless this situation was meliorated, the consequences to the Indian patient would only worsen. The group then presented a litany of five appalling incidents at three facilities, including the Lawton Indian Hospital. They added a plea to the director of the Indian Health Service to remedy the deficiencies in medical personnel "in time to avoid a calamity in the medical services of the Oklahoma Area Indian Health Service."[48]

All of these rumblings stimulated the press to examine Indian health care more closely. A story in March 1972 in the *Daily Oklahoman* brought the need for more Indian health funds to a wider audience.[49] Horrible reports prompted yet another story to burst into the spotlight in spring 1972. In Anadarko, the local hospital refused treatment to an Indian youth with a deep cut in his forearm. No doctor came to the emergency room, and no one tended to his wound. A nurse told his parents to take him to the Lawton Indian Hospital, forty miles away. At that facility the youth was given emergency treatment, and a physician put sixteen stitches into his arm. The incident prompted a wide-scale debate. Many people called for improved procedures in the Anadarko hospital. There local doctors were called upon to decide whether an emergency existed, and local Indians cited a need for an Indian clinic. As a result, the hospital board agreed to study long-range plans to provide free medical treatment for area Indians. In addition, the Oklahoma Human Rights Commission, holding its May meeting in Anadarko, was influenced by complaints from Indians who alleged that the municipal hospital discriminated against them. Then the mayor of Anadarko announced that his constituents had expressed their overwhelming desire for a new hospital by approving a $2.2 million bond issue. As a matter of economic survival, he asserted, "hospital needs must be met with some type of assistance." The searchlight of public attention was focusing on Indian health care, and change was being effected.[50]

Changes came at a higher administrative level as well. Calvin Beames, appointed director of the Oklahoma Indian Health Area in January 1971, was the first person of Indian descent to serve in that position in the entire United States. Throughout the state, as service units and advisory boards became operational, Indians assumed larger roles in the selection of program priorities. By the end of 1972, seven of the nine service unit directors and many hospital administrative officers were of Indian descent, selected through Equal Employment Opportunity methods with Indian Advisory Board reviews. In addition, qualified Indian men and women were in special programs, being groomed to fill management posts throughout the Oklahoma Indian Health Area. Increasing Indian involvement was clear evidence that self-determination, despite appalling conditions at some health installations, was beginning to take hold.[51]

Despite a shortage of funds, on March 23, 1973, Oklahoma City followed Tulsa's example and established a volunteer health clinic. Very quickly, more than 850 patients sought service from the 20 doctors and 10 registered nurses, as well as the practical nurses, laboratory technicians, pharmacists, physician assistants, medical students, and receptionists who participated. Advancing from virtually no medical care, Indians in Oklahoma City now had access to a clinic far superior to that offered by any IHS clinic in the state, thanks to the volunteer staff. Church groups supported the clinic and the Native American Center associated with it. Of the more than twenty-five different tribal groups who patronized it, 45 percent had an income level of less than $1,000 a year. The Native American Center clinic provided only a small improvement to health care for the 12,000 Indians living in the city in 1973. Yet within a year, the Native American Center moved into larger, more adequate quarters. By February 1974 the clinic had already served about 2,000 patients.[52]

Even more impressive was an announcement in March that an IHS contract with the six-tribe North Central Oklahoma Inter-Tribal Health Council would allow the group to employ a full-time staff to direct its health program. It was the first program in the state that allowed Indians to direct, develop, and evaluate their health services.[53]

As events unfolded, tribes that had earlier been terminated now began to play a role in the health care delivery debate. The three already-terminated tribes in northeastern Oklahoma (the Ottawa, the Peoria, and the Modoc) and one that was about to be terminated (the Wyandotte), all of which were small tribes, petitioned through the Inter-Tribal Council of Northeast Oklahoma to have the federal government reinstate their tribal status. The object of their request was to position each tribe's members to receive the services of the Bureau of Indian Affairs and the Department of Indian Health. The tribes then would be able "to work toward self-determination at the speed they choose."[54]

The call for change in Oklahoma became more strident and stimulated more public interest as more evidence became available. A House subcommittee heard testimony about the situation in Claremore. If construction began in summer 1974, Indian Health director Emery Johnson told the congressmen, a new hospital could open there in late 1976—provided they approved the $8.4 million appropriation. Witnesses from Oklahoma testified at Senate hearings about the critical need for an intense effort to change the low health status of American Indians. Proponents of change continued to deluge the state's congressional delegation with letters and resolutions depicting deplorable health conditions and calling for increased funding to remedy them.[55]

Even more significantly, militants took to the streets. Tulsa's Indian residents held demonstrations, protesting being forced to seek health care at the Claremore Indian Hospital. They also objected to that facility's negligence in treating its patients. In 1968 the hospital had maintained a nursing staff of fifty, but by 1974 the staff had declined to forty-one, who struggled to cope with a work load that had probably tripled. No one in the Oklahoma City Area Office, which was in nominal charge of the Claremore unit, ever indicated any awareness of the problems. Investigators confirmed this by proving that there was no communication between the office in Oklahoma City and the local hospital officials. The Tulsa protestors also charged that improper sterilizations had been performed on Indians.

Following the demonstrations and the allegations released during that episode, an outside team, headed by a fellow of the American College of Obstetrics and Gynecology, reviewed the sterilization charge but could not validate it. Nevertheless, reports of the terrible conditions at Claremore and throughout Oklahoma Indian country now had people in an uproar. The staff of the Senate's Indian affairs subcommittee was convinced that American Indians had by far the worst health of all Americans. Chaired by Senator Henry Jackson, of Washington State, the subcommittee now began a thorough investigation.[56] Hearings formally commenced on September 16, 1974.[57]

Thanks to the recent publicity, Director John W. Davis of the Oklahoma Area Indian Health Service, now aware of the appalling conditions at Claremore, met with the hospital's general staff to consider the circumstances that had spawned so much unfavorable press. Davis's belated action could cover some of the dilemmas at the Claremore Indian Hospital, but the need for a new hospital could only be resolved in the nation's capital, where Senator Jackson's subcommittee on Indian affairs continued to seek the facts about Indian health care.[58]

Despite lengthy study and deliberation, Jackson's subcommittee failed to produce a bill that could pass muster, but Congress soon enacted a law that more than any other single action reversed the nation's ignominious history with regard to Indian people. The 1975 Indian Self-Determination and Education Assistance Act gave tribes the option of administering programs currently under the purview of the Bureau of Indian Affairs. As self-determination took root, the bureau's role would become one of facilitating and providing assistance. The government now pledged itself officially to working "more closely and effectively with the tribes for all the Indian people by assisting them in meeting goals they themselves have set."[59]

The lot of urban Indians improved as clinics in Tulsa and Oklahoma City, relying largely on donations and volunteers, provided first aid, referral, diagnoses, and lab work. The situation at Claremore continued to be investigated. A special committee, for example, found no evidence of illegal or harmful medical practices. To direct attention away from conditions at the hospital, area director John Davis extolled the fact that on March 1, 1975, ground would be broken for the new Claremore Comprehensive Indian Health Facility, adding that a bevy of prominent individuals, including numerous tribe leaders, would be on hand to celebrate the event.[60]

Tribes became more assertive in presenting their concerns. The Osage Tribal Council, rather than petitioning the IHS or the Oklahoma delegation, wrote their own proposal for a new health clinic and submitted it directly to Robert C. Byrd, chair of the Senate Subcommittee on Interior Affairs. The North Central Inter-Tribal Health Council also appealed directly to Byrd and called for a new Indian hospital. The state's congressional delegation continued to get mail complaining that hospitals and clinics "don't help us a bit" and that most Indians could not afford "the gas expense to go." Oklahoma tribes and individuals were now seeking greater responsibility and increasing involvement in their health programs.[61]

The Area Office in Oklahoma City, which in 1970 served 112,977 Indians in thirty-six tribes, now sought to involve the existing tribal health committees and the more directly elected tribal leaders. In 1969 the Area Indian Health Advisory Board had been organized as a mechanism for seeking input from Indian people. By 1975 all thirty-six tribes had a member on that board, and each service unit had its own board. In addition, eight tribes and four intertribal groups had community health representatives who sought federal funds for family planning and a variety of development projects, and training in various aspects of health care management was offered to tribes that requested it. Tangible evidence of the mutual efforts of Indian community development and management concepts was best reflected by the experience of the Northeastern Inter-Tribal Council, which received funds from the IHS to establish a health management office.[62]

In 1975, while tribes were discussing the technicalities of implementing self-determination, Congress again considered a health care measure. S.B. 522 would have sufficient options to permit maximum tribal involvement to unfold within a policy of self-determination. An exemplary circumstance was cited in Senate committee hearings: in Oklahoma a number of communities were building health facilities using tribal construction workers with expertise. The completed buildings were leased to the Indian Health Service for delivery of health services. Leasing included a full complement of costs for drug inventories, equipment, supplies, and personnel salaries and benefits.[63]

S.B. 522—virtually identical to S.B. 2938, which had been presented in the previous (Ninety-third) Congress—was introduced on February 3, 1975. A report issued by the Committee on Interior and Insular Affairs made abundantly clear that the vast majority of Indians still lived in an environment characterized by understaffed and inadequate health facilities, improper or nonexistent water supply and waste disposal systems, and continuing dangers of disabling or deadly diseases.[64]

The House and Senate versions coalesced in the Indian Health Care Improvement Act. It fully launched Oklahoma Indians on the road to self-determination with regard to their health care. Increased funding would expand health services, build and renovate medical facilities, and facilitate construction of drinking water and sanitary disposal systems.[65] The law also called for programs designed to increase the number of Indian health professionals and most notably to improve health care for the approximately 500,000 Indians living in urban areas across the country. More and more, the overall program would be planned and carried out in cooperation with organizations, Indians, and others interested in improving the health of all Indian peoples.

While complaints about service did not disappear, new clinics were opened, and urban Indians in both of the state's major cities actively pressed for increased funding to allow the free clinics associated with their Native American Centers to expand their services. And in Washington, Senator Bartlett and other members of the subcommittee that had helped prepare the Health Care Act now sought an amendment that would allow the Indian Health Service to utilize funds from the private sector to assist in recruiting physicians and other key personnel.[66]

While the Indian Health Care Act allowed Indians to assume responsibility for programs administered by the IHS, funding shortages imposed limitations on Oklahoma tribes seeking to manage their health programs. The Creek tribe, however, did take advantage of the opportunity for self-determination. It proposed a community hospital that would be operated by the Creek Nation to serve Indian and non-Indian residents. In another example, in 1977 the Absentee Shawnee Tribe initiated construction of a new medical-dental health center. Poor, uneducated, and unhealthy as most Oklahoma Indians were, they were nevertheless exercising more control over health matters. While complaints about health care still predominated, the counter theme of self-determination was emerging as well. The lack of funding and underfunding continued to impede or stall the implementation of plans and programs throughout Oklahoma.[67] While change came slowly, tribes obviously knew that they would need "to take independent action to get anything done."[68]

As Indians in Oklahoma assumed responsibility for or exercised oversight in health services, tribal and regional debates and inconsistencies emerged. The problem of blood quantum among the Five Tribes, which comprised nearly two-thirds of the entire Indian population in Oklahoma offers an example. The Five Tribes were the only ones to have a self-imposed blood quantum, but the hospitals on the east side of the state at Claremore and Tahlequah were used by other tribes that counted members with less than one-quarter degree of Indian blood. Then, when the Five Tribes virtually eliminated the quantum requirement, the situation at the east side facilities became acute.

Other factors also led to disparities between eastern and western Oklahoma Indians. On November 19, 1977, the Absentee Shawnee Tribe of Oklahoma celebrated the grand opening of its newly constructed Shawnee Indian Health Center. Owned by the tribe, the facility would be leased and operated by the IHS and was expected to serve approximately 20,000 Indians within a large radius of Shawnee. Nearby, the Kickapoo Home Start Project had begun to operate by September 1. The program provided help for mentally handicapped Kickapoo children. Tensions arose when the Western Indian Health Advisory Board complained that the IHS favored Indians in forty-one eastern Oklahoma counties over those in western counties. The Eastern Oklahoma Indian Health Advisory Board in turn insisted, because the National Indian Health Advisory

Board seated only one delegate from Oklahoma, that it be represented on the national board every other year.[69]

By the late 1970s solutions to ongoing problems were being implemented in various ways as health care facilities and service continued to expand and improve. The University of Oklahoma Health Sciences Center established an American Indian Graduate Program in Health Education as part of the School of Public Health. In the Anadarko Service Area, a new health center was planned to be constructed and operated by the IHS. The facility would provide about 6,300 people with a full range of medical, dental, optometric, ambulatory, and community health services. The health center would replace the existing facility serviced by a physician who was based at the Lawton Indian Hospital and who drove to Anadarko to hold office hours at the clinic. Tribal leaders testified in support of this proposal and for another clinic at Concho in western Oklahoma. These proposals were designed to address the imbalance between facilities available to Indians in eastern and western Oklahoma. While the perceived disproportion was not markedly corrected, at the end of 1978 the IHS maintained six Indian hospitals in Oklahoma and was constructing one at Ada on land obtained by the Chickasaw Nation.[70]

Self-determination was taking firm hold. By 1980 the tribes employed more than three hundred community outreach workers and fifty health administrators. Community Health Representatives, as previously noted, were tribal members employed by their respective groups to prompt community action in the launching of a broad range of health activities. The representatives also served as liaisons between their communities and health care providers, constructing a bridge between the community and non-Indian staff. In addition to the Indian hospitals, by 1980 there were thirteen health centers, most of which were new facilities owned by local tribes but leased to the IHS. More limited services were available at nine smaller health clinics that operated on a regular weekly schedule.

A singular piece of evidence of the tribes' assertion of self-determination came early in 1980. The principal officers of the Five Tribes called for the removal of area director John Davis because he had "continued to demonstrate his lack of concern and indecisiveness toward any health problems." Davis was charged with showing "no leadership in the area of Indian self-determination" and with being evasive in his dealings with tribal leaders. The tribes' officials insisted they had a right to play a role in planning health services for their people and "to expect cooperation in working out any problems that arise." The request for removal was sent to Dr. Emery Johnson, the director of the Indian Health Service, in Rockville, Maryland.[71]

An evaluation of Indian self-determination was undertaken by the National Indian Health Board and the American Indian Technical Services in 1984. Their report, titled "Evaluation Report: The Indian Health Services Implementation of the Indian Self-Determination Process," reviewed the situation in the Oklahoma City Area. The study indicated that 638 contracts were used by the tribes to provide limited services such as community health programs.

More important, the report detailed the reasons that some tribes did not contract extensively for the takeover of IHS facilities. First to be noted was the fact that many existing facilities were multitribal service units and that the organizational requirements for putting together the necessary community and tribal support was proving difficult to develop. Second, while there was evidence of tribal satisfaction with prevailing facilities, some tribes ranked securing health care below their economic development priorities. Finally, a number of smaller Oklahoma tribes had concluded that they could not bear the additional burden and responsibilities involved in assuming a major Indian Health Service operation. The report helped mitigate some of the criticism of the Area Office and its director, John Davis, by noting that personnel "readily provided information" and that there was "little tribal interest in contracting other than for the renewal of existing programs." Several tribes, however, called for major assumptions of IHS functions: "the operation of hospitals and clinics or the provision of major health care." The 1984 report articulated the realization that self-determination was an unfolding process. The study made clear, however, that within the space of a little more than two decades Indian health care in Oklahoma had moved from termination to self-determination. Much had been accomplished; much remained to be done before Indian health approached equality with the prevailing status of general health care in Oklahoma. Self-determination gave Oklahoma Indians an increasingly significant voice in promoting and taking responsibility for their own health care.[72]

Notes

1. Indian Health Care Improvement Act, Hearings before the House Subcommittee on Indian Affairs, May 23, 1975, 94th Cong., 1st sess., passim.

2. While data on Indian health are readily available, the source of this information is an April 21, 1977, statement by a Kiowa delegation testifying in the Senate before the American Indian Policy Review Commission, copy in Folder 11, Box 32, Dewey Bartlett Collection, Congressional Archives, Carl Albert Center, University of Oklahoma, Norman [Carl Albert Center is hereafter cited as CAC]. For a more official statement, see *Overview of the Indian Health Service Program: Indian Health Trends and Services* (Washington, D.C.: U.S. Department of Health, Education, and Welfare, Public Health Service, 1978).

3. A Review of the Indian Health Program, Hearing before the House Subcommittee on Indian Affairs, May 23, 1963, 88th Cong., 1st sess., passim.

4. Fred Harris to Dr. Erwin S. Rabeau, August 1, 1966, Folder 10, Box 74, Fred Harris Collection, Congressional Archives, CAC. Beginning salary for physicians in the Indian Health Service was from $6,400 to $7,600 a year. See story by Howard Rusk in *New York Times*, March 15, 1954. For an explanation of the goal and philosophy of the Oklahoma City Area Indian Health Service, the largest of the eleven Indian Health Service Areas in the nation, see the statement by Calvin G. Beames, Director, in Folder 10, Box 74, Harris Collection. In 1971 there were twenty branch chiefs serving under an assistant director or an executive officer. See Folder 16, General Box 52, Tom Steed Collection, Congressional Archives, CAC.

5. "What's Happening with the Indians," *Health Services and Mental Health Administration* 4 (September–October 1969): 30.

6. *Daily Oklahoman* (Oklahoma City), May 30 and June 30, 1954. U.S. Representative Ed Edmondson attacked the bill as leading to "a great government bureau for a socialized medicine program in this country." N. B. Johnson, vice chief justice of the Oklahoma Supreme Court and president of the Inter-Tribal Council of the Five Civilized Tribes, which had been formed in 1950 to promote Indian rights, likewise added his voice in opposition. He asserted that "the class of Indians for whom the Indian hospitals are most needed are the backward and retarded groups residing in remote areas and who do not understand the ways of the communities about them."

7. *Daily Oklahoman*, December 16, 1955; *Plan for Medical Facilities Needed for Indian Health Services* (Washington, D.C.: U.S. Department of Health, Education, and Welfare, 1958), 83–86.

8. Petitions abound in the papers of all members of the Oklahoma delegation. Some will be specifically cited in the course of this article.

9. Carl Albert to To Whom It May Concern, February 2, 1967, copy in Folder 8, Box 93, Mike Monroney Collection, Congressional Archives, CAC. For a discussion of the Shawnee Tuberculosis Sanatorium, see Johnnie Naneato to Floyd Maytubby, January 19, 1960, copy in Folder 13, Departmental Box 13, Robert S. Kerr Collection, Congressional Archives, CAC. See also *Daily Oklahoman*, May 11 and 13, 1961, and December 10, 1961, and Rex Whistler to Kerr, August 21, 1962, Folder 9, Box 14, Kerr Collection.

10. Patient complaints abounded. See for example Benjamin L. Henry to Kerr, January 21, 1961, Folder 37, Departmental Box 13, Kerr Collection, and Harry Belvin to Hubert Hudgens, June 23, 1939, Folder 5, Departmental Box 33, Albert Collection. For the Talihina situation, see Mary C. Hammack to Tom Steed, December 5, 1943, and Jamie M. Thompson to Steed, December 5, 1963, Folder 2, Box 24, Steed Collection.

11. This lengthy discussion is based on a penetrating report titled "Application of Construction Criteria to Talihina Indian Hospital" [n.d., ca. 1963], 1–12, Folder 11, Departmental Box 52, Carl Albert Collection, Congressional Archives, CAC. Indigent whites in the area served by the Talihina hospital were unable to utilize its services. Their health care was considered substandard and often nonexistent. For their plight see Morton Glasser to Albert, January 19, 1964, Folder 37, Departmental Box 47, Albert Collection. Glasser was a physician stationed at Talihina. For the removal of tuberculosis patients from Talihina to state hospitals, see Benjamin McBrayer to Monroney, June 5, 1963, Folder 22, Box 32, Monroney Collection. For an example of Indian loyalties to their regional hospital despite its recognized deficiencies, see Col. M. A. Hagerstrand to Anthony Celebreeze, January 11, 1963, Folder 22, Box 32, Monroney Collection. Hagerstrand was calling for an expansion of the Tahlequah Indian Hospital, which was vital to the Indian community in northwestern Oklahoma.

12. Herbert A. Hudgins to Kerr, August 15, 1961, Folder 24, Departmental Box 13, Kerr Collection. See also James R. Shaw to Rev. E. Russell Carter, December 20, 1961, Folder 6, Departmental Box 44, Albert Collection. Hudgins was the medical officer for the Oklahoma Indian Health Area Office. Shaw was the chief of the Division of Indian Health in the Department of Health, Education and Welfare.

13. McBrayer to Monroney, October 18, 1963, Folder 22, Box 32, and McBrayer to Monroney, November 19, 1963, Folder 21, Box 32, Monroney Collection. See also Dolores Murray to Harris, January 23, 1967, and Rabeau to Harris, April 7, 1967, Folder 10, Box 24, Harris Collection; Shaw to Carter, December 20, 1961, Folder 6, Departmental Box 44, Albert Collection.

14. Carruth Wagner to Monroney, June 20, 1963, and Monroney to Mrs. Bennie Jones, June 21, 1963, Folder 16, Box 32, Monroney Collection.

15. Lewis Zadoka to Monroney, February 11, 1964, Folder 14, Box 44, Monroney Collection. Zadoka was chair of the Wichita Executive Committee. Indians had a slight voice in the planning for a new eighty-bed Indian hospital in Lawton. *Daily Oklahoman*, March 11, 1964. See also Indian Health Area Director, press release, April 1, 1964, for a meeting with chiefs of the Five Tribes to review Indian health plans, copy in Folder 12, Box 44, Monroney Collection, and McBrayer to B. Frank Belvin, April 6, 1964, copy in Folder 11, Box 44, Monroney Collection. Belvin was president of the Inter-Tribal Council of the Five Tribes; McBrayer was the Indian Health Area director. For a further report on a special meeting of the Inter-Tribal Council, see Belvin to Monroney, July 8, 1965, Folder 15, Box 54, Monroney Collection.

16. McBrayer to Albert, April 7, 1964, Folder 55, Departmental Box 47, Albert Collection; McBrayer to Walter Kuchee, April 14, 1964, Folder 12, Box 44, Monroney Collection. Relations with private hospitals when Indians were admitted in emergencies often resulted in payment disputes between the Indian Health Service and the hospital. For an example see McBrayer to Steed, February 17, 1965, Folder 23, Box 29, Steed Collection. See also Chickasaw Nation of Oklahoma: Resolution: August 21, 1965, Folder 34, Box 12, Harris Collection. The resolution called attention to the acute needs of Chickasaws for improved clinical and hospital service. The lack of funds was the essence of every complaint the Division of Indian Health received. See, for example, Wagner to Harris, October 12, 1965, Folder 34, Box 12, Harris Collection.

17. E. S. Rabeau to Harris, May 6, 1966, and V. F. Melot to Harris, June 29, 1966, Folder 5, Box 42, Harris Collection. Melot said a clerk decided that his grandson was not eligible even though he had previously received medical care.

18. *Daily Oklahoman*, January 8, 1966; press release from the office of Congressman Ed Edmondson, March 8, 1966, copy in Folder 19, Box 69, Monroney Collection. See also Mike Mansfield to Carl Hayden, April 15, 1966, copy in Folder 16, Box 69, Monroney Collection. Mansfield was informing the chair of the Interior Appropriations Subcommittee of funds to meet "gross sanitation deficiencies" throughout Indian country. By the end of 1966 plans for replacing or updating other Indian hospitals were already underway. See Rabeau to Harris, November 1, 1966, Folder 5, Box 42, Harris Collection, and "Talihina Hospital: Construction Funds for Alterations," [n.d., ca. 1966], copy in Folder 15, Departmental Box 63, Albert Collection.

19. See story in *Oklahoma City Times*, April 27, 1966. LaDonna Harris, Comanche wife of Senator Fred Harris, was an activist for improved Indian health care in her own right. President Lyndon Johnson appointed her to the National Indian Opportunities Counsel, and she worked closely with Michael Mahsetky, who served as staff attorney for the Senate Committee on Indian Affairs and later on the board of directors of the American Indian Health Care Association. Together

they lobbied for numerous health care bills. See her autobiography, *LaDonna Harris: A Comanche Life*, Bison Books, 2006.

20. Fred Hinchee to Steed, August 26, 1966, Folder 8, Box 33, Steed Collection. Another small but significant change, one assisted by Harris's staff, was the transfer of a Northern Cheyenne woman, Bessie Elk Shoulder, who neither spoke nor understood English, from the Public Health Service Sioux Tuberculosis Sanatorium to one in Clinton, Oklahoma, a state-administered facility. Due to its proximity to the Southern Cheyenne Nation, she could speak and be understood. By 1966, as previously noted, the state provided all tuberculosis care. Memorandum, September 16, 1966, re: Bessie Elk Shoulder, Folder 5, Box 42, Harris Collection.

21. Rabeau to Harris, October 10, 1966, Folder 9, Box 74, and Charles Duffy to Harris, October 24, 1966, Folder 10, Box 74, Harris Collection. For an overview of the problems and concerns of Oklahoma Indians see the Report of the Indian Leaders' Conference held in Oklahoma City, October 31 to November 2, 1966, copy in Folder 3, Box 37, Steed Collection.

22. Dr. Benjamin McBrayer, Indian Health Area Director, presentation to Intertribal Health Council, December 12, 1966, copy in Folder 10, Box 74, Harris Collection. For a general overall statement, see McBrayer's form letter, April 20, 1962, copy in Folder 11, Departmental Box 63, Albert Collection.

23. The controversy can be followed in Steed to Rabeau, February 24, 1967, copy in Folder 13, Departmental Box 63, Albert Collection; F. L. Lewis to Albert, February 28, 1967, Albert to Harry J. W. Belvin, March 2, 1967, and V. H. Bointy to Albert, March 3, 1967, Folder 14, Departmental Box 63, Albert Collection; Resolution of Intertribal Council of the Five Civilized Tribes of Oklahoma, March 2, 1967, copy in Folder 4, Box 37, Steed Collection. The lengthy resolution details their health concerns. See Rabeau to Page Belcher, March 22, 1967, Folder 66, Box 115, Page H. Belcher Collection, Congressional Archives, CAC, in which Rabeau announces his selection of Calvin Beames as the area executive officer of the Public Health Service Indian Health Area Office, Oklahoma City.

24. *Daily Oklahoman*, April 1, 1967; *Oklahoma Health Bulletin* (April–May 1967): 1.

25. Sula Goodman to Albert, April 24, 1967, Folder 12, Departmental Box 63, Albert Collection.

26. Ben Choate to Monroney, April 28, 1967, Folder 5, Box 83, Monroney Collection; Lee Motah to Monroney, Folder 4, Box 83, Monroney Collection; Resolution: Robert Whitebird, et al., [n.d., ca. July 1967], Tray 47, Departmental Box 63, Albert Collection; Robert Drew to Mrs. Fred R. Harris, June 19, 1967, and Stanton Young to Mrs. Harris, June 23, 1967, Folder 10, Box 74, Harris Collection. Young, a prominent civic leader in Oklahoma City, thought Indians living in the city would best be served at the University Medical Center. He chaired the

Health Hospital Planning Committee and believed an Indian health clinic could be coordinated with the range of facilities available in Oklahoma City. See also Paul Attocknie to Harris, September 19, 1967, Folder 9, Box 74, Harris Collection. Indian Health officials were now proclaiming, "The Federal Indian Health program is your program, and will be carried out in accordance with your wishes and your requirements." Speech by H. V. Chadwick before a Creek Meeting in Holdenville, October 8, 1967, copy in Folder 12, Departmental Box 63, Albert Collection. See also *Norman* (Okla.) *Transcript*, August 16, 1968. The *Transcript* reported the story of Indians telling Mrs. Harris of Indian hospitals refusing to admit them.

27. Overton James to Rabeau, June 30, 1967, copy in Folder 4, Box 37, Steed Collection; Thelma Morton to Harris, [n.d.], Folder 9, Box 74, Harris Collection; Monroney to Rex Privett, July 7, 1967, and Mrs. David C. Pruet to Monroney, May 8, 1967, Folder 8, Box 83, Monroney Collection. On another matter on behalf of the Inter-Tribal Council of the Five Tribes, James wrote directly to the president. See James to Dear Mr. President, July 29, 1967, Folder 7, Box 83, Monroney Collection.

28. Amos Maxwell to Harris, September 22, 1967, Folder 9, Box 74, Harris Collection; Memo, CLW [Charles L. Ward] to Albert, October 20, 1967, Folder 4, Departmental Box 63, Albert Collection. See also Rabeau to Harris, November 28, 1967, Folder 9, Box 74, Harris Collection, for an explanation of other changes in health services offered in southeastern Oklahoma. A further indication of inadequate health care is the fact that funds were unavailable to provide dental work for adults that was not an emergency. See Orvil Wilson to Belcher, November 27, 1962, Folder 66, Box 115, Belcher Collection.

29. Rabeau to Harris, November 17, 1967, and Robert Allison to Mary McCormick (copy), November 20, 1967, Folder 9, Box 74, Harris Collection.

30. Resolution, January 19, 1968, copy in Folder 12, Box 167, Belcher Collection; Memo from Indian Health Area Director, Oklahoma City Area Office, to Director, Division of Indian Health, PHS, Silver Spring, Maryland, January 25, 1968, Folder 66, Box 115, Belcher Collection. Even the National Congress of American Indians saw fit to commend the Division of Indian Health for seeking to involve Indians in planning and carrying out their program. See Resolution, May 18, 1968, copy in Folder 9, Box 93, Monroney Collection.

31. L. J. Bernard to Belcher, July 23, 1968, Folder 66, Box 115, Belcher Collection; Bernard to Steed, July 23, 1968, Folder 1, Box 41, Steed Collection.

32. Pauline George to Albert, August 28, 1968, Folder 62a, Departmental Box 75, Albert Collection; Resolution, Inter-Tribal Council of the Five Tribes, September 11, 1968, Folder 17, Box 162, Belcher Collection; W. W. Keeler to Belcher, October 16, 1968, Folder 66, Box 115, Belcher Collection. Keeler, principal chief of the Cherokee Nation, called for further funds to improve services at the Indian Hospital at Tahlequah. That Congress was responding to these petitions

is evident in Monroney to Overton James, October 17, 1968, Folder 8, Box 93, Monroney Collection. James was president of the Inter-Tribal Council of the Five Tribes. See also a story entitled "Hospital Conditions at W. W. Hastings are Overcrowded" from "The Official Publication of the Cherokee," February 1969, and a Chickasaw Resolution delineating "Unmet Health Needs at Tishomingo Service Unit," February 15, 1969, copies in Folder 13, Box 139, Belcher Collection.

33. Rabeau to John R. "Happy" Camp, February 14, 1969, Folder 33, Box 2, John R. "Happy" Camp Collection, Congressional Archives, CAC; Rabeau to Albert, February 11, 1969, Folder 62b, Departmental Box 75, Albert Collection.

34. An article in the *Daily Oklahoman*, May 25, 1969, discusses Indian health care improvements. See also "Program Status: Comparative Trends and Operational Problems, Oklahoma City Area, Spring, 1969," copy in Folder 62, Departmental Box 75, Albert Collection.

35. "Program Status: Comparative Trends and Operational Problems, Oklahoma City Area, Spring 1969." See also Harry Belvin to Emory Johnson, November 4, 1969, Folder 17, Box 167, Belcher Collection, wherein the Five Tribes ask that the Indian hospitals in their area be rebuilt or modernized.

36. Ed Edmondson and "Happy" Camp to James A. Haley, September 5, 1969, Folder 3, Box 67, Camp Collection. Haley was chair of the Subcommittee on Indian Affairs. See also a story in the *Tulsa* (Okla.) *Daily World*, August 22, 1969, titled "Indian Health Services Said Seriously Curtailed by HEW." For the situation in the Pawnee Service Unit where clinic hours were being curtailed and services cut back, see "To Indian People of The Pawnee Service Unit," May 26, 1969, copy in Folder 34, Box 2, Camp Collection. For the effort of the Cheyenne and Arapaho Tribes not to lose the services of a valued doctor, see John Washee, Jr., to Jack C. Robertson, August 8, 1969, copy in Folder 13, Box 139, Belcher Collection. In the *Daily Oklahoman*, September 5, 1969, is a story entitled "Indian Health Probe" discussing the efforts of the Oklahoma delegation to meliorate the deplorable health care situation in the state. A story on October 12, 1969, titled "Indian Health Units Reported Needing of Drugs" and an undated clipping from a *Tulsa World* story by Alex Gowan, titled "Indians Air Dilemma in Washington," copies are also found in Tray 7, Box 45, Steed Collection. See also Ed Edmondson, "Report on Oklahoma Indian Hospitals," *Indian Affairs* 76 (October–December 1969).

37. *Sunday Oklahoman*, November 9, 1969; Alma Chapman to Camp, October 28, 1969, Folder 34, Box 2, Camp Collection. Chapman was the Community Health Representative of the Pawnee Tribe; the *Oklahoman* of November 21, 1969, ran a story titled "Indian Health Effort Hailed," relating the efforts of Representatives Edmondson and "Happy" Camp for calling attention to Indian health problems in Oklahoma. See also a statement by Arthur Thomas to Honorable Members of Congress, [n.d.], that discusses additional resources needed for the Indian Health Program, copy in Folder 28a, Box 132, Belcher Collection. See also

Congressional Record, 91 Cong., 1st sess., December 18, 1969, 39975–76 and *Daily Oklahoman*, December 19, 1969. See also To Dear Mr. President, January 23, 1970, copy in Folder 13, Box 139, Belcher Collection, and *Tulsa World*, January 23, 1970.

38. Resolution of the Eight Area Indian Health Advisory Boards to the U.S. Indian Health Service, January 30, 1970, copy in Folder 13, Box 139, Belcher Collection; Resolution of the Inter-Tribal Council of the Five Tribes of Oklahoma, February 6, 1970, copy in Tray 3, Box 67, Camp Collection.

39. Memo from the Office of Congressman Tom Steed, re: Partial Victory Gained in Fight for Indian Health Funds, February 6, 1970, Folder 3, Box 49, Steed Collection; Emery Johnson to Harris, April 7, 1970, Roy and Rosella Ussrey to Harris, May 4, 1970, and Mark Weiss to Harris, May 11, 1970, Folder 6, Box 197, Harris Collection. Weiss was the chief medical officer at the Claremore Indian Hospital.

40. Mrs. Sherman Wilde to Dear Sir, July 14, 1970, Folder 13, Box 139, Belcher Collection; Resolution, Inter-Tribal Council of the Five Tribes, July 10, 1970, copy in Folder 3, Box 49, Steed Collection; staff memorandum attached to Camp to Neal McCaleb, August 3, 1970, Folder 3, Box 67, Camp Collection; Daisy Romano to Louis Bruce, August 13, 1970, copy in Folder 6, Box 197, Harris Collection. Bruce was commissioner of Indian affairs. See also Inter-Tribal Health Committee of the Lawton Indian Hospital to Harris, September 24, 1970, Folder 21, Box 235, Harris Collection.

41. *Public Papers of the President of the United States: Richard Nixon, 1970* (Washington, D.C.: GPO, 1971): 564–76. See also Thomas Clarkin, *Federal Indian Policy in the Kennedy and Johnson Administrations* (Albuquerque: University of New Mexico Press, 2001).

42. Resolution of the Northern Oklahoma Intertribal Health Committee, September 14, 1970, Folder 3, Box 49, Steed Collection; To Whom It May Concern: Letter to personnel at an October 5, 1970, meeting held at Lawton USPHS Hospital, Folder 21, Box 235, Harris Collection; Resolution, Advisory Board, Claremore Service Unit, October 19, 1970, Folder 22, Box 235, Harris Collection; *Daily Oklahoman,* November 12, 1970; press release, Public Health Service, Indian Health Service, November 12, 1970, copy in Folder 8, Box 8, Camp Collection.

43. Elmer Manatowa, Jr., to Dr. Emery Johnson, April 9, 1971, copy in Folder 6, Box 168, Belcher Collection; Matilda M. Harjo to Harris, April 23, 1971, Folder 20, Box 235, Harris Collection.

44. "Tulsa City County Health Department," [n.d.], 22, Folder 6, Box 178, Belcher Collection; Lee L. Chupco to Phil C. Howell, June 5, 1969, in Tulsa Area Health and Hospital Planning Council, "Metropolitan Indian Health Case Study (June 1971)," 52, copy in Folder 6, Box 178, Belcher Collection. Chupco was president of the Tulsa Indian Center. Howell was president of the Health and Hospital Planning Council.

45. In 1960 Indians residing in the Tulsa Standard Metropolitan Statistical Area comprised 12 percent of the state's Indian population. Approximately 1.4 percent of the nation's total Indian population resided in Creek, Osage, and Tulsa Counties (however, Oklahoma County had the largest Indian population in the state). In 1960, 62.9 percent of all Oklahomans lived in urban areas, and 63 percent of Indians lived in rural areas. In fiscal 1970 the state counted 65,600 Indian residents; of the estimated 7,900 living in Creek, Osage, and Tulsa Counties, more than 40 percent lived within the city of Tulsa. "Metropolitan Indian Health Case Study," 3–4; Schlezinger to Howell, June 24, 1971, Folder 6, Box 178, Belcher Collection.

46. Patsy Thomas to Harris, July 23, 1971, Folder 22, Box 235, Harris Collection. I relied heavily on this letter for the thoughts suggested in this paragraph. See also Bertha Katcher to Harris, May 7, 1971, and Emery Johnson to Harris, July 28, 1971, Folder 21, Box 235, Harris Collection, for an example of the director of the Indian Health Service explaining why the Tahlequah Indian Hospital refused to admit a seriously ill Indian who died within hours after being refused admission. For instances of patients dying because of callous treatment or lack of attention at an Indian hospital, see Sallie Davis to Harris, August 27, 1971, Folder 20, Box 235, Harris Collection, and Calvin Beames to Steed, September 30, 1971, Folder 17, Box 52, Steed Collection.

47. The Inter-Tribal Health Committee of the Lawton Indian Hospital to Camp, January 6, 1972, Folder 17, Box 19, Camp Collection. For further complaints about the Lawton Indian Hospital see Harriet Moore to Steed, January 7, 1972, Folder 19, Box 58, Steed Collection.

48. Louis Fazen III to Emery Johnson, January 25, 1972, copy in Folder 25, Box 266, Harris Collection. The principal chiefs of the Five Tribes of Oklahoma were "unqualifiedly supporting" the views expressed by the twenty physicians. See Overton James et al. to Johnson, February 10, 1972, copy in Folder 14, Box 165, Belcher Collection.

49. *Daily Oklahoman*, March 20, 1972. Although the newly elected president of the IHS's Indian Advisory Board, Reverend Morgan Burgin, a member of the Ottawa tribe, was generally complimentary to the Indian Health Service, he nevertheless noted that there was only one mental health coordinator for the state, despite the fact that mental health workers and psychiatrists were desperately needed in each of the service units. He noted that the creation of advisory boards had represented another step toward self-determination. Now, he said, starting with these boards and through their Community Health Representatives, Oklahoma Indians were beginning to express their needs more directly to health officials.

50. Ibid., April 5, 1972; *Anadarko* (Okla.) *Daily News*, April 20, 1972; "Oklahoma Human Rights Commission: Complaints Against Anadarko Municipal

Hospital, June 20, 1972," copy in Folder 19, Box 58, Steed Collection; E. E. Otey to Steed, April 23, 1973, Folder 22, Box 67, Steed Collection. See also the report of the Anadarko Indian Affairs Committee's September 1973 meeting in Folder 22, Box 67, Steed Collection. See also "Public Notice: USPHS Indian Hospital Lawton, Oklahoma, December 1, 1972," in which hospital officials explain how contract funds were to be allocated. Copy in Folder 19, Box 58, Steed Collection.

51. Calvin Beames, press release, December 5, 1972, copy in Folder 19, Box 58, Steed Collection.

52. Native American Center Clinic Statement, March 23, 1973, copy in Folder 22, Box 67, Steed Collection; *Oklahoma City Times*, February 9, 1974.

53. *Daily Oklahoman*, March 28, 1973; "Programs Generated by North Central," [n.d.], copy in Folder 10, Box 74, Steed Collection; Calvin Beames, press release, April 8, 1973, copy in Folder 7, Box 66, Steed Collection.

54. Resolution: Inter-Tribal Council, Inc., of Northeast Oklahoma, December 5, 1973, copy in Folder 9, Box 24, Steed Collection.

55. "Health Service Presses for New Indian Hospital," clipping from *Tulsa World*, Folder 9, Box 32, Bartlett Collection; *Daily Oklahoman*, April 4, 1974; Harry Belvin to the Oklahoma Congressional Delegation, June 5, 1974, copy in Folder 17, Box 36, Camp Collection; Lee Motah to Johnson, August 21, 1974, Tray 10, Box 74, Steed Collection. Belvin was principal chief of the Choctaw Nation. Motah, president of the United Indian Tribes of Western Oklahoma and Kansas, assured the director of the Indian Health Service "that our Congressional delegation" will be informed of the tribes' request for an Indian Health Service hospital facility at Shawnee.

56. Delbert Horsechief to Abourezk, August 30, 1974, copy in Folder 9, Box 32, Bartlett Collection; *Daily Oklahoman*, September 14, 1974; *Washington Post*, September 15, 1974. Horsechief was head of the Pawnee Indian Tribal Business Council.

57. *Daily Oklahoman*, September 17, 1974.

58. John W. Davis, press release, October 2, 1974, copy in Folder 9, Box 32, Bartlett Collection; *Daily Oklahoman*, October 3, 1974, and October 16, 1974. The latter article charged that nurses at the hospital performed minor surgeries such as circumcisions and episiotomies. See also *Daily Oklahoman*, October 27, 1974, and October 31, 1974.

59. *Public Papers of the Presidents of the United States: Gerald R. Ford*, Book 1 (Washington, D.C.: GPO, 1977): 10–11.

60. *Daily Oklahoman*, January 31, 1975, and February 7, 1975; John W. Davis, press release, February 26, 1975, copy in Folder 12, Box 82, Steed Collection.

61. Sylvester Tinker to Robert C. Byrd, March 13, 1975, and Bates Shaw to Byrd, March 26, 1975, copies in Folder 14, Box 32, Bartlett Collection; Shaw to Sidney Yates, March 26, 1975, copy in Folder 8, Box 84, Steed Collection. Yates was chair of the House Subcommittee on Interior and Related Agencies. Mrs. R. L.

Smith to Steed, March 27, 1975, Folder 8, Box 84, Steed Collection. See also United Tribes of Western Oklahoma and Kansas Position Paper [Washington, D.C.], April 7–12, 1975, copy in Folder 8, Box 15, Steed Collection.

62. "Tribal Involvement in the Oklahoma Area Health Program," [1975], copy in Folder 14, Box 32, Bartlett Collection. For the efforts of the Cheyenne and Arapaho Tribes of Oklahoma to improve their health care, see Virgil Franklin to Mr. Chairman, May 12, 1975, copy in Folder 12, Box 82, Steed Collection.

63. *Indian Health Care Improvement Act: Report of the Committee on Interior and Insular Affairs*, May 13, 1975, 94th Cong., 1st sess., S. Rpt. 94–133 (Washington, D.C.: GPO, 1975), p. 143, relates the Oklahoma example.

64. Ibid., 36, 23. For a brief review of the report see "Proposed Indian Health Care Project," [1975], copy in Folder 12, Box 32, Bartlett Collection.

65. "Statement on Signing the Indian Health Care Improvement Act, October 1, 1976," *Public Papers of the Presidents of the United States: Gerald R. Ford*, Book 3: 2384.

66. Ibid., June 16, 1975; Hickory Starr to Steed, July 2, 1975, Folder 12, Box 82, Steed Collection. Starr was director of the Oklahoma City Urban Indian Health Project. For a story on the Tulsa Indian Health Center, see *Oklahoma City Times*, September 15, 1975. See also Bartlett, et al., to Edward Kennedy, September 29, 1975, Folder 10, Box 32, Bartlett Collection. The Oklahoma Federation of Indian Women called for the construction of a new Indian Health Service hospital. See Mary Crowe to the Oklahoma Delegation, copy in Folder 8, Box 84, Steed Collection.

67. Henry M. Jackson, et al., to Joseph Califano, February 11, 1977, copy in Folder 14, Box 32, Bartlett Collection; John W. Davis, press release, February 16, 1977, copy in Folder 6, Box 99, Steed Collection; Claude Cox to Bartlett, February 28, 1977, Folder 11, Box 32, Bartlett Collection; Danny Little Axe to Steed, May 19, 1977, Folder 6, Box 99, Steed Collection; Starr to Bartlett, September 9, 1977, Folder 11, Box 32, Bartlett Collection. Califano was secretary of health, education, and welfare. Cox was principal chief of the Creek Nation. Little Axe was chair of the Absentee Shawnee Tribe of Oklahoma.

68. *Chickasaw Newsletter*, January/March 1976, 2. For instance, the Chickasaw prompted a change that brought health care to members of the Five Tribes not previously qualified. A resolution presented by Chickasaw Nation governor Overton James to the Inter-Tribe Council of the Five Tribes declared that all Indians whose names appeared on the Dawes Commission rolls would be eligible for IHS care, regardless of blood quantum. Members not on the rolls would still be required to prove one-quarter blood quantum. The quote is from the April 9, 1976, resolution of the Inter-Tribal Council of the Five Tribes calling for a major medical facility in eastern Oklahoma. The Creeks, however, rejected the resolution at a council meeting several months later. See *Muskogee* (Okla.) *Phoenix and Times*, October 2, 1977.

69. Little Axe to Steed, November 9, 1977, Folder 15, Box 109, Steed Collection; *Shawnee* (Okla.) *News Star*, November 17, 1977; Overton James to John Davis, December 7, 1977, copy in Folder 6, Box 9, Steed Collection.

70. "Proposed New Anadarko Health Center," [n.d.], copy in Folder 5, Box 108, Steed Collection; Statement by Lawrence Snake before Senate Appropriations Subcommittee, April 18, 1978, and Statement by Joe Pedro before Senate Appropriations Subcommittee, April 20, 1978, copies of both in Folder 12, Box 32, Bartlett Collection. Snake, testifying on behalf of the proposed Anadarko clinic, was president of the Delaware Tribes of Western Oklahoma; Pedro, testifying in behalf of a clinic in Concho, was chair of the Business Committee of the Southern Cheyenne-Arapaho Tribes of Oklahoma. See also Statement by John Davis, Indian Health Area Director, December 20, 1978, copy in Folder 5, Box 115, Steed Collection, and *Daily Oklahoman*, February 12, 1979. For a further listing of proposals considered by the appropriations subcommittees in 1978, see Folder 12, Box 32, Bartlett Collection. For a summary of the requested appropriations of the Tulsa Indian Health Care Center in 1979, see Folder 5, Box 32, Bartlett Collection. For Kiowa concern about an Indian Health Service Clinic see "Subjects of Interest to the Kiowas," [n.d. (1979)], copy in Folder 17, Box 116, Steed Collection. Many tribes submitted health plans for congressional consideration.

71. Overton James to Emery Johnson, February 11, 1980, copy in Folder 12, Box 123, Steed Collection. For a story lauding Davis, see "Indian Health Care Measure Draws Praise" by Gail Mitchell in the *Daily Oklahoman*, February 9, 1980.

72. Oklahoma State Department of Health, "Health Care Information 2004, Summary," 7–8 and passim; Oklahoma State Department of Health, Chronic Disease Service, "Behavioral Risk Factors Among American Indians in Oklahoma," April 2004, passim.

« 6 »

Forty Feet Under

Kaw City and the Kaw Project on the Arkansas River, 1957–1976

Kaw City, established in the Oklahoma Territory in 1902 at the oxbow bend of the Arkansas River, lay in an area ideally suited for farming and cattle raising. The town, located about nine miles east of Ponca City, first served as a center for oil operations. In 1950 it had a population of 809 and housed a notable art collection in the Clubb Hotel, a plain, three-story red-brick building. The entire area was subject to periodic flooding, and in 1956 the U.S. Army Corps of Engineers completed the construction of just over two miles of levee for Kaw City's protection. Yet within two decades the town was abandoned, making way for a dam that was part of a master plan to promote flood control and improve navigation on the Arkansas River, the last major undeveloped river in the United States.[1]

Arkansas River development was divided between the Army Corps of Engineers, which represented downstream interests encompassing the state of Oklahoma, and the Bureau of Reclamation (Department of the Interior), which was primarily concerned with irrigation and upstream problems. Kay County, where the major part of the Kaw Reservoir would be located, is classified as an urban county (where more than half of the population resides in towns of more than 2,500 inhabitants). The primary reason for this designation is that Ponca City, home of the Continental Oil Company, contains about 60 percent of the county's population. During the years this project was under way, Kay County experienced a net outmigration, due to a lack of job opportunities.[2]

Water policy for the Arkansas River Valley had largely been formulated by both geographical and vested-interest-group politics: agriculture in the upper valley (Bureau of Reclamation), business and industry in the lower valley (Corps of Engineers). Upstream interests wanted federal funds for watershed development and irrigation; downstream groups called for large dams for flood control and navigation. Following severe flooding in 1943, Robert S. Kerr, as governor of Oklahoma, awakened to the opportunity to control the state's water resources for multiple purposes. Working with members of the Tulsa business community and a state engineer, Don McBride, Kerr began to contact federal agencies, administration officials, and key legislators to involve the federal government. He was not interested in a river valley authority comparable to the Tennessee Valley Authority (TVA), preferring instead to have the governor and executive agencies involved in the process. Water development, Kerr recognized, would create jobs, attract industry, assist agriculture, and possibly one day surpass oil revenues. It would be the catalyst of prosperity.

With his failure to win the presidential nomination in 1952, Kerr determined that he would spend his tenure as a United States senator furthering his state's interests. He was especially interested in bringing to Oklahoma a seaport for ocean-going vessels through the federal development of the Arkansas River Valley. As a member of the Public Works Committee and, after 1955, chair of the Subcommittee on Rivers and Harbors and Flood Control, with an ex-officio seat on the Appropriations Committee, Kerr was situated as the most powerful member of the Senate to further water development in Oklahoma, let alone the United States. In this capacity he was instrumental in removing Kaw City in order to further the development of the Arkansas River Valley. In this decision the people in Kaw City had no voice other than bargaining with the Corps of Engineers for a meaningful price for their property. Modernization signified progress and prosperity, and in this instance the people of Kaw City would pay the price. Community leaders in Ponca City and in Newkirk, the county seat, endorsed and actively supported Kerr's efforts, although he was a Democrat and Kay County traditionally cast its votes for the Republican ticket.[3]

Kerr was alerted early in 1956 that "a large number of people in Kay County, particularly in Kaw City," were alarmed by the action of the Arkansas River changing its course at several points. They were seeking aid in protecting bank-side property. Federal funds to curb bank caving, Kerr knew, could only be secured if transportation arteries were in danger or if the caving affected flood control. An earlier authorized project for protection of Kaw City was deferred for lack of local interest. If anything was to be accomplished in Kay County, concerned groups would have to become involved.[4]

A year later the interest had materialized. Bank protection was replaced by a proposal for a Kaw reservoir as a means of expanding water facilities for the entire county. A grateful mayor of Ponca City was delighted with Kerr's "generous and heartening cooperation" in endorsing the proposal, formally entitled "Reconnaissance Report on the Kaw Project, Arkansas River," that was forwarded to the Corps's Chief of Engineers, General E. C. Itschner. The proposal was formally accepted at a meeting held by the Arkansas Basin Development Association to discuss the possibility of securing a survey and report on the feasibility of the new project. In attendance were U.S. representatives Ed Edmondson and Page Belcher, representatives of the governor of Kansas, and delegates from Kay County. If the project was deemed attractive, Kerr's endorsement asked General Itschner to provide "some indication of the economic benefit" that might accrue from it.[5]

News of the proposal and its filing with the Corps of Engineers spread quickly throughout the county and aroused the interest and enthusiasm of individuals and groups who corresponded with Kerr and Belcher. All were pleased when Brigadier General J. L. Person, responsible for civil works in the Corps of Engineers, asserted that a favorable benefit-to-cost ratio could be achieved if, in addition to flood control and power benefits, water supply and recreational purposes were factored into the proposal. However, additional detailed studies would be required before a definite determination could be made. A long process now began. Kerr thought the Corps of Engineers would be favorably impressed once "the Recreational Bill and the Omnibus Rivers and Harbors and Flood Control Bill" were enacted. He hoped that once these bills were law, the Corps would respond favorably to the Kaw proposal.[6]

The situation became acute in May 1957, when thousands of acres of Kay County's fertile farmlands, rich with the promise of a bumper wheat crop, lay beneath flood waters. Scores of farms and homes were inundated or isolated. Transportation was disrupted, and bridges were closed. The newly organized Kaw Dam and Reservoir Association (KDRA), already boasting forty thousand members, hoped that Kerr could "immediately help" secure an appropriation of $25,000 and request a feasibility study by the Tulsa District of the Corps of Engineers. Kerr informed the president of KDRA that the Corps of Engineers had promptly launched a survey "to determine the extent of the damage and projects which would have eliminated it." The Kaw Project could supply needed additional storage to prevent flooding. In addition, Kerr would bring the association's concern to his Public Works Subcommittee on Appropriations.[7]

Thus far, no one in Kay County or in Washington were paying attention to the residents of the old Kaw Indian Nation in Washunga, or to the people of Kaw City, whose homes and businesses would be submerged if and when the proposed dam and reservoir became realities. Residents adopted a "wait and see attitude," but construction and home improvements virtually ceased in these two Kay County communities that faced each other across the river.

The project's success would mean that water up to thirty-four feet deep would cover Kaw City's main street, leaving only the top of the three-story hotel not submerged. Residents were already concerned about the seventy-five or eighty pensioners who would not be able to replace their modest homes, valued "anywhere from $3,000–$4,000." However, Dale Shackelford, the mayor, believed it was "too early to be upset," because in 1957 the project's feasibility was yet to be determined. In effect, a time bomb was ticking, as the proposal's promoters were relentlessly enthusiastic.[8]

To influence public opinion throughout the region, among the officers of the Tulsa District of the Corps of Engineers, and in Washington, the newly incorporated KDRA launched a massive campaign to secure funding for a feasibility report. The association reported in a 1958 newsletter that besides the benefits emanating from flood control, the dam and reservoir were necessary for "the preservation of the welfare of our people, our refineries and other industries during the drought years to come." In May success seemed possible when Belcher testified before the

Public Works Subcommittee on Appropriations to urge the inclusion of a $100,000 survey of the Kaw Project. If this effort failed, Kerr would seek its inclusion in the Senate "and then get the Conferees of the House and Senate to agree."[9]

News that the appropriations committees might consider this request sent three association members to Washington. There they joined a host of delegates from Oklahoma, Kansas, and Arkansas, all emphasizing the need for the Arkansas River basin projects. The three KDRA representatives were distressed to learn that Belcher's request for $100,000 had been reduced to $25,000. The members returned home, tired but confident that planning would soon be under way. Don Hoye of the Newkirk Trust Company told Representative Tom Steed that "without water the industries that we now have will not expand and we know that no new industries will come in," and there was a chance "we could lose the industries we have." As an indication of how alarming the situation was, he noted that in the past two weeks not a single new car had been sold in Ponca City. People, Hoye concluded, simply did not have any money to spend. Another Ponca City resident observed that well water was being pumped into Lake Ponca to reduce the hardness of its water and, at the same time, to afford recreational facilities on a lake already congested with boats. In addition, the Research Department for Continental Oil Company noted that drinking water in the city "was approaching a serious health hazard for internal consumption." All were further reasons for the project's construction.[10]

However, despite the efforts of the Washington delegates, the House Appropriations Committee did not include funding for the feasibility study in their bill. Kerr promised to do his best to persuade the Senate Appropriations Committee to include the item, and he was successful. Ponca City Chamber of Commerce President Don Wright exulted that "this is one of the most significant things that has ever taken place in our community."[11]

While they awaited the Corps's study, KDRA's supporters mounted a barrage of resolutions and membership drives (annual membership cost was $2). In late April 1959, in Ponca City, members packed the Corps's public meeting, held so that the feasibility report could reflect the attitude of local interests. The association made every effort to ensure that members of the congressional delegation, state officials, and Kansas representatives were on hand.[12]

An unintended consequence of all this activity had occurred on April 14, 1959, when eighty-eight affected property owners formed the Anti–Kaw Dam Association. Keith Fruits, a Kaw City–area farmer and president of the new organization, said the group would proclaim their opposition at the public meeting, and they did. One farmer said it had taken him a decade to improve his land to its present state and that it would take another decade to get another farm to the point of productivity of his present operation. Another observed that farmers did not want to improve their land if they would be forced to move. Still another said it was almost impossible to sell property or secure a loan. In addition, the men pointed out that many of Kaw City's almost seven hundred residents had moved there upon retiring.[13]

Shortly after the meeting, the Anti–Kaw Dam Association enumerated in a notice, in bold print, the devastation that would probably occur. Fertile land would be lost; dwellings and other improvements, including places of business, would be abandoned. Services would be impaired and huge costs incurred to pay for inundated land, to rebuild county roads, and possibly to build a bridge. The notice inquired, "Who Do You Think Will Pay for This?" and "Where Will You Replace This God-Given Land?" Members of the Anti–Kaw Dam Association found it "difficult to understand how businessmen at Ponca City, Newkirk or other cities in this area can favor the Kaw Dam project, since it is clearly a socialist project which will undeniably and definitely destroy a large part of the best tributary farmland in the respective trade territories."[14]

Before the meeting, Continental Oil Company of Ponca City had expressed its concerns in a communication to Corps district engineer Colonel John Bristor, who was to preside at the meeting. The company cited its expanding needs for good-quality water beyond the "2.1 billion gallons" already available and thus its "vital interest" in the completion of the KawProject. An adequate water supply constituted "a basic condition for the development of a substantial petrochemical industry." Furthermore, the construction of the Kaw Dam and Reservoir would obviate "the devastating effects of flood and drought" upon the region's economy and improve Continental's role as "one of the principal suppliers of petroleum products in this primarily agricultural region." Moreover, through water-flooding practices, a number of oil fields in the area could be made to produce great quantities of additional crude, ventures that could not otherwise be undertaken. Construction of the project, in brief, "would both permit and encourage industrial growth," attract "tourist travel," and stimulate "recreational activities" that "would create substantial new sources of income to the suppliers of petroleum products."[15]

Couched in terms relevant to the concerns of the Continental Oil Company, the letter reflected the views of KDRA and all who supported the proposal. It would benefit the region's economy and provide recreational facilities beyond those offered at the already overcrowded Lake Ponca. In fulfilling Kerr's broad vision of developing the Arkansas River Valley, the project would be good for business. It also meant that the anti–Kaw Dam group would pay the price of progress, because the Corps of Engineers, in the general information it received and in the testimony presented, said, in greater detail and with different specifications, what the Continental Oil Company had related to the district engineer. Namely, the project would promote the area's industrial development, bring additional job opportunities, provide flood control, greatly enhance the water supply, and possibly develop the fish and wildlife potential. In his statement at the public hearing, Senator Kerr had commented on "the vigor, the enthusiasm, and the precise planning" demonstrated by the project's backers. He further announced that the entire Oklahoma congressional delegation "pledged their whole hearted support." He related this project to his work in promoting water development throughout Oklahoma and called upon the Corps of Engineers "to again demonstrate here their usual and thorough manner of expediting vital surveys."[16]

A survey would take time in working its way through the bureaucracy. With the Eisenhower administration unenthusiastic about endorsing public works proposals, Kerr realized, as did most area residents, that a decision would be arrived at later rather than sooner. He, however, took some satisfaction when, for the first time during Eisenhower's tenure, Congress in 1959 overrode his veto of a water resources bill and appropriated funds for fifteen new reclamation project starts. As chair of the newly created Senate Select Committee on National Water Resources, Kerr was ideally situated to secure authorization for the Kaw Project, once the survey report reached Congress.[17]

Chambers of Commerce in nearby Kansas communities also expressed an interest in the project, and several sent delegates to the public hearing held in June 1959 in Ponca City. Meanwhile, residents of the area began addressing letters of inquiry directly to the Tulsa District Office of the U.S. Corps of Engineers. The Chamber of Commerce of Newkirk, the Kay County seat, was particularly concerned with "whether or not a bridge across the proposed reservoir at a point where a bridge is now located, due east of Newkirk was part of the feasibility study." The chamber considered the bridge vital to the community. Ponca City's mayor wrote to the director of the Bureau of the Budget to explain how his community depended upon industry for its economy and how industry in turn depended upon water. Mayor Dale Shackleford of Kaw City had more immediate concerns. District engineer Colonel Howard Penney had informed him that the report "under study" would set the flood control pool for the Kaw Reservoir "at about elevation 1,044, which is much higher than the lands in and around the City of Kaw," thereby inundating the community. If deemed feasible, the project could take from "three to five years or more to obtain authorization." If authorized, the mayor was informed, the government could provide assistance in removing publicly owned facilities to a new site. Private property, however, would not be relocated but would be purchased. Conditions at the time of removal would determine the purchase price of land and improvements. If a favorable feasibility report was presented, Kaw City was doomed.[18]

With Kerr handily reelected in 1960 (he lost Kay County despite the enthusiastic support his efforts always received in Ponca City), he could now devote more attention to the proposal and a request from Carl Cramton, vice president of Kaw City's First National Bank. The bank was "doing very nicely," he noted, but everybody in Kaw City was "very concerned as to their position in regard to proposed dam." A number of retired people were worried that if forced to sell their homes, they would not be able to replace them if the selling price was based on the market value. Actually, the banker noted, there was no market of any kind, due to the possibility of a dam being constructed. No one wanted to buy, and there was "not a single lender" willing to loan on Kaw City property. While, he said, farms and ranch land would be appraised and something approaching an equitable value could be determined, he worried about residents who owned and lived in homes that now had no sale value. A new house in Ponca City would cost them four or five times what they could get for their Kaw City home. The banker needed advice as to how "the home owner might be treated and the choices he might have." Kerr, of course, was of little help. He could only relay the information to District Engineer Penney, and that information was not reassuring to Kaw City homeowners.[19]

Anxiously awaiting word on the project's feasibility from the Corps of Engineers, Kay County residents received a tremendous boost from the "Special Message to the Congress on Natural Resources" by newly elected President John F. Kennedy. In his message Kennedy announced that "we reject a 'no new starts' policy" and that he had requested the director of the Bureau of the Budget to schedule new projects to meet accumulated demands. The reluctance evident during the Eisenhower presidency would end with the new administration. During the campaign, Kennedy had wired people in Ponca City that he endorsed the Kaw Dam and Reservoir proposal. The supporters responded to his pledge in an exuberant telegram proclaiming that the people of northern Oklahoma were "happy" with his message on natural resources. The telegram further expressed the hope that "with your helping Senator Kerr the report from the Army engineers should be forthcoming immediately." The telegram contained the names of fourteen prominent members of the Ponca City business community, including the presidents of both oil companies.[20]

Proponents of the projects received a boost of another sort in May 1961, when violent thunderstorms, accompanied by heavy rains, hail, strong winds, and rising streams, wrought havoc throughout the county and forced the evacuation of homes in parts of Ponca City. At Kaw City, where three inches of rain fell, the Arkansas River rose slightly, but no serious flooding was reported. While flooding from the Arkansas River was not a major factor, other water-gorged streams emptied into the river, arousing concern and helping maintain interest in the project.[21]

The disastrous rains possibly prompted a story in the *Daily Oklahoman* that focused on Kaw City, claiming that it "refuses to give up, either to water and silt on the angry Arkansas River. . . ." The story noted that while once there were more than 2,500 people living there, the 1960 census listed 457 persons. The three-story Clubb Hotel, with its famed art collection, was now a rest home, and most of the art resided in Tulsa's Philbrook Museum. While there was talk of moving the First National Bank, founded in 1902, away from Kaw City, it continued to function as proof of business stability and as a vital part of town life. Its deposits and loans were up, a savings department had been added, and the lobby modernized. There were even some new jobs in the area. All was evidence of a slowing rate of decline, but all was threatened if the forthcoming feasibility report favored the project. Nevertheless, individuals who wanted to keep Kaw City alive still could have possibly a decade "before anything more definitive than discussion" about the reservoir was concluded. They resolved to keep active during that time.[22]

So too did supporters of the project. In late May KDRA's directors announced their intention to flood the Oklahoma congressional delegation's Appropriations Committee members, as well as the Corps of Engineers office in Tulsa and Dallas, with letters calling for authorization of the proposed dam and reservoir. The recent downpour and flooding made it a propitious time to launch such a campaign, with the impulse emanating, as in the past, from the Ponca City business elite. This time, however, the association's leaders would seek greater support throughout the county and in Kansas. While it was known that the engineer's preliminary report had reached Washington, no one in Ponca City knew how it had been received. The coming letter-writing campaign could speed the process and help secure a favorable report.[23]

To no avail. It soon became known that the preliminary evaluation indicated the need for "more detailed studies" before "firming up [the project's] economic feasibility." The Corps's director of civil works, Major General William F. Cassidy, explained that further study would necessitate "a careful review of major cost items" and a further assessment of project benefits to determine how they juxtaposed "with the goal of national economic growth recently set by the President." The statement nevertheless revealed that the proposal was being seriously considered and that the Tulsa District Engineers would be fine-tuning it, a task that could take several months.[24]

Anticipating a favorable response and to manifest massive support, KDRA scheduled a rally for the evening of October 9 in Ponca City. To lure a large audience, the association would provide "piping hot barbeque." Senators Kerr and Mike Monroney and Representative Belcher would speak, kicking off an intensive effort to secure the project's authorization. At the rally, Kerr assured the crowd of approximately eight thousand people that the project would be approved in January [1962], but he added that this "would be only the beginning." Appropriations would have to be made before the Corps of Engineers could launch the project. Kerr's remarks indicated his optimism, bordering on certainty, that with a Democratic president and Congress, and with his dominant position on the Public Works and Appropriations committees, the slogan "the Kaw Dam for You in '62" would become reality.[25]

By this time, opposition to the project was rarely noted in the press and was confined largely to letters to officials. These were directed primarily to Republican Page Belcher, who represented the First District, extending across northern Oklahoma roughly from Woodward to Tulsa. Correspondents included farmers whose lands would be taken, ultraconservative Republicans resentful of any intrusion by the federal government, and Kaw City residents. Their voices were lost in the general enthusiasm evident at the Ponca City meeting and even more so following another startling announcement. In November they received notice of a public hearing to discuss a proposal offered by the Bureau of Sport Fisheries of the U.S. Fish and Wildlife Service to develop a national wildlife refuge in conjunction with the Kaw Reservoir. This new proposal would generate considerable controversy, but it also implied that a favorable feasibility report was forthcoming. Indeed, in scheduling the meeting for late November in Ponca City, the district engineer said that the survey studies were nearing completion.[26]

On December 12, 1961, the results of the report were formally announced by Major General Robert J. Fleming, Jr., heading the Corps' Southwestern Division, which included the Tulsa Division of the Corps of Engineers. Calling for the construction of the Kaw Dam, the reporting officers approved a multipurpose reservoir that would provide storage for flood control, municipal and industrial water supply, water quality control, and conservation uses. The officers further recommended that careful consideration be given to the Fish and Wildlife Service's request. In accordance with law, the report would be referred for review to the Board of Engineers for Rivers and Harbors in Washington. Hearings would be held on January 3, 1962.[27]

Before the meeting in Washington, the parameters of a major battle among friends of Kaw Reservoir were already outlined. For example, Mayor William Kasl of Blackwell, in Kay County, expressed opposition to the proposed refuge because it would include the entire area of the lake from Kaw City to the Kansas line. This, he insisted, would destroy recreational opportunities and "cost the City of Blackwell and surrounding area many dollars in retail business, derived from recreation and the development of cabins and boat docks." That there was an opposing side to this was evident in a resolution from the Tonkawa and Ponca City chapters of the Izaak Walton League of America. They endorsed the proposal and called for specific access points to be made available for fishing, hunting, and boating.[28]

With the December announcement, the first phase, that of securing approval for the Kaw Project, concluded. Opposition became negligible. Arguments for the project's economic and recreational potential had produced a substantial result in a favorable feasibility report, and construction of the Kaw Dam and Reservoir now was assured. Supporters would contend among themselves about the virtues of a game preserve, a contest that soon extended beyond Kay County. Kerr and other members of the Oklahoma delegation considered this a distraction, as did KDRA. In a formal resolution, the directors unanimously opposed "the inclusion of a wildlife refuge as an adjunct of the Kaw Reservoir," a view endorsed by the chambers of commerce of most towns within Kay County.[29]

Throughout 1962, before action occurred in Washington to start funding the project, the Kaw Reservoir game preserve controversy raged. Members of the Oklahoma delegation received hundreds of postcards and letters on the subject as well as petitions, illustrating a lively debate in Kay County and increasing interest elsewhere. Kerr indicated that his mail "from the cities and towns and individuals in the area" indicated "almost 100% opposed" to the refuge. Belcher was informed that interested groups were circulating petitions among county residents in opposition, in all suggesting that it was general and not limited to an isolated few.[30]

In late February the project moved a step further when the Army Engineers Board of Rivers and Harbors approved the project. Once approval was announced, Senators Kerr and Monroney said they would attempt to get the project in the Omnibus Rivers and Harbors Bill in time to obtain preconstruction funds in 1962. Before that could occur, the chief of engineers and the Budget Bureau would have to approve the proposal. The chief of engineers did so in March, submitting a report for transmission to Congress. In September the Budget Bureau advised the Senate and the House Public Works committees that it had approved the multimilliondollar Kaw Reservoir project. But it was too late for the Eighty-Seventh Congress to act.[31]

Between February and September debate raged on over the merits of the refuge, and pressure to launch the project intensified. Spokespersons for the Branch of Wildlife Refuges again met with groups throughout the county. When asked at a meeting of the Tonkawa Chapter of the Izaak Walton League if reaction against the Branch of Wildlife Refuges coming into the Kaw debate was typical, the spokesperson replied, "We only get this type of reaction where people are trying to make a lot of money." Senator Kerr, who had no need to make a lot of money, quickly concluded that "since there has been so much opposition to the wildlife refuge," he would "favor the project without the refuge." KDRA endorsed his view, as did most chambers of commerce and business people in the county, with one notable exception. The Tonkawa Chamber of Commerce reflected the opposition of the local chapter of the Izaak Walton League. Although Representative Belcher and Senator Monroney were in accord with Kerr's views, it was also evident that the refuge fight would only intensify in the coming months.[32]

The strides toward realization of the project prompted the Kaw Indian tribe to consult with the Bureau of Indian Affairs on the problems it sought to have resolved. Sixteen Kaw Indian families resided on lands to be submerged, and the tribe requested that the bureau seek an appraisal enabling them to secure comparable property nearby. The tribe also sought aid in selecting a new burial ground for the cemetery that would be inundated. However, concerns of soon-to-be displaced people attracted little attention. It would be several years before their problems would be addressed. The immediate concern was the wildlife refuge itself, which drew the attention of a growing constituency outside of Kay County.[33]

Within the county a class cleavage could be discerned. While more affluent individuals would bear no financial hardship in finding a place to hunt and fish, and could afford to travel some distance to find it, the "poorer people" were denied many such opportunities. In addition, organizations such as the Oklahoma State Division of the Izaak Walton League, the Oklahoma Academy of Science (Conservation Section), the Oklahoma Division of the Outdoor Council of America, and numerous Sportsman Clubs had acquired an elitist image. Owing to their lower economic status, Kay County residents recognized that their recreational opportunities, unlike those of members of the supporting organizations, were largely limited to those offered in the vicinity.[34]

Meanwhile, despite the fact that the Budget Bureau had not officially accepted the project, Kerr continued discussing it. His assistant provided an outline of points that the KDRA leadership should make in its presentation before the Public Works Committee. Besides a general statement relating to the need for the project, the Corps's report should be characterized as "ultra conservative" in its assessment of potential benefits such as flood control and recreation. Benefits included in the report should be evaluated. Strong statements "reinforced by appropriate resolutions" relative to water supply requirements and "the willingness of local communities to participate on a contract basis" for such supplies should be stressed. Other points in the presentation could mention how the Kaw

Reservoir, through silt control, would extend the life of the downstream Keystone Reservoir. Above all, anticipated industrial development should be stressed as a primary benefit. In short, an elaborate presentation embellished with supporting data would be of great assistance to the committee. No mention was made of a wildlife refuge.[35]

A further hurdle was cleared in June 1962 when Oklahoma governor J. Howard Edmondson informed the acting chief of engineers, Major General Keith Barney, that all agencies having responsibility regarding construction of the project had now concurred in the report. Edmondson urged the acting chief to forward the report to Congress at the earliest possible date. Shortly thereafter, Secretary of the Interior Stewart L. Udall informed Lieutenant General Walker Wilson, the chief of engineers, that "the proposed national wildlife refuge would be of substantial value in the national program for the management of the waterfowl resource." The secretary challenged the district engineer's report on the estimates of fish and wildlife utilization, claiming it was not in agreement with those of the Bureau of Sport Fisheries and Wildlife. Moreover, he was specific in requesting that the district engineer consult with the Bureau of Indian Affairs regarding effects that the policy might have on "restricted Indian lands in Kay County."[36]

At the end of August the U.S. Army Corps of Engineers asked Congress for funds to launch new water projects in Oklahoma. The Kaw Reservoir would furnish municipal water to Ponca City and Newkirk, as well as to Arkansas City, Kansas. It would also control floods, improve water quality, and provide fish and wildlife habitats. The order for construction of the several projects, however, would be left to the discretion of the Corps, leaving the contentious issue of the wildlife refuge unresolved. All that Kerr could offer at this point was that authorization was necessary to continue the program of developing natural resources in Oklahoma. In September, as previously noted, the Kaw Dam and Reservoir had been approved by the Bureau of the Budget. But this approval made no mention of a wildlife refuge, while that of the Corps called for the provision of fish and wildlife benefits, leaving the matter up to a new Congress, scheduled to convene in January 1963. However, thanks to the strenuous efforts of Senator Kerr, the Eighty-seventh Congress, just before it adjourned, had appropriated an additional $75,000 for the project. Delighted, KDRA's directors said that in five years it had reached a level of accomplishment generally not seen in such a program until twelve or fifteen years of work had been done.[37]

Project supporters' exuberance dimmed somewhat with the death of Senator Kerr, whose arduous efforts had been responsible for the progress thus far achieved. Fortunately, every member of the Oklahoma delegation would continue to back the project. Belcher in the House and Monroney in the Senate took the lead. Thanks to Kerr's efforts, the project now entered a decisive stage, namely that construction money had been handed to the Corps of Engineers.[38]

A more immediate matter needed clarification, namely the status of the wildlife refuge. While the Corps of Engineers recommended the proposal, the Bureau of the Budget hesitated to utilize funds for acquisition of lands for wildlife purposes. As the Department of the Interior and the Bureau of the Budget sought to resolve their differences in the summer of 1963, Congress had already appropriated $75,000 for advance planning and engineering, and the president had requested $200,000 for similar use in the next fiscal year. Only after this work was completed would construction funds be allocated; at least another year of engineering would be required before a contract could be let. The envisioned target date to get under way, KDRA officials claimed, would be July 1, 1965, with the major construction contracts awarded a year later. The Tulsa district engineer, Colonel John W. Morris, in March 1964 amended the starting date to July 1967. He further indicated that residents of the areas to be inundated would not know when they must move until about six months after the construction of the dam. Kaw City residents now knew that a wait-and-see attitude had become precarious.

On the other hand, Ponca City residents envisioned the project "as a bonanza which will mean untold millions in recreational and industrial profits for future generations." Don McBride, now assisting Senator Monroney on water issues, insisted that maintaining the project would sustain jobs and a continuous annual payroll. Tourism would increase, as would private investments, and per capita income would rise. But high hopes alone would not translate McBride's views into reality. Congress still had to vote the construction funds, an amount estimated at $83 million by the Corps. As soon as money was available, land would be purchased, and access roads, project buildings, and construction areas would be developed. If anything, KDRA would have to work even harder than it had when Kerr, with his powerful committee assignments, had been there to assist.[39]

A waiting game now ensued: waiting until preconstruction planning was completed, waiting before being forced to move, waiting for contracts and the employment opportunities that would follow. Kaw City's leaders understood that the whole town would be lost if it were abandoned, but that relocation would secure government aid to grade new roads and move utilities, roads, schools, and churches. To assist in the process, the Kaw City Council hired a Tulsa engineering firm to plan and supervise the town's relocation. In Ponca City, Newkirk, and elsewhere, the debate between "wildlifers" and opponents renewed with some intensity, but most people were seemingly willing to let Congress, the Corps of Engineers, and the Bureau of the Budget resolve the issue. In addition, lobbying was renewed to secure supplemental appropriations so that the project could proceed on schedule.[40]

In May 1965 Belcher appeared before the House Appropriations Committee to request additional funds to complete the planning and initiate the construction for the Kaw Project. Senator Fred Harris made the same appeal before both the House and Senate appropriations subcommittees on public works. He, like Kerr, ardently supported the project and, like Kerr in 1960, failed to carry Ponca City and Kay County in 1964 when he succeeded in winning Kerr's Senate seat. Nevertheless, like Kerr, he endorsed KDRA's views, because both senators deemed the project vital to the enhanced prosperity of the state. Harris's efforts convinced the Senate to include a provision for the Kaw Dam in its Public Works Appropriations Bill. The conference committee accepted the provision, which meant that construction could get under way by 1967.[41]

While the approval of the appropriation aroused enthusiasm in Ponca City and throughout the county, such was not the case in Kaw City. There, more than 75 percent of residents owned their own homes, and two-thirds of the inhabitants were more than sixty-five years old. At the time (1965), there were only 323 Kaw City residents of voting age. All were eligible to vote on the site proposed by the city council for relocation. It was located three miles west of the original town, on a bluff overlooking the Arkansas River Valley, and would be surrounded on three sides by the waters of the Kaw Reservoir. By a vote of 155 to 10, voters approved the new site.[42]

Meanwhile, the other concerned party in the controversy, the Fish and Wildlife Service, launched a last-ditch effort to secure the creation of a refuge. Regional Director John G. Gatlin claimed that at the 1961 public hearing strong support had been evident. Since that time, the service had restudied the proposal and developed a revised plan that "we feel will remove almost all of the opposition to the refuge." Excluded from the refuge boundary was "a tract desired by local interests as a summer home area." In all, the service reduced the area for the refuge to approximately twelve thousand acres. An important part of the new plan called for developing recreational facilities on land that would not be subject to periodic flooding. With the next public hearing scheduled by the Corps of Engineers for the following spring, the service intended to work closely with all concerned groups in an "attempt to resolve as many difficulties as possible."[43]

Monroney tried to quash this effort by reminding the director that Kerr had found it necessary "to exclude the proposed wildlife refuge in order to secure local support for the project." Congress had authorized it without the refuge, and funds available to the Corps of Engineers "for advance engineering and design" made no mention of one. While Monroney did not commit himself, he recognized that a replay of the earlier debate would ensue, probably with greater intensity. But this was of little concern to KDRA members, who planned a "victory dinner" to celebrate the start of construction early in 1966. The meeting would also provide an opportunity for "the local folks" to meet new the new district engineer, Colonel George A. Rebh.[44]

The debate, however, was a matter of grave concern to numerous farmers, ranchers, and businessmen. Many of them feared that a new proposal was being made to establish a wildlife refuge. They worried about crop depreciation by "the fowls using the Refuge." In addition, the people of

Newkirk complained that the area would be fenced and placed under the jurisdiction of the Department of the Interior, thereby precluding "any reasonable opportunity" for them to take advantage of commercial development. For opponents of the refuge, it was "same song, second verse."[45]

At the end of 1965 the issue was far from resolved. District Engineer Rebh let it be known that his division planned "to give full consideration to the establishment of the national wildlife refuge in developing the best uses for project lands." What was decided was that ground-breaking ceremonies for the start of construction would occur with ample pomp and ceremony in the spring of the new year. Construction time for the project was estimated to be at least five years, after which the reservoir would be ready for filling.[46]

Once a starting date, May 21, was announced, a Kay County steering committee was organized to coordinate opposition to the proposed refuge. Eliminating public use of approximately forty miles of shoreline would remove a huge acreage available for private and commercial use. One critic noted that "the general attitude in this country is that we are against passing out any federal funds unless you pass it out here and give us the authority to use it as we please and to hell with anybody else," adding that "you would think, by the attitude here, that Kay County was paying the entire cost of the reservoir."[47]

Meanwhile, the Oklahoma Department of Wildlife Conservation, claiming the support of twenty-two thousand sportsmen in the state, announced its intention to be heard at the public hearing. However, at gatherings held throughout the county and in Arkansas City, Kansas, with "Wildlife representatives" present, the pros and cons were presented, and in every instance by a margin of five to one, the vote went against a federal wildlife refuge. Most local residents remained opposed to it.[48]

At the same time, enthusiastic support for the project permeated the KDRA-sponsored Victory Dinner to celebrate the receipt of $500,000 in construction funds. The dinner honored the men who had led the eight-year-long drive, and special tribute was paid to Fred G. Fellows, consulting engineer, who had first called attention to the possibility of a large dam and reservoir. The guest speaker was Tulsa district engineer Rebh, who predicted that in time the Kaw Reservoir would attract "two million" visitors each year. To cement the cordial relations, Rebh and his wife were made honorary chief and princess of the Poncas.[49]

Despite strong opposition to the refuge, the Corps of Engineers announced that it was still considering "all elements" in its planning to secure "maximum benefits from the project lands." So heavy was the mail pouring into Monroney's office that he insisted that a public hearing be held before a decision was announced. As Monroney understood the matter, funds were not available for the creation of a wildlife refuge, thereby necessitating a congressional appropriation. His sympathies, in accord with other members of the Oklahoma delegation, were hostile to the refuge. Therefore, he was surprised to learn that after hearing a full explanation, audiences were withdrawing their opposition. The Oklahoma Department of Wildlife Conservation promised to furnish him with the names of the ninety thousand individuals who favored the refuge. In Kay County, the only people who consistently endorsed it were in Tonkawa, the community furthest from the project, and where the Kiwanis Club and the Izaak Walton League played a leading role.[50]

Spokespersons from the Bureau of Sport Fisheries and Wildlife, part of the Fish and Wildlife Service, worked hard to get their message across to audiences throughout the county early in 1966. They met with some success among groups previously opposed. After discussing both sides of the issue, the Ponca City Chamber of Commerce went into executive session to consider a motion by a prominent business leader who had spoken extensively against the refuge. Nevertheless, the group declined to oppose it. So too did farmers and other landowners who learned that they could grow crops under agricultural allotment with bureau management. Land owners were surprised to learn that they would have preference in grazing and sharecropping leases under bureau direction. Now prominent members of KDRA spoke in favor of the proposal. However, the naysayers still insisted that the area would be fenced and restricted, precluding cabins, boat ramps, docks, and other structures connected with recreation.[51]

Ignored during the refuge controversy was the plight of Kaw City. Its continued existence, the mayor reflected, could depend on the interest of outside investors. Most residents wanted to move the town and had already approved a site on the ridge of hills three miles northwest of the present boundaries. While people from many communities had inquired about lots, the mayor said the people of Kaw City would have to decide on a specific course of action.

A major blow to the community had occurred several months previously, when Kaw City's First National Bank had moved to Ponca City and opened for business with a new name. Departure of the city's main financial institution was the most recent example of the way in which the impending dam and reservoir was curbing progress in a once prosperous and lively community. Early in 1966 there were only ten functioning business establishments. Brick buildings along Main Street were vacant and deteriorating. The Santa Fe depot was already dilapidated, servicing one freight train daily, and the railroad indicated that it might not relocate. Spot appraisals of property were under way, but the main appraisal of residential properties would occur early in 1967, at which time the mayor expected the city to have a contract with engineers for municipally owned property.

The former Clubb Hotel, once the area's showplace but now functioning as a rest home, would have to be razed before the Kaw Dam backed up forty feet of water over the surface of Main Street. While most Kay County residents anticipated the project's launching, with or without the refuge, with excitement, Kaw City residents awaited the outcome with feelings of despair. Many, including Mayor J. H. Humphrey, believed that outside money was the only hope.[52]

Another potential loser was the farmer who did not want to be forced to sell land for the refuge, even though he would be allowed to plant in designated areas under careful supervision. With farmland making a good return and with mounting opposition to federal purchase of farmlands, farmers in the vicinity generally opposed the refuge. The Oklahoma Farmers' Union entered the fray in their support. The controversy headed toward resolution at a public meeting scheduled by District Engineer Rebh for March 31 in Kaw City. At this meeting, land requirements, acquisition procedures, and other matters, including the refuge, would be discussed. Rebh made it clear that the Corps would not purchase more land than absolutely necessary.[53]

Days before the meeting, Regional Director Gatlin of the Bureau of Sports Fisheries and Wildlife announced that his agency was postponing immediate establishment of the Kaw National Wildlife Refuge. Convinced of the ultimate local benefits from the proposed refuge, the director recognized that "questions have arisen regarding the effect that the refuge might have on possible commercial development and other private opportunities." Thus ended a controversy that disappointed supporters of the refuge but pleased most of the landowners and local villagers, especially those who might profit "from the various beer and bait joints" envisioned in or near the proposed preserve (and provide the clutter that spoiled many lakes in Oklahoma).[54]

With the matter of the refuge now resolved, the overflow crowd of nine hundred who filed into the Kaw City High School gymnasium on March 31 learned that residents would have to start evacuating their town by late 1967. Colonel Rebh informed the audience that land purchases were already being made in the dam and reservoir area and that funds already received meant that ground breaking for roads and project buildings soon would be scheduled. June 1972 was cited as the target date for completion of the reservoir. Several days after this meeting, Kaw City residents learned that a federal grant had been prepared for a comprehensive plan to move their city to higher ground.[55]

May 21, 1966, would be a great day: ground would be broken for the Kaw Dam and Reservoir. The day was deemed so important that its sponsors, KDRA, invited President Lyndon B. Johnson to attend the ceremony. They had to settle for Chief Francis Pipestem of the Otoe-Missouria tribe, who delivered the invocation. An estimated fifteen hundred persons witnessed the ceremonies and heard Brigadier General Richard Free, Southwest Division engineer, proclaim that "the Kaw project has come about, not just as a result of technical studies by engineers, but through the strong, persistent effort of local people who visualized the project as catalyst to the economic growth of this area." As master of ceremonies, Representative Ed Edmondson praised the project as a tribute to Senator Robert S. Kerr. Also on hand were members of the congressional delegation, Governor Henry Bellmon, and leading citizens of Ponca City who had been involved since 1957 in planning for the project. Most business establishments in Ponca City closed their doors so that merchants and employees could attend the ceremonies.[56]

Those present learned about the dimensions of the project that was about to get under way. The Kaw Dam site would be located 654 river miles above the mouth of the Arkansas River and about seven miles east of Ponca City on the Kay County-Osage County line. At the top of the flood control pool, at elevation 1,004.5 feet, the reservoir would extend upstream to the vicinity of Arkansas City, Kansas. The project would be utilized for flood control and would stand ready to supply the area's anticipated population and industrial growth with its water needs and recreational opportunities. The size of the lake at the flood control pool would encompass 38,000 acres.[57]

Residents of Kaw City, recognizing that their community would be inundated before 1967 was out, became increasingly apprehensive. City officials complained that the Corps of Engineers, while cooperative, was not providing adequate information about relocation planning, and residents worried that their homes would not bring enough to replace them. Information received by city officials and residents was not entirely satisfactory. While the government would buy all land within the existing city limits, it would not purchase the land for the new town site, claiming that so doing would constitute double payment. The purchase price of private properties would be negotiated with each owner, while municipally owned real estate would be included in the relocation contract between the government and Kaw City. In addition, the government would pay for the grading necessary in relocating these facilities, including sidewalks, streets, and gas, sewer, and water lines. But such services would not be offered to properties to be developed as business or residential areas. The government, of course, was embodied in the U.S. Army Corps of Engineers. Among other things, it could not pay more than fair market value to homeowners, a sum that would not enable them to relocate without going into debt. However, residents learned that the Farmers Home Administration could possibly provide them with loans that might help ease their plight.[58]

Most of the public's attention focused on dam construction and securing continuous appropriations for the project, despite the rising demands of the war in Vietnam and the heavy commitment to domestic programs. The Oklahoma congressional delegation worked assiduously to avoid budget slashes. Despite this concern, army engineers considered including a hydroelectric power plant in the Kaw Dam. Adding power would push the cost of the project from an estimated $86.6 million to almost $100 million. Local interest was manifest in the placement of roads and bridges in and around the area adjacent to Kaw City. The location of one or more bridges across the reservoir concerned residents, who might have to travel roundabout routes to reach recreational sites, as it did farmers, who would need to haul grain out of the area to grain elevators. In 1967 three bridges across the Arkansas River were serving the needs of northern Oklahoma. The Corps of Engineers planned to build only two bridges across the Kaw Reservoir, insisting that "three multi-million dollar bridges so close together, each of them serving east-west traffic, is not justified." Bridges quickly became a topic of debate. But satisfaction was evident throughout the county in June when a brief ceremony celebrated the completion of the first major contract on the Kaw project.[59]

By midsummer 1967 Kaw City residents had to resolve another problem. The site of the new town, selected several years earlier, involved excessive costs in securing the tract. A new site had to be chosen, so that it could be "entered, surveyed, appraised and clear title ascertained" before the Corps of Engineers would provide funds to develop the property. Kaw City officials claimed they were unable to find a suitable site because they could not convince an owner to sign "any form of agreement" until he received the money. Moreover, to get a site they would need a "condemnation proceeding," the cost of which would likely be prohibitive. The Federal Housing Administration, which wanted to help, was barred from providing a loan unless title to the site could be obtained at the same time the loan was made so that the land could be mortgaged to FHA. Officials of Kaw City quickly agreed on a new site, and the Corps of Engineers began preparing a "design memorandum" for it. Until the plan was completed, the site could not be approved. And because Kaw City was in the first stage of land acquisitions now scheduled for 1968, a sense of urgency permeated the proceedings. To make their case as effectively as possible, residents created the Kaw City Corporation to apply for a guaranteed loan from the Federal Housing Administration. All of the people involved in relocating the town were of the opinion that the federal government had "some degree of obligation" other than the Corps' responsibility to provide utilities and streets at the new location.[60]

At year's end, as a headline in the *Tulsa Tribune* announced, Kaw City was a "Town Awaiting Date with Death." Appraisers roamed the town seeking to purchase homes and property. One resident ran the appraiser out of his home, complaining that "you can't even move out of this place for the price they are offering." While property was being appraised and purchased, the town still did not have the land for relocation. Mayor Humphrey acknowledged that "we have an option, but we're working against a January 15 [1968] deadline to raise the balance of the money—$62,000." The town had already paid $12,000 down on the 160-acre tract that people hoped to occupy. Previously, in July 1964, residents had signed a petition stating that they wished "to stay with our friends and family and not be forced to make new homes among strangers." Containing 242 signatures, it had been forwarded to the Corps of Engineers. The Corps now requested a new petition to ascertain how many individuals still wished to relocate. As of December 21, 1967, 250 had signed.[61]

But Kaw City, the mayor, and the residents had not received much help. If the government, Mayor Humphrey complained, could take their homes and their lands, "that same Government should be able to give us a loan to take care of our people." Now the mayor sought private financing. An investor would purchase the site for the new town. The citizens would then authorize the city to assume the mortgage. The land, which would be bought for $500 an acre, could then be divided into three lots per acre, about three hundred lots in all. The lots would then be sold to Kaw City residents for the price it cost the city to develop them, and those not purchased would be available to outsiders. All of this had to be accomplished before April 1968, when the Corps of Engineers was scheduled to sign a contact purchasing all municipal property in Kaw City. Grading on the new site would then get under way. The new town, Humphrey proclaimed, would be better than the old one. Already, outside people were "coming in looking for lots, especially lakefront lots." Not all the people in Kaw City were as optimistic as their mayor about the promised resurrection of their community. They were uncertain about their futures and sad about the fate of the place in which they had lived a good portion of their lives.[62]

By mid-February more than 50 percent of the townspeople had been bought out by the Corps of Engineers and were anxious to get settled in the new location. The town had indebted itself in excess of $80,000 for the new town site. Once the plat was filed, residents would have their choice of lots in the new Kaw City. The community's application for public housing there, however, had been delayed. The mayor hoped "to get the public housing project coordinated on a time schedule with the Corps of Engineers relocation design memorandum" and asked Representative Belcher to look into the matter.[63]

For its part, the Corps of Engineers planned on beginning "firm contract negotiations" with Kaw City officials in April. Within sixty days after an agreement was reached, "preparation of plans and specifications could be completed by early Fall 1968," with construction started the following January. In a last hurrah for the old town, former and remaining residents planned to join for a reunion early in June at the high school from which many of them had graduated. About two thousand were expected to attend. If further reunions were to occur, participants would have to wait until 1970 for the completion of the new site, on higher ground about one mile west of their soon-to-be inundated hometown.[64]

At this juncture Dave Morgan, a Ponca City philanthropist, came to Kaw City's rescue after the federal agencies found themselves unable to be of assistance. He paid $500 an acre for the 160-acre site and then deeded it to the town. Reimbursement would come from the proceeds of the sale of lots in the new Kaw City. An additional piece of good news came when the Corps in Tulsa announced that Kaw Citians would be allowed to remain in the old town until the new town site was ready and that they would get two weeks' exclusive choice before the lots went on sale to the public. Lots would cost between $450 and $700. By the end of May a hopeful spirit pervaded Kaw City that the community would bounce back.[65]

If hope was on the rise in Kaw City, exuberance prevailed among the four thousand members of KDRA on Saturday, June 22, 1968, at the ground breaking. U.S. Senator Mike Monroney boarded a huge earth-moving machine to launch "Operation Bulldozer" and to begin the mammoth construction project. Dignitaries on hand harangued the crowd, most of whom had driven to the site in a 112-car caravan from Ponca City. A similar ceremony at the same site two years earlier had marked the actual ground breaking. On this occasion, 1968 being an election year, Monroney in his remarks took note of a telegram from President Johnson. Of greater interest to the large crowd was the information, conveyed by one of the speakers, that the initial project could be completed in fewer than two and a half years.[66]

Equally promising was the progress being made to provide for the addition of power-generating facilities. Secretary of the Army Stanley Resor approved, and Fred Harris introduced, a bill to so modify the project. It was referred to the Public Works Committee, where Kerr had once been the most influential member and where Harris now served. But this was as far as the proposal went. Also stalled was the effort of Kaw City mayor Martin Branch to secure public housing funds to assist families being displaced "because of a mammoth Government project." It would seem, the mayor asserted, "that the citizens of our community should be given the same attention as the city people."[67]

Delayed too was the start of construction work. It could not get under way until municipal facilities were relocated at new Kaw City. A federal contract with Kaw City was awarded at the end of January 1969. But before moving could occur, the water, gas, and sewer systems, as well as streets, had to be laid out. Plans and specifications were developed, and prospective bidders would compete. Construction of the systems was expected to start later in the year. Some owners were still holding out, but their claims for replacement costs, as previous residents learned, could not be met by the Corps of Engineers.[68]

By August 1969 most of these pressing issues had been resolved. The last of the residential lots in the new town site had been sold, utility installation was completed, and street construction was being readied. A temporary water system would be provided by the Corps of Engineers, with a more permanent one to be established later. The removal process merited a headline in the *Sunday Oklahoman:* "Rebirth of Dying Kaw

City Underway on New Site." The new town site, it was expected, would be ready for occupancy in six to eight months. When completed, it would be on a peninsula extending into the Kaw Reservoir.[69]

If the people of Kaw City were pleased, though far from satisfied, that the ordeal of relocation was being concluded, the five thousand members of the Kaw Dam and Reservoir Development Association, as well as most people in Kay County, parts of Osage County, and southern Kansas, were exuberant. In October the House Appropriations Committee allocated $6,850,000 for constructing the project, and several months later President Richard M. Nixon recommended that Congress allocate it $11.1 million. Funding would enable the Corps to start the spillway, purchase necessary lands along the river, realign highways, and complete the relocation of Kaw City. In addition, all the storage water in the Kaw Reservoir, still under construction, had been apportioned based on population and use over a period of one hundred years. The target date for starting the impoundment of Arkansas River water, originally programmed for 1972, was moved forward to 1975. Inflation had boosted the initial cost estimate of the project from $83 million up to a 1970 estimate of $103 million.[70]

In October 1970 President Nixon signed the Public Works Appropriation Bill, which included the $11.1 million that he had requested for the Kaw Reservoir. Advertising for bids on the remaining construction, the concrete spillway, and the earthen dam could get under way once design plans were resolved. Completion of the reservoir with final closure and start of impoundment was forecast for June 1975. Whether or not this forecast proved valid would depend upon the Corps's acquisition "of the approximately 1,800 tracts needed for Kaw Lake." By late 1970, 607 tracts had been secured, 528 by purchase and 79 by condemnation proceedings; the Corps also acquired easements, over 15 by purchase and 5 by condemnation.[71]

On June 5, 1971, the president dedicated the Arkansas River Navigation System before a jubilant crowd gathered at the Port of Catoosa, at the head of the 448-mile-long waterway. The Kaw Project, about 21 percent completed at this time, would take its place as a unit helping coordinate flood control within the Arkansas River basin, as well as serving as vital storage for water needed periodically for successful operation of the

McClellan-Kerr Arkansas River Navigation System. The opening of the waterway, plus the onset of drought, prompted the leadership of the Kaw Lake Association, formerly KDRA, to intensify their efforts in urging Appropriations to secure maximum funding for the project.[72]

With construction well under way, steps were taken to save the old stone tribal council house of the Kaw Indian Agency from inundation. Residents of Arkansas City, Kansas, wanted to remove it stone by stone and transfer it to the grounds of the Cherokee Strip Living Museum in their community. A state historical marker was also being planned in commemoration of the former Kaw capital, located in the Washunga community that would be flooded. The plight of the Indians received almost no public attention, most of which was focused on its southerly neighbor Kaw City, which would soon join the list of Oklahoma ghost towns.[73]

In new Kaw City at the end of 1971, thirty-two of the fifty-three homes were already connected to utilities. Some municipal buildings were in place, and several commercial enterprises were open for business. Most residents were among the estimated four thousand people crowded among the downtown ruins of old Kaw City for a last homecoming and reunion, including a parade. Before the celebration, the City Council officially turned the town over to the U.S. Army Corps of Engineers. The day-long observance was climaxed with a street dance in new Kaw City. To reverse the words of the poet T. S. Eliot, old Kaw City ended with a bang and not a whimper. Meanwhile, not too far away, concrete was being poured for a portion of the dam.[74]

Another task the Corps had to consider was road relocations for Kaw Lake, a process worked out with Kay County officials. A county road extending across the Arkansas River was on a school bus route. Since officials considered use of the bridge hazardous, the Corps awarded a construction contract for repair. The bridge was expected to be operational at the onset of the new school year. The Corps also arranged for the dead to be disinterred at the Kaw Indian tribal cemetery and moved to a new burying ground near Newkirk.[75]

As already noted, residents of Kaw City were far from satisfied with the sums they had to accept when the Corps of Engineers acquired their property. Under the terms of the Uniform Relocations Assistance and Real Property Acquisition Policies Act of 1970, many residents applied for, and hoped to receive, financial aid. The Corps interpreted the law "as meaning that the applicant whose property was acquired before January 2, 1971, but who did not vacate the property until after that date, was eligible for benefits under the Act." While the law and the official interpretation assisted many residents, others complained that because they had sold their properties and relocated prior to January 2, 1971, they had not received any payment. The law was not retroactive. Residents whose property was acquired after January 2, 1971, were receiving sums considerably in excess of the funding provided people who relocated before the designated date. To remedy this situation, Representative John N. "Happy" Camp introduced a measure that would provide payment to all persons relocated from Kaw City, a process that had begun in 1966. While legislation was enacted, the Corps requested a ruling from the comptroller general that suggested a broader interpretation of the 1970 law. It provided benefits to homeowners whose property was acquired before the effective date of the act, although "substantially less than those persons whose property was acquired subsequent to that time" in most instances.[76]

While these matters were being concluded, construction of the Kaw Project approached completion. The Corps announced that while it always responded to the nation's changing needs for the various benefits of water resources development, it was also sensitive to the American public's growing concern with environmental quality. Manifesting that interest, the Ponca City Chamber of Commerce wanted to know if the Corps of Engineers planned to locate a marina on Kaw Lake near Ponca City and, if so, who would own and operate it. In addition, chamber members inquired whether federal funding was available for building a lodge comparable to state lodges on other Oklahoma lakes.[77]

At this time, in the spring of 1973, the Kaw Dam was half finished. Workmen were installing structural steel for a power plant in the project, now estimated to cost $116 million. The first water was expected to start backing up in 1975 and to raise a pool fifty-five feet deep. Meanwhile, the matter of county roads providing access to the public areas of the soon-to-be-completed Kaw Reservoir was a matter of increasing urgency, as county commissioners anticipated being unable to maintain these roads with increased traffic going to the lake. The county hoped the Corps of Engineers would assist. Some needed to be widened, and culverts and bridges provided. Traffic connected with the project already accentuated the problem, which would become acute when the public gained access.[78]

The public, particularly the Kaw Lake Association, was disturbed to learn that appropriations for some of the public-use areas had been cut back. If the Kaw Lake Association members and others were disturbed, those who grazed cattle in unauthorized areas of the project were equally distressed to learn that unless the cattle were removed within two weeks, the owners would be issued citations. Cattle, the district engineer asserted, damaged work areas, including road grading projects, resulting in liability to the government.[79]

When the cattle were removed and concern for public-use areas was expressed, the Kaw Project was 82 percent complete. Although a power station was being constructed as part of the dam, a Congressional appropriation would be needed to install production facilities. More significant was the fact that Kaw Lake would provide about 920,000 acre-feet of flood control storage to the Arkansas River system and serve as the major water supply for communities throughout north-central Oklahoma, along with Arkansas City, Kansas. As the new year, 1976, the nation's bicentennial, got under way, work on the Kaw Dam was winding down. Engineers said they needed to plug two temporary sluices in the concrete spillway. Thereafter impoundment would begin. Clearing the lake area was virtually complete, while the public-use areas were expected to be open before the onset of spring. Almost all the road relocations were completed, and construction of municipal water-supply facilities for the new Kaw City were nearly finished. Yet to be constructed was the road across the dam.[80]

The project, authorized by the Flood Control Act of 1962, had been proposed almost a decade earlier. Construction started in June 1966, and the project was placed in useful operation in May 1976. The earth-fill dam is 9,466 feet long, including the spillway, with a crest height of 121 feet above the original stream bed. Kaw Lake, covering an area of 38,000 acres, controlled the runoff from a drainage area of about 7,250 square miles and would provide flood protection for roughly 39,000 acres of agricultural and urban land. The lake and the government-owned lands around it were developed and managed for public use. Six public-use areas were available when the project became operative; five more were being completed. All would include boat ramps, picnic tables, campsites, motorcycle trails, water supply, and sanitary facilities. Concerned about the environment, the Corps assured visitors that the clearing within the public-use areas would be held to a necessary minimum to provide pleasant, usable space. All desirable vegetation would remain in the natural state, and a program of reforestation and turfing would be maintained throughout the life of the project. Its estimated cost at this time was $111.1 million.[81]

Yet to be resolved was the matter of generating electricity, and the power station to be constructed as part of the Kaw Dam. Before a final decision would be reached, though, the Corps wanted to institute a "marketability study" in the summer after the ceremonies marking completion of the project.[82]

On May 21, 1976, a huge "get-acquainted" party honored people who, in one way or another, had participated in the development of the dam. Dedication ceremonies the following day began with a morning parade featuring Senator, formerly Governor, Henry Bellmon, the parade marshal. On the speakers' platform, among the numerous dignitaries only one, Commissioner of Charities and Corrections Jim Cook, was a Democrat. As Kay County voted overwhelmingly Republican, and as Kerr had been instrumental in launching the project, and as both Monroney and Harris were unflinching in their support in the Senate, as was Speaker of the House of Representatives Carl Albert, Cook requested that Albert send greetings and regrets that he could not be present. Cook intended to read the Speaker's message before the distinguished guests began their orations.[83]

To complete the project, in July 1976 President Gerald R. Ford signed the bill appropriating funds. The legislation included items for rural road relocation and recreation development. With no resolution on the generation of hydroelectric power, the issue quickly disappeared from public view. Also disappearing was the request of the Kaw Indians in 1977 for approximately a thousand acres of public land for a marina and recreational park, a proposal considered excess to project requirements.[84]

With Kaw Lake now in operation, the long battle of KDRA, the current Kaw Lake Association, to secure federal funds of $111.1 million in total, to promote the welfare of their business interests came to a successful conclusion. The project welcomed 1,657,000 visitors in 1979, and the dam assuredly fulfilled part of Senator Kerr's broader vision of utilizing water resources for developing, maintaining, and promoting prosperity in Oklahoma. And on July 4, 1977, even some of the opponents found reason to celebrate. About three thousand people crowded into the new Kaw City to celebrate Independence Day, as well as the seventy-fifth anniversary of the founding of the original town. In addition, several thousand more spent the holiday on the nearby shores of Kaw Lake. There was a parade through the downtown area, followed by the presentation of a golden shovel that had been used eleven years earlier by Chief Francis Pipestem in the official ground breaking for the Kaw Dam. The shovel was presented to the Kaw City Museum, housed in the Santa Fe depot, which had been moved from the old town site, already under forty feet of water.[85]

Notes

1. *Oklahoma: A Guide to the Sooner State* (Norman: University of Oklahoma Press, 1941), 355; *Report of Chief of Engineers, U.S. Army, 1957* (Washington, D.C.: GPO, 1957), 2: 871. In a 1957 revision of *Oklahoma: A Guide to the Sooner State*, edited by Kent Ruth, Kaw City's population is listed at 561 and the art collection of more than 200 paintings had already been moved to the Philbrook Museum in Tulsa (pp. 418–19).

2. Untitled booklet on the Kaw Reservoir, prepared for the Kaw Tribe by McCaleb, Nussbaum Thomas, QME Inc., July 1976, 3, Dewey Bartlett Collection, Box 34, Folder 10, Carl Albert Congressional Research and Studies Center Congressional Archive at the University of Oklahoma. Hereafter, unless otherwise noted, all cited manuscript collections are housed in the Carl Albert Center.

3. For my discussion of the role of Robert S. Kerr, I have relied on Anne Hodges Morgan, *Robert S. Kerr: The Senate Years* (Norman: University of Oklahoma Press, 1977), a penetrating study of Kerr's senate career, and John Robert Ferrell, "Water Resource Development in the Arkansas Valley: A History of Public Policy to 1950" (PhD diss., University of Oklahoma, 1968), which offers

incisive insights into Kerr's role. See also an article by Walker in the *Lawton Constitution*, November 2, 1958. The article originally appeared in the *Dallas News.*

4. Robert S. Kerr to David Ross, January 27, 1956, Robert S. Kerr Collection, Departmental Series, Box 5, Folder 36.

5. L. A. Needham to Kerr, March 12, 1957, and Kerr to General E. C. Itschner, March 12, 1957, both in Kerr Collection, Conservation Series, Box 3, Folder 11.

6. Mrs. R. E. Brook to Page Belcher, March 21, 1957, Page H. Belcher Collection, Box 28, Folder 15d; General J. L. Person to Kerr, April 19, 1957, Kerr Collection, Conservation Series, Box 3, Folder 11; Kerr to Fred G. Fellows, April 23, 1957, Kerr Collection, Conservation Series, Box 3, Folder 4.

7. *Ponca City* (Okla.) *News*, May 19, 1957; Lawrence Cannon to Kerr, June 5, 1957 (telegram), and Kerr to Cannon, June 12, 1957, both in Kerr Collection, Conservation Series, Box 3, Folder 11. Cannon was president of the Kaw Reservoir Development Association.

8. *Oklahoma's ORBIT* [magazine], *Sunday Oklahoman* (Oklahoma City), August 25, 1957, 5; *Ponca City News*, September 17, 1957. In the latter article, Representative Belcher advised boosters that a long battle was expected "if we are going to get more water storage, the place to get it is here."

9. For examples of the promotional work, see Cannon to Colonel John Bristor, District Engineer, September 20, 1957, Kerr Collection, Conservation Series, Box 3, Folder 11; Cannon to Belcher, February 28, 1958, Belcher Collection, Box 184, Folder 2; Statement on Proposed Dam and Reservoir to the Public Works Subcommittees on Appropriations, n.d. [1958], Kerr Collection, Conservation Series, Box 3, Folder 11; Belcher to Gerald Nield, May 9, 1958, Belcher Collection, Box 184, Folder 3.

10. *Newkirk* (Okla.) *Herald Journal*, May 16, 1958; Dean Hoye to Tom Steed, May 16, 1958, Tom Steed Collection, General Series, Box 11, Folder 7. Hoye was vice president of Newkirk Trust Company. Perry Whiting to Kerr, May 17, 1958, Kerr Collection, Conservation Series, Box 3, Folder 11. Whiting owned a furniture company in Ponca City.

11. Kerr to Cannon, June 17, 1958, and Don Wright to Kerr, August 26, 1958, both in Kerr Collection, Conservation Series, Box 3, Folder 11.

12. See for example Resolution No. 1834 [April 20, 1959] by the Ponca City Board of Commissioners [copy], Toby Morris Collection, Topical Series, Box 2, Folder 10; Continental Oil Company letter to their employees March 25, 1959 [copy], Belcher Collection, Box 184, Folder 4; Bristor to Carl Albert, March 26, 1959, Carl Albert Collection, Departmental Files, Box 32, Folder 33; Cannon to Belcher, April 7, 1959, Belcher Collection, Box 184, Folder 4. In addition, the *Ponca City News* every Sunday in March ran full-page campaign spreads to solicit support for the project.

13. *Ponca City News*, April 15, 1959.

14. See *Ponca City News*, April 20, 1959, for both the broadside and a story on the Anti–Kaw Dam Group.

15. Vice president, Continental Oil Company to Bristor, April 23, 1959 [copy], Belcher Collection, Box 184, Folder 6. The copy in Belcher's files was not signed. For a similar letter from the manager of the Cities Service Refinery in Ponca City to the Director of the Bureau of the Budget, see H. W. Targeson to Charles Warner, September 24, 1960 [copy], Belcher Collection, Box 184, Folder 6.

16. For the April 24 public meeting see "General Information" [copy], Albert Collection, General Files, Box 14, Folder 54; Statement of Senator Robert S. Kerr, April 24, 1959, Kerr Collection, Conservation Series, Box 3, Folder 12.

17. Kerr to Mr. and Mrs. Charles, May 4, 1959, Kerr Collection, Conservation Series, Box 3, Folder 12. See *Reclamation News*, September 1959, for stories about overriding a presidential veto and Kerr's becoming chair of the Senate Select Committee on Water Resources. See *Tulsa Tribune*, October 17, 1959, for a story about Kerr's promoting numerous state water and military projects. For additional stories about Kerr's promotion of Oklahoma water projects, see Kerr Collection, Clipping Series, Box 1, Folder 46.

18. Floyd Amsden to Toby Morris, May 13, 1960, Morris Collection, Topical Series, Box 2, Folder 10; Don Andrews to U.S. Corps of Engineers, May 19, 1960, Albert Collection, General Files, Box 17, Folder 5; Colonel Howard Penney to Dale Shackleford, July 14, 1960, and F. Q. Jennings to Charles Warner, September 28, 1960, both in Belcher Collection, Box 184, Folder 6. Amsden was president of the Wichita Chamber of Commerce. Andrews was the president of the Newkirk Chamber of Commerce. Jennings was the mayor of Ponca City, and Warner was the director of the Bureau of the Budget.

19. Carl Cramton to Kerr, November 18, 1960, and Penney to Kerr, December 2, 1960, both in Kerr Collection, Conservation Series, Box 3, Folder 12. For the vote in Kay County see Richard Scammon et al., *America Votes*, vol. 4 (Pittsburgh: University of Pittsburgh Press, 1960), 333.

20. Telegram to Hon. J. F. Kennedy [n.d., March 6, 1961?, copy], Belcher Collection, Box 184, Folder 7. See also *Public Papers of the Presidents of the United States: John F. Kennedy, 1961–1963*, 3 vols. (Washington, D.C.: GPO, 1962–63), 1:114–21, for the special message on Natural Resources.

21. *Ponca City News*, May 8, 1961.

22. *Daily Oklahoman* (Oklahoma City), May 14, 1961.

23. *Ponca City News*, May 25, 1961.

24. Major General William F. Cassidy to Belcher, July 26, 1961, and Penney to Belcher, September 1, 1961, both in Belcher Collection, Box 184, Folder 7.

25. *Newkirk* (Okla.) *Herald-Journal*, October 5, 1961; *Shidler* (Okla.) *Review*, October 12, 1961; *Fairfax* (Okla.) *Chief*, [n.d.], *Osage* (Okla.) *Journal*, October 13, 1961. All are available in Kerr Collection, Clipping Series, Box 1, Folder 36.

26. Dale Orr to Belcher, October 24, 1961, Belcher Collection, Box 55, Folder 16C; Belcher to Jerome Peterson, September 12, 1961, Belcher Collection, Box 184, Folder 7; "Notice of Joint Public Hearing," November 1, 1961 [copy], Belcher Collection, Box 55, Folder 16C; Penney to Albert, November 6, 1961, Albert Collection, Projects Files, Box 10, Folder 10.

27. "Notice of Survey Report on Kaw Reservoir . . . ," December 12, 1961, Albert Collection, Departmental Series, Box 37, Folder 54.

28. William M. Kasl to Belcher, December 30, 1961, Belcher Collection, Box 183, Folder 33; Resolution by Tonkawa and Ponca City chapters, Izaak Walton League, Belcher Collection, Box 183, Folder 31.

29. Resolution, January 16, 1962, Kaw Dam and Reservoir Development Association, Inc. [copy], Kerr Collection, Conservation Series, Box 3, Folder 13; *Ponca City News*, January 12, 1962; Belcher to John Gardner, January 16, 1962, Belcher Collection, Box 183, Folder 33. In this letter to the mayor of Newkirk, Belcher said he had discussed the matter with Kerr "and, upon investigation, we find that the justification for the project does not require the Fish and Wildlife Refuge."

30. Kerr to Wendyl Watts, February 16, 1962, Kerr Collection, Conservation Series, Box 3, Folder 13; John Warren to Belcher, Box 183, Folder 32. See also Mrs. C. E. Doyle to Albert, February 20, 1962, Albert Collection, Projects File, Box 10, Folder 10. Mrs. Doyle was president of Oklahoma Gardens and Clubs, Inc. More of Albert's correspondents favored the refuge than opposed it.

31. *Ponca City News*, February 28, 1962; *Daily Oklahoman*, February 28, 1962; General W. K. Wilson, Jr., Chief of Engineers, to the Secretary of the Army [March 1962, copy], Belcher Collection, Box 184, Folder 8; *Shawnee News-Star*, September 14, 1962.

32. *Tonkawa* (Okla.) *News*, [n.d. (March 1962)], Kerr Collection, Clipping Series, Box 1, Folder 36; Kerr to Brown, March 5, 1962, Perry Whiting to Kerr, March 10, 1962, and Dennis Impson to Kerr, March 10, 1962, all in Kerr Collection, Conservation Series, Box 3, Folder 14; *Daily Oklahoman*, March 6, 1962.

33. Frank Kunc to Albert, March 9, 1962, Albert Collection, Projects Files, Box 10, Series, Box 3, Folder 14. Kunc was vice president of the Mid-Continental News Company in Oklahoma City; Sushnik was a retired accountant living in Bartlesville. See *Daily Oklahoman*, March 16, 1962, for a story titled "Refuge Battle Line Drawn" (p. 10).

34. Ray Hamilton to Belcher, March 20, 1962, Belcher Collection, Box 183, Folder 32. Hamilton, a teacher at the junior college in Tonkawa, was also an officer in the Oklahoma Division of the Izaak Walton League.

35. McBride to Dean Hoye, May 23, 1962, and Fred G. Fellows to Chairman of Public Works Committee (with copy of report), June 11, 1962, both in Kerr Collection, Conservation Series, Box 3, Folder 14. In addition, Fellows informed McBride that statements from many people would be submitted to the chairs of the Public Works Committees in both houses of Congress.

36. J. Howard Edmondson to Major General Keith Barney, June 18, 1962, and Kenneth Holm to Lieutenant General Walker Wilson, Jr., June 26, 1962, both in Kerr Collection, Conservation Series, Box 3, Folder 14.

37. *Bartlesville* (Okla.) *Examiner Enterprise*, August 30, 1962; Wilson to Orville Freeman, September 13, 1962, 87 Cong., 2d Sess., S. Doc. 143, xix; John Gardner to Kerr, September 14, 1962, Kerr Collection, Conservation Series, Box 3, Folder 14; *Daily Oklahoman*, October 22, 1962. Incidentally, Lieutenant General Wilson had to satisfy the secretary of agriculture that a minimum of agricultural land would be permanently flooded.

38. *Daily Oklahoman*, March 6, 1963; *Ponca City News*, May 26, 1963.

39. Clarence Pantzke to Belcher, August 1, 1963, Belcher Collection, Box 77, Folder 21; Belcher to Thomas Lamb, November 12, 1964, Belcher Collection, Box 77, Folder 21; *Sunday Oklahoman*, November 17, 1963; *Daily Oklahoman*, March 4, 1964. Pantzke was a commissioner in the U.S. Fish and Wildlife Service.

40. *Oklahoma's ORBIT* [magazine], *Sunday Oklahoman*, January 10, 1965, 12; Herman J. Smith to McBride and Monroney, January 28, 1965, A. S. Mike Monroney Collection, Box 76, Folder 27; Belcher to LaVera Sheeks, March 12, 1965, Belcher Collection, Box 184, Folder 10; Harper Baughman to Albert, March 15, 1965, and John Gardner to Albert, March 15, 1965, both in Albert Collection, Projects File, Box 10, Folder 10; L. Enloe Baumert to Fred Harris, March 22, 1965, Harris Collection, Box 25, Folder 21. Baughman was president of the Kaw Dam and Reservoir Development Association.

41. Statement of Page Belcher, May 17, 1965, and Belcher to Harper Baughman, October 18, 1965, both in Belcher Collection, Box 184, Folder 11; Statement of Fred Harris, May 17 and 18, 1965, Charles Duffy to Harris, July 6, 1965, and Baumert to Harris, August 27, 1965, all in Harris Collection, Box 15, Folder 25.

42. *Daily Oklahoman*, September 9, 1965, p. 12; *Sunday Oklahoman*, September 12, 1965.

43. John G. Gatlin to Monroney, November 1, 1965, Monroney Collection, Box 60, Folder 9; H. O. Crowley to District Engineer, December 9, 1965 [copy], Monroney Collection, Box 76, Folder 27; Information, For Release, November 4, 1965, and "Proposed National Wildlife Refuge: November 18, 1965" [copy], both in Harris Collection, Box 26, Folder 6. Gatlin headed the Albuquerque Office of the Fish and Wildlife Service. Crowley was acting regional director of the Fish and Wildlife Service.

44. Monroney to Gatlin, November 8, 1965, Monroney Collection, Box 60, Folder 9; Cannon to McBride, November 9, 1965, Monroney Collection, Box 58, Folder 17.

45. John W. Warren to Monroney, November 9, 1965, Monroney Collection, Box 6, Folder 9; David Ross to Harris, November 12, 1965, Harris Collection, Box 26, Folder 6.

46. Colonel George A. Rebh to Belcher, December 23, 1965, Belcher Collection, Box 133, Folder 34; *Daily Oklahoman*, December 16, 1965.

47. *Ponca City News*, January 2, 1966; Mills Garrison to Harris, January 4, 1966 [copy], Monroney Collection, Box 76, Folder 27.

48. John Warren to Monroney, January 10, 1966, Beaver to Monroney, January 6, 1966, and William Johnson to Monroney, January 10, 1966, all in Monroney Collection, Box 66, Folder 27; Johnson to Belcher, January 12, 1966, and H. Drew Owen to Belcher, January 20, 1966, both in Belcher Collection, Box 183, Folder 36. Beaver was with the Oklahoma Department of Wildlife Conservation. Owen was president of the state wildlife federation.

49. *Ponca City News*, January 10, 1966.

50. Rebh to Belcher, January 19, 1966, Belcher Collection, Box 183, Folder 36; Monroney to John Gardner, January 19, 1966, Jay Wilson to Monroney, January 20, 1966, and Monroney to William Johnson, January 26, 1966, all in Monroney Collection, Box 76, Folder 27. Colonel Rebh was the district engineer. Wilson was secretary of the Kiwanis Club.

51. Gatlin to Belcher, January 31, 1966, Belcher Collection, Box 183, Folder 36; Gatlin to Monroney, February 1, 1966, Monroney Collection, Box 76, Folder 27; *Ponca City News*, February 6, 1966; Duane Palovik to Belcher, February 11, 1966, Belcher Collection, Box 183, Folder 36; Stanley Spencer to Monroney, February 18, 1966, Monroney Collection, Box 76, Folder 27. Gatlin was regional director of the Bureau of Sport Fisheries and Wildlife. Spencer was with the Arkansas City, Kansas, Chamber of Commerce.

52. *Sunday Oklahoman*, February 13, 1966.

53. George Stone to Monroney, March 4, 1966, Monroney Collection, Box 76, Folder 28; Rebh to Monroney, February 11, 1966, Monroney Collection, Box 76, Folder 27.

54. Gatlin to Editor, *Ponca City News*, March 25, 1966 [copy], Harris Collection, Box 85, Folder 6; Harold Jones to Monroney, March 29, 1966, Monroney Collection, Box 76, Folder 28.

55. William H. Robertson, Jr., to Monroney, April 1, 1966, Monroney Collection, Box 76, Folder 28; *Daily Oklahoman*, April 1 and 6, 1966.

56. Ray Eisele to Lyndon Johnson (telegram, 1966, copy), Steed Collection, General Series, Box 100, Folder 17; *Sunday Oklahoman*, May 22, 1966.For Chief Pipestem, see clipping in John N. "Happy" Camp Collection, Box 74, Folder 14a.

57. "Kaw Dam and Reservoir," May 1960, U.S. Army Engineer Corps of Engineers Tulsa District [copy], Camp Collection, Box 74, Folder 14a; "On This Site," U.S. Army Corps of Engineers Tulsa District [copy], Belcher Collection, Box 184, Folder 11.

58. Joe P. Walcott to Belcher, January 26, 1967, Rebh to Belcher, February 6, 1967, and Belcher to Walcott, February 13, 1967, all in Belcher Collection, Box 183, Folder 29.

59. "Army Engineers Studying Power Plant at Kaw Dam," Newspaper clipping, ca. 1967, Belcher Collection, Box 135, Folder 13; Belcher to A. B. Alcott, April 10, 1967, Belcher Collection, Box 184, Folder 11; Fred G. Fellows to F. L. Vogler, May 15, 1967, and Vogler to Harris, May 15, 1967, both in Harris Collection, Box 65, Folder 2; Rebh to Belcher, May 31, 1967, Belcher Collection, Box 184, Folder 11. See *Ponca City News*, May 11, 1967, and *Daily Oklahoman*, June 15, 1967, for stories about dam construction.

60. Conference with officials of the Corps of Engineers, H.U.D., et al., July 25 and July 27, 1967, and J. D. Check to Federal Housing Administration, August 16, 1967, both in Belcher Collection, Box 183, Folder 29. For a further indication of the inability of the government to be of assistance to Kaw City, see F. N. Brownstein to Belcher, January 24, 1968, J. H. Humphrey (mayor of Kaw City) to Belcher, January 4, 1968, and W. B. Breisch to Belcher, January 26, 1968, all in Belcher Collection, Box 183, Folder 29, and Belcher to Breisch, May 3, 1968, Belcher Collection, Box 183, Folder 30.

61. "Kaw City—Time Awaiting Date with Death," *Tulsa Tribune*, December 29, 1967.

62. Ibid.

63. J. H. Humphrey to Belcher, February 15, 1968, Belcher Collection, Box 183, Folder 30.

64. Colonel Harley Ladd to Belcher, March 6, 1968, Belcher Collection, Box 183, Folder 30; Guy McCune to Harris, March 9, 1968, Harris Collection, Box 105, Folder 10. For the final reunion in Kaw City, see *Daily Oklahoman*, May 9, 1968, p. 28, May 10, 1968, p. 11, and June 3, 1968, p.16.

65. "Kaw City Will Live; May Even Have Boom," *Tulsa World*, May 26, 1968.

66. *Daily Oklahoman*, June 23, 1968.

67. *Congressional Record*, 90th Cong., 2d sess., September 12, 1968, 26665; Harris to Colonel Vernon Pinkey, September 16, 1968, Harris Collection, Box 116, Folder 23; R. A. Lindquist to Martin Branch, February 28, 1968, and Branch to Belcher, March 7, 1969, both in Belcher Collection, Box 183, Folder 30.

68. Lieutenant Colonel Edward Fike to Belcher, May 1, 1969, and Pinkey to Belcher, May 13, 1969, both in Belcher Collection, Box 183, Folder 30; Roy Grantham to Camp, July 18, 1969, Camp Collection, Box 74, Folder 14a.

69. *Sunday Oklahoman*, August 3, 1969; *Daily Oklahoman*, January 11, 1970.

70. Herman J. Smith to Albert, October 5, 1969, Albert Collection, Legislative Series, Box 114, Folder 35; Herman J. Smith to Chairman of the Public Works Subcommittee, April 15, 1970, Belcher Collection, Box 184, Folder 12; *Ponca City News*, October 3, 1969, and February 2, 1970; *Daily Oklahoman*, January 11, 1970.

71. *Ponca City News*, October 12, 1970; Woodrow Berge to Belcher, October 28, 1970, Belcher Collection, Box 135, Folder 13.

72. *Report of the Chief of Engineers, U.S. Army, 1971* (Washington, D.C.: GPO, 1971), 2: 19–29; Ellsworth Rains to Chairman of the Public Works Subcommittee, Appropriations Committee, House of Representatives, May 6, 1971 [copy], Belcher Collection, Box 184, Folder 12.

73. *Daily Oklahoman*, March 28, 1971, and August 9, 1971. For a photo of the Kaw Indians' historic council house, soon to be removed and restored so that it could again be used for tribal functions, see *Annual Report: Chief of Engineers on Civil Works Activities, 1975* (Washington, D.C.: GPO, 1975), 1:59.

74. *Ponca City News*, December 29, 1971, and May 5, 1972; *Sunday Oklahoman*, May 14, 1972. A few die-hard residents still remained in old Kaw City. They were notified that all utility services would be cut off at the end of June and the lines removed shortly thereafter. See *Daily Oklahoman*, June 16, 1972, p.11.

75. Colonel William E. Read to Camp, March 10, 1972, Camp Collection, Box 74, Folder 14b; *Daily Oklahoman*, July 17, 1972, p. 13. Kay County later complained that the road to the bridge was hazardous. See Gerald LeValley to Camp, September 18, 1972, Camp Collection, Box 74, Folder 14b.

76. Camp to Earnest Wolfenbarger, August 10, 1972, J. F. Kaskiewicz to Camp, August 15, 1972, Otto and Ethel Burtscher to Camp, August 16 and September 2, 1972, Jean Southard to Laverna McCune, October 20, 1972, and Nikki McNiece to Paul Smith, September 20, 1972, all in Camp Collection, Box 84, Folder 19; Colonel John Driskill to Camp, March 6, 1973, Camp Collection, Box 74, Folder 14b.

77. Water Resources Development . . . in Oklahoma, "Environmental Statement," January 1973 [copy], Albert Collection, Departmental Series, Box 106, Folder 44; Raymond Shaffer to Dewey Bartlett, February 16, 1973, Bartlett Collection, Box 63, Folder 8.

78. *Daily Oklahoman*, May 6, 1973; Dorothy Conaghan to Bartlett, September 27, 1974, Bartlett Collection, Box 63, Folder 8; LeValley to Camp, October 4, 1974, and Driskill to Camp, October 16, 1974, both in Camp Collection, Box 33, Folder 4.

79. David Beard to Bartlett, March 24, 1975, Bartlett Collection, Box 63, Folder 8; *Tulsa World*, May 1, 1975.

80. *Tulsa World*, September 7, 1975; *Daily Oklahoman*, January 29, 1976.

81. Water Resources Development by U.S. Army Corps Of Engineers in Oklahoma (Tulsa: U.S. Army Corps Engineers, Southwestern Division, Dallas, Texas, January 1977), 11–12; Annual Report of the Chief of Engineers on Civil Works Activities, 1976 (Washington, D.C.: GPO, 1976), 2:19–13, 14.

82. Ed King to Bartlett, February 25, 1976, Bartlett Collection, Box 43, Folder 42; Colonel Anthony Smith to Bartlett, April 23, 1976, Bartlett Collection, Box 61, Folder 9.

83. *Tulsa Tribune*, March 5, 1976; Helen [Newman] to Charlie [Ward], May 20, 1976, Albert Collection, Departmental Files, Box 137, Folder 3.

84. *Tulsa Tribune,* July 15, 1976; M. M. Chouteau to Colonel Smith, May 3, 1977, and Colonel Smith to Bartlett, May 6, 1977, both in Bartlett Collection, Box 34, Folder 10. The installation of a generating unit at the dam began commercial operation in August 1989.

85. *Daily Oklahoman*, July 5, 1977; *Water Resources Development in Oklahoma* (Tulsa: U.S. Army Corps of Engineers, Southwestern Division, 1981), 30–31.

« 7 »

Power for the People

Developing the Grand River Dam Authority, 1935–1964

The Grand River Dam, constructed with federal funds and costing Oklahoma taxpayers nary a penny, helped turn northeastern Oklahoma green and transformed an economically deprived, poverty-stricken area into a thriving, generally prosperous region. The Grand River Dam Authority, the state agency overseeing the dam's operation, would never have been developed if not for the arduous efforts of U.S. Representative Wesley Ernest Disney (1883–1961), a member of Congress who is all but forgotten today. Disney served Oklahoma's First District for seven terms (1931–45) and devoted an inordinate amount of his time to shepherding the project through a maze of New Deal agencies that were required to sign off on it. Although a settlement that sprang up near Pensacola Dam assumed his name, by his own request the name of Wesley Disney does not appear on any of the plaques recording the names of the founding fathers of the Grand River Dam Authority.

The major figure in Oklahoma water history has been Robert S. Kerr (1896–1963), and rightfully so. But Kerr, who was governor of the state from 1943 to 1947, did not enter the U.S. Senate until 1949. In that half of Congress, Elmer (John William Elmer) Thomas (1876–1965) played a key role in furthering projects to develop the Arkansas River. When possible, Kerr assisted Disney's efforts in pushing for the creation and development of the Grand River Dam Authority. He devoted his energies to making the Arkansas River, the nation's last major undeveloped river, a viable waterway, one that helped change the course of Oklahoma history. Kerr was instrumental in bringing this project to fruition, but Disney was a key at the outset.

Interest in developing the Grand River, which was a part of the Arkansas River system, dated from the early twentieth century. Historically, floods had repeatedly devastated crops and homes in the Grand River drainage system. Originating in central Kansas, the Neosho River flows in a southeasterly direction, joining the Spring River in northeastern Oklahoma, where it becomes the Grand River. It retains that name until it flows into the Arkansas River near Fort Gibson, Oklahoma. The Grand registered a watershed length of more than 250 miles and a maximum drainage width of approximately 100 miles near the Kansas-Oklahoma border. Though comprising only one-thirteenth of the Arkansas Basin area, the Grand River produced one-fourth of the flood control problems on the lower Arkansas River. The U.S. Army Corps of Engineers in 1935

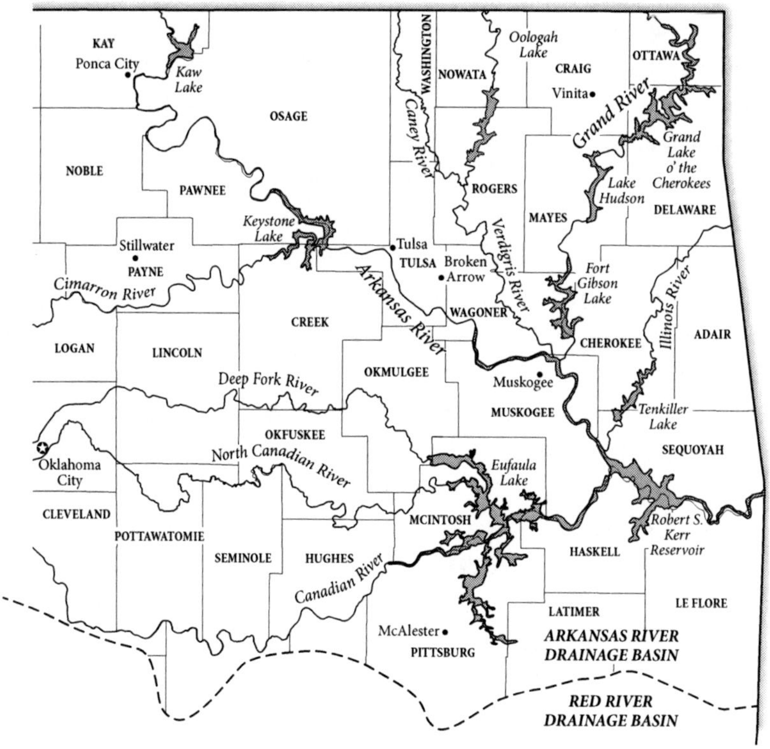

Arkansas River–Grand River watershed

recommended that the United States participate in controlling floods in the Grand water bed by building a dam that served for both flood control and power generation.[1]

Neither a local market nor funding for multipurpose river valley development became available, however, until the Great Depression spawned the New Deal in the 1930s. In 1935 Representative Disney began advocating the development of the Grand River. A committee for the Proposed Arkansas River Development approved a dam on the river, and the Mississippi Valley Committee gave the project an A rating. Groups throughout the region clamored for initiating development, and for several years Senator Elmer Thomas tried to persuade the Franklin D. Roosevelt administration to commit to constructing dams and reservoirs as flood control projects. Thomas's approach left the Grand River project to rest on its merits as a state-approved power site.[2]

On April 9, 1935, Senator Jack L. Rorschach of Vinita introduced Senate Bill 395, creating the Grand River Dam Authority (GRDA) and defining its powers, rights, and responsibilities. A state agency, GRDA would manage "a conservation and reclamation district" that encompassed fourteen counties of northeastern Oklahoma. The agency was to have a nine-member board of directors, three of whom were to be appointed by the governor, three by the attorney general, and three by the commissioner of labor. As the bill moved through the legislature in the spring of 1935, however, Glade R. Kirkpatrick, a state representative from Tulsa, attached an amendment requiring that all power generated by the project be sold at the turbines and only to utility companies that would then resell it to consumers. Thus, the Authority was to be denied the right to develop its own distribution system that would sell electricity directly to the public.[3] The Kirkpatrick Amendment would permit the selling of power only to organizations that built transmission lines to the proposed Pensacola Dam. To overcome this obstacle, the Grand River Dam Authority needed to be able to provide transmission and distribution lines to reach customers in distant markets and to reduce rates in other markets. In brief, it needed to engage in the retail sale of power. Disney thought Secretary of the Interior Harold Ickes would have been willing to approve the project despite the objection but for the fact that he needed routine endorsements from several department heads. Securing these endorsements would entail some delay in Public Works Administration approval and provide time for the Oklahoma Legislature to repeal the Kirkpatrick Amendment or initiate a petition to achieve that end.[4]

In the interim, Disney was encouraged when the Senate and House Commerce Committees included in the 1935 flood control bill not only Pensacola but also Markham Ferry and Fort Gibson dams on the Grand River. These three dams would complete the Grand River power project and would lead to electrification of farms and help establishment of new industries. Disney announced that he would "concentrate all my energy and abilities looking forward to the final approval" of the Grand River Dam project and would not involve himself in the 1936 U.S. senatorial campaign.[5]

Disney was jubilant over the Supreme Court's decision that upheld the government on questions raised in the TVA case (*Ashwander et al. v. Tennessee Valley Authority* [1936]). He announced his intention to call on the president to discuss prospects for a grant of several hundred thousand dollars for a preliminary survey of the Grand River project. Roosevelt was unavailable, however, and Secretary Ickes flatly refused Disney's request. Impasse ensued. That the project had been formally proposed and investigated gave proponents some solace.[6] Disney persisted, hoping that the application for a $16 million loan and grant would be favorably reported to Secretary Ickes. Disney prodded PWA officials and secured an interview with the president. All expressed interest, but Secretary Ickes declared that "we don't have money for such a big project now."[7]

Nonetheless, as a result of Disney's efforts, Roosevelt called in June 1936 for a complete engineering survey of the Pensacola Dam project to ascertain the feasibility of both flood control and hydroelectric power. Campaigning for reelection, the president paused long enough at Vinita, headquarters of the Grand River Dam Authority, to call for Disney's return to Washington and to acknowledge the project promisingly. With a favorable report ready to present to Congress when it convened in January, Disney was confident that "we can go right to bat for necessary authorization and appropriations for the project." *Harlow's Weekly*, a statewide journal that at times had opposed the project, admitted that

"Mr. Disney appears to have detoured the War Department and won his case at the White House."[8]

When the Natural Resources Board reported to President Roosevelt that the project was feasible from both an engineering and economic standpoint and recommended a PWA loan for immediate construction, Disney's optimism seemed justified. One snag remained: the Kirkpatrick Amendment forbidding the Authority to sell power at retail. The National Resources Board insisted that the amendment be replaced before work started.

While Disney remained in Washington to lobby for the biggest federal project his state had ever requested, Governor Ernest W. Marland sought to convince a majority of state legislators to repeal the Kirkpatrick Amendment. The proposed change would permit GRDA to distribute electricity at retail, as TVA did. By the end of September 1936 Secretary Ickes had informed Disney that because of the complications pertaining largely to the Kirkpatrick Amendment, Pensacola had been put on a deferred list to be considered after the national election. Having "put in several years on this matter," Disney said he did not "intend to quit now." Like the president, he was up for reelection, in his case, to a fourth term representing the First Congressional District.[9]

The Democratic landslide in 1936 gave advocates of public power in Oklahoma, backed strongly by Disney and Governor Marland, their greatest victory. Before the legislature repealed the Kirkpatrick Amendment, the Oklahoma Public Works Administration director took the GRDA plan to Washington because Disney was confident that President Roosevelt would sign the order starting work. Shortly thereafter, the legislature revised the GRDA Enabling Act to permit the agency to build transmission lines. Marland signed the law on January 2, thus ending Disney's long ordeal to get the project launched.[10]

Although Disney was the key figure in securing federal support for the project, he was not alone. Senator Elmer Thomas rendered yeoman service in June 1937 when he secured an amendment to a War Department appropriation bill of $16 million for the project. With this boost from Thomas, who now joined forces with Disney, starting work on the project appeared to be a matter of time. It did not quite happen as Thomas envisioned, but it did happen. In September the president approved the Pensacola Power Project (Public Works Administration docket 1097P) in the amount of $8,437,000 as an outright grant and $11,563,000 as a loan. The loan would be used to issue bonds, which in turn would be sold to the PWA.[11]

Earlier in the year army engineers conducted field surveys of the three dam sites: Pensacola, Markham Ferry, and Fort Gibson. This work was performed in conjunction with the massive flood control program being conducted throughout the Arkansas River basin. Disney initially hoped to have the dams included in this program, with the government assuming the expense of flood control, and his efforts kept the project in the mix of several federal proposals. Thanks to the district's state senator, Jack Rorschach, the original sponsor of the Grand River Dam Authority Act, the Oklahoma Planning and Resources Board made $7,000 available to help start the project, possibly the only state money ever contributed to the project.[12]

The dam, at that time projected to be 6,150 feet in length and 157 feet high, would create a huge artificial lake containing upwards of 2 million acre-feet of water. The lake would be approximately 57 miles long and would range from a few hundred feet to possibly 7 miles in width, with 1,300 miles of shoreline. The first 135 feet of height would be for power production, an estimated 283 million kilowatts annually. An additional 15 feet would facilitate flood control, which engineers calculated as furnishing one-fourth of the flow for the Arkansas River (the other 7 feet would complete the platform needed at the top of the structure). Disney estimated that the project would take approximately two thousand men off relief rolls for four years, and the Federal Power Commission estimated revenue from power and the sale of water at more than $1 million annually. Power would be sold to utility companies with existing transmission lines. The Grand River Dam Authority also could construct its own lines to furnish power to cities and rural sections. One town, Bernice, would be inundated by the backed-up water, along with an estimated 44,600 acres, including about 35,000 farms.[13]

The onset of the Grand River Project, Disney reflected, "amply repays the long, hard work I have done, amidst discouragement, political backbiting, and other wrong thinking about the subject. It has taken patience and perseverance in large quantities." He was delighted that the greatest "flood control-water conservation power project in the southwest was now under way." Henceforth, as Disney informed the nine men of the GRDA board of directors, "Gentlemen, I leave in your laps the Grand River Dam project, your judgment must control from this day on."[14] Newly appointed general manager Robert Van Lear Wright became the chief spokesman, but as long as he served in Congress, Disney remained vigilant on behalf of the project's interests.

Although it would take two or more years before the big lake actually took form, preparations of all kinds were under way even before formal papers were received from the PWA. As soon as Wright was on the job, land acquisitions and timber clearance began, as did hiring a labor force. New highways to the dam were surveyed, and new county roads, as well as a railroad spur, were either under way or being considered. At the same time, hordes of people—land speculators, investors, businessmen seeking to relocate, workers in search of jobs, and tourists by the thousands, all fully awake to the possibilities of cheap power, irrigation, and recreational attractions that would be available—trekked into the Grand River Valley.[15]

As a precaution, and wanting no challenge to the Grand River Dam Authority's legality, Ickes called for a court review of the 1935 enabling law. Until a decision on the validity of the Grand River Dam Authority bonds was resolved, no portion of the PWA grant would be advanced. The contract contained a clause that the Authority could demand a test case to establish the validity of the 1935 law by the Oklahoma Supreme Court, which was the provision that had prompted Ickes's action.[16] Compliance required Wright to adjust the height of the dam to 147 feet and to draft an employment policy with a wage schedule.[17]

On February 1, 1938, in a 7–2 decision the Oklahoma Supreme Court upheld the constitutionality of the Grand River Dam Authority Act. The decision cleared the way for construction of Pensacola Dam with funds furnished by the federal government. The Kassman Construction Company of Kansas City won the contract. As the earth-moving equipment began to roar, residents of nearby communities, including the newly created town of Disney, began to cast aside the gloom and tediousness of the Great Depression. The largest federal project thus far to receive approval in Oklahoma would serve as the engine for developing its northeastern counties.[18]

At the same time, the Authority's chief engineer readied his plans for the dam at Markham Ferry. Congressman Disney soon reported that the application for a $2.025 million PWA grant for Markham Ferry was virtually assured. The third dam, at Fort Gibson, would be undertaken later, as GRDA anticipated asking the state legislature for funding. By early 1939, through the efforts of Disney and with the backing of the Army Corps of Engineers, the Tri-Dam proposal had expanded into a $51 million federal power and flood control project.[19]

As fund-raising progressed, a new controversy arose. Early in his tenure, Oklahoma governor Leon Chase Phillips, elected in 1938, emerged as an adamant New Deal critic. Arguing that "neither the views, concerns, objections nor advice of the sovereign state of Oklahoma have been invited or heard in Washington," he criticized the board of the Grand River Dam Authority and urged the legislature to change the Grand River Dam Authority Enabling Act to reduce board membership from nine to five. In his most dramatic act, he called out the Oklahoma National Guard to halt work on Pensacola Dam.[20]

Phillips insisted it was the duty of Grand River Dam Authority to relocate roads, some of which were being flooded by water backing up behind the closed gates of the partially completed dam. The governor wanted the PWA to pay $800,000 for road and bridge damages caused by the rapidly growing lake, asserting it was the duty of the Grand River Dam Authority to relocate all roads in the reservoir basin. A full panoply of guardsmen, replete with machine guns, rifles, and other weapons, appeared to shut down work on the dam and keep the gates open, but one of their commanders, Major H. B. Haws, was able to achieve the same objective when he and two other unarmed National Guard officers met with the construction foreman, who quickly complied with the orders not to close the gap in the dam. With the matter on a state district court docket, Phillips's declaration of martial law, although still in place, was only a threat. The three officers enforcing it promised that their only order—to keep the river flowing—would be observed. The troops were withdrawn when the governor was enjoined from interfering with the construction of the project by a three-judge federal court. The conflict seemed resolvable when Phillips was urged in May to accept Grand River Dam Authority bonds in settlement of the claim.[21]

As the controversy wore on, Disney introduced a measure authorizing construction of the Markham Ferry and Fort Gibson Dams. He left open the question of how the projects were to be built but said the Grand River Dam Authority should supervise them. Unlike Pensacola, these dams would serve hydroelectric and flood control purposes equally. The question of who would eventually build the dams remained a matter of contention between those favoring the Grand River Dam Authority and those willing to accept the Corps of Engineers.[22]

Although not as active as Disney, Senator Elmer Thomas sought PWA funding to construct Markham Ferry and conferred with the chief of army engineers for a special study of several proposed reservoir, flood control, and power projects in eastern Oklahoma. Because Disney and Thomas were political rivals, they never coordinated their efforts, although each claimed credit for the Grand River Dam Authority. Thomas alone merited credit in one area that never concerned Disney or most of his constituents. In the hiring of workers, Thomas said, discrimination was "being made in favor of the white race and it is only fair that negroes be called according to their percentage of population and given as much consideration with reference to wage scales as everyone else."[23]

The tension over who should control the project, already evident in 1939, would be central to the construction of the Markham Ferry and Fort Gibson Dams. Markham Ferry and Fort Gibson were attractive to the Grand River Dam Authority because, utilizing water that passed over the spillways or through the turbines of Pensacola Dam, they would produce electricity at a lower cost than did the larger Pensacola Dam. The important point was that these dams function as a unit of the Grand River Dam Authority and not be integrated into the Corps of Engineers' program to develop an Arkansas River waterway. Although debate was already under way, neither dam was yet authorized by Congress or approved by the PWA.[24]

By 1940 the discussion took on concerns for national defense and the war effort, especially evident when U.S. Army officials promised to consider a proposal to construct a government arsenal in the Grand River Dam area. The offer was made before Pensacola Dam was operative. Quick to grasp the possibility of the area as a vital center for the defense program, Disney conveyed his enthusiasm in a long letter to the president (copied to other officials and industrial leaders), explaining that the location offered the advantages of a wide range of energy resources, including coal, natural gas, oil, and water power.[25]

By June 1940 rumors were swirling that an aluminum plant would be located in the area. Clark Foreman, chief of the PWA power division, indicated that only a community using Grand River Dam Authority power would be considered. If industrial plants were to be located in the area, Disney was confident that prospects for Markham Ferry and Fort Gibson Dams would be greatly enhanced through loans from the Reconstruction Finance Corporation.[26]

In October 1940 Disney's seven-year effort was realized. The PWA underwrote the project by advancing $11,563,000 as a loan and $8,437,000 as an additional grant, with another $2,750,000 loan and grant allotted in 1941. The loaned money was to be repaid by GRDA through the annual sale of approximately 200 million kilowatt hours of low-cost power. Pensacola Dam, 1.25 miles in length, was the largest in the Southwest. The directors did not name the lake after a particular Indian tribe, for fear of offending other tribes, but instead called it Grand Lake. With fifty-one arches resting against hollow buttresses placed fifty-four feet from center to center, the structure was the longest multiple-arch dam in the world. Filling steadily behind it, Grand Lake already contained more water than all the other lakes in Oklahoma combined. It would eventually cover about 52,000 acres. The project was placed in commercial operation on May 1, 1941.[27]

Throughout 1941 GRDA's plans moved forward slowly. In Washington, D.C., the House Appropriations Committee provided funds for four Oklahoma dams, including Markham Ferry and Fort Gibson. At the same time, the chief of army engineers outlined plans for completion of the Grand River dams' development. The Federal Power Commission also recommended the immediate construction of Markham Ferry and Fort Gibson so that power could be available for distribution in 1943. Further impetus for these dams came with word that federal officials were seriously discussing plans to alleviate a national shortage of electrical power for defense industries. Of more immediate significance was a story that broke in August 1941: the federal government would build a $51 million smokeless powder plant. The facility, covering six thousand or more acres, would employ approximately five thousand men in its construction. The same number would be hired for its operation, under the management of E. I. Dupont de Nemours and Company. To be located near Chouteau, the plant would use power generated by Pensacola Dam. Selected after months of lobbying by Disney, Thomas, and Senator Josh Lee, among others, it would be Oklahoma's largest defense project. At that time, the community of Chouteau had a population of four hundred, seven business houses, and no industries.[28]

In 1941, as armed conflict in Europe and Asia escalated, and the United States stepped up its defense measures, the federal government assumed control of the Grand River project. By Executive Order, President Roosevelt federalized Pensacola Dam and its reservoir on November 21, 1941, integrating its power into defense efforts. In January 1941 an engineering contract had been awarded for construction of both the Fort Gibson and Markham Ferry Dams. They would be built by the Corps of Engineers and operated in concert with GRDA. The dams would embrace both flood control and power, and work was to start on Markham Ferry in May 1942.[29]

Following the December 7, 1941, attack on Pearl Harbor, and the nation's entrance into the war, individuals in northeastern Oklahoma strove mightily for new projects to assist in the war effort and accelerate the region's economic development. Early in 1942, for example, the government approved plans for a railroad line to be built from a point near Tulsa to the powder plant near Chouteau. To counter dispatches from Washington that the War Production Board would not allow location of any more war industries in the state for a lack of power, the president of the Oklahoma Gas and Electric Company (OG&E) asserted that no such shortage existed. Yet another dispute arose over project purpose and control.[30] The Grand River Dam Authority was strictly an Oklahoma corporation in the power business and not concerned with flood control. The Federal Works Agency, as it took over the facility, agreed. The army engineers concerned themselves primarily with flood control along the Arkansas River and along the lower Mississippi. The two priorities never melded perfectly, but the issue was resolved through compromise after the war.[31]

Local groups favored flood control. In early 1942 the Tulsa Chamber of Commerce and its president, Newton Graham, called for creation of an Arkansas River waterway. The group sharply opposed the Federal Works Administration and the Pensacola project because both the dam and the agency ignored the needs of flood control. When the chamber learned that the Bureau of the Budget had frozen funds appropriated for Markham Ferry, Graham protested. He called for construction of the dam and that at Fort Gibson by calling attention to the disastrous floods in the lower Arkansas River Valley, and by citing the importance of flood control in the nation's defense.[32]

The Grand River Dam Authority and the Federal Works Administration also had their advocates in Tulsa who expressed their views through the Arkansas Valley Electric Power Association. The association's vice president insisted that public power was important not only "as a war measure" but for the future as well. If Oklahoma did not industrialize and stop importing finished commodities and exporting raw material, he said, "we will always be an ideal field for the W. P. A. and other relief organizations." He criticized the army engineers' greater interest in flood control and castigated the private utilities for "exercising every means of opposition at their command to prevent the development of hydroelectricity as a competitive measure."[33]

Hopes for rapid construction of both the Fort Gibson and Markham Ferry Dams faded when the Bureau of the Budget concluded that neither project was necessary to the war effort. The Corps of Engineers said power was necessary to produce munitions and instruments of war, however, and declared its intent to complete the dams as rapidly as possible. It was not to be. Congressional funds were impounded, and Markham Ferry and Fort Gibson became casualties of war. Pensacola would be the public engine furthering the war effort in Oklahoma.[34] On September 1, 1943, with revenues of about $160,000 a month, the Grand River Dam Authority became part of the federal Southwestern Power Administration.[35]

As the federal government took over the power project, nature intervened to cause havoc. Unusually heavy rains fell for three days in May 1943 throughout the Grand and Arkansas River Valleys, and flooding was extreme. To protect the properties of the Oklahoma Ordinance Works, that is, the powder plant near Chouteau, GRDA temporarily raised the pool level at the dam from between 744 and 745 feet to an elevation of 754.5 feet above sea level. The flood and GRDA's action prompted a heated exchange between GRDA administrator Wright and Newton Graham, serving as chair of the board of the Southwest Valley Association.

Graham criticized GRDA's flood control action. Long an advocate of flood control and power dams, the formula utilized by the Corps of Engineers, Graham charged that "every person who advocated the building of this [Pensacola] dam [was] promised flood control and that promise is not being kept." With a power pool level of 745 feet approved by the Federal Power Commission over the published objections of the Corps of Engineers, the commission, in disregarding these objections and raising the elevation, bore prime responsibility for the devastation. In addition to loss of life, thousands of acres of crops were ruined and many homes destroyed. In Graham's view, the loss, numbering "well above a million dollars," could have been avoided. Power was needed for war, Graham said, but "so are potatoes, corn and livestock."[36]

Responding on behalf of the Federal Works Administration, Douglas Wright said the main question was whether the reservoir elevation should have been held at 745 feet or at 735 feet. Citing channel capacity and cubic feet of water per second, he insisted that an additional ten feet of storage would not have been of "any material assistance in controlling the flood." Offering a "very simple description of the flood," Wright asserted that "the Grand River Valley was completely full of water from the Grand River Dam to the end of the watershed" and was roughly one-third to one-half full from the [Pensacola] dam to Fort Gibson, where the Grand River entered the Arkansas. Had Fort Gibson Dam already existed, the flooding of the Fort Gibson and Muskogee areas and on the

Arkansas River could have been minimized, while the water level in the Grand River Valley from Fort Gibson to Pensacola Dam would have increased. "There was no other place left in the entire water shed to have put the water," Wright said. The one way to beat a seventeen-inch rain, an editorial in the *Tulsa Tribune* concluded, would be "to construct the Fort Gibson and Markham Ferry dams on the Grand as soon as possible."[37]

Senator Thomas devoted his energies to expediting the construction of Fort Gibson Dam. Its location near the mouth of the Grand River would play a major role in curbing one of the major flood-producing streams in the Arkansas River basin. The 1943 flood devastated crop production in eastern Oklahoma and in western Arkansas, along with many homes and barns. Nineteen individuals lost their lives, and livestock losses possibly ran into the thousands. The Corps of Engineers had actually started work on the project shortly before the war, only to have it stopped by the War Production Board. Thomas and others called for resumption of the project, and the Corps of Engineers was fully prepared to renew construction on an expedited schedule. However, the War Production Board remained opposed because no material was available to build Fort Gibson and other dams.[38] Flood control failed to spur dam construction, and an Executive Order from Roosevelt on September 1, 1943, emphasized the primary purpose of producing hydroelectric power.[39]

The region's need for power became increasingly obvious as the war progressed. By October 1943 GRDA was purchasing coal-generated power from private utilities to meet customer demands. This situation led OG&E president George Davis to crow, "It would appear that the dam failed as a flood control project last spring in the flood, and now is failing as a source of power in the drought—all in the same year."[40] Meanwhile, the Oklahoma Ordnance Works (the smokeless powder plant) near Chouteau on Grand Lake was nearing completion. The Authority stood ready to provide it with power and in doing so would bring itself "out of the red ink." Happily, that occurred early in 1944; in March, Douglas Wright, serving as Southwestern Power administrator, announced that the Grand River Dam "has 'licked' the worst period of low water recorded." Thanks to a rising water level at Pensacola, Wright said, the project was expected to "carry practically all its own loads." Boosting his optimism was the exciting news that B. F. Goodrich would construct a $5 million tire plant in Miami to take advantage of cheap Grand River power.[41]

Less exciting, but of great significance, was Wesley Disney's defeat in the primary election as he sought to replace Elmer Thomas in the United States Senate. Replaced by a Republican hostile to the Authority, Disney, the "father" of the Grand River Dam Authority and largely responsible for obtaining government funds to build the project, gradually faded into obscurity. Because he refused to allow his name to appear on any of the five plaques on the Pensacola cornerstone, visitors saw embossed only the names of other public officials. The nearby town of Disney is the only recognition he received, and most residents now would have trouble recognizing his remarkable contribution in launching the project. The election, however, brought into the Congress from the Second District a new member, William G. Stigler, who was keenly interested in the project.[42]

Meanwhile, Senator Thomas, now assured of another term, recognized that construction of Fort Gibson would have to wait until the war ended. It was also evident that army engineers, who would emphasize flood control and relegate power production to secondary status, would direct the project. But, with the war still raging and the demand for energy constantly increasing, GRDA accepted bids to construct a fifth generating unit at Pensacola, along with improvements to the spillways.[43]

In 1945 Thomas said he would try to ensure "that any future dams built on the Arkansas or any of its tributaries, will be designed primarily for flood control purposes and power will be incident to flood control." He wanted the Corps of Engineers to manage all future dams on the Arkansas River, and he objected to any being "constructed like the authority of the Grand River Dam." In fact, he was informing his constituents that Pensacola "was constructed largely for the control of floods," even though some people insisted it was designed primarily for the generation of hydroelectric power.[44]

Without a member in Congress to champion their view, groups in communities bordering or near Grand Lake continued to support the construction of Markham Ferry and Fort Gibson "chiefly for the production of electrical energy." They argued that the Grand River "is the best, if not the only real 'power stream' between the Mississippi River and the Rocky Mountains." Markham Ferry and Fort Gibson were designed as "power dams" so that water stored at the Pensacola reservoir could again be utilized in the production of electrical energy, assuring an ample supply of firm power. Using the river for power purposes ensured that lakes would remain at constant levels and create natural recreation areas. In the postwar years, the Grand River Dam Authority's supporters would carefully hone and elaborate these views.[45]

With the end of World War II, the dispute over power and flood control was embedded in the broader issue of returning the Authority to Oklahoma. Although President Harry Truman agreed to return Pensacola Dam to the Grand River Dam Authority "as soon as that may be done," numerous agencies would be involved in the process. By the end of January 1946, besides Secretary Harold Ickes, the Federal Power Commission and the Bureau of the Budget were expected to sign off. Early in February Thomas introduced a bill (S. 1816) transferring control, and Stigler followed shortly thereafter with an identical House measure (H.R. 5508).[46]

While Congress would legislate the return of Pensacola Dam to GRDA, the Authority was prepared to purchase the Oklahoma Ordnance Works from the newly created War Assets Corporation so that its steam plant could provide low-cost electric energy for domestic and industrial uses as well as for distribution by rural electric cooperatives.[47] But it was not to be, because the War Assets Administration began to cannibalize parts of the Oklahoma Ordnance Works. The Authority urged Governor Kerr to pursue the matter with the War Assets Administration when he was in Washington.[48] The Rural Electrification Administration also pursued the matter, its administrator asserting that sixteen rural electric cooperatives in Oklahoma and three adjacent states had a vital interest in the disposition of the steam plant. To aid the Authority in furthering peacetime activities, the state legislature in 1947 amended the Grand River Dam Authority Act by granting it power to issue bonds up to $25 million to acquire the steam plant and related facilities at the Oklahoma Ordnance Works.[49] Although assuming additional bonded indebtedness, the

Authority gained the ability to provide a growing number of consumers, both public and private, with cheap and abundant hydroelectric power.

With Pensacola again under the aegis of the Authority and with construction of Fort Gibson Dam already approved, the Oklahoma Legislature authorized GRDA to issue revenue bonds in the amount of $10 million to launch Markham Ferry for power generation. The Authority, meanwhile, applied to the Federal Works Administration for a $90,000 advance-planning loan. The application indicated that GRDA would actively seek to realize its vision of an integrated system of dams on the Grand River with possibilities for industrial and recreational development. The Authority was more cautious than in the past, however. The dam would be planned in such a way that the army could use the reservoir for flood control by purchasing additional land, if and when flood control was included in the project. By so doing, GRDA hoped to win the support of the state's senior senator, who had committed himself to flood control in constructing dams by the Corps of Engineers. All of these efforts soon hit a snag, however. In the 1946 election the Republican Party regained control of Congress after more than a decade and threatened to cut federal appropriations by as much as $10 billion.[50]

Resolution of concerns requiring congressional approval was slow to come. A trickle of funds in 1947 allowed work on Fort Gibson to continue and for planning studies on Markham Ferry. Constructing Markham Ferry required a permit from the Federal Power Commission because it would affect lands acquired by the government. Roy J. Turner, Kerr's successor as governor, was equally desirous of working out an arrangement whereby the Authority would build the dam with privately financed revenue bonds. Elmer Thomas contested this view, however, vowing there would be no appropriation for Markham Ferry while he served in the U.S. Senate unless people in the area agreed with his opposition to projects not primarily concerned with flood control.[51]

Thomas's views gained support among area residents. Some of them desired Markham Ferry regardless of who built it and for what primary purpose. Thomas believed that if the Grand River Dam Authority stepped aside and permitted the Corps of Engineers to submit an estimate, Congress would appropriate funds to start construction. With the Democrats regaining control of Congress in 1948, and with Kerr now joining Thomas in the Senate, more adequate funding for Oklahoma projects seemed assured.[52]

Recognizing that public sentiment was changing, and anxious to get construction under way now that congressional appropriations were increasing, GRDA modified its position on Markham Ferry. Unable to obtain a permit from the Federal Power Commission because the 1941 Flood Control Act authorized the War Department to construct the project, GRDA was willing to accept the engineers' contention that the project should provide for no less than 233,000 acre feet of flood storage, but the government should contribute a portion of the construction costs for providing this amount of flood storage. As 1948 came to an end, the question remained whether Thomas or Kerr or both would accept the proposal and seek legislative approval.[53]

At the time this proposal was drafted, Fort Gibson Dam, providing for flood control, power, and irrigation, was roughly 33 percent complete. With Fort Gibson becoming a major component of the developing Arkansas River waterway, GRDA's vision for Grand River was changing. Nevertheless, GRDA was determined to maintain its integrity as a state agency devoted to the generation of public power.[54] It already owned a large transmission line that furnished power to contractors involved with the construction of Fort Gibson. GRDA filed a claim with the Corps of Engineers seeking compensation for rights assumed by the government in producing power at the dam. It cited Section 10 of the Federal Power Act as justification, noting that Fort Gibson's power would be produced by the waters released through the turbines at Pensacola Dam. Given the validity of the position it presented, the Grand River Dam Authority insisted that it would be only "right and equitable" for the government to deliver to it the power generated at Fort Gibson, receiving in return "reasonable and just" compensation.[55]

Without Wesley Disney to battle on its behalf, and with Thomas at best lukewarm, the Authority had little choice but to pin its hopes on newly elected Senator Robert S. Kerr. It did so with some measure of optimism because, as governor, Kerr had been a staunch friend, and it was correct in doing so. Early in 1949 Thomas opted out, suggesting that the Grand River Dam Authority work with Kerr, who had joined the committee that authorized flood control projects. In opting out Thomas claimed that he "could have had the [Markham Ferry] dam well under way to completion at the present time had it not been for the controversy over who should build the dam." Because the state of Oklahoma found itself unable to finance construction, Thomas hoped that the Grand River Dam Authority would stand aside and let the Corps do the job and thus relinquish its claim to all the power generated. If the Authority did so, Thomas indicated he would be in a position to secure funds to start Markham Ferry "exactly similar to the Fort Gibson project," which would emphasize flood control first and power second. Thomas had no answer to local concerns that construction of Markham Ferry primarily for flood control "would mean the loss of thousands of acres of additional land."[56]

Governor Turner impressed upon both of Oklahoma's senators the benefits of Markham Ferry being developed by the Grand River Dam Authority. The project, he argued, would benefit the people of Oklahoma, and the power produced at Markham Ferry and Pensacola would provide additional income to the state. The Authority could provide the same amount of flood control for an approximate cost of $7 million to the government, whereas if the military constructed the project, it would cost $32 million. The Authority would fund the project from the sale of revenue bonds, whereas the army's construction would require tax money. Also, GRDA would bear all administrative and operating expenses. Already, Turner said in conclusion, the Authority was operating Pensacola for flood control under the direction of the army engineers. If this model could be pursued at Markham Ferry, the top of the flood pool would be at least seventeen feet higher than the top of the power pool. In asking the senators to support GRDA, Turner reinforced views that others at the Authority already preached. By early 1950 the contours of the legislative battle for Markham Ferry and Fort Gibson were clear, but GRDA would have little direct control over how long it would take to realize them.[57]

In 1950 Congress, a body that did have a direct voice, limited funds for new dams. One possibility for constructing Markham Ferry, as Thomas saw it, was to secure "as liberal a contribution as possible" from the U.S. Army Corps of Engineers with the Grand River Dam Authority defray-ing all the power expenses, thereby avoiding the legislative process. In spelling out the details for construction, Senator Kerr's S.B. 3432 called on the Authority to construct the project in accordance with the recommendations of the chief of engineers pertaining to flood storage and pool elevation. It authorized the appropriation of $7 million to the Grand River Dam Authority as the federal government's total contribution for flood control storage at Markham Ferry. Kerr followed with a public hearing, where he affirmed a state's right to develop its own resources.[58]

The Public Service Company of Oklahoma helped build sentiment for Kerr's bill. Headquartered in Tulsa, Public Service contracted with GRDA for electric power. Each party agreed to cooperate in conserving natural resources, in fostering industrial and agricultural development, and "in the development and construction of additional hydroelectric facilities for Grand River Dam Authority." Private utility support was balanced by the loss of Thomas's reluctant, but nonetheless powerful, endorsement. His primary defeat in July 1950 deprived Oklahoma of the third-ranking Democrat in the U.S. Senate. He left knowing that Fort Gibson would go forward and that Congress would reconsider Markham Ferry.[59]

When the new Congress convened, Kerr introduced S.B. 272, providing once again for the construction of Markham Ferry by the State of Oklahoma through the Grand River Dam Authority. As hearings got under way, Fort Gibson Dam, the second of the three dams and reservoirs authorized for the Grand River and a unit of the comprehensive plan for flood control and navigation in the Arkansas River basin, was about 75 percent complete.

The watershed above Fort Gibson contained 12,615 square miles and comprised more than 99 percent of the drainage area of the Grand River, which joined the Arkansas River approximately eight miles below the dam. Fort Gibson Reservoir was expected to provide flood protection to about 3,000 acres in the Grand River Valley below the dam site and aid in protecting the flood plain below the mouth of the Grand River. Constructed by army engineers with a different set of priorities, Fort Gibson nevertheless allowed the Grand River Dam Authority to fulfill its primary mission of generating electric power even as it provided a measure of flood control. Indeed, when completed, Fort Gibson together with Pensacola would provide sufficient flood control capacity to have restricted all floods of record to bank-full stage, except for the massive floods that had occurred in April 1927, October 1941, and May 1943. When completed, the reservoir would have a permanent pool of 365,000 acre-feet, which would provide head for generating electric power.[60]

As construction of Fort Gibson Dam continued, Markham Ferry slowly made its way through Congress. Several federal officials questioned various provisions of S.B. 272, while GRDA argued for a substitute measure that would have the same number of acre-feet of flood storage and the same pool elevation as the chief of engineers recommended.[61] A dispute from 1941 also cropped up. In that year, Governor Leon Phillips had sent members of the National Guard to Pensacola to curtail filling of the reservoir and prevent flooding of state roads. To resolve the matter, Senator Mike Monroney introduced a bill in October 1951 calling upon the secretary of the treasury to appropriate to the state of Oklahoma $656,500 for the use and benefit of the Oklahoma Highway Commission. At the same time, GRDA, with the notable assistance of Senator Kerr, was striving to resolve contentions with other federal agencies. This suggested that soon the Authority could function as a self-sustaining state agency.[62]

But not yet. In 1952 the Authority, with major corporations contemplating operations in the area, was stalled in purchasing tracts of land from the Corps of Engineers. Monsanto Chemical Company was interested in leasing plants from the government and building an additional plant in a tract the Authority was trying to buy from the Corps. In another instance, a fertilizer company was considering building an anhydrous ammonia plant. For GRDA in all these matters—approval of S.B. 272, reimbursing the state for road construction, and securing tracts of land to attract major corporations—time was of the essence. Frustration was the lot of many state officials and of Senator Kerr.[63]

By the end of the year the Authority's general counsel, in accordance with the directions of all the involved federal agencies, had revised and redrafted Monroney's measure to clarify the technical details for the Public Works Subcommittee to consider. The governor of Oklahoma then advised the president that the revised bill was satisfactory. Accordingly, at the outset of the Eighty-third Congress, Kerr introduced S.B. 119, authorizing state construction of Markham Ferry at an estimated cost of $21 million, financed by the sale of revenue bonds and a federal appropriation of $6.5 million for flood control. "The anticipated addition of Markham Ferry to the other facilities on Grand River," Kerr confidently exclaimed, "would open up a great new source of power and water at reasonable rates and accelerate the industrial growth in the area" as well as "provide a greatly needed power source for the rural co-ops."[64]

Kerr wrote to every member of the committee that was reviewing S.B. 119 in June to note that several days hence the full committee in executive session would consider Markham Ferry. A few days thereafter the Senate approved the measure, authorizing construction by the Grand River Dam Authority with $6.5 million as the federal government's contribution for flood control. A year later, on July 6, 1954, the bill gained congressional approval. Soon the Authority began acquiring necessary rights-of-way and making financial arrangements for construction. GRDA continued to call on Kerr for assistance in resolving problems, one of which involved securing easements from the Corps of Engineers for construction of facilities to transmit steam from the former Oklahoma Ordnance Works to industries. One of these was John Deere and Company, then in the midst of constructing a $20 million plant located near the Authority's industrial tract.[65]

The 1956 Public Works Appropriation Bill, which included the Markham Ferry Dam, "is one of the greatest boosts of the Federal power construction and marketing program that has come from the Congress during the past decade," Kerr proudly announced. Congress added eleven new projects in the bill, and the Eisenhower administration, which had recommended no new starts, approved it with great reluctance. If construction of Markham Ferry was now possible, reimbursement to the state for $656,500 for roads that had to be relocated was not. At the request of newly elected governor Raymond Gary, Kerr and Monroney reintroduced the measure to attempt to secure favorable action during the Eighty-fourth Congress.[66]

Satisfied that the matter of reimbursement would be reviewed once more as the bill worked its way through Congress, the Grand River Dam

Authority filed an application with the Federal Power Commission in April 1955 for a license to construct and operate Markham Ferry Dam. The structure would have a maximum height of eighty feet, and it would include penstocks, a substation and switchyard, and transmission lines. Markham Ferry Reservoir would have a capacity of 420,000 acre-feet. The powerhouse would include three units, with two more proposed as needed. Once the licensing process was complete, GRDA could begin selling $6.5 million worth of bonds.[67]

By July 1955 the process was completed. The Federal Power Commission had issued the license, and the Bureau of the Budget approved allocation of funds once it secured the "supplemental request" from the president. All of this happened in time for consideration by the Senate. Congress only approved $6.3 million instead of the $6.5 million requested to pay the government for lands it owned in the reservoir area. Construction could now begin in January 1957. While Kerr recognized that securing the appropriation was "a team accomplishment," he took credit for assuring that the money in the bill was not seriously deleted.[68]

Exuberance prevailed in Vinita, Oklahoma, where GRDA maintained its headquarters. The Authority's directors were equally pleased that the agency's financial condition had been steadily improving, that water elevation in Pensacola Reservoir was very favorable, and that their longstanding plan to add a 30,000-kilowatt generating unit at the Chouteau Steam Plant could now be undertaken. Markham Ferry would be designed for an ultimate installed power capacity of 72,000 kilowatts. Its operation for flood control purposes would be tied in with the already functioning Pensacola and Fort Gibson reservoirs so that flow releases from the power plants, together with natural flows, were sufficient to maintain the navigation pools below Fort Gibson on the Arkansas River.[69]

When, on August 5, 1957, a contract was agreed upon between the Grand River Dam Authority and the Public Service Company of Oklahoma, a suit to validate the contract was filed in the Oklahoma Supreme Court. For it to become effective, the Federal Power Commission, following court approval, would have to favorably review it. In 1958, two years after Congress approved Markham Ferry, the contract still had not been approved, nor had construction started. Writing to Kerr, an area chamber of commerce manager complained, "The future industrial development in Northeast Oklahoma depends greatly upon the construction of Markham Ferry Dam and the approval of the power exchange contract." Until these matters were thrashed out, the project was at a standstill.[70]

One vexing matter relating to the pending contract with the Public Service Company was the requirement that GRDA only purchase electricity from the Public Service Company and limit its future power production to hydroelectric. The contract, which awaited Federal Power Commission approval, blocked construction of a 50,000-kilowatt nuclear power plant at Pensacola. Some legislators believed the deal would make GRDA a captive of a private utility company, and that the low-cost power it provided, the yardstick that kept rates competitive, would disappear. If Markham Ferry was held in abeyance, the Authority would never be able to carry its own load without the aid of the private company. Resolving the situation without impairing GRDA was imperative.[71]

In addition, as Governor Raymond Gary recognized, before any contract could become effective and bonds sold, the legislature would have to increase the Authority's bonded debt limit. Drafted in consultation with investment bankers and the General Services Administration, who would buy many of the bonds, a bill raising the debt limit from $50 million to $133 million was introduced in March 1957. Although the measure sailed through the Oklahoma Senate, W. R. Holway, in his detailed history of the Grand River Dam Authority, suggests that there were at least two requests for bribes to insure safe passage of the bill.[72]

Although the debt limit bill passed easily, conflict arose again when the contract with the Public Service Company was signed by GRDA later that summer. The rural electric cooperatives charged that the contract favored the Public Service Company, and they wanted changes that would permit the Authority to purchase electricity "from anyone except the one source which is its sole competitor." However, the Oklahoma Supreme Court, reviewing the entire matter in December 1957, unanimously upheld the contract.[73] The Markham Ferry Coordinating Agreement then became the subject of extended hearings before William J. Costello, a Federal Power Commission examiner, who eventually concluded that the contract was "just and reasonable." The Authority and Public Service Company arrangement governing Pensacola, which allowed them to exchange "peak" and "firm" power, could now be extended to Markham Ferry.[74] Costello also approved increasing the hydroelectric capacity at Markham Ferry from 45,000 to 100,000 kilowatts.[75]

The Grand River Dam Authority now endeavored to improve its revenue streams. First, it sought to purchase from the Southwestern Power Administration the electricity generated at Fort Gibson. Doing so would better serve GRDA's municipal and Rural Electric Administration customers.[76] The next major task was to issue bonds and, with luck, start work on the dam in 1961. As the General Services Administration held a majority of the outstanding bonds, Governor J. Howard Edmondson and a group of bankers sought to further the bond sale. In December a company syndicate purchased a $50 million bond issue to finance the project. Soon thereafter, Grand River Dam Authority announced that the eight-year struggle to find the funds to build Markham Ferry appeared to be over.[77]

By January 1962, thanks to the General Services Administration, the way was cleared, and groundbreaking ceremonies were held. Construction bids were awarded, and the chair of the Authority asserted that the project would be in operation "sometime between May 1 and July 1, 1964." Expected to produce 100,000 kilowatts of electricity, Markham Ferry would nearly double the Authority's power capacity, which was then limited to 140,000 kilowatts from Pensacola, located forty-seven miles up the Grand River. Recognizing the efforts of Senator Kerr in championing the project and supporting the Authority, it adopted a resolution signed by Governor Edmondson naming Markham Ferry the Robert S. Kerr Dam.[78] Speaking at the start of construction on the dam that would bear his name, Kerr said it had involved three presidents (Truman, Eisenhower, and Kennedy), countless members of Congress, seven governors, numerous state legislative sessions, and the determination of many citizens, all of whom sought "to make Oklahoma an even better land in which to live." In his remarks Kerr reviewed the history of the development of the Grand River for hydroelectric power, culminating with the 1954 bill he had sponsored. While he congratulated numerous individuals and groups, one name—that of Congressman Wesley E. Disney—was conspicuously absent from his remarks.[79]

Already an almost forgotten individual in Oklahoma, Disney died in Washington, D.C., about two months after Kerr spoke at the dam site. His lengthy battles had helped launch the Grand River Dam Authority as a state agency, with all its facilities constructed with federal funds, generating its own revenues, and costing the state almost nothing, yet yielding immeasurable benefits, most notably in northeastern Oklahoma. Although Disney helped launch the Authority, Kerr was the major factor in enabling it to complete its mission of utilizing the Grand River for the generation of hydroelectric power, thereby turning a blighted and poverty-stricken section of Oklahoma into a productive, prosperous, and attractive recreational area. Kerr did not see the completion of Markham Ferry, but his efforts made it possible for the Grand River Dam Authority to fulfill its mission and thereafter sustain itself as the lone state-owned and state-operated public power project in Oklahoma.

Notes

1. For a discussion of the early efforts to develop the Grand River, see W. R. Holway, "Dams on the Grand River," *Chronicles of Oklahoma* 26 (Autumn 1948): 329–34. Holway was a consulting engineer long connected with the Grand River Dam Authority. He is the author of *A History of the Grand River Dam Authority: State of Oklahoma, 1935–1968* (Tulsa: Privately printed, 1968). See also Wash Hudson to Elmer Thomas, May 12, 1933, for a previous proposal to build dams on the Grand River, in Folder 24, Box 24, Subject Files, Elmer Thomas Collection, Congressional Archives, Carl Albert Center, University of Oklahoma, Norman [hereafter cited as CAC]. For discussions of U.S. Army Corps of Engineers assessments of the extent of flooding in the river systems, see "Reservoirs on the Grand (Neosho) River," 1939, H. Doc. 107, 76th Cong., 1st sess., Serial 10331, and "Report of the Corps of Engineers on the Arkansas Rivers and Its Tributaries," 1935, H. Doc. 308, 74th Cong., 1st sess., 3 vols., Serial 9936-1, 9936-2, 9936-3.

2. C. A. Stanfield to Thomas, January 28, 1935, Folder 57, Box 10, Projects Files, Thomas Collection; Resolution: Democratic County Wide Precinct Organization of Tulsa, April 3, 1935, Folder 42, Box 16, Legislative Files, Thomas Collection; Thomas to George Schaefer, August 14, 1935, and Business Mens' Club of Spavinaw to Thomas, August 16, 1935 (telegram), Folder 14, Box 6, Projects Files, Thomas Collection. Early in 1935 every Chamber of Commerce in northeastern

Oklahoma had joined a movement to aid Disney in the Pensacola Dam fight. As early as January 1935 Disney had brought the matter to the attention of the president, who indicated he did not favor the construction of new hydroelectric power projects at this time. See story in the *Vinita* (Okla.) *Journal*, January 31, 1935. For discussions of U.S. Army Corps of Engineers assessments of the extent of flooding in the river systems, see "Reservoirs on the Grand (Neosho) River," 1939, H. Doc. 107, 76th Cong., 1st sess., Serial 10331, and "Report of the Corps of Engineers on the Arkansas Rivers and Its Tributaries," 1935, H. Doc. 308, 74th Cong., 1st sess., 3 vols., Serial 9936–1, 9936–2, 9936–3.

3. *Journal of the Senate of the Fifteenth Legislature of the State of Oklahoma, Regular Session* (n.p., 1935), 1375, 1412, 1468, 1479, 1853–65, 2054–55; *Journal of the House of Representatives, Regular Session, Fifteen Legislature of the State of Oklahoma, 1935* (n.p., 1935), 2793, 3396, 3488, 3490, 3550, 3613–15, 2968–69. See *Journal of the House of Representatives* for April 24, 1935, p. 1855, for the text of the Kirkpatrick Amendment.

4. *Tulsa Tribune*, September 12, 1935; unidentified clipping, September 16, 1935, Folder 5, Box 1, Wesley Disney Collection, CAC. The Wesley Disney Collection in the CAC consists almost entirely of press clippings, many of which include his weekly newsletters. "The Political Bird's Eye," a column by R. M. McClintock, which appeared in the *Pawnee* (Okla.) *Dispatch* on October 31, 1935, indicated that Grand River Dam Authority officials had conferred with Governor Ernest W. Marland, who had gone on record enthusiastically for the project. Clipping, Folder 5, Box 1, Disney Collection.

5. *Tulsa Tribune*, November 20, 1935, column by McClintock, and unidentified November 1935 clipping, Folder 5, Box 1, Disney Collection.

6. *Tulsa World*, February 19, 1936; *Daily Oklahoman*, February 21, 1936, clipping in Folder 6, Box 1, Disney Collection. See also the February 1936 clipping in Disney, Folder 6, Box 1, covering his activities at this time.

7. Quote is from an unidentified March 1936 clipping in Folder 6, Box 1, Disney Collection. This paragraph is based on perusal of clipping in Folder 6, Box 1, Disney Collection. See also *Harlow's Weekly*, April 18, 1936, for the article titled, "With the Oklahoma Delegation at Washington."

8. "Capital Topics," by McClintock, in *Ponca City* (Okla.) *News*, June 26, 1936, *Shawnee* (Okla.) *News*, June 25, 1936, plus late June clipping, Folder 7, Box 1, Disney Collection. The quote from *Harlow's Weekly* is in the *Grove* (Okla.) *Sun*, July 9, 1936.

9. *Tahlequah* (Okla.) *Star*, "The Political Bird's Eye," September 13, 1936, and *Ponca City News*, "Capital Topics, September 27, 1936, and Disney's "Weekly Washington Letter," in P*ryor* (Okla.) *Democrat*, September 19, 1936, and his newsletter in *Nowata* (Okla.) *Star*, September 19, 1936, *Nowata* (Okla.) *Times*, Disney's "Weekly Washington Letter," October 3, 1936, and *Heavener* (Okla.) *Ledger*, "The Political Bird's Eye," October 3, 1936, These and other relevant clipping can be found in Folder 8, Box 1, Disney Collection.

10. *Medford* (Okla.) *Star*, "This Week at the Capital," November 21, 1936, Folder 7, Box 1, Disney Collection; *Muskogee* (Okla.) *Phoenix*, January 29, 1937, Folder 2, Box 1, Disney Collection.

11. *Nowata Times*, July 1, 1937, clipping in Folder 30, Box 11, Legislative Files, Thomas Collection; Virginia Smith to Thomas, September 16, 1937 (telegram), Folder 16, Box 6, Projects Files, Thomas Collection; Holway, *History of the Grand River Dam Authority*, 7; Holway to Thomas, November 10, 1937, Folder 16, Box 6, Projects Files, Thomas Collection. Holway wrote, "I appreciate the important part you played in getting the Grand River Project over." *Tulsa Tribune*, January 25, 1937, and related clippings in Folder 1, Box 2, Disney Collection. Thomas called for the Public Works Administration to fund the construction of Pensacola Dam. See also *Ryan* (Okla.) *Democrat*, June 24, 1937, and related June clippings.

12. *Vinita Journal*, February 2, 1937, "News from the Capitol," by Wesley Disney, and *Vinita Journal*, February 4, 1937, *Vinita Journal*, August 4, 1937. Related clippings can also be found in Folder 1, Box 2, Disney Collection.

13. *Grove Sun*, July 29, 1937, *McAlester* (Okla.) *Capital*, July 27, 1937, and related clippings in Folder 2, Box 2, Disney Collection.

14. For Disney's remarks in full see his article in the *Afton* (Okla.) *American*, September 23, 1937. For stories of celebrations throughout the area see clippings, most notably *Harlow's Weekly*, September 18, 1937, Folder 3, Box 2, Disney Collection.

15. *Harlow's Weekly*, October 2, 1937, and October 30, 1937, for perceptive stories. The *Tulsa World*, October 16, 1937, published the complete text of the Public Works Administration contract. See related clippings in Folder 4, Box 2, Disney Collection.

16. *Oklahoma City Times*, November 6, 1937, *Daily Oklahoman*, November 9, 1937, *Muskogee* (Okla.) *Democrat*, November 6, 1937, and related clippings in Folder 5, Box 2, Disney Collection.

17. *Tulsa Tribune*, November 28, 1937, Folder 5, Box 2, Disney Collection; *Tulsa World*, January 6, 1938, and *Oklahoma City Times*, January 6, 1938, clippings in Folder 6, Box 2, Disney Collection.

18. *Daily Oklahoman*, February 2, 1938; *Oklahoma City News*, February 2, 1938; *Tulsa World*, January 2, 1938; and clippings in Folder 6, Box 2, Disney Collection. See also *Daily Oklahoman*, February 24, 1938, for pictures and stories about five individuals already benefiting from the approval of the project, Folder 6, Box 2, Disney Collection.

19. *Tulsa World*, June 18, 1938, story by R. P. Matthews; *Pryor Democrat*, July 21, 1938, clippings in Folder 10, Box 2, Disney Collection; *Tulsa World*, July 21, 1938, and January 15, 1939; *Oklahoma City News*, August 7, 1938; *Miami Record*, January 15, 1939, clippings in Folder 1, Box 3, Disney Collection.

20. *Oklahoma City Times*, February 2, 1939; clippings (no newspaper cited) March 29, 1939, Folder 1, Box 3, Disney Collection; Quince Biffle Boydstun,

Growing Up With Oklahoma (Oklahoma City: Oklahoma Historical Society, 1982), 120–21.

21. *Tulsa World*, March 1, 3, 1940, *Okmulgee* (Okla.) *Daily Times*, March 9, 16, 1940, *Oklahoma City Times*, March 16, 1940, *Miami Record*, March 8, 1940, *Mangum* (Okla.) *Star*, March 13, 1940, *Muskogee Democrat*, March 8, 1940, *Durant* (Okla.) *Democrat*, March 18, 1940, *Newkirk* (Okla.) *Daily Reporter*, March 9, 1940, all in Folder 4, Box 2, Disney Collection. See also *Tulsa Tribune*, April 19, 1940, Folder 5, Box 3, Disney Collection; *Tulsa World*, May 23, 1940, Folder 1, Box 2, Disney Collection. The Leon Phillips Papers in the Western History Collections at the University of Oklahoma contain a mass of scrapbooks and clippings. There is one folder in Box 21 pertaining to the Grand River Dam Authority. It contains several letters requested by the governor from Authority officials providing him with information about their assignments. "No governor," said Federal District Court Judge Robert L. Williams, himself a former governor, "has the power to declare martial law until the civil Authority has failed." See story in *Daily Oklahoman*, March 26, 1940, "Gov. Phillips Criticized for Calling Out Troops," copy in Folder 23, Box 6, Projects Files, Thomas Collection. The preliminary injunction enjoining any interference with the construction of the Pensacola Dam can be found in Holway, *History of the Grand River Dam Authority*, Section 9, 16–18.

22. *Vinita Journal*, May 4, 1939, *Pryor Democrat*, May 4, 1939, *Tulsa Tribune*, May 3, 1939, *Daily Oklahoman*, May 2, 1939, and related clippings, all in Folder 1, Box 3, Disney Collection. See *Tulsa Tribune*, August 23, 1939, in Folder 3, Box 2, Disney Collection. Elmer Thomas talked about the possibility of trying to develop a number of Oklahoma projects into a small TVA. See Thomas to R. L. Davidson, October 10, 1938, Folder 10, Box 11, Projects Files, Thomas Collection.

23. M. E. Pool to J. C. Wilkerson, October 10, 1938, Folder 15, Box 9, Projects Files, Thomas Collection; Thomas to R. Y. L. Wright, October 31, 1938, Folder 6, Box 18, Projects Files, Thomas Collection; *Mayes County* (Okla.) *Daily Democrat*, January 16, 1939, story entitled "Senator Elmer Thomas Back of Grand River Development," copy in Folder 73, Box 40, Legislative Files, Thomas Collection.

24. For some of the dimensions of this tension, see Thomas to M. S. Kreiger, June 27, 1939, Folder 10, Box 5, Projects Files, Thomas Collection. For a discussion by the chief of engineers, viewing these dams as serving the dual purpose of flood control and power development, see H. Doc. 107, 76th Cong., 1st sess. The document was transmitted to the Speaker on January 12, 1939.

25. *Muskogee Democrat*, March 30, 1940, *Tulsa Tribune*, April 19, 1940, and unidentified clipping, "Disney Seeks Arms Plant for GRD Area," Folder 5, Box 3, Disney Collection. See also *Vinita* (Okla.) *Star*, June 1, 1940, Folder 6, Box 3, Disney Collection, and Everett Bateman to Thomas, June 1, 1940, Folder 85, Box 4, Subject Files, Thomas Collection.

26. *Vinita Journal*, June 13, 1940, *Tulsa World*, June 12, 1940, Folder 5, Box 3, Disney Collection; *Tulsa Tribune*, July 11, 1940, Folder 6, Box 3, Disney Collec-

tion; *Miami Record*, July 17, 1940, Folder 7, Box 3, Disney Collection; *Pryor Democrat*, August 12, 1940, Folder 6, Box 3, Disney Collection; *Tulsa World*, October 27, 1940, Folder 8, Box 3, Disney Collection.

27. *Mayes County Democrat*, Special Edition, November 1940, Section E, "Romantic Story of Grand River Dam," Folder 8, Box 3, Disney Collection.

28. *Pryor Democrat*, March 27, 1941, and *Tulsa World*, March 27, 1941, Folder 1, Box 4, Disney Collection; *Tulsa World*, June 1, 1941, Folder 2, Box 4, Disney Collection; Thomas and Jack Nichols to Victor Barnett, telegrams, n.d., [1941], Folder 33, Box 5, Projects Files, Thomas Collection; *Grove Sun*, July 31, 1941, Folder 3, Box 4, Disney Collection; *Tulsa Tribune*, August 4, 1941, *Daily Oklahoman*, August 2, 1940, Folder 3, Box 4, Disney Collection; C. A. West to Lyle Boren, October 9, 1941 (telegram), Folder 35, Box 12, Lyle Boren Collection, CAC.

29. *Pawhuska* (Okla.) *News*, December 5, 1941, Folder 4, Box 4, Disney Collection; *Wagoner* (Okla.) *Tribune*, January 6, 1941, Folder 5, Box 4, Disney Collection; Boren to C. C. Grimes, November 12, 1941, Folder 35, Box 12, Boren Collection; Thomas to J. P. Arnold, December 12, 1941, Folder 18, Box 9, Projects Files, Thomas Collection; *Tulsa Tribune*, December 15, 1941, Folder 18, Box 9, Projects Files, Thomas Collection. See also *Daily Oklahoman*, November 22, 1941. Details about the takeover can be found in Holway, *History of the Grand River Dam Authority*, Section 12, 4–10.

30. *Pryor Democrat*, March 10, 1942, Folder 5, Box 4, Disney Collection; *Duncan* (Okla.) *Banner*, April 16, 1942, Folder 6, Box 4, Disney Collection.

31. *Tulsa World*, April 21, 1942, Folder 6, Box 4, Disney Collection. Disney declared that he did not care who built the dams "just so long as someone does." *Enid* (Okla.) *Morning News*, April 28, 1942, Folder 6, Box 4, Disney Collection.

32. N. R. Graham to Harold L. Smith, February 18, 1942, Folder 19, Box 9, Projects Files, Thomas Collection. Smith was director of the Bureau of the Budget. See also the resolution adopted by the Waterways Committee of the Tulsa Chamber of Commerce, April 20, 1942, copy in Folder 34, Box 5, Projects Files, Thomas Collection.

33. T. W. Stallings to Thomas, April 21, 1942, Folder 34, Box 5, Projects Files, Thomas Collection.

34. Holway to Board of Directors, Tulsa Chamber of Commerce, April 21, 1941, and Thomas to Holway, April 24, 1942, Folder 34, Box 5, Projects Files, Thomas Collection.

35. For details of "Government Takeover and Occupancy," see Holway, *History of the Grand River Dam Authority*, Section XII, 1–10, and "Grand River Dam Project [brief statement]," (n.d.) in Folder 13, Box 2, Conservation Files, Robert S. Kerr Collection, CAC.

36. N. R. Graham to Board of Directors, Tulsa Chamber of Commerce, May 18, 1943, copy in Folder 12, Box 2, Conservation Files, Kerr Collection. Similar environmental issues had occurred in 1927 when the Mississippi River rampaged

across the southern states. See Philip Scarpino, *Great River: An Environmental History of the Upper Mississippi, 1890–1950* (Columbia: University of Missouri Press, 1985), and Chris Morris, *The Big Muddy: An Environmental History of the Mississippi and Its Peoples from Hernando De Soto to Hurricane Katrina* (New York: Oxford University Press, 2012).

37. *Tulsa Tribune*, May 19, 1943, copy in Folder 35, Box 12, Boren Collection.

38. Thomas to War Production Board, July 18, 1943, Thomas to Reybold, July 15, 1943, Reybold to Thomas, July 21, 1943, Folder 35, Box 5, Projects Files, Thomas Collection. In his letter to the War Production Board, Thomas provided three pages of data pertaining to agricultural losses and damage caused by flooding. Thomas to Hub Adams, September 22, 1943, Folder 36, Box 5, Projects Files, Thomas Collection. Thomas to Major General Eugene Reybold, June 16, 1943, and Reybold to Thomas, June 24, 1943, Folder 35, Box 5, Projects Files, Thomas Collection, for both items; Thomas to Witt Dill, July 6, 1943, Folder 36, Box 5, Projects Files, Thomas Collection.

39. Earl Ward to Kerr, August 6, 1943, Folder 12, Box 2, Conservation Files, Kerr Collection; Harold Ickes to Thomas, August 11, 1943, Folder 36, Box 6, Projects Files, Thomas Collection. A copy of Executive Order No. 9373 can be found in Folder 12, Box 2, Conservation Files, Kerr Collection.

40. *Oklahoma City Times*, October 11, 1943, copy in Box 38, Folder 10, Boren Collection; Edward P. Marshall to Kerr, October 15, 1943, and November 2, 1943, Folder 12, Box 2, Conservation Files, Kerr Collection. Marshall was general counsel of the GRDA. See also a brief prepared by Marshall, "In Re: The Proposed Construction of The Markham's [*sic*] Ferry and Fort Gibson Dams by the United States Insofar As Their Construction Constitutes a Taking of Water Right in Grand River Vested in the Grand River Dam Authority by the Grand River Dam Authority Act" [November 1943], copy in Folder 12, Box 2, Conservation Files, Kerr Collection. See also Marshall to Reybold, December 17, 1943 (draft), in Folder 12, Box 2, Conservation Files, Kerr Collection.

41. *Daily Oklahoman*, November 15, 1943, Folder 25, Box 4, Boren Collection; *Tulsa World*, March 6, 1944, Folder 2, Box 5, Disney Collection; *Tulsa Tribune* (editorial), January 4, 1944, Folder 2, Box 35, Gubernatorial Files, Kerr Collection. For an analysis of the Goodrich decision and of its impact, plus a discussion of public power, see Wright to Kerr, March 8, 1944, Folder 2, Box 35, Gubernatorial Files, Kerr Collection.

42. See *Tulsa Tribune*, April 2, 1941, Folder 2, Box 4, Disney Collection, for a story about the plaques on the dam cornerstone. Howard Maginniss to Disney, January 2, 1941, Folder 1, Box 4, Disney Collection. Maginniss, a reporter on the *Tulsa Tribune*, asked why he "emphatically insisted" that his name be withheld from the "dedicatory emblems."

43. Thomas to C. R. Sallee, July 31, 1944, Folder 31, Box 5, Projects Files, Thomas Collection; Thomas to Reybold, August 16, 1944, and Wright to Thomas,

November 10, 1944, Folder 69, Box 4, Projects Files, Thomas Collection; France Paris to Thomas, August 29, 1944, Folder 18, Box 11, Projects Files, Thomas Collection. Paris was chair of the State Highway Commission. For Thomas's Senate remarks, see *Congressional Record*, 78th Cong., 2nd sess., November 24, 1944, 8488.

44. Thomas to W. H. Breedlove, February 17, 1945, Folder 70, Box 4, Projects Files, Thomas Collection; Thomas to F. M Baumgartner, February 21, 1945, and Thomas to R. Guy Scott, February 20, 1945, Folder 40, Box 6, Projects Files, Thomas Collection; Thomas to Mrs. R. W. Armstrong, February 17, 1945, Folder 7, Box 8, Subject Files, Thomas Collection. See also N. R. Graham to Thomas, February 9, 1945, Folder 44, Box 59, Legislative Files, Thomas Collection. Graham wrote, "You and I are in complete accord in our desires for river development."

45. "Chamber of Commerce Resolution, February 27, 1945, adopted at Pryor, Oklahoma," copy in Folder 71, Box 4, Projects Files, Thomas Collection. See also Haskell Gaither et al. to Thomas, August 27, 1945, Folder 21, Box 9, Projects Files, Thomas Collection.

46. Boydstun to Thomas, January 28, 1946, Folder 43, Box 6, Projects Files, Thomas Collection; Boydstun to Stigler, February 11, 1946, copy in Folder 45, Box 6, Projects Files, Thomas Collection.

47. Paris to War Assets Corporation, March 20, 1946, copy in Folder 15, Box 2, Conservation Files, Kerr Collection.

48. Paris to John J. O'Brien, May 29, 1946, Folder 15, Box 2, Conservation Files, Kerr Collection. O'Brien was director of the Office of Real Property Disposal, War Assets Administration. Paris to Kerr (telegram), June 12, 1945, Folder 15, Box 2, Conservation Files, Kerr Collection.

49. Claude Wickard to Robert M. Littlejohn, September 24, 1947, Folder 74, Box 2, Stigler Collection. Littlejohn was administrator of the War Assets Administration. Grand River Dam Authority Fact Sheet [n.d. , 1947], copy in Folder 12, Box 2, Conservation Files, Kerr Collection; Thomas to Graham, February 20, 1947, Folder 62, Box 12, Projects Files, Thomas Collection.

50. McBride to W. H. Sindt, July 19, 1946, Folder 22, Box 9, Projects Files, Thomas Collection. Sindt was division engineer for the Bureau of Community Facilities, Federal Works Administration. See also Kerr to Sindt, July 19, 1946, Folder 15, Box 2, Conservation Files, Kerr Collection. See also Paris to Thomas, October 26, 1946, Folder 22, Box 9, Projects Files, Thomas Collection; Thomas to W. E. Apperson, November 13, 1946, Folder 39, Box 5, Projects Files, Thomas Collection; and Thomas to Clarence Burch, November 18, 1946, Folder 4, Box 5, Projects Files, Thomas Collection.

51. Thomas to A. G. House, July 26, 1947, Folder 23, Box 9, Projects Files, Thomas Collection; C. H. Chorpening to Boydstun, September 8, 1947, copy in Folder 35, Box 66, Legislative Files, Thomas Collection. Chorpening was the district engineer in the Tulsa Office. Paris to Thomas, February 6, 1948, Folder 23,

Box 9, Projects Files, Thomas Collection; Thomas to Paris, February 18, 1948, Folder 25, Box 11, Projects Files, Thomas Collection.

52. J. C. Wilkerson to Thomas, December 17, 1948, Folder 23, Box 9, Projects Files, Thomas Collection; Graham to Thomas, November 27, 1948, Folder 23, Box 9, Projects Files, Thomas Collection; Thomas to J. T. Buckner, November 29, 1948, Folder 23, Box 9, Projects Files, Thomas Collection.

53. Boydstun to Thomas, December 27, 1948, copy in Folder 6, Box 4, Gubernatorial Files, Kerr Collection. Kerr was elected to the U.S. Senate in 1948.

54. Stigler Statement, January 29, 1948, Folder 70, Box 1, Stigler Collection.

55. Boydstun to Thomas, December 27, 1948, copy in Folder 15, Box 2, Conservation Files, Kerr Collection. Copies of the two bills were sent to Stigler by Governor Turner. Turner to Stigler, January 6, 1949, Folder 85, Box 2, Stigler Collection.

56. Thomas to Boydstun, January 27, 1949, Folder 6, Box 4, Gubernatorial Files, Kerr Collection; Thomas to Kerr, January 27, 1949, Folder 6, Box 4, Gubernatorial Files, Kerr Collection; H. H. Taylor to Thomas, March 5, 1949, Folder 24, Box 9, Projects Files, Thomas Collection.

57. Turner to Thomas, February 15, 1950, Folder 37, Box 90, Legislative Files, Thomas Collection; Turner to Kerr, February 15, 1950, Folder 6, Box 4, Conservation Files, Kerr Collection. Both senators supported Markham Ferry. Both placed the proposal in a broader context. See Thomas to Turner, March 6, 1950, Folder 25, Box 9, Projects Files, Thomas Collection; and Kerr to Turner, February 17, 1950, Folder 6, Box 4, Gubernatorial Files, Kerr Collection.

58. Thomas to Paris, March 31, 1950, Folder 49, Box 6, Projects Files, Thomas Collection. For a copy of S. 3432, introduced April 14, 1950, see Folder 6, Box 4, Gubernatorial Files, Kerr Collection. See also Hearing Before A Sub-committee On Public Works, United States Senate, 81st Congress, 2nd. sess. on S. 3432 May 25, 1950, copy in Folder 6, Box 4, Conservation Files, Kerr Collection; Kerr to Sheridan Downey, June 7, 1950, Folder 6, Box 4, Gubernatorial Files, Kerr Collection. Downey was chair of the Senate Subcommittee on Rivers and Harbors and Flood Control. See also Kerr to James N. Rutledge, June 12, 1950, Folder 6, Box 4, Conservation Files, Kerr Collection.

59. R. K. Lane to Dennis Chavez, July 11, 1950, Folder 6, Box 4, Conservation Files, Kerr Collection. Chavez chaired the Senate Committee on Public Works. Thomas to Joe Franks, August 28, 1950, Folder 26, Box 5, Projects Files, Thomas Collection.

60. For general information on Fort Gibson Dam and Reservoir, I have relied on *Civil Works News Bulletin* 1 (April 1951), copy in Folder 8, Box 2, Conservation Files, Kerr Collection. Additional information was gleaned from a lengthy report titled "Fort Gibson Project, Oklahoma," July 6, 1951, prepared for the commissioner of the Bureau of Reclamation and emanating from the regional director of

Region 5 in Amarillo, Texas, 11–12, passim, copy in Folder 9, Box 2, Conservation Files, Kerr Collection.

61. S. D. Searles to Chavez, August 20, 1951, Folder 6, Box 4, Conservation Files, Kerr Collection. Searles was acting secretary of the interior. Paris to Kerr, August 30, 1951, Folder 6, Box 4, Conservation Files, Kerr Collectiion; E. G. Herb to Paris, September 13, 1951, Folder 6, Box 4, Conservation Files, Kerr Collection. Herb was the Tulsa district engineer.

62. S. 2200, "A Bill for the Relief of the State of Oklahoma," Folder 16, Box 2, Conservation Files, Kerr Collection; "Statements re: controversy pertaining to Governor Phillip's actions re: Grand River Dam Authority," copy in Folder 49, Box 6, Projects Files, Thomas Collection. Unfortunately, the Department of Justice claimed that the Circuit Court of Appeals held that the state acknowledged full satisfaction of all claims for damages. See William Rogers to William Langer, July 6, 1953, copy in Folder 16, Box 2, Conservation Files, Kerr Collection. Rogers was deputy attorney general. Senator Langer chaired the Judiciary Committee. Oklahoma disputed the court decision and called for a hearing on S. 377. See LeRoy Powers to Langer, May 1, 1954, copy in Folder 17, Box 2, Conservation Files, Kerr Collection.

63. Paris to McBride, January 18, 1952, Folder 16, Box 2, Conservation Files, Kerr Collection; Boydstun to George Meier, January 25, 1952, Folder 16, Box 2, Conservation Files, Kerr Collection. Meier was deputy chief of real estate in the Office of the Chief of Engineers. LeRoy Powers to McBride, March 7, 1952, Folder 23, Box 23, Legislative Files, Kerr Collection. Powers was an attorney for Governor Johnston Murray. Lawton to Chavez, February 4, 1952, Folder 23, Box 23, Legislative Files, Kerr Collection. In this letter the director of the Bureau of the Budget suggests further fine-tuning of S. 272. Kerr to G. W. Terry, March 25, 1952, Folder 4, Box 7, Conservation Files, Kerr Collection. See also Paris to C. D. Williams, April 17, 1952, Folder 16, Box 2, Conservation Files, Kerr Collection. In this letter the Grand River Dam Authority sought to purchase a tract of surplus land of the Oklahoma Ordnance Works from the General Services Administration.

64. Kerr Press Release, January 22, 1953, Folder 35, Box 22, Political/Campaign Files, Kerr Collection.

65. Boydstun to Thomas H. Kuchel, June 22, 1953, Folder 4, Box 7, Conservation Files, Kerr Collection. Senator Kuchel was a member of the Committee of Public Works. Kerr and Monroney to United Press (telegram), July 6, 1953, Folder 4, Box 7, Conservation Files, Kerr Collection; Boydstun to Kerr, January 26, 1954, Folder 10, Box 2, Conservation Files, Kerr Collection; Kerr to Samuel Sturgis January 29, 1954, Folder 17, Box 2, Conservation Files, Kerr Collection. Sturgis was chief of engineers. How complicated the matter of easements could become is cited in T. A. Young to Kerr, February 15, 1954, Folder 25, Box 5,

Departmental Files, Kerr Collection. Young was a special assistant to the secretary of the army.

66. [Speech, untitled] (1955), p. 1, Folder 36, Box 12, Kerr Speeches, Kerr Collection; Kerr to Raymond Gary, February 28, 1955, Folder 41, Box 23, Legislative Files, Kerr Collection; Kerr to Nelle Penney, March 31, 1955, Folder 8, Box 4, Conservation Files, Kerr Collection. Kerr thought that under normal procedure construction of the Markham Ferry Dam could get under way within eighteen months.

67. Federal Power Commission: Project No. 2183, Release No. 7842 April 4, 1955, Folder 8, Box 4, Conservation Files, Kerr Collection; Kerr to Fred Qualls, April 5, 1955, Folder 8, Box 4, Conservation Files, Kerr Collection.

68. Kerr to Boydstun, July 13, 1955, Folder 31, Box 5, Legislative Files, Kerr Collection; Kerr to Francis Wilson, July 18, 1935, Folder 31, Box 5, Legislative Files, Kerr Collection.

69. Boydstun to Robert S. Mikesell, August 3, 1955, Folder 31, Box 5, Legislative Files, Kerr Collection; "Six Oklahoma Public Works Projects Listed," *Daily Oklahoman* (Oklahoma City), July 10, 1955.

70. Lyman Beard to Gary, June 28, 1957 (telegram), copy in Folder 8, Box 4, Conservation Files, Kerr Collection. Beard was mayor of Muskogee. J. B. Martin to Kerr, February 18, 1958, Folder 9, Box 4, Conservation Files, Kerr Collection. Martin was manager of the Miami Chamber of Commerce. Kerr to Ace Forman, February 11, 1958, Folder 9, Box 4, Conservation Files, Kerr Collection; Kerr to Hunter Martin, May 15, 1958, Folder 9, Box 4, Conservation Files, Kerr Collection. In 1959 the contract between the Grand River Dam Authority and the Public Service Company was still pending before the Federal Power Commission. See Kerr to Roy McGhee, February 4, 1959, Folder 10, Box 4, Conservation Files, Kerr Collection.

71. Wheeler Mayo to John Moore, May 8, 1951, copy in Folder 5, Box 3, Kerr Addition Series, Kerr Collection. Mayo was a former Grand River Dam Authority director and executive secretary of the Oklahoma Power Users Association, which opposed the contract and endorsed the Markham Ferry Project. Moore was administrator of the General Services Administration. *Daily Oklahoman*, October 9, 1956.

72. *Daily Oklahoman*, March 6, 1957, April 16 and 30, 1957; Holway, *History of the Grand River Dam Authority*, Section 15, Markham Ferry Project, 64. Holway, a consulting engineer, was associated with the Authority. His history, covering the years 1935–68, is a dense, complex volume long on detailed documentation.

73. *Daily Oklahoman*, May 16, 1957, August 1, 1957, September 21, 1957, December 18, 1957, and March 17, 1958.

74. *Daily Oklahoman*, May 12, 1960. This article by Allan Cromley contains a succinct summary of the controversy. Another story by Cromley on October 23, 1958, discusses facets of the contract.

75. *Daily Oklahoman*, July 3, 1959, December 6, 1959, May 12 and 13, 1960. See also an April 18, 1961, article by Allan Cromley.

76. C. J. Dugan to Frank Pittman, July 18, 1961, Folder 5, Box 3, Kerr Addition Series, Kerr Collection. Dugan was general manager of Grand River Dam Authority. Pittman was an official in the Atomic Energy Commission. Boydstun to Kerr, July 20, 1961, Folder 5, Box 3, Kerr Addition Series, Kerr Collection; Boydstun to Douglas Wright, August 7, 1961, Folder 5, Box 3, Kerr Addition Series, Kerr Collection. Wright was now administrator of the Southwestern Power Administration. Dugan to J. M. Hicks, November 15, 1961, Folder 5, Box 3, Kerr Addition Series, Kerr Collection.

77. *Daily Oklahoman*, August 15, 1962, December 6, 1961, and November 16, 1961.

78. Ben Owens to Bernard L. Boutin, January 6, 1962, Folder 5, Box 3, Kerr Addition Series, Kerr Collection. Boutin was administrator of the General Services Administration. Kerr to Owens, January 11, 1962, Folder 10, Box 4, Conservation Files, Kerr Collection.

79. A copy of Kerr's remarks at the start of the construction of the Markham Ferry Dam can be found in Folder 35, Box 7, Kerr Speeches, Kerr Collectiion. How rapidly construction was proceeding a half year after Kerr's speech is evident in Holway's July 15, 1962, Quarterly Progress Report, copy in Folder 10, Box 5, Conservation Files, Kerr Collection. Holway was construction engineer for the Markham Ferry Project. One of Kerr's last acts on behalf of the project was to prod the Interstate Commerce Commission to allow the Kansas, Oklahoma and Gulf Railway Company to abandon its tracks in the construction area of the dam site. Kerr to Robert Murphy, July 13, 1962, Folder 6, Box 3, Conservation Files, Kerr Collection. Murphy was chairman of the Interstate Commerce Commission. Charles Ingersoll to Kerr, December 27, 1962, Folder 10, Box 4, Conservation Files, Kerr Collection. Ingersoll was board chair of the Kansas, Oklahoma and Gulf Railway Company.

« 8 »

The 1969 Oklahoma City Garbage Strike

The turmoil and strife accompanying the efforts of African Americans to secure justice and equality in the 1960s largely evaded Oklahoma. By the latter years of the decade the state was well along on the road to integration in its schools and public accommodations. Thanks to Governors Johnston Murray and more notably Raymond Gary, Oklahoma had no Birmingham. Their efforts helped achieve the peaceful admission of blacks into the state's public schools. And also notably, two years before the sit-in in February 1960 in Greensboro, North Carolina, African Americans through an impressive series of sit-ins had won the right to be served in Oklahoma City on the same basis as white customers. By 1964 Oklahoma City had adopted a public accommodations ordinance. But even before the 1958 sit-ins, segregation in city theaters and city buses had ended quietly. Indeed, in 1957 the director of the Department of Commerce and Industry found Oklahoma's record on racial integration an important factor in contacts with prospective new industries.

The successful sit-ins were due largely to the strenuous efforts of Clara S. Luper working with the Youth Council of the National Association for the Advancement of Colored People (NAACP). She devoted fifteen months to planning and training its members in civil disobedience. Thanks in good part to her efforts a harmonious atmosphere of negotiation, compromise, and acceptance helped dampen threats of extremists who sought to curb these developments. But with the racial turmoil following the assassination of Martin Luther King, Jr., in Memphis on April 4, 1968, communities and states, especially in the South, enacted laws and ordinances designed to curtail rioting. Oklahoma and its capital city approved such legislation. Intended to limit race riots, the legislation proved equally effective against angry opponents of the escalating war in Vietnam. At the same time in Oklahoma, Governor Dewey Bartlett issued a proclamation designating the last week in April as Oklahoma Equal Opportunity Week.

But an Equal Opportunity Week did not resolve the concerns of many African American residents of Oklahoma City, of which adequate housing was among the most prominent. This concern focused on realtors' opposition to the civil right legislation that called for open housing, allowing individuals to live wherever their means would allow. Add inadequate education, poor city services, and recognition that practically every troubled situation that arose quickly involved the police. Despite much visible progress, African Americans were far from satisfied with their lot. Minor incidents could spark serious disturbances.[1]

On July 24, 1969, on a back page of the *Daily Oklahoman* appeared a story that could spark a serious disturbance. Sanitation workers, unhappy with their lot, were calling for improvements. A garbage strike inevitably conjured up memories of the 1968 strike in Memphis that cost Martin Luther King, Jr., his life and led to rioting that scourged numerous urban areas. A strike in New York City saw some one hundred thousand tons of garbage heaped high on city streets and prompted a health emergency. And with Clara Luper serving as spokesperson for the Oklahoma City workers, their dissatisfactions would be heard.

Luper was responding to a decision of Robert Oldland, the city manager new to his job from Miami, where he had held a similar position, to resurrect a minority employment committee. As a member of the committee, Luper responded that since there were no black supervisors in the Sanitation Department, before creating a minority committee this issue should be addressed. Thus, at the outset it was clear that a garbage strike would be a racial issue even more than a labor dispute.

After some discussion, 276 sanitation workers told Luper they wanted her as their leader. She agreed, set about organizing a steering committee, and sought a meeting with the city manager to present a list of grievances. Among them was a call for a five-day work week, specific job assignments, and elimination of the practice of making workers help out on other collection routes after completing their assignments. The workers also called for improved conditions at the municipal garages and, most important, a pay raise of $100 a month over the $360 pay minimum they were then only recently receiving. Oldland told Luper he would look at the demands and respond to them in writing.[2]

His response failed to satisfy the workers, though the city administration agreed to institute a five-day week on a trial basis in one area of the city. After due consideration the committee rejected the report on Monday, July 28, and agreed to meet later in the week to determine how to proceed. To a charge by Oldland that she was misinformed, Luper replied, "The city council is being asked by the city manager to raise the salaries of some big shot city workers, and I think it's time for the same city to give that long overdue raise for all city workers."[3]

At a Saturday meeting the sanitation workers voted to again ask the city manager for specific changes in their working conditions and for higher pay. If their requests were not answered by August 19, employees of the department would remain away from their jobs. While Oldland at first refused to recognize Luper as the sanitation employees' spokesperson, he made it clear that workers who left their jobs would be fired. In all there were about 360 workers, mostly African Americans, in the Sanitation Department; only about 40 who attended meetings with Luper agreed to strike if their requests for higher salaries and work changes were not met. They claimed to represent more than 300 sanitation workers.

At the same time, the City Council as well as city officials were discussing possible pay revisions for sanitation workers, firemen, police, and other city employees. Councilman A. L. Dowell, the lone black member, voiced concerns about revision of lower-echelon pay raises while discussing pay-range changes for higher-paid employees. And Luper announced that the NAACP Youth Council had voted to stand or lie down in front of garbage trucks if the workers' demands were not met. Some white workers assured Luper they were with her in endorsing the workers' demands. But Oldland, following an hour-long meeting with Luper, NAACP officials, and a representative of the Black Panthers (at least ten more waited outside the manager's office), insisted that "this city will not operate on a demand basis.[4]

"A man [Oldland] who makes $30,000 a year . . . should be more flexible and understanding of problems," exclaimed state representative Archibald Hill, a leader in the black community. Following the meeting and several days before the strike deadline, Oldland indicated some flexibility. He met with sanitation workers and agreed to most of their terms, with the exception of the demand for a salary increase that would have to await the completion of a salary review of city workers due at the end of the year. Flexible though he was, the city manager did not back away from his assertion that he would fire workers who refused to work on August 19.[5]

As the strike deadline approached, leaders sought to assure the black community that the dispute could be resolved without a confrontation that might get out of hand. The presence of Black Panthers outside the meeting in the manager's office had prompted some of this concern. To help insure a nonviolent outcome, NAACP headquarters in New York agreed to send two specialists, one an attorney, to assist leaders in the black community and pledged its support of the sanitation workers. In a roll-call vote, members of the Civic Leadership Coalition (CLC), composed of representatives of all major civil rights, social, and civic organizations, largely located on the east side of Oklahoma City, promised their support of the NAACP Youth Council's pledge to stand or lie down in front of garbage trucks if sanitation workers went on strike. The vote was unanimous. Prior to the vote, CLC leaders listened to five City Council members and the city manager present their side in the controversy. A large number of sanitation workers accompanied Clara Luper to this meeting, where the central issues were again discussed. Once again it was asserted that all the issues raised by the workers had been or were being resolved except demands for salary increases and for five-man crews instead of three-man work units. If the issues were not resolved, a minister at the meeting informed the audience that his fellow clergymen would be creating a fund to aid striking workers.[6]

While the CLC supported the sanitation workers, Mayor James Norick and the City Council lined up solidly behind the city manager. One by one the mayor and the council members endorsed the manager's edict that those who went on strike would be fired. Councilman

A. L. Dowell noted that most of the workers' issues had been resolved, except that of salary. He concluded that it was time for the workers to "yield something." While he acknowledged their "real" and "legitimate" demands, he contended that the men should consider "past and proposed progress in raising salaries and benefits." Thus, while some middle ground existed, proponents on both sides committed themselves on what each considered central issues: one involving wages, the other the illegality of the contemplated strike and the refusal to bargain. As the August 19 strike date approached, on August 15 its onset appeared inevitable.[7]

Yet on the weekend before August 19, Councilman Dowell urged Oldland to meet with Luper to cobble together a measure to raise workers' wages through a small increase in the monthly garbage rate of $2.50 for twice-weekly service. Dowell asserted that the dispute had become one of personalities and that the sanitation workers and their families had been largely forgotten. In a statement issued from his office, Oldland said that the city was continuing to evaluate the contentious issues and was in the process of establishing a fact-finding citizens committee to assist in resolving them.

Since the wedge between the two parties showed no last-minute signs of narrowing, Luper now spelled out some of the actions the black community would take. "The east side community will not allow others to pick up our garbage and members would give up things: new clothes, necessities of all kinds, in sympathy with the men if they were fired." In addition, members of the NAACP Youth Council paraded through downtown Oklahoma City on the Saturday morning preceding the strike. And at a church service the next day, Phil Savage, a NAACP official from Philadelphia and a cofounder of the Student Non-Violent Coordinating Committee, told the workers and their supporters that they "have just begun what you should have started years ago." All the community leaders who spoke throughout the weekend deplored violence yet were firm in their support of the sanitation workers. Also, the Interdenominational Ministerial Alliance sent telegrams to the mayor and city manager expressing concern about the "threat of a strike or violence in our streets."[8]

On August 19 a majority of the more than 300 city employees seeking a $100 per month wage increase were African Americans. The walkout affected approximately 450,000 city residents. At no time during its course did Oklahoma City enjoy full, twice-a-week garbage service. Efforts were made to provide once-a-week service, and on one occasion for a brief period in one part of the city full service was available. In addition, garbage trucks were parked at fire stations for residents to deposit their refuse. The police, most of whom were white and who like the sanitation workers were affected by inflation and anticipated a pay raise, were assigned to accompany garbage trucks and to guard the truck barns all night. But on the first day of the strike there were no incidents. Fifty-six volunteers manned thirty-three trucks aided by forty-three men who remained on their jobs. No incidents occurred because the committee studying city salaries suggested that the city give the striking workers until 5:00 P.M. Friday to seek reinstatement "without loss of accrued benefits." At a marathon meeting before the scheduled strike, the men decided instead to march on City Hall. They were encouraged by the progress of the fact-finding committee in seeking to improve salaries and working conditions. The one hundred workers who marched wanted to recommend that the council move a pay raise (not yet determined) scheduled for January 1 back to September 1. Council members, however, insisted they could not consider giving a pay raise to any segment of city workers without considering all city employees.

After the sanitation workers indicated they could not accept the promise of a raise in 1970 as a reason for calling off the strike, a meeting of council members, sanitation workers, strike committee leaders, and NAACP officials was called at the Oklahoma City Chamber of Commerce offices. Here once again the entire situation was thrashed about. No side was willing to make any concessions on the crucial issue of a pay raise. At the end of the first day of the walkout, then, no serious incidents had occurred, Oldland had offered an olive branch to the workers, and city residents had been alerted on how to handle their refuse. Now officials could only await the response of the disgruntled workers and their supporters.[9]

Early Wednesday morning outside the Westwood garage, severe disturbances occurred. Only twenty-two of the city's sanitation trucks were in service, while thirty-seven persons were arrested for obstructing the street, disorderly conduct, or inciting to riot. Among those arrested were Luper, the spokesperson for the workers, and two NAACP officials: James Brown from New York and Richard Dockery from Dallas. With the strike under way, the citizen fact-finding committee recommended $40 raises, by September 1, of $40 for all municipal employees making less than $500 a month and $20 for those earning more than $500, to be financed by a modest increase in monthly sewer and refuse rates. Coupled with an already budgeted $20 across-the-board annual rate slated for January 1970, the proposed increase would mean a total $60 per month increase for the Sanitation Department and for other workers making less than $500 by that date. Though the workers rejected this proposal, it was accepted by the City Council, which started to improve the facilities workers used, such as providing showers and lockers. Though the committee proposal became central to the final outcome of the strike, neither the city nor the strikers and their supporters at this time accepted it.[10]

Meanwhile, that Wednesday evening—August 20, 1969—at the Greater Cleaves Memorial CME Church, about four hundred people, many forced to stand, heard state senator E. Melvin Porter and state representative Archibald Hill assert that they would be on hand early the following morning to block movement of garbage trucks. They were joined by Luper, who urged supporters to meet at the nearby Freedom Center, from whence they would go in a caravan to the two city garages—one on Classen Boulevard and the nearby one on Westwood. Porter promised to stand in front of a garbage truck. Hill went further and told the cheering crowd that he was willing to lie in front of one of those trucks. Brown, the national youth secretary of the NAACP, criticized the police for overreacting and said they should understand that if sanitation workers got a raise, they would too. Both were in the same situation.[11]

While these officials and fifteen other men were arrested on Thursday morning, six of the eight City Council members agreed to the citizen council proposed pay raise; two council members were not present, but as Dowell said, "the six votes are enough to pass it." At another packed church meeting, sanitation workers agreed to meet near the Westwood garage to vote on the proposal. One of the strikers said earlier in this meeting that the workers would hold out for a $100 increase. But both Dowell and Luper expressed hope for a prompt settlement. More important, Luper, a high school history teacher, announced she would be returning to the classroom and that the leadership of the strike would change. To offset, in part, the loss of her leadership, the Oklahoma Bar Association offered free legal representation to all city sanitation workers, an indication that there was some sympathy for their cause in the broader community.[12]

By Friday the strike seemingly stalled, as sixty-nine workers applied for reinstatement, joining at least thirty who were already rehired or had applied for reinstatement. Meanwhile, new workers (scabs) were being hired, and some of those who remained on the job were being promoted. Employees from other departments were used to drive fifty of the eighty-three available garbage trucks. After four days, as the strike appeared to be collapsing, leaders in the black community at various meetings insisted that too much was at stake, that the effort should not be abandoned.[13]

It was not. Sanitation workers demonstrated by marching on City Hall, holding meetings, attending rallies, and listening to Luper and Porter whip up enthusiasm. Seeking to curb that enthusiasm and possibly end the strike, Oldland announced that the city would reinstate all but thirty-three of the strikers because that number of new refuse collectors had already been hired. Though those rehired might not be placed in their former jobs, the city manager pledged that every effort to do so would be made. Thus, while the strike situation appeared stalled, it was clear from Oldland's offer that it was having an effect. As one striker observed, "We know what conditions filth brings and that is what Oklahoma City is experiencing now."[14]

Without a union and without a strike fund, sanitation workers had to rely on community leaders for guidance and supporters for funds. It was understandable that many workers sought their jobs back and why a week after the strike was launched they yielded their demand for a $100 per month increase and settled for a $40 raise effective September 1 and an additional $20 raise effective January 1. Their only proviso was that they return to their same jobs. At this point, if the City Council and Mayor

Norick had assumed the initiative, the strike could have ended to the satisfaction of all concerned.[15]

Instead, the situation became more intense as a permit was granted for a parade in support of the city manager and the chief of police. On the other side, the CLC now assumed a broader role in the dispute. The coalition, composed of representatives of forty-two black community organizations, was headed by the Reverend W. K. Jackson, minister of St. John's Baptist Church, which served as strike headquarters. A strategy committee headed by Urban League director Frank Cowan sought further meetings with city officials to end the strike now that most of the workers' demands had been met and more workers had returned to their jobs. Ten days into the strike 175 men were at work. The Sanitation Department now employed 284 garbage collectors compared to 35 at the beginning of the work stoppage two weeks previous.[16]

To prompt a resolution of the strike, CLC leaders called early in September for a general boycott of downtown stores and shopping centers. A march on the city Police Department was planned to protest the different handling of demonstrations by blacks, who were closely monitored, and those by whites, who were not. Moreover, Oldland and the City Council appeared to backtrack on the citizen committee's proposal by now insisting that active leaders of the strike or men who had been arrested during demonstrations not be rehired. On both sides feelings became more intense. Leaders became more determined and more firmly locked in their positions.[17]

Excitement mounted in the black community when it was learned that the Reverend Ralph Abernathy, the successor of Martin Luther King, Jr., as president of the Southern Christian Leadership Conference (SCLC), would be in Oklahoma City to march in support of the workers' demands. Excitement mounted also because the CLC was striving to expand the economic boycott. In addition to the forty-two original groups making up the coalition, eighty additional organizations, including several unions, were expected to join the mass efforts of the coalition and to assist in contributing funds and food. Excitement faded when it was learned that Abernathy, "due to emergency situations in Atlanta at the Southern Christian Leadership Conference," would not visit as planned. It faded even more when two of the demonstrators at the Westwood Sanitation Department compound weeks previously were found guilty of obstructing a city street and fined. Luper was required to pay two $30 fines, while the Reverend Norbert Kabelitz, pastor of Redeemer Lutheran Church, guilty of the same offense, was ordered to pay two $20 fines. Kabelitz was one of a handful of white people who were actively engaged with the CLC.[18]

Despite setbacks with the strike diminishing in intensity, the CLC could note some positive signs. The Saturday boycott of downtown stores was beginning to have an impact. Merchants reported light business and some harassment of customers, such as being photographed by boycott backers or handed leaflets. A social club volunteered to operate a carpool to take shoppers to nearby communities. By mid-September no blacks were evident at any downtown restaurant. Even more positive was the City Council voting a pay raise for sanitation workers, though it was not as high as the one recommended by the citizens fact-finding committee. By mid-September the difference between the contending parties was narrowing. The peaceful marches and the boycott were beginning to have an impact even beyond Oklahoma City. In nearby Norman students at the University of Oklahoma were urged to support the strikers. Further evidence was an announcement in September and quickly endorsed by the CLC that a drive to organize a local union of city employees would soon be launched.[19]

On Sunday, September 21, at the Will Rogers World Airport, the president of the SCLC was greeted by a group of about sixty people. He would participate in a march the following day but refused to talk about the strike until he conferred with the CLC leaders. Instead, Abernathy spoke briefly about the SCLC and nonviolence. At a CLC public meeting at St. John's Baptist Church that evening, Abernathy said, "I came to tell old Pharaoh mayor and the Pharaoh city manager to let the sanitation workers go." But at the end of a march estimated at about eight hundred people, with others watching and cheering them on, "old Pharaoh mayor" James Norick was nowhere to be seen, and the Pharaoh city manager agreed to see Abernathy for the purpose of welcoming him to Oklahoma City but not to discuss the sanitation strike. Frustrated by no reception at City Hall Abernathy, before departing the city, expressed confidence in the local leaders and the "excellent cooperation from the various levels among the community in Oklahoma City." His visit would be followed by one from another SCLC official, whose mission, Abernathy said, would be to determine how the SCLC could best aid the striking sanitation workers.[20]

Oldland's refusal to meet with Abernathy and strike leaders suggested increasing intransigence on the city's part. Mayor Norick, the city manager said, was "busy at the plant [his printing business] and with prior commitments [at the State Fair of Oklahoma]." In a memorandum to department heads for posting in city buildings and offices, Oldland prohibited union organizing "on city property on city time." For their part, the Reverend W. K. Jackson, chairman of the CLC, said the coalition looked forward to the aid forthcoming from the SCLC. Meanwhile, the boycott and the marches continued, including a march of about sixty strike supporters intending to call on Oldland's home, only to learn that they'd gone to the wrong address.[21]

After Abernathy's visit, enthusiasm and support seemed to wane. By early October about half of the more than 200 workers who had walked off the job had returned to work, while the city had been hiring new men. But the division staff was still below "the some 275 workers who were on the job before August 19." Nevertheless, an optimistic assistant city manager announced twice weekly sanitation service for the central area of the city on Monday, October 6. The central city was the heaviest work area, but it was less than a third of the total area serviced by the city. As more workers returned or were recruited, service would be expanded, depending on the tempo of the strike.[22]

That the tempo would change became evident that same week, when Roland Betts, a field staff representative of the SCLC, and his wife moved to Oklahoma City. Betts would assess the situation and remain in the city "until this thing is over—until it's won." Another SCLC official who accompanied Betts argued that the sanitation strike was essentially "a trade union fight" and should receive their support, a development that never occurred. To many city officials the strike had ended a scant four or five days after it began, but to the CLC leadership in mid-October, the strike was entering its third month with no end in sight.[23]

On October 21 Oldland sent a memo to the mayor and City Council in which he addressed "legitimate sanitation employee grievances and . . . implement[ation of] changes recommended by the Citizens Fact-Finding Committee." In particular, the memo called for a five-day work week, increased minority employment in administrative positions, overtime payment for crews volunteering for additional work, improved grievance procedures, the construction and improvement of shower and crew room facilities in the truck yards maintained by the Sanitation Department—and most important, a pay plan along the lines suggested by the citizens committee. Oldland further proposed a policy of reinstatement of which 128 workers had already taken advantage. As of October 20, he wrote, "there were a total of 219 sanitation employees working." With this report, if approved by the City Council, the sanitation dispute could have been resolved. Instead, a spokesman for the CLC called for a new walkout on Monday, October 27.[24]

In calling for the walkout, Archibald Hill, chairman of the CLC's strategy committee, told a news conference that sanitation workers still demanded "reinstatement of all workers without loss of benefits and at least a $60 [monthly] raise." Aware of the city manager's memo, Hill said the workers disagreed with the pay scales it presented. He called Oldland "an enemy of ours" and that workers who remained at their jobs would "be labeled 'Uncle Toms.'" In addition, he asserted that demonstrations would be increased and not be announced before they took place. Betts, the field organizer for the SCLC, insisted that "it is necessary to intensify demonstrations and strike activities." Others, including a representative of the workers along with a Black Muslim, issued statements suggesting a black community that was strongly coming together. Any grounds for using Oldland's memo as a base for discussing and resolving the issues on which they were not far apart had disappeared.[25]

To intensify their efforts, Hill attacked Oldland, saying he had handled the situation in an irresponsible manner, "with a deep southern approach." But he insisted that, despite the city manager's refusal to negotiate, violence would not resolve the workers' problems. Moreover, he argued, it would not be necessary to raise taxes to improve employees' wages, since "the sanitation department brings in about $3.6 million per year and costs only $1.3 million to operate." Oldland, in turn, called Hill's remarks "irresponsible," adding that all who strike would be fired. But he did not think the announced walkout, if it ever occurred, would be as extensive as the one that had begun on August 19.[26]

It would occur. Strikers and their supporters were urged to be on hand at the Westwood garage, where Reverend Jackson would lead the demonstration that was to begin at 5:00 A.M., or before the trucks left the garage. For some time after August 20, which was the date of the initial effort to stop the trucks, police patrol cars had escorted the trucks on their appointed rounds, and that was the case today. All the forces were now in play for the dramatic confrontation that next occurred.[27]

A bold newspaper headline blared "Demonstrators Block Trucks; Eight Jailed." Reading from the Bible, Reverend Jackson was dragged by two officers from the front of a garbage truck to a paddy wagon. Twice groups of four demonstrators knelt in line in front of trucks leaving the compound and were arrested. Some like Reverend Jackson resisted passively and were carried or dragged to waiting paddy wagons. Jackson, holding an open Bible, repeated over and over, "The Lord is my refuge and strength." All were African Americans; all but Representative A. Visanio Johnson were jailed in lieu of bonds ranging from $40 to $100. While six were soon released on cash bonds, Representative Johnson on his own recognizance, Reverend Jackson, the head of CLC, refused bond and remained in jail, saying "I just want to get some rest." Roland Betts, carrying a sign that read "Nigger Get Off That Truck," was one of the arrested men.[28]

Demonstrators who were not arrested left the compound at about 7:00 A.M. Most of the garbage workers interviewed indicated that they wanted to work. Some crossed the picket line; others were pleased with the prospects of improved working conditions; most were disillusioned. And so was Robert Oldland. While the city manager had expressed doubts that demonstrations would be effective, now he reversed himself. Strikers would not be rehired, as they were after August 19. At the other end of the spectrum, Representative Hill proclaimed that the demonstration that put eight men in jail would be "only kindergarten" in comparison to forthcoming actions, and he explained that workers who collected garbage would not be threatened with actual harm but were certain to be ostracized by the black community.[29]

That evening, following a peaceful City Hall demonstration, the City Council agreed by consensus to keep lines of communication open but to make no overtures to strike supporters. The city would meet with CLC leaders but would not initiate a meeting. Mayor Norick said he did not know when a proclamation of emergency for various locations, including fire stations and other city property, would be lifted. While tensions seemed to ease at City Hall, such was not the case at a Sunday evening meeting called by the CLC. When Reverend Jackson addressed the less than two hundred people in attendance, he asked all sanitation workers to stand. Three men rose. Nevertheless, CLC leaders said a demonstration would occur the following morning. Strikers were to meet at 4:00 A.M. at the same church, St. John's Baptist. Jackson said workers "don't have a reason to be afraid to walk off the job." "The City Manager," he continued, "can't fire you. He's doing the same thing they were doing a hundred years ago in Georgia and Mississippi—trying to frighten the black man." Much was at stake. Despite rousing rhetoric, the two-month-old sanitation strike was clearly at a crossroads. Without mass community support, the upcoming walkout could fail, a point emphasized by Representative Johnson in his remarks: "If the strike effort fails Monday, then the black community has lost the struggle, lost the strike, and lost the city. If we lose now, Oklahoma City black people will be ignored by City Hall from now on."[30]

Early Monday morning, forty-four out of forty-six garbage trucks, each with a police car escort, rumbled out of the Westwood compound. About twenty-five workers walked off their jobs. Fourteen demonstrators were arrested, most of them ministers. And the district attorney announced he was considering felony charges against Betts, the SCLC field organizer, and Representative Hill. Among the demonstrators was Mrs. Clare Robertson, who was thrown from a garbage truck when she tried to prevent it from leaving the compound. Once again Reverend

Jackson, holding a Bible, was dragged to a paddy wagon. Most of those arrested, after posting $20 bonds, were released. But three ministers, including Jackson, wanted no bonds posted and intended to fast "until justice is done," according to Senator Melvin Porter, a strike leader. Roland Betts, however, received special treatment. He was arraigned in district court and released from county jail on $1,000 bond on a misdemeanor charge. In all there were more police (around sixty) than demonstrators (about forty) on hand as anger flared on both sides. But, it should be noted, most of the trucks left the compound after the demonstration had been quelled by the police. For over an hour more than a hundred sanitation workers, mostly African Americans, had milled around the crew room and refused to take out trucks, all but twenty-five doing so after the demonstration abated.[31]

Meeting that evening, strike leaders told a mass meeting that they would intensify "direct action" until the workers' demands were met. To assist them in these efforts was the Reverend T. Y. Rogers, Jr., of the SCLC. On the platform with Rogers was Theodore GX, leader of the Oklahoma City Black Muslim Mosque. Strike leaders announced that demonstrators on the following day would try again to keep the trucks from rolling and would be on hand when the City Council met later in the day. Reverend Rogers told a hand-clapping audience, "Praying is OK, but you've got to march and fight a little, too." Theodore GX went further and argued that before they could win concessions, they needed to learn that "the white man is your enemy." But Representative Hill, emphasizing the premise of the CLC leadership, stated boldly that if there is violence, "the violence will come from the policemen. . . . They're out there armed and violent." And the police were working twelve-hour shifts instead of their regular eight-hour stints.[32]

In answer to a telegram from Reverend Rogers asking that the governor intervene to head off possible violence, Governor Dewey Bartlett said, "Jurisdiction in the matter between the sanitation workers and officials of the city of Oklahoma City rests with those city officials." Bartlett parried questions from newsmen, all answers indicating he had no intention of involving himself. The governor's press conference in effect diverted attention from the demonstrations called for Tuesday, October 28. The demonstration, in which seven protestors were arrested, was followed by strike supporters appearing before the City Council to protest the failure of the police to investigate the incident in which a garbage truck "ran down" a woman demonstrator (Mrs. Robinson). A. L. Dowell, the lone black City Council member, acutely observed that the dispute now revolved around one main issue—the rehiring of the workers who acted as leaders in the strike movement. What did get attention was another mass meeting at St. John's Baptist Church, where strike leaders called for a "Black Friday" in Oklahoma City. They asked that black school children and black workers in all positions stay at home in a show of support. "We have to take radical action," asserted Reverend Rogers, "because we have a radical problem." And those in attendance learned that Ralph Abernathy, head of the SCLC, would return to Oklahoma City to support the strike.[33]

On Wednesday about 130 workers refused to board garbage trucks, while in a drizzling rain 15 demonstrators, including 4 high school students, were arrested at the Westwood compound. About 120 policemen confronted 80 or more demonstrators. Tempers flared on both sides. By midmorning only twelve of the trucks scheduled to leave the yard were on the road, seven of which were manned by volunteer crews from the city's Street Department. Clara Luper and Representative Hill demonstrated but were not arrested while Reverend Jackson remained in jail. At one point, Luper led demonstrators in a "snail dance" in front of the main gate. A white man who was a high school teacher said he'd joined the demonstration "because I am a Christian." Another demonstrator was Mrs. Robertson, who had been bumped by a truck earlier in the week and was again arrested. She was photographed and fingerprinted by officers in the compound. She then dropped to the ground and was dragged to the paddy wagon. Another demonstrator, clutching a small American flag, lay on his back on the ground and was also dragged to the paddy wagon. With the demonstrators for the first time were Councilman Dowell and Representative Hannah Atkins.[34]

About half of those who walked off the job appeared at the NAACP Freedom Center for a rally led by Roland Betts. He urged the men to "stop believing white folks" and urged them to join the morrow's demonstration. "If we stay on till Friday this will be over by Monday and everyone will be back to work," he predicted, presciently. Meanwhile, Sanitation Department supervisors reportedly asked the city manager to rehire the strike leaders who had walked off their jobs on August 19.[35]

As the black community and a handful of white supporters increased the pressure on behalf of the strikers, so too did Mayor Norick and some City Council members toughen their stance. They called for felony charges against demonstrators and sought to determine if Dowell could be removed from the council. Both Dowell and Atkins had addressed the rally at St. John's Baptist Church before appearing with the demonstrators the following morning. Dowell, an optometrist whose name often appeared in print as Dr. Dowell, told the rally, "The only conclusion I can arrive at is that it is time for the entire black community to take a stand," while asserting "we are tired of asking, we are tired of begging." Representative Atkins went further and said to the black community that the city had reached an "all-time low" when at the previous City Council meeting "the skunks in City Hall showed their stripes." Both, as already noted, demonstrated the following morning, and Dowell was arrested at the Westwood site on October 30. While the mayor and several council members considered calling for more severe measures, there was growing recognition that the crux of the matter was no longer wages but the retention of the twelve strikers (the number varied at times) who had walked off their jobs on August 19, more than two months past.[36]

Finally, on October 29, Robert Oldland said openly what everyone understood but none had proclaimed, namely that Oklahoma City faced "a major racial crisis." The sanitation strike had never really been a labor dispute, as officials previously argued, but an effort on the part of black sanitation workers to secure a greater measure of human dignity by achieving parity in the workplace. But Oldland went on to reaffirm the council's policy of not rehiring the leaders who had urged the walkout of two hundred workers on August 19. "This city," he insisted, "cannot and must not be subjected to the violence and risks that have plagued other cities across the nation," nor could the city "be administered on the basis of threats or coercion." While its comprehension of the situation had increased, the city government manifested little sensitivity or knowledge in seeking to cope with it.[37]

On Thursday morning Reverend Jackson paid a $20 bond and left the jail, while Dowell and Atkins were arrested, along with five others, at the Westwood compound, where many teenagers were among the demonstrators. That afternoon six hundred Douglass High School students marched on City Hall before holding a rally at a nearby park. And there were rumors that the National Guard would be on hand in case anything got out of hand on "Black Friday." Some Street Department employees who worked out of the Westwood compound refused to go to work that morning, indicating the possibility of a sympathy strike. Hannah Atkins, refusing to post bond, told the judge she wanted to stay in jail "awhile." The *Black Dispatch* devoted a full page and part of another to listing the names of individuals who supported the sanitation workers and called for "1. Every Man Reinstated," and "2. Issue the $60 Dollar Monthly Raise Now!" Later that evening Mayor Norick declared a state of emergency in limited areas of the city.[38]

But the *Daily Oklahoman* also reported that Norick was prepared to tell Reverend Jackson and other black leaders that a majority of the council would vote at a special meeting to change the policy against rehiring the twelve workers by allowing them to return to work on six months' probation before receiving full reinstatement. Unable to attend this meeting owing to a mass meeting of about seven hundred people at his church, Jackson and other leaders prepared for the march to be led by Ralph Abernathy, while the city prepared to cope with a dire emergency.[39]

Clara Luper, in charge of organizing students for the march, said there would be one central leader and one from each of the five city high schools participating. Earlier Black Student Union members at Oklahoma City University announced that they too would march. Finally, at this rally Reverend Jackson denied the strike was racial in nature, claiming it was merely "a fight for the sanitation workers." Earlier at the rally he had told the group that the CLC would apply for a parade permit the following morning, several hours before the march was scheduled.[40]

On Friday a crowd estimated by police at fifteen hundred marched three abreast on City Hall. They marched without the presence of the head of the SCLC, who was coping with another emergency situation. No arrests were made; no violent incidents were reported. Most stores in the downtown area along the parade route were closed. Helmeted officers, some with shotguns, others with tear gas and mace, awaited the marchers near City Hall.

About four hundred city police and highway patrol troopers were assigned to the march that got underway from Washington Park on the east side in the early afternoon when the state NAACP youth adviser called out "All right. Let's go, brothers." As they marched across town for about ninety minutes toward City Hall, they were joined by some observers. Several marchers carried signs proclaiming their concerns. A lone police car preceded the procession, which wended its way past tumbled-down houses and shabby shops, past a tavern where men were already drunk early in the afternoon, past frowsy prostitutes and ragged kids, while marchers sang "We Shall Overcome" and some of the youth chanted "Black Power." Up front with Reverend Jackson and Luper were Representative Atkins and Senator Porter. Two white ministers marched alongside Jackson. The line of the march extended close to five city blocks.

Near City Hall uniformed and plainclothes police armed with heavy wooden riot sticks and joined by all the law enforcement officials in the city awaited the marchers. "Anybody who doesn't want to be arrested, stay back" blared forth from a loudspeaker as the marchers approached the off-limits area. Asked if the marchers intended to continue to City Hall, Jackson nodded, Luper uttered an inarticulate cry and clasped the hand of Atkins, and the marchers moved forward toward the massed force of police. At the last possible moment, the police stepped aside and let the demonstrators pass. As they crowded the east steps at City Hall, armed and helmeted officers formed a ring around the protestors. As the chief of police handed Reverend Jackson a portable megaphone, Jackson and Luper turned to face the crowd. Jackson asked the mayor and city manager, neither of whom were evident, to "keep the faith with these men in order that our city may have the proper image in America," then added, "We are going to be orderly and non-violent."—whereupon the demonstration took on an aspect of a love-in. The police chief thanked the marchers for their nonviolent attitude. Jackson then asked that "each and everyone of us peacefully now disperse on the sidewalks in groups of not more than three." He asked that people meet again that evening at his church. Policemen then moved aside and let the demonstrators depart. In all, the confrontation lasted about twenty minutes. Governor Bartlett, who had carefully monitored the situation, thanked all involved parties for the manner in which they conducted themselves. But even as tension abated and everyone dispersed, the plight of the sanitation workers was still unresolved.[41]

District Attorney Curtis Harris sought to resolve the situation by filing felony riot charges against four strike leaders and in so doing angered and solidified strike supporters. The four were Representative Hill, who was serving as chief strategist and attorney for the strikers; City Councilman Dowell, an intermediary who had forcefully argued the strikers' case; Betts of the SCLC; and William Woodward, a respected member of the black community who had not played a prominent role in the strike. After arraignment, they were represented by Senator Porter, who hurriedly raised the bonds set at $5,000 each and arranged a date for a preliminary hearing. The bonds were signed by the operators of a funeral parlor. Both Representative Atkins and Luper, who witnessed these proceedings. offered brief remarks; Luper's were most telling: "Oklahoma City lacks leadership in the white community at this time. I think the silence of the white churches, labor leaders, political leaders, business leaders and plain white people has created a climate where professional bigots"—and here she rattled off the names of several city officials from the mayor on down—"can practice their bigotry under the flag of law and order."[42]

Though the four released on bail were not on hand for the march, strike leaders justifiably were pleased with its outcome. At the rally held Friday evening, Betts mentioned the emergency meeting that had prevented Abernathy from participating. He was in Dallas and had purchased an airline ticket to Oklahoma City before the emergency that sent him to Memphis. While there was much to celebrate, steps toward resolution would have to come from the white community, and its concerns soon became evident. Hundreds of city residents wanting to know when and where they could dump garbage flooded the Fire Department's alarm headquarters. And the *Daily Oklahoman*, which had faithfully covered the dispute with front-page stories, finally committed itself with a front-page editorial in the Sunday issue, where it would attract widespread attention.[43]

Boldly titled "Let's Settle It Now," the editorial asserted that Oklahoma City was "setting a time bomb" with a short fuse as it escalated a dispute over wages "into a contest as to whether blacks or whites would win." Recognizing that "the cooperation and goodwill of the blacks" was important to the city's future, the editorial claimed that an offer from the City Council to rehire former sanitation workers could settle the dispute. While it was not important which side won, it was important "that the public wins." To reach that goal, the editorial observed that "council members are meeting today in Gov. Bartlett's house" with some "dedicated citizens" serving as mediators, adding, "Both sides should give enough to reach an agreement."[44]

The story accompanying the editorial stated that strike leaders and council members would meet that afternoon at the Executive Mansion. Bartlett still insisted that the dispute was a local problem, but that he certainly wanted to assist in seeking a solution can be inferred from the fact that he had hastily canceled a planned vacation trip. Both sides were amenable to the meeting, which had been prompted by a group of business and civic leaders who were initially contacted by the governor.[45]

After two and a half months, the two sides were now seriously negotiating. For about nine hours, until 12:30 the following morning of November 3, the two groups were closeted in separate rooms on the first floor of the mansion, with mediators carrying messages back and forth. Mayor Norick did not attend, nor did one councilman who was out of the city. But the city manager and his top assistant were with the council. By 4:30 on Sunday afternoon the CLC delegation of about twenty members representing the strikers had presented its proposal for reaching a settlement to the three mediators. Reportedly it contained eight terms, the key issue calling for reemployment of all strikers with full benefits. If the council accepted the proposal, everything could be quickly resolved, since it had already addressed many of the issues, including a $60 raise. The mediators, shuffling between rooms, were the president of the Oklahoma City Chamber of Commerce, a former district judge, and a prominent city businessman.[46]

By the end of the second day the talks had broken off. Both sides refused to yield on the rehiring of eleven strike leaders. Calling the talks "fruitless," the chairman of the CLC said, "When they get ready they'll call us." Though he did not elaborate, he insisted that demonstrations would continue, while a spokesman for the absent mayor indicated that the limited state of emergency was continuing. And Oldland observed that the primary methods of garbage collection would continue to be the twenty-four trucks placed at fire stations. About eight hundred tons of garbage had been collected over the past weekend.[47]

The vice mayor, speaking for a majority of the council, argued that reinstatement of the strike leaders "would establish a precedent that would destroy city government." Reverend Jackson argued that the strike leaders were Clara Luper, the adviser of the NAACP Youth Council and subsequently the CLC, and not the eleven workers. The previous offer to take the eleven workers back on probation for six months and then reinstating them with full benefits was not discussed. While it was offered by the council to the CLC with the premise "that there would be no Black Friday," it was not renewed, and there was no mention of it in reports emanating from the Executive Mansion. Almost every other point of contention had already been agreed to or was under consideration by the council. To the CLC leaders the views expressed by the vice mayor and others stirred deep chords of memory within the black psyche.[48]

One CLC member articulated this view by asserting that city officials, in seeking to make eleven men "whipping boys," were utilizing tactics similar to those used on some antebellum plantations. When a black man had the nerve to speak up, "he was . . . broken by his master in the face of all other black people to create fear in them." As during slavery days, some in the CLC believed, so too were city officials attempting "to dehumanize and stifle the conviction of an individual." The question was simply "whether a Negro is a man." For hundreds of years, whenever an African American stepped forward, seeking to be treated as a man, he had been slapped down. In Oklahoma City, eleven men had stepped forward, and they did not want to be put down for it. This, according to Ira D. Hall, who articulated these views on behalf of the CLC, "is the whole issue."[49]

The Oklahoma City Chamber of Commerce, which had offered jobs to the eleven strikers the city considered a dire threat, found the workers instead capable of advancement and noted that some had college degrees. Strike leaders, however, felt there was a more fundamental issue involved, although they appreciated the concern of the chamber. And the workers were dubious about job offers from white businessmen they had no reason to trust. Stanton Young, the president of the Chamber of Commerce and a mediator at the failed meetings at the Governor's Mansion, now faced a challenge he sought to resolve before a renewed demonstration threatened to destroy whatever racial equilibrium still existed in Oklahoma City. And most ironic was the fact that the one issue that did not exist when the strike got underway was the lone issue now preventing a resolution of the crisis. Progress had been made on every other issue: salaries, hours, working conditions, grievance machinery, showers, and locker rooms.[50]

At a rally after the collapse of the negotiating sessions, strike leaders called for a series of night marches. So sparse was the attendance, about one hundred people, that Betts said he and other SCLC representatives now in the city would return to Atlanta if more support was not forthcoming. Both Betts and Reverend Jackson called on black students to stay out of school, join the march, and urge other students to do the same. "There won't be anymore going to school in Oklahoma City," Betts added, "until this [strike] business is over."[51]

The following evening a crowd of about two hundred people, chanting and clapping, bunched in front of the Governor's Mansion for a "prayer vigil." The mansion was heavily guarded by troopers, spaced about twenty feet apart and wielding heavy riot sticks, just outside the steel fence surrounding the governor's residence. Troopers and city detectives buzzed in and out, while Reverend Jackson in his clerical robes led the demonstrators in singing "We Shall Overcome." Governor Bartlett was nowhere in sight, though some spectators thought they saw him briefly on the mansion porch, some ninety yards distant. A chilling north wind made for a short vigil. But Reverend Jackson, before the march got under way, called for another Black Friday, intensifying the black boycott of downtown stores and extending it to shopping centers.[52]

The mansion got an encore call the following evening, and strike leaders prepared for a demonstration the next morning at the Westwood compound. At the same time, the city manager announced that workers who had recently walked off their jobs would have until the following Monday to return before being terminated, unwittingly allowing these workers to participate in the upcoming Black Friday. Meanwhile, anti-strike forces were busy seeking volunteers to man garbage trucks and to demonstrate in support of the City Council's stand. On the other hand, the commander of a local white American Legion Post urged city officials to meet with members of the predominantly black post to seek a settlement.[53]

As tensions mounted in anticipation of a second Black Friday, suddenly on Thursday evening strike leaders announced a resolution of the key issue in the dispute. To understand what had occurred, one can follow the activities of Stanton Young during the previous week. On Thursday, October 30, he left for a week's vacation in San Diego. That evening from the Dallas airport, having learned there would be a march the next day, he phoned a fellow member of the chamber of commerce and told him he wanted to get the city and the CLC together. From California he phoned back and learned of the limited emergency set by the city. In turn, he received a call from the governor, who was concerned because of the announced march. Young told Bartlett he was coming home. He arrived in Oklahoma City that evening, and after much phoning back and forth found that he could not set up a meeting for Saturday, thereby losing a day before workers went to their compounds on Monday morning. But a meeting was held on Sunday and again on Monday at the mansion, as already noted. Since August, Young revealed, the chamber of commerce had been trying to find jobs for the strike leaders, but, he recalled, "We really did not know who we were talking about." At first they believed the city manager indicated thirty men were involved, but "by screening" the number was reduced to twelve and then eleven leaders because one was not a city employee. After the failure of the first agreement, Young learned that the men feared they might be fired from their new jobs.

Young felt that if the eleven men knew that the jobs were not just assigned to them but were suited to them, that there was opportunity for advancement, and that they were wanted and not being placed in a make-work program, their outlook would change. The businessmen who were offering jobs agreed with Young. All recognized that educationally the men were well qualified: four had gone to college; the others had all attained or gone beyond the eleventh grade. Young further claimed that the businessmen understood that those workers who spoke for others when "improper" conditions existed were the best employees when the conditions were corrected. The best employees were the smart employees, an asset to any thriving enterprise. He candidly admitted that though the business community was aware of the poor conditions sanitation workers experienced, it had not reacted fast enough to the last alternative the workers had offered.

Young said it was through the chamber's response at the Wednesday meeting that Reverend Jackson, the CLC leaders, and the eleven strikers realized that they were wanted. On Thursday, Young met twice with Jackson and at 6:00 P.M. brought him a list of sixteen jobs from which the men could select their employment. Moreover, the corporate board of the chamber assured the eleven men that if they were terminated their case would be reviewed and they would be offered other employment. Young concluded that the resolution came about "only after certain people in this community stood up and let it be known that things were not right." In his public remarks on Thursday evening, Young credited the role of the black community with bringing the city's attention to shortcomings in the Sanitation Department.[54]

Thereafter, the state of emergency was lifted. At a rally Young told those in attendance that the vice mayor had asked him to call all city workers who had left their jobs "to please come back." He also called attention to an eight-member committee, four appointed by the CLC and four by the chamber, that would review any termination, if it arose, among the eleven and if necessary find the man another job. A headline in the *Daily Oklahoman* proclaimed, "Everybody Loves Everybody Now." The governor, city officials, and CLC leaders all expressed relief, gratitude, joy, and jubilation that the long ordeal was over, each contending group finding something positive in its resolution.[55]

With everybody on speaking terms with everybody, with sanitation workers returning to their jobs, with the strike leaders settling into new positions, with school children returning to the classroom, the eleven-week ordeal came to an end to the satisfaction of all parties, including the residents of Oklahoma City, who no longer would have to take their garbage to one of twenty-five fire stations because of the lag in regular pickups. Most city employees were enabled to enjoy a four-day holiday from Saturday through Tuesday, being granted Monday off, which preceded Veterans Day, an official holiday. Those sanitation workers required to be on the job would receive double pay. The only points of contention that remained were the felony charges against four strike leaders.[56]

Until these charges were dropped, Reverend Jackson told 250 persons at a rally, "the fight really isn't over yet," a point reiterated by the Reverend T. Y. Rogers of the SCLC. He called for a more belligerent black community: "Don't sit down and let the white folks in this city misuse you. . . . You've got to fight the racist system, even if it means resorting to violence." And District Attorney Curtis Harris made clear his intentions to proceed against the four leaders facing felony charges growing out of demonstrations at the Westwood garage. "Neither the city of Oklahoma City nor the chamber of commerce are running my office," Harris asserted. In turn, Senator Porter, who represented the four men, called for a court ruling on the charges leveled against them. He preferred to see the charges dismissed after being proven "without merit in the court." And that is what occurred several weeks later, when Special Judge Robert Berry dismissed the "riot" charge at the end of a preliminary hearing, ruling that there was not enough evidence to support it.[57]

The eleven-week strike that disrupted garbage collection in Oklahoma City was quite remarkable in several ways. To start, there were winners and no losers, except for the hard-pressed residents of Oklahoma City, who never enjoyed full service throughout its duration. Further, at a time when big-city riots were a common occurrence, when violence frequently accompanied demonstrations against the Vietnam War, numerous racial incidents, and strikes, there was no violence, though the police, helmeted and armed, had arrested demonstrators, some of whom practiced passive resistance. Credit for the nonviolent approach must be accorded to Clara Luper and the NAACP Youth, well trained in the ways of passive resistance, and to the Reverend W. K. Jackson and the CLC, who proclaimed their faith and never relented in their support of the strikers and the fight for human dignity, which they considered a cultural issue. The strike also commanded the attention of the national NAACP and the SCLC, both of whom sent individuals from their headquarters to aid in the effort. Moreover, every black official in the legislature and on the City Council had endorsed the strike, and all had been arrested. The black community emerged from the strike a more unified, self-confident, and proud sector of Oklahoma City.

City officials, too, could claim victory. They did not yield in their insistence that "leading strikers" not regain their jobs. It took a while until they settled on eleven men. While the city was in the process of raising wages and meliorating working conditions, they would do so at their own pace and not appear to be yielding to striker demands. At times they were truculent, and at other times they seemed more receptive to workers' concerns, but when push came to shove on Black Friday, the city yielded. And when it was all over and the city celebrated, the mayor, the city's official leader, was nowhere to be seen.

What made the strike unique was the role of the chamber of commerce, which negotiated a resolution that brought the strike to an end. Its role was especially significant because chambers traditionally shunned such involvement. That its leaders exhibited concern for the plight of distressed garbage workers and in turn involved some of their associates in the chamber was most unusual, in that the chamber crossed a racial divide to assist the beleaguered black community and in doing so recognized that hitherto unrecognized municipal workers provided vital services necessary in a thriving urban community.

That the strike was a racial matter and not primarily a labor dispute there can be little doubt. Reverend Jackson insisted that it was not, but no union local or any other labor group came to the support of the garbage workers. To be sure, there were some white supporters at the rallies, and a Lutheran minister was active in the CLC. And while a handful of white garbage workers openly agreed with the aspirations of their black brethren, these were few and far between. The garbage strike originated with and was conducted almost exclusively by blacks, who quickly saw or came to conclude that beneath the debatable issues it had been a fundamental struggle to achieve a greater measure of human dignity.

Notes

1. Discussion of background material in these early paragraphs is based on Paul English's draft of a United Press International (UPI) story, April 3, 1968, Box 11, Folder 13, Harry Culver Papers, Carl Albert Center, University of Oklahoma, Norman (hereafter cited as Culver Papers). On housing see Gilbert Hill, "Negroes Keep Up Fight for Better Housing," *Oklahoma City Times*, July 3, 1964; and draft of February 15, 1968, story on housing in Box 7, Folder 15, Culver Papers. For school integration, see *Oklahoma Integration Report as of October 1961*, Box 7, Folder 7, Culver Papers. For the remarks of the director of the Department of Commerce and Industry, see UPI story, October 4, 1957, Box 7, Folder 25, Culver Papers; "Executive Department Proclamation," April 24, 1968, in which Dewey Bartlett called for an equal opportunity week, Box 7, Folder 25, Culver Papers. For Clara Luper, see story by Jack Taylor in *Oklahoma City Times*, July 1, 1964, Box 7, Folder 25, Culver Papers; and UPI story. September 11, 1958, Box 7, Folder 25, Culver Papers.

2. For this and the preceding two paragraphs: *Daily Oklahoman* (Oklahoma City), July 24, 1969, 41; Clara Luper, *Behold the Walls* (Oklahoma City: Jim Wire, 1979), 211–15.

3. *Daily Oklahoman*, July 29, 1969, 15; ibid., August 2, 1969, 17; Luper, *Behold the Walls*, 215.

4. For this and the preceding paragraph: *Daily Oklahoman*, August 3, 1969, 1; ibid., August 5, 1969, 13; ibid., August 7, 1969, 1; ibid., August 8, 1969, 33; *Black Dispatch* (Oklahoma City), August 7, 1969.

5. *Daily Oklahoman*, August 12, 1969, 13; ibid., August 13, 1969, 1. For the remarks of Archibald Hill, see story "Oldland Stand on Sanitation Issue Rapped," unmarked clipping, Box 5, Folder 27, Culver Papers.

6. *Daily Oklahoman*, August 12, 1969, 13; ibid., August 13, 1969, 1; ibid., August 14, 1969, 1.

7. Ibid., August 15, 1969, 1; *Black Dispatch*, August 16, 1969.

8. For this and the preceding paragraph: *Daily Oklahoman*, August 17, 1969, 1; ibid., August 18, 1969, 2; ibid., August 16, 1969, 1; ibid., August 19, 1969, 27. In an editorial on August 19, 1969 (p. 8), the *Daily Oklahoman*, without mentioning the strike situation, noted how inflation "was putting the squeeze on everyone and everything today." The editorial focused on the impact of inflation on education.

9. For this and the preceding paragraph: *Daily Oklahoman*, August 19, 1969, 1; ibid., August 20, 1969, two stories on p. 1.

10. Ibid., August 21, 1969, 53; *Black Dispatch*, August 21. 1969.

11. *Daily Oklahoman*, August 21, 1969, 1.

12. Ibid., August 21, 1969, 5; ibid., August 22, 1969, two stories on p. 1. For greater detail on Clara Luper in jail, see Luper, *Behold the Walls*, 220–22. Luper was the first African American admitted to the history graduate program at the University of Oklahoma.

13. *Daily Oklahoman*, August 23, 1969, two stories on p. 1.

14. Ibid., August 24, 1969, 1; ibid., August 25, 1969, 1; ibid., August 26, 1969, 1.

15. Ibid., August 26, 1969, 1, story by John Greiner noting the workers' shifting wage demands.

16. Ibid., August 28, 1969, 1; ibid., August 29, 1969, 5; ibid., September 1, 1969, 2; *Black Dispatch*, August 28, 1969.

17. *Daily Oklahoman*, September 6, 1969, 1; ibid., September 8, 1969, 1; ibid., September 9, 1969, 1.

18. Ibid., September 10, 1969, 1; ibid., September 13, 1969, two stories on p. 1; *Black Dispatch*, September 11, 1969.

19. *Daily Oklahoman*, September 14, 1969, 1; ibid., September 16, 1969, p. 1; ibid., September 18, 1969, 13; ibid., September 20, 1969, 1.

20. *Black Dispatch*, September 23, 1969; *Daily Oklahoman*, September 22, 1969, 1; ibid., September 23, 1969, 1.

21. *Daily Oklahoman*, September 23, 1969, 1; ibid., September 24, 1969, 17; ibid., September 26, 1969, 1; ibid., September 20, 1969, 1.

22. Ibid., October 2, 1969, 1.

23. Ibid., October 11, 1969, 22; see also *Oklahoma Observer* (Oklahoma City), October 17, 1969, 16–17, for a story by Rhoda Clary reviewing the situation.

24. Memorandum, "Council Memo No. 1708–69," October 21, 1969, Box 5, Folder 17, Culver Papers; *Daily Oklahoman*, October 22, 1969, 1.

25. *Daily Oklahoman*, October 22, 1969, 1.

26. Ibid., October 23, 1969, 1; *Oklahoma City Times*, October 23, 1969, story by Tom Boone.

27. *Daily Oklahoman*, October 24, 1969, 1.

28. Ibid. W. K. Jackson left the city jail around 6 P.M. on October 24 after an unidentified man posted a bond of forty dollars for the minister.

29. *Daily Oklahoman*, October 25, 1969, 1.

30. *Oklahoma City Times*, October 25, 1969, 1; *Daily Oklahoman*, October 27, 1969, 1. Undated clipping, *Oklahoma Journal* (Oklahoma City), October 1969, story by Paul Cartledge, Box 5, Folder 27, Culver Papers.

31. *Oklahoma City Times*, October 27, 1969, two stories on p. 1; *Daily Oklahoman*, October 18, 1969, 1.

32. *Daily Oklahoman*, October 28, 1969, 1.

33. Ibid., October 29, 1969, 1. For Governor Dewey Bartlett's response, see draft of UPI story, October 29, 1969, Box 5, Folder 27, Culver Papers. See also *Oklahoma Journal*, October 29, 1969, story by Paul Cartledge, Box 5, Folder 27, Culver Papers.

34. *Oklahoma City Times*, October 29, 1969, 1.

35. Ibid.

36. Ibid., October 30, 1969, 1.

37. *Daily Oklahoman*, October 30, 1969, 1.

38. *Black Dispatch*, October 30, 1969.

39. *Daily Oklahoman*, October 31, 1969, two stories on p. 1 and p. 19; *Oklahoma Journal*, October 31, 1969.

40. *Daily Oklahoman*, October 31, 1969, 1, story by Dave Dryden.

41. For this and the preceding two paragraphs: ibid., November 1, 1969, two stories on p. 1. Clara Luper's detailed and dramatic account is related in *Behold the Walls*, 229–37. See also the account in the *Tulsa World*, November 1, 1969, story by Roy Bode.

42. *McAlester* (Okla.) *Democrat*, November 1, 1969; *Oklahoma Journal*, November 1, 1969, story by J. Nelson Taylor.

43. *Daily Oklahoman*, November 2, 1969, for editorial and story.

44. Ibid.

45. Ibid., 8. See also *Sapulpa* (Okla.) *Daily Herald*, November 3, 1969, where the story by Harry Culver details the role of Governor Bartlett.

46. *Daily Oklahoman*, November 3, 1969, 1.

47. *Oklahoman Journal*, November 4, 1969, story by Rhoda Clary.

48. Draft of UPI story by Harry Culver, November 4, 1969, Box 5, Folder 27, Culver Papers.

49. Ibid. See also *Oklahoma City Times*, November 4, 1969.

50. Draft of UPI story, November 4, 1969, Box 5, Folder 27, Culver Papers.

51. *Daily Oklahoman*, November 4, 1969, 1.

52. Ibid., November 5, 1969, 1.

53. Ibid., November 6, 1969, 1; ibid., 49, for a review of the week's development. See also *Black Dispatch*, November 6, 1969.

54. For this and the preceding two paragraphs: Stanton Young, draft of interview by Harry Culver, November 7, 1969, Box 5, Folder 27, Culver Papers; *Daily Oklahoman*, November 7, 1969, 1, story by Nancy Kell.

55. *Daily Oklahoman*, November 7, 1969, 1. See also *Oklahoma Journal*, November 7, 1969, 1.

56. Draft of UPI story by Gary Goodine, November 7, 1969, Box 5, Folder 27, Culver Papers; *Daily Oklahoman*, November 8, 1969, 1.

57. *Daily Oklahoman*, November 11, 1969, 7; ibid., November 12, 1969, 1; ibid., November 22, 1969, 1; *Oklahoma Journal*, November 11, 1969, 1; *Black Dispatch*, November 13, 1969.

« 9 »

The Farm Crisis in Oklahoma

For two decades, during the 1970s and 1980s, farmers throughout the bread basket of America, as well as cattlemen, grain producers, and the communities that served them, experienced severe economic distress that played havoc with their lives. While farmers protested, organized (some even went on strike), and went deeper into debt, Washington seemed indifferent to their plight. Its policies threw the agricultural sector off balance and created a cost-price situation that devastated all but the largest producers.

What caused this crisis? To start, one can note that military operations in Vietnam were conducted with no tax increases to cover their staggering cost. As a result, inflation began to mount. In 1971 President Richard M. Nixon sought to dampen rising prices by briefly instituting wage and price controls. At the same time, the U.S. Department of Agriculture (USDA) and its allies sought a general loosening of crop and price controls with increased emphasis on sales abroad, thereby abandoning the supply-management approach of the preceding Democratic administrations. Opponents feared that the increasingly efficient American farming methods, without adequate planning and controls, would produce huge surpluses, driving prices down, depleting farm profits, and creating serious problems for the rural economy. Earl Butz, secretary of agriculture during the Nixon and Ford administrations, exemplified the new approach, urging farmers "to get big or get out" and to plant commodity crops from "fencerow to fencerow."

This article examines the unfolding of this approach as it affected primarily Oklahoma cattlemen and grain producers. By the 1970s the state was among the nation's top producers of winter wheat, with cattle joining wheat as major commodities. While the trend in agriculture had been toward a reduction in the number of farms, larger acreages per farm plus an increase in their value was evident both in the nation as a whole and in Oklahoma. In the 1970s over 80 percent of Oklahoma's land was used for agricultural production.[1]

On June 18, 1974, Carl Albert sought permission to address the Committee on Agriculture, an unusual request by the Speaker of the U.S. House of Representatives. Albert asserted that the cattle industry was in "a financial squeeze," experiencing "the worst decline in twenty years, while at the same time the worst peace-time inflation in history causes production costs to sky-rocket." What disturbed Albert was the fact that the administration was giving every evidence that it understood neither the depth nor the meaning of the problem. The same could be said for every administration from Nixon on into that of Ronald Reagan.[2]

Ranchers were faced with declining cattle prices, while feed and other costs were continually rising. Everything was out of balance. Many in the business blamed beef imports, which had a direct impact on the domestic price. Albert cited Nixon's decision in 1972 to lift the quotas imposed by the Meat Import Act of 1964. And in the face of decreasing demand and increasing production, several nations had instituted import quotas on foreign beef, and some, Albert claimed, were prohibiting beef imports altogether, leaving the United States with the only open market "quickly becoming the dumping ground for world beef producers." Owing to rising imports, increased domestic production, and decreased demand, Albert said, "the beef market has become glutted." Adding to the cattleman's woes was "the soaring increase" in the cost of production. Along with cow-calf producing costs, fuel, fertilizer, baling wire, and feed costs had "increased dramatically" and continued to soar. Nixon's placing a price ceiling on beef in 1973 served only to totally disrupt the cattle industry, in that, as Albert explained, many farmers and ranchers held cattle "off the feed lots and out of the slaughter houses," hoping to turn a profit when the price freeze was lifted.[3]

A final factor disrupting the agricultural economy, Albert continued, was "the cash situation of our producers and feeders." Through normal banking channels, cattlemen secured "mortgages on their cattle, their land and everything else they own." With lack of available cash, the whole credit system could grind to a halt as the numbers of defaulting borrowers mounted. As their cash supply was depleted, their debts accumulated, and many sought to refinance their loans. Having neither cash nor equity, increasing numbers of debtors faced bankruptcy or liquidation. Moreover, Albert insisted, cattlemen could not be divorced from the rest of the economy. Small-town businessmen, local bankers, agriculture-related industries—all were impacted as the domino effect extended out into the broader economy.[4]

Earlier Governor David Hall had sent an urgent letter to President Nixon, indicating that Oklahoma, along with other cattle-feeding states, faced a "pending disaster of crisis proportions." After briefly delineating the situation, Hall asked the president to designate cattle-feeding sectors of the nation as "severe economic impact areas" and thereby qualify cattlemen for long-term, low-interest loans available to businessmen and citizens when a natural disaster occurred. But the concerns of both governor and Speaker fell on deaf ears.[5]

For over a decade it had been evident to members of the Oklahoma congressional delegation that no administration had any intention of coping with the mounting concerns of cattlemen and farmers. For as long as they served in the United States Senate, both Dewey Bartlett and Henry Bellmon called for the reinstitution of import quotas on beef. Beginning in 1974, and for as long as he remained in the Senate, Bartlett introduced a bill to curb meat imports. He noted that "there are many beef producers who are losing $100 or more for each animal that is now sent to market."[6]

Tumbling prices for beef on the hoof was playing havoc with the cattle industry. "It just doesn't make sense," remarked Johnny Hafner, Jefferson County extension director. "Eveything else is going up. Feed, seed, fertilizer, interest, you name it. Prices for other things have doubled and tripled but cattlemen are watching a year of work go down the drain." Paul Hammonds of the Waurika Livestock Market asserted that some cattlemen were "losing thousands of dollars a day." Sooner or later, he said, "the smaller fellows are going to quit and the bigger boys are going to cut back." In Jefferson County and throughout Oklahoma, feed lots were seriously impacted. Some closed down. Then the stocker-feeder operations, grazing heifers for a year prior to sending them to feed lots, lost their markets, with the cattlemen working a year for nothing.[7]

People pointed to the 1973 freeze on beef prices ordered by President Nixon. With the industry thus singled out, cattlemen started holding back until the freeze was over. That created a shortage followed by skyrocketing prices. By late summer 1973 consumer demand for beef had waned, and the backlog of cattle held off the market began to go to slaughter, causing a glut of overfinished beef and tumbling cattle prices. While supplies leveled out, farm prices, led by beef, continued to fall. The Oklahoma Crop and Livestock Reporting Service said that the livestock index plunged 50 points in May 1974, 16 percent below the previous year. At the same time the index of prices paid by farmers and ranchers was up 16 percent over the previous year. While most observers expected the larger operators to handle the situation, consumers could look forward to stringier beef and higher prices. But for smaller communities, such as those in Jefferson County that used to produce 50,000 calves a year, selling them at 40 cents a pound at an average of 500 pounds, the loss of income could be a disaster.[8]

Because of continual high losses and the drain of cattlemen's equity, the banks and financial institutions on which cattlemen depended were finding it difficult, if not impossible, to make new loans and extend existing loans. With both the Congress and the administration interfering with the market, farmers and ranchers were unable to gain meaningful relief.[9]

In June of 1974 about 200 ranchers signed petitions protesting the quality of beef imports, which Representative Clem McSpadden claimed could amount to 12 percent total U. S. consumption. He suggested curbing beef imports, exporting beef to Canada, and lowering grading standards to reduce time on feed without reducing beef quality. But as with most such proposals, few, if any, gained approval while the cattleman's dilemma continued: animals going for less than 40 cents a pound and stockmen considering holding their product off the market as the cost of the things they purchased continued to increase.[10]

To dramatize their plight, some 160 Oklahoma ranchers made plans to join in a mass beef slaughter if President Gerald Ford took no cognizance of their problems. By October 1974 some ranchers were losing their homes and selling off their herds. Francis Stagna, the group's organizer, said he had sold 800-pound yearlings for only 18 cents per pound. "You can't stay in business spending a year or more to raise a calf you're selling at that price" he declared. While not all Oklahoma cattlemen agreed with Stagna's notion of slaughtering cattle, many, along with cattlemen in other states, did.[11]

Out in the panhandle, Duty Rowe, determining the feed lot business was no longer profitable, along with his neighbors, closed down the Frontier Feed Lot in Guymon. "Eighteen months ago," Rowe exclaimed, "we had a 49 percent equity in our cattle. Today that margin is gone and we even are experiencing a negative margin." Rowe claimed this situation was "eating up our reserves" and that their only recourse was "to mortgage the land to satisfy our bankers." At his prime Rowe was handling anywhere from 3,000 to 5,000 head of cattle. In October 1974 he had 700.[12]

With the value of cattle declining roughly by two-thirds of their cost in a single year, small operators were being wiped out. Dumping cheap beef on the American market only exacerbated the situation, as did remarks by Earl Butz, the secretary of agriculture, to the effect that there was going to be plenty of beef and that it was going to be cheap. But consumers in Oklahoma saw little, if any, decline in prices at their local meat counter. Inflation forced stores to keep beef prices steady, despite a drop in suppliers' prices.[13]

Unfortunately in 1974, cattlemen were not the only agricultural sector experiencing declining commodity prices and rising costs. "There is no way," warned Henry Bellmon, that American producers "could provide an abundance of food for consumers while being forced to pay higher prices for their supplies and then selling their products at artificially low domestic prices." Farmers, like any other consumer group, were affected by rising prices for food, clothing, and other day-to-day needs; they were also hit by rising prices for things they secured from other farmers, as well as costs of new combines and coveralls. As a producer-consumer the farmer was balanced between profits and losses when things were on an even keel. When they got out of whack, he could go over the brink. And by late 1974 such was the case, the price of everything a farmer needed, for example, from tractors, to tires for older tractors, to labor costs for motor tune-ups, and diesel fuel and other petroleum products, all jumped in price. Virtually no industrial product needed by farmers failed to rise.[14]

The plight of grain producers, the largest group of Oklahoma farmers, will be the other sector of the agricultural economy to be discussed in this article. Speaking for them, Billy Ray Gowdy, president of the State Board of Agriculture, called President Gerald Ford's decision to block the sale of 34 million bushels of wheat to the Soviet Union "very poor public relations as far as world trade is concerned," because foreign officials worried whether the United States would be a dependable commodity supplier. Gowdy and fellow wheat farmers were concerned, "confused and really scared" because only about a third of the nation's wheat harvest was used domestically. Grain growers complained their marketing system had been taken away, while 6th District congressman Glenn English proclaimed what was already becoming self-evident; namely, the absence of a strong vocal representation in the Congress. Overnight, as a result of Ford's action, the state wheat trade markedly declined. An agronomist associated with Oklahoma State University argued that the president had "sold out the breadbasket of the nation to soothe the consumers." Previously the federal government had encouraged farmers to increase production for export. It now turned around and placed limits on exports. While only a temporary measure until the administration presented a modified system of export controls, confusion reigned among Oklahoma wheat growers.[15]

Depressed prices now were the lot of the two major sectors of Oklahoma agriculture. As Oklahoma wheat farmers in 1975 looked forward to a bumper crop, concern mounted as prices dropped from about $3.60 a bushel in April to about $3.11 a bushel a month later. Critics insisted that the goal of the administration, personified in Earl Butz, the secretary of agriculture, was to tilt agricultural policy so large corporations could make the marketing decisions and Oklahoma, let alone other mid-America cattlemen and farmers, many of whom were already struggling for survival, would eventually be eliminated as a significant part of American agriculture.[16]

And by 1975, producers of food were already being forced out of business. On into the next decade, administrations manifested little concern about the depression in American agriculture while concerned members of Congress were unable to secure effective legislation restoring a balance to the economic climate. One constituent informed Carl Albert, "You can't raise twenty dollars a hundred calves and pay one hundred and eighty dollars a ton for feed, five thousand dollars for a pickup, and twenty five dollars a roll for barbed wire where you can find it. A new tractor will cost eight to fourteen thousand dollars and about everything else used on the ranch has gone up while cattle prices have gone down since the government has stuck its nose into the business," in its effort to placate large corporations and urban consumers. This cost-price freeze created a "state of near panic" among Oklahoma cattlemen, several of whom, along with some state legislators, went to Washington seeking legislation.[17]

Indicative was a 1975 article, "Price Perspective on Agriculture," that cited farm prices rising 72 percent in the previous two decades, almost 25 percent more than industrial prices. While farm prices moved in two directions, farmers' costs went only one way—up. This development was spelled out in considerable detail in the letters pouring into Washington from distressed farmers and ranchers.[18]

Carl Albert received one such letter from a friend who had recently traveled throughout southeastern Oklahoma with a farm editor. What he heard and saw "was not only shocking but sickening": namely, thousands of cattle malnourished or starving, in either case dying because the owners had neither means nor credit to feed them properly. What was clear to Albert was that without the federal government responding promptly, many rural Oklahomans faced the loss of their entire capital investment and productive capacity. What particularly grated on many rural residents was the failure of Presidents Ford, Carter, and Reagan to approve omnibus bills or to seriously raise the loan and target price on farm commodities because such actions would be too inflationary.[19]

With agriculture the largest single industry in the state's economy, accounting for more than one-fourth of the jobs and personal incomes, there was ample cause for concern. Governor David Boren worried about the impact of a projected record wheat crop depressing prices and causing producers' gross income to drop. This situation, combined with low cattle prices, would cost the state millions of dollars in lost tax revenue. Boren, like members of the congressional delegation, called for a government action, but to no avail.[20]

But it was Carl Albert who understood most clearly the dramatic reversal in agricultural policies "away from efforts aimed at curtailing excess production to avoid surpluses," the New Deal approach, "toward the new goal of maximizing the nation's agricultural production to avoid shortages." The farm programs launched during the New Deal contained "built-in incentives not to produce." The new programs sought to achieve "greater production from the nation's agricultural acreage." Besides coping with the devastating cost-price squeeze, and mounting farm debt, Congress would also, in "light of the nation's present and future requirements," have to grapple with ways and means of securing enhanced soil conservation.[21]

Meanwhile, a new dimension was added when a group called the National Farm Coalition, citing the precipitous decline in farm prices, called on the government to provide "meaningful price protection." All to no avail, as were the penetrating remarks of Carl Albert endorsing the 1975 farm bill. Opponents called it inflationary and outrageous, as did the president when he vetoed the measure.[22]

The farm bill called for an increase in target prices, a concept introduced in 1973 wherein the government would pay the farmer the difference when the sale price was less than the target price. With the cost squeeze farmers were experiencing, higher price supports were a high priority for farm state legislators and their constituents. Oklahoma farmers by 1975 were no longer seeking comforts but were struggling for their survival. Despite being deluged by rural legislators, the president vetoed the 1975 Emergency Farm Bill largely on the premise that it would encourage inflationary spending and add to the deficit. Thus by the end of the Ford administration the pattern was set for almost another decade. Agricultural distress could not prompt meaningful legislative redress. The most lasting criticism of this pattern came from Senator Henry Bellmon, the only member of the delegation, and one of very few members of Congress, who rode a tractor and farmed for a living. Calling Ford's veto "indefensible," he noted, "This is the same President who last October ordered a virtual embargo on wheat exports which caused a sharp break in wheat prices." For the remainder of his tenure, Bellmon remained the sharpest critic of the nation's farm policies.[23]

The veto, and the pattern it encouraged, left the farmer without price protection at a time when high costs were already going higher and the government was calling for an all-out effort in production. Bankruptcy loomed for many Oklahoma producers. Then a ray of hope for wheat producers occurred when it appeared that the Soviet Union would be purchasing over 2 million metric tons of hard winter wheat, the kind grown in Oklahoma. With a wheat crop in 1975 expected to yield a record 59.5 million tons, up 10.7 million from 1974's record harvest, the sale to the Soviet Union, while good news for Oklahoma wheat farmers, was no more than a ray of hope.[24]

The wheat sale prompted members of the longshoremen's union to refuse to load American wheat for export. Urban newspapers speculated that the sale might cause higher prices for consumers. And Earl Butz admitted that the longshoremen's action came shortly after he and the administration had decided upon a moratorium on grain sales. Throughout the ensuing decade, Oklahoma producers concluded that political considerations were a primary factor affecting their access to free export markets. They were being tested and frustrated by these developments: first believing they would have free access to world markets and then finding a year later that export wheat sales were curbed, especially after the AFL-CIO endorsed the activities of the longshoremen. Many argued that consumer-oriented groups were depriving rural producers of their share of profit. Since the bulk of Oklahoma's grain needed to find a market with less productive nations, there was mounting agreement that government catered to urban groups and interests.[25]

The focus on the distressed grain market diverted attention away from the collapsed cattle feeder industry. Thanks to the efforts of Senator Bellmon, President Ford, who was in Oklahoma City for a series of campaign appearances, met with leaders in the cattle industry. The United States, Bellmon observed, was the only country with borders open for unrestricted import of foreign beef. If the United States demanded reciprocity from foreign nations in exchange for trade concessions, then, Bellmon said, American beef producers could compete in expanded foreign markets, thereby ensuring an adequate beef supply and a healthier industry. At the time of this meeting with the president, wholesale prices of beef were so low that cattlemen were selling their breeding herds. In short, by the last year of the Nixon-Ford administration, cattlemen and farmers felt betrayed by their government. Maximum production was not insured with protection, as Earl Butz had promised. And the beef industry, the largest segment of American agriculture, already sustained over a two-year period unprecedented losses and faced at the end of 1975 many more months of uncertain fluctuations.[26]

With wheat it was a similar story. The Treasury, the State Department, and the Department of Agriculture all engaged in efforts that in effect helped depress prices. With a record wheat harvest in 1975 and an equally abundant one in 1976, increased sales to the Soviet Union and other foreign buyers, plus expanded Food for Peace commitments, would be necessary to sustain sagging domestic wheat prices and reduce wide price fluctuations in the U.S. grain markets. To help producers avoid ceasing operations, rural bank loans rose at a rapid rate. Banks in Oklahoma increased their agricultural lending at a 13.2 percent annual rate over the previous decade, the highest of any state within the Tenth Federal Reserve District.[27]

It was becoming an all too familiar pattern. Oklahoma farmers and ranchers asked for help and waited, only to endure continuing delays and denials. Various groups then began to offer proposals, as did members of Congress. Thousands of individual farmers in the 1970s and 1980s appeared to lobby in Washington. Many no longer trusted top officials: "People out here" wrote a wheat farmer to Carl Albert, "are so distrusting of our government it is shameful." By far the angriest critic was Senator Bellmon, who bitterly denounced administration farm measures proclaimed by the president on down to the secretary of agriculture and to the "instant agricultural experts" in the White House and Commerce and State Departments. Their policies and actions ignored or gave short shrift to the desperate situation of farmers and cattlemen in Oklahoma. The unfolding system of boom and bust was showing signs of wrecking major segments of the agricultural economy.[28]

Federal meddling with the export sales of Oklahoma wheat and beef penalized farm families and placed a serious burden on small rural banks. The government, for example, set a wheat loan rate as well as a target price, almost always too low to encourage farmers. While many farmers had difficulty maintaining their operations with the loan rates and target prices imposed throughout the 1970s and 1980s, administration officials claimed that if they raised loan rates and called for higher target prices, they would place themselves in an untenable position by encouraging wheat production for government support rather than profit. While the beef embargo was soon lifted, beef imports continued to enter the American market easily, keeping prices depressed both in grain and livestock. Bellmon claimed that "wheat prices are a dollar a bushel below cost, [and] cattle probably $50 a head below cost of production." Production costs kept increasing while farm income tended to stay level.[29]

As governor in 1976, Boren noted that agricultural advisers had informed him that inflation was "eroding farm income at an alarming rate" because farmers, unlike most businessmen, had no means of passing higher costs on to consumers. As governor there was little he could do to meliorate the situation except to call for officials in Washington to act.[30]

The Carter administration, like its predecessor, did little to alleviate the concerns of Oklahoma producers. The president and his secretary of agriculture appeared unwilling to cope with low beef prices and high grain costs. It made little sense, for example, to increase beef imports when there was greater domestic beef production and to allow less imported beef when there was declining domestic production. The reverse, the sensible approach, would take over a decade to achieve. For the administration to call for an economic stabilization program to curb inflation would be of little assistance to farmers and ranchers in Oklahoma, who were increasingly dependent on foreign markets for the sale of their products and keeping the nation in a favorable balance of payments position.

To reduce the supply of wheat—the 1976 wheat crop was one of the largest ever produced in Oklahoma—farmers grazed out or baled their seeded wheat acres. They soon learned that only acres harvested for grain could qualify for target payments. Reducing the abundance of wheat penalized producers, who complained bitterly that the restriction only added to their woes. By 1977 farm numbers in the state, according to the *Oklahoma Farmer-Stockman*, were down a thousand from the average number in the 1973–75 time frame, and farm sales and public auctions of equipment by farmers were becoming increasingly evident. This situation was only exacerbated by the fact that in 1977 farmers were holding a surplus of over one billion bushels with a good part of the excess due to government embargoes. Moreover, prospects for selling carryover wheat were not good because the world's wheat-producing countries, notably Canada and the Soviet Union, had also produced bumper crops.[31]

For Oklahoma cattlemen the situation was equally bleak. Most were seeking to cut production. Indeed, herds in 1977 had been reduced by about 10 million head. As cattlemen struggled to get supply in reasonable balance with demand, the State Department through voluntary agreements with meat exporters agreed to import 1,281,900,000 pounds of beef in 1977, the equivalent of 6 to 7 percent of domestic consumption. Imports in this year either equaled or exceeded all the dairy cows, beef cattle and heifers weighing over 500 pounds in the state. This situation, plus adverse weather conditions added to low cattle prices, high feed costs, and short hay stocks in some localities, led to severe culling and in some instances the complete liquidation of herds.[32]

In 1977 Carter vetoed a major farm bill that took into account the plight of distressed Oklahoma producers. Bumper crops continued to depress prices as production costs continued to increase. A local farm official summed up rural grievances when he wrote his congressman that "farmers in general are thoroughly disgusted because they have seen for many years improper supply management on farm products, gross pay acre reductions . . . unintelligible ASC [agricultural stabilization and conservation] formulas, mock target prices, high interest rates on so-called emergency livestock loans, uncontrolled acreages and surpluses, wheat embargoes, and beef imports." Moreover, he asserted, "policy makers gave little consideration to the current cost of production, including land, machinery, and general agricultural inputs." While it was relatively easy for wheat growers and cattlemen to agree on the problems they faced, the solution wasn't that obvious when it came to favoring a strict acreage control plan or agreeing on how high loan rates or target prices should be set. There were many different suggestions on the farm and the ranch, in the USDA and Congress.[33]

However, in one sector of the rural economy by the spring of 1977 there was an encouraging sign. The National Cattlemen's Association reported that "cow slaughter" was continuing at a rate that was putting the basic herd into better balance with the demand for beef. Since 1975 over 22 million cows had been slaughtered. The president of the association announced that "the cow herd has now returned to the trend line." While the situation was improving, the issue of beef imports continued to plague cattlemen, and the association's president said the cow herd would have to further decline before the "total" industry could expect favorable returns. Many cattlemen were still losing anywhere from $20 to $100 every time they sold an animal and had stretched their borrowing, as had wheat farmers, to the limit as they attempted to continue operating.[34]

Furthermore, concern was mounting in that fewer sons would follow their fathers into farming. And farm women, equally concerned, wrote about family members seeking work off the farm and the difficulties they faced in maintaining the family farm and enjoying life in a rural community. No one expected to get rich, but they did hope "to see ends meet once in a while" and resented the large operator who plowed under "a better crop of wheat than we harvested just so he could collect the government payment." One couple wrote that "every day for the last two months there are ten to twelve public auctions in our paper of farmers selling out or taking bankruptcy because they haven't been able to continue under present day prices." Comparable letters, increasingly written by farm women, were beginning to pour into congressional offices.[35]

A growing sense of desperation was evident in these letters. Farmers were beginning to feel that their representatives had let them down. All were concerned that they were losing money on every bushel of wheat they sold. Some were willing to cut acreage, hoping in this way to get supply and demand in line to gain a fair return on labor and investment. Most recognized that government policies were causing their problems and were increasingly frustrated that no resolution was evident.[36]

Disillusioned though they might be, groups of Oklahoma farmers still flocked to Washington to lobby for higher wheat prices. One group carried 61,000 letters from wheat growers. Another group included 120 farmwives, all seeking a greater level of support for wheat. At a meeting in Tonkawa, farmers filled a pickup truck with about 60,000 letters to send to Washington, most asking for higher loan and target prices. Later a group of 90 women made a three-day trip to Washington. Governor Boren also went to Washington to inform President Carter that Oklahoma's 3,200 farmers were in dire financial straits. All to no avail. At the same time a survey by the Economic Research Services of bankers in the Great Plains region revealed Oklahoma to be "in the most serious plight" of all the states surveyed. It indicated that 3,200 farmers would not be able to refinance their loans through any lending agency.[37] A chart prepared by the National Farmers Union in 1977 dramatically illustrated the cost-price squeeze that was devastating farmers in Oklahoma and throughout the breadbasket of the nation.[38]

Following the veto of the 1975 farm bill, the situation for wheat producers deteriorated further. By July 1977 the price of wheat had fallen to less than half of the 1974 level, while farmers' direct costs continued to rise sharply. The Department of Agriculture estimated that 13,000 farmers in Oklahoma were unable to repay their loans. Glenn English noted that "this agricultural disaster is threatening many small businesses in rural areas." Accompanying depressed wheat prices was a huge, 1.1 billion bushel surplus.[39]

What puzzled and aggravated farmers was the government bestowing billions in aid to foreign countries while denying aid to embattled farmers. The situation was "especially tragic" for "the new generation of young men and women who purchased their land" at prevailing high prices. Carter's veto of the 1977 Farm Bill on grounds that it was too costly and could trigger further inflation did not go down easily with producers in Oklahoma. They wanted improved target prices for wheat, and their Congressmen called for a loan rate which would immediately rise to 90 percent parity, while hundreds of Oklahoma wheat producers and farmwives visited Washington to lend their support. The fact that the secretary of agriculture did not call for a large enough acreage set-aside to help get the wheat surplus under control further disillusioned farmers.[40]

On a more limited scale, Bellmon sought to use set-aside wheat acreage for cattle grazing. His initial task was to convince farm organizations to change their stance and then to pressure the administration to allow grazing on wheat acreage taken out of production under its recently announced wheat set-aside program. Bellmon argued that southern wheat producers, the large purchasers of stocker cattle, heifers and calves raised to round out or replenish depleted herds, would be the chief users of these lands. Bellmon argued forcefully for his proposal, but it was several years before it was accepted.[41]

The same could be said for his colleague, Dewey Bartlett, who sought to correlate world beef supplies with domestic supplies. He recognized that peaks in beef available for importation coincided with peaks in domestic supply, a situation further amplified by the fact that the United States was the lone large market in foreign beef. Thus, as the domestic market showed an increase in domestic production, the same message was transmitted to foreign producers. Oklahoma cattlemen were caught in a vise preventing them from climbing out of their depressed state. Through a series of measures, Bartlett sought to achieve a stabilizing influence for domestic beef producers by measures that would approach an inverse of the total beef production; an inversion was achieved during Reagan's second term. Meanwhile, peak imports continued at times of herd liquidations, further exacerbating falling prices and making it exceedingly difficult, if not impossible, for producers to cover their costs while other countries involved in the international meat trade imposed quotas, tariffs, and other barriers that helped keep American beef from gaining access to their markets. What Bartlett and his fellow cattlemen set as their goal was for imports to be increased when domestic supplies were short and decreased when domestic production was excessive.[42]

By year's end in 1977, the USDA acknowledged that "some 14 thousand Great Plains farmers" were unable to pay their loans and "about 60 thousand" would be forced to renegotiate their loans or sell some of their assets. At the time, wheat producers were losing anywhere "from $1.00 to $1.50 per bushel" and were distressed upon learning that the People's Republic of China, suffering a serious crop failure, was purchasing possibly 500 million bushels of wheat, the bulk of which was not being purchased in the United States. Farmers slowly but surely were losing confidence in their government, a sentiment expressed in a letter to Congressman Thomas Jefferson Steed: "The people of my community, farmers and businessmen alike, are fed up with the indifferent bureaucratic treatment of our number one industry."[43]

Late in 1977 a new organization, American Agriculture, quickly gained supporters throughout Oklahoma. As farmers became more desperate, they became more belligerent. Younger and college-educated farmers took the lead in demanding governmental action. Some called for a strike to help realize American Agriculture's primary goal of 100 percent parity. It further advocated farmers having more authority in the Department of Agriculture. These were bold and aggressive proposals, yet labor unions and legislators already enjoyed comparable benefits. Not having the numbers or the money to compete in a consumer-oriented Congress, farmers did have power as food producers to use as a weapon for their own protection. This was the message of American Agriculture that resonated throughout rural Oklahoma.[44]

To many it seemed that every time a bill came out of Washington, it created more problems for the famer. Such was the case with the 1977 farm bill, with its set-aside provision requiring a cover crop without compensation, thereby limiting or prohibiting growing wheat or grazing cattle on the land. And as in all farm bills, producers in Oklahoma insisted that the target prices did not approach their cost of production.[45]

Unexpected support came when Governor Boren asked Oklahomans to write letters to national leaders urging action to correct "the desperate financial condition" of farmers. The governor endorsed a farm strike "as a demonstration to the American people that American agriculture is in deep trouble." He commended the leadership of American Agriculture because the movement thus far remained voluntary, nonviolent, and responsible. With only 4 percent of the population actively engaged in farming, Boren asserted that "dramatic demonstrations" were needed to arouse "fellow citizens and Washington leaders." He further noted that "every banker, small business person, teacher and factory worker will feel the pinch, because when farmers can't earn, they can't buy as customers." Already 3,200 farmers faced the loss of their farms because they could no longer refinance loans, while another 40 percent had to refinance loans. And, Boren added, "if things don't change soon thousands will be forced to put the product of their life's work on the auction block." In endorsing the farm strike, he observed that national income of farms in 1973 was $73 billion; in 1977 it was only $17 billion, while investments and operating costs had skyrocketed since the 1950s.[46]

Boren's speech before more than a thousand farmers in Enid highlighted a gigantic strike rally where more than seven hundred farm vehicles, chiefly large, expensive tractors, jammed the streets before merchants opened their stores. While most farmers in attendance were from grain-rich north-central Oklahoma, some came from as far away as Minnesota and Virginia. Meanwhile, 130 miles south of Enid, striking farmers paraded through Apache in Caddo County, while officials in other counties pledged "sympathy and support." In Guymon, officials of the Panhandle Livestock Commission Company announced they would shut down operations for ten days as a gesture of sympathy with striking cattle operators and growers.[47]

Assuredly, the strike with its demand for 100 percent parity helped bring the plight of farmers to public awareness, but there was no assurance of widespread understanding of the problem. Representative Tom Steed noted that only forty-eight members of Congress could be defeated by the farm vote; the rest were from city and suburban areas. Moreover most consumers, unaware of the farmers' situation, never called their congressmen to support legislation to resolve the cost-price squeeze or to increase price supports and alleviate the crisis.[48]

Members of American Agriculture recognized that if something was not done to change the trend in Oklahoma agriculture, it would soon be in corporate hands. For the present, its leaders presented farmers with detailed knowledge of their plight and the significant economic impact of agriculture on the American economy. When fully organized, it promised, if necessary, to "paralyze this whole country" by plowing up wheat and otherwise halting production. Organizers in communities throughout the state stressed the five-point program of their demands revolving around 100 percent parity for all domestic agricultural products and halving all agricultural imports until 100 percent of the parity price was achieved. All contracts for food reserves should also call for 100 precent parity. In addition, it wanted farmers to devise and approve policies affecting agriculture. To express these views, the movement launched a statewide letter-writing campaign asking farmers, merchants, and citizens to bombard officials in Washington expressing their concerns.[49]

Soon members of the Oklahoma delegation again found themselves deluged with letters from constituents calling attention to their plight and the program of American Agriculture. They wanted equality in return for providing food for the American people and others throughout the world. The letters came from residents young and old, men and women, city dwellers and folks in small towns and rural areas, plus others in all walks of life. Some delineated their personal histories, others simply called for 100 percent parity, some were formally typed, others were in semiliterate scrawls. All desired greater equality for agriculture, summed up in the call for 100 percent parity.[50]

And there was no end in sight. For example, the market price for cattle went from about $44 in 1974 to $39 in 1977, not an extreme price drop, but the effect of inflation made it more difficult for cattlemen to stay in business. More dire was the drop of 1 percent in land values in midwestern states during a three-month period in 1977. Without inflating land prices, many farmers would be unable to secure credit to cover future borrowing. In Washington, one hundred Oklahoma farmers, young, middle-aged, and old, spent hours with Bellmon in his Senate office relating their coping with high operating costs, low market prices, and unfair exporting practices. Most wore work jackets and caps with the American Agriculture logo and faces drawn with worry. They were among thousands of farm families who journeyed to Washington to demand parity. Most rallied in subfreezing weather on the Capitol steps for two hours to hear speeches. Aside from genuine concern, Bellmon could provide little assurance of prompt remedial action. However, at the state capitol American Agriculture got encouragement from legislators, the governor's office, and the state Department of Agriculture. A spokesman for the state beer industry, a major purchaser of grain, endorsed the movement. "What American Agriculture has done," said Governor Boren, "is to allow farmers to rally around a cause." Realizing that cause was the problem.[51]

Harvey Gardner, a farmer and rancher, devoted hours to championing the cause of American Agriculture by noting how closely beef production was tied to grain production. If the cattle price was fair, grain prices took a beating. If the reverse occurred and grain prices came close to parity, cattle prices plummeted. "In order for cattlemen to pay parity for grain," Gardner insisted, "beef imports have got to come to a halt." With the number of beef cattle being raised in the United States at a low ebb, beef imports, Gardner claimed, comprised "the most severely overlooked aspect of the whole thing." The United States, as the largest beef producer, was also the biggest importer. To resolve this situation and others, Gardner, speaking for American Agriculture, called for greater input by farmers. Parity, Gardner explained, essentially meant "equality." Achieving it would release farmers from the handicap of being treated like "second-class citizens." While Gardner and others were bringing the message of American Agriculture to farmers and lawmakers in Washington, budget estimates indicated that payment to farmers would decline from $7.3 billion in 1978 to $4.3 billion in 1979.[52]

While Oklahoma producers recognized they could not continue farming and ranching under current conditions and most endorsed the efforts of American Agriculture and its call for a farm strike, there were no mass plow-ups or other efforts to curb production and no violence. Complaints, pleas, and suggestions continued to pour into congressional offices and increasingly irate farmers appeared on Capitol Hill, but nothing seriously changed. American Agriculture, however, continued to make headway among Oklahoma farmers, some of whom began to consider crop cutbacks. All become better informed about their plight and the significant role of agriculture in the functioning of the economy.[53]

Well aware that the American Agriculture Movement had aroused both public and congressional sympathy for the American farmer, Bellmon wrote the secretary of agriculture, Bob Bergland, urging him to allow farmers greater flexibility in the set-aside program as a step toward balancing production and demand. Bellmon admired Bergland's insistence that available legislation provided sufficient vehicles to stimulate the agricultural economy. His suggestions were offered to help Bergland in this endeavor.[54]

When Bellmon wrote Bergland, the USDA estimated that nearly 5 percent of all American farmers were facing immediate bankruptcy. Many of the younger farmers in Oklahoma who paid high prices and high interest rates for their land, according to Representative Glenn English, had lost so much money that many would be forced to abandon farming altogether. Since one-third of the gross national product came from the agricultural sector, English said the farm crisis jeopardized the entire economy. Meanwhile, the president of the Federal Land Bank of Wichita wondered "if for a few years farmers will have to accept a lower standard of living." National farm debt in 1960 was about $25 billion, in 1978 he cited $180 billion, adding that in 1977 total farm debt rose at a rate of about $1.3 billion per month. And in Oklahoma, he observed, the debt against land was worth more than the land was worth in 1945.[55]

Seeking flexibility, Bellmon viewed the administration's announcement that farmers must remove cattle from wheat set-aside acreage as a further example "of President Carter's amazing lack of understanding of the present farm situation." Thus, while many members of Congress introduced measures seeking to do something about the farm situation, and a handful of farm organizations were openly courting or working with the American Agriculture Movement, little understanding and no gleam of support emanated from the executive branch of government.[56]

Thus far the farm crisis was long on talk but devoid, despite calls for a farm strike, of any violence. This situation changed in March 1978, when violence erupted in South Texas. Farmers from Oklahoma, Louisiana, Missouri, Kentucky, and Georgia had traveled to the town of Edinburg to protest Mexican farmers bringing their produce across the Rio Grande. After a confrontation with police, strike leaders estimated that of the more than two hundred strikers jailed in Edinburg, twenty-five to thirty-five Oklahoma farmers were among them, six of them from northwestern Oklahoma. Alberta Leierer, the wife of one, was hospitalized for injuries inflicted by a police officer's billy club as she attempted to escape from a cloud of tear gas. Leierer, whose husband was jailed, asserted, "We have just as much at stake in this farm strike as our husbands do. If they lose everything we lose everything." Three northwestern Oklahoma wives accompanied their husbands to Texas; only Leierer was assaulted, but another wife was briefly jailed. All who went to Edinburg were members of the American Agriculture Movement. The jailed strikers insisted that the fines leveled against them be dropped before they left the Edinburg jail, secure in the knowledge that their cause would receive widespread attention in distressed rural regions.[57]

In one sector of the Oklahoma agriculture, however, there was marked improvement. Cattle numbers in 1978 were generally below earlier estimates. As cattle numbers dropped, value per head steadily increased. An inventory showed 2.3 million cows in Oklahoma on January 1, 1978, a 3 percent decrease from a year earlier. Inventory value of all cattle and calves on Oklahoma's 71,000 cattle operations showed a 23 percent increase over the previous year's value. The substantial reduction in cattle numbers meant a much improved market. While cattlemen's difficulties were far from over, by reducing their herds they were in the process of resolving them. But there was no end in sight to the depressing conditions their neighboring grain farmers were enduring.[58]

Although many in Congress now agreed on the necessity of farm aid, there was an inability on the part of its proponents to agree on a specific measure, and no president showed any inclination to endorse congressional proposals. In 1978 the Senate managed to cobble together a farm bill that dealt with crucial aspects of the farm problem, and after listening patiently to twenty-one agricultural leaders in the White House, the president indicated he understood the broad dimensions of the situation. Yet despite these endeavors, no agreement could be reached.[59]

Just how wheat farmers in Oklahoma were coping was vividly portrayed in a penetrating story in the feature magazine of the *Tulsa Tribune*. Ralph Marsh related the predicament of several farmers in Kingfisher County, along with the views of the banker who handled their accounts. The cost-price situation, along with Russian grain deals and beef imports that depressed cattle prices, affected them all. Marsh related how the local banker viewed the situation, with younger farmers among the hardest hit.

On certain farms the wife went to work off the farm, and some of his male clients got jobs as roughnecks on an oil rig, while others expanded into the hog business. To keep afloat, some farmers refinanced their farms, using higher land evaluation to borrow more money, at the same time facing the specter of losing the land. Overall, the banker concluded that the young progressive farmer was trapped by interest on money he borrowed to purchase machinery to work the land. At the other end of the spectrum, the old, established farmer was borrowing against the land his father gave him. If a farmer expanded operations, he ran up his interest money, while cutting back drove up production costs per acre. The goal of farmers in keeping their land and maintaining their way of life was at stake. And the country banker, who provided access to credit and who at times had to foreclose, was both keen observer and key player. He was also vulnerable if he overextended his operations and was unable to collect interest on them.[60]

To resolve the crisis, it was clear to all concerned that the impetus would have to come from Washington. After meeting with a delegation of Panhandle members of American Agriculture, a member of Steed's staff informed him that they were most concerned about the flexible supports principle. If that concept could be achieved, they could live with any bill Congress approved. Flexibility was a premise stridently called for by Bellmon as a tool in bringing supply and demand into balance. Like most Oklahoma farmers, especially leaders of farm organizations, Bellmon argued against proposals that made food producers dependent on subsidies for their income, concluding that they were much better off when they could get fair prices in the marketplace. All the efforts to start resolving the crisis came to an abrupt end in 1978, when Carter vetoed the Emergency Farm Bill.[61]

The failure to achieve remedial legislation led the American Agriculture Movement to increase its efforts in calling for 100 percent of parity at the marketplace. Now, however, some members characterized opponents as part of a vast conspiracy. "I am convinced," wrote a member from Amber, Oklahoma, "that the Carter Administration and their promoters are only interested in controlling food, energy and the money or wealth of this nation in order to establish world government" controlled by multinational corporations and banks. Congress now had to do more than seek 100 percent parity, it now had to pass laws "to prevent communism and socialism taking over our democracy." While desperate residents in rural Oklahoma, out of utter frustration, found a simple answer that could explain the failure to secure salutary legislation, there is no evidence to suggest that the American Agricultural Movement endorsed such views.[62]

Recognizing that significant assistance would not be forthcoming from Washington, producers sought different ways to survive. While 100 million bushels of wheat moved out of Oklahoma each year into the export market, farmers were reducing acreage formerly devoted to wheat and showing an interest in other commodities, particularly alfalfa. Other farmers harvested their wheat with cattle as grain prices remained below production costs. Although cattle offered a way out, securing cattle was a problem, since their numbers, as already noted, had been greatly reduced. In the Panhandle some farmers plowed wheat under; others were fencing wheat fields for cattle grazing. Further indications of a shift in outlook were evident when an American Agriculture spokesperson in Oklahoma claimed that the movement was seeking to reduce wheat production in the state.[63]

A sign of improved conditions for cattlemen was a story in the *New York Times* entitled "Wholesale Prices for Beef Set Record." And even more positive was a story in the *Oklahoma Farmer-Stockman* that the wheat outlook was improving, thanks to a substantial drop in production, and the fact that the People's Republic of China had purchased one million metric tons in April 1978. A USDA official on a visit to Oklahoma predicted increased progress in developing markets for U.S. wheat overseas.[64]

Despite encouraging signs, Bellmon was far from satisfied. He observed that farm real estate debt had risen to more than $15 billion and that Oklahoma farmers were facing bankruptcies at four to five times the normal rate in the High Plains. On his own farm, he acknowledged, he had lost money for the previous three years and that few young farmers could survive such losses. He blamed the policies pursued by every administration since he entered the Senate in 1968 for the intolerable markets farmers faced. Since no one farmer or group of farmers could have an appreciable effect, leadership from the administration was necessary "to bring supply and demand into balance and strengthen farm prices." Unfortunately, such leadership was lacking. While Bellmon did not want Congress "to get into the business of administering programs, . . . because of lack of action by the Administration," he concluded, "we have no choice." But his proposal indicated that Congress had too many choices and could not muster enough support to confront the administration.[65]

To add to producers woes, grain shipments to the Soviet Union were suspended by the president early in 1980. The embargo drastically upset the market, even though the administration pledged to purchase grain already under contract. Carter initiated the embargo following the invasion of Afghanistan by Soviet troops in December 1979. Fraught with political implications, the embargo imposed just prior to the Iowa caucuses primarily impacted corn belt farmers. Less impacted Oklahoma wheat producers, nevertheless, were concerned that farmers could not bear an unfair share of the burden.[66]

With the number of family farms declining and with an embargo on Soviet grain sales in place, Bellmon pointed to an estimate of the World Food Council that within the next fifteen years the demand for food grains worldwide would increase "by some 550 million tons" and that American farmers would be called upon to provide the largest share. This estimate served to further his concern that legislation be enacted to assist family farmers. Though Congress did discuss numerous measures, little was accomplished in this year. Indeed, the *National Journal* in a feature article reported that the grain embargo had no serious impact on either the Soviets or the farmers. As the nation prepared for a presidential election, significant agricultural legislation no longer seemed possible, though there was speculation that the administration would take some action to bolster support in the farm belt. On the other hand, Bellmon, who had worked tirelessly on behalf of his rural constituents, decided to retire to his farm in Billings, Oklahoma. The Congress did produce one piece of important agricultural legislation which was important but not central to the squeeze crippling and crushing many grain farmers. Legislation was enacted creating a Food Security Reserve of 4 million metric tons of wheat to help alleviate famine in what was then called the Third World.[67]

The new Congress quickly got to work on a farm bill. Oklahoma's new senator, David L. Boren, as governor had endorsed the platform of the American Agriculture Movement and supported the farm strike. In the Senate he offered an amendment to prohibit the importation of Soviet agricultural products as long as the grain embargo continued. While the Senate approved his proposal, the amendment was changed to reflect only "a Sense of the Senate" and thus lost its mandatory impact. Boren found it incredible that "the U.S. government, on the one hand, denies our farmers access to the Soviet market, while on the other hand we keep our markets open to the Soviets." In addition, he sought fair income levels rather than more credit in an economy where total farm debt was ten times the level of net farm income. While Boren had fears of an impending collapse of major sectors of the farm economy, the Reagan administration viewed larger farms and growing dependence on exports as requiring less federal aid. Such an approach tied together both the administration's "free market" rhetoric and its budget constraints.[68]

The farm bill that made its way through Congress approved wheat support prices of $4.20 (House) and $4.00 (Senate) per bushel, the closest target prices came to the $5.00 level equated to what grain farmers deemed their cost of production. But what rankled Oklahomans, and did not bode well for the farm bill, was the president's refusal to meet with a group of congressmen to discuss the sagging farm economy. High interest rates, huge commodity surpluses, soaring production costs, and depressed market prices accelerated large-scale delinquencies in government loan programs. This situation led Boren to introduce a measure calling for a one-year moratorium on foreclosures of farm loans by the Farmers Home Administration.[69]

It also led Bellmon, in his retirement, to offer the Senate Budget Committee a firsthand report "from down on the farm." Having established himself during his tenure "as a budgeter of the old school," he now presented his credentials as a farmer who was losing money on his wheat and cattle. He discussed how rising land values led hard-pressed producers to borrow against their land to cover operating deficits, just like the federal government. But in Bellmon's case, his land bank manager had informed him that this was the last time he could borrow against his land. If farmers could not meet interest payments on their land, Bellmon indicated that "many farms would have to be sold over the next 12 to 18 months." A glut of such sales would cause land prices to fall, further reducing a farmer's equity and leading to "even more liquidation, a snowballing effect." To stall this collapse, Bellmon called for prompt action by the Farmers Home Administration and other agencies to lower interest rates. He asserted that he did not want to "whine and complain" but rather inform members "how it is down on the farm," and to say "straight out" that two more years like the previous two "and the U.S. will no longer be the bread basket of the world." He concluded his analysis by criticizing the Reagan administration, stating that high interest rates were "killing agriculture" and that supply-side economics "has meant less for the tax collector and more, much more, for the money lenders." The idea of stimulating an economic recovery by reducing deficits and increasing revenues in the depth of a recession appeared to Bellmon "an unproven radical economic theory."[70]

Both Boren and Bellmon expressed anxiety about the impending crisis in farm credit that threatened increasing numbers of producers with bankruptcy and foreclosure and even the collapse of the farm economy. During the 1970s, the Farm Credit System, the nation's leading supplier of agricultural credit, had been especially rapid in funneling large amounts of money into agriculture. The FCS comprised three types of lending institutions: (1) Federal Land Banks and the Federal Land Bank Associations, (2) the Federal Intermediate Credit Banks and the Production Credit Associations, and (3) the Banks for Cooperatives. Overall supervision was provided by the Farm Credit Administration, an independent agency in the executive branch. With growing demands for credit, the FCS in 1980 was sorely pressed. As debate over a proposed Farm Crisis Act became more intense, and with farm income at its lowest point since the Depression, farm credit crept into the debate with pleas for shoring up the sagging agricultural economy. Boren warned that without immediate action excess supplies of wheat and corn would combine to have an adverse effect on market conditions.[71]

He was successful in securing an amendment requiring the secretary of agriculture to permit deferral of payments for Farmers Home

Administration loans to creditors temporarily unable to make payments through no fault of their own. It took Boren seven months to achieve this goal. He was disturbed that the administration had not used its authority to ease the farm credit situation, noting that from October 1, 1981, to August 31, 1982, there were 776 foreclosures, 5,501 voluntary liquidations, and 1,156 bankruptcies compared to 300 foreclosures in 1981. And he was more disturbed by a recent study demonstrating that Oklahoma farm incomes tended to decline faster and more drastically than farm incomes in the United States as a whole.[72]

With the failure of his amendment to achieve fruition in legislation, Boren tried again to incorporate it into the Emergency Agricultural Credit Act of 1983, which he cosponsored. He observed that "in Oklahoma, the average net farm income in 1981 was only $14 per farm, the lowest in the entire nation." In 1982, he maintained, "that figure will register in the red." Since the president in his State of the Union message had stated that he was directing the USDA to work with farmers directly to help them stay in business, Boren believed the measure he cosponsored would allow the USDA to do what Reagan requested.[73]

He went one step further and introduced a comprehensive farm bill, stating that "unless we take drastic action now, it does not appear the situation will be reversed." What concerned Boren was the estimate that about two thousand Farmers Home Administration borrowers in Oklahoma would not have financing unless additional funds became available. He called upon the secretary of agriculture to reallocate funds to meet this situation, because enacting a supplemental appropriation bill would be time consuming when swift action was necessary. What made the situation most precarious in Oklahoma was the sagging demand for natural gas and the "shutting in" of many gas wells, causing "a staggering increase in the number of bankruptcies among independent oil men and their support industries." Adding to this crisis was the failure in 1982 of the Penn Square Bank in Oklahoma City. The confluence of these failures left the economy in shambles.[74]

The Farm Credit Banks of Wichita, a major source of credit for farmers, ranchers, and cooperative agribusiness, whose district included Oklahoma, reported that "net farm income remains depressed for the fourth consecutive year, and we see little chance for near-term improvement." Severely hot, dry weather compounded the problem for some producers; in many instances their financial position had eroded to the point that the banks could not survive an additional debt load, while the borrower might "be well advised to liquidate some land.[75]

Owing to these difficult conditions, ranchers and farmers reduced their demand for products and services. Resolving the problems confronting producers hinged on increased export demand to reduce supplies of many commodities. In addition, the report concluded, a general improvement of the domestic economy plus individual attention to reducing heavy debt loads would help meliorate the situation. One positive action in Oklahoma was the successful effort of the Oklahoma Wheat Commission, meeting in Enid with officials of the People's Republic of China, in convincing them of the virtues of hard red winter wheat. The visit resulted in the sale of 4.5 million bushels.[76]

Despite the coup of the grain sales, the outlook in Oklahoma remained bleak. The Tenth Federal Reserve District, which included Oklahoma, reported that loan repayment rates had dropped sharply across the Farm Belt. In the district, the population of farmers who left farming during the fourth quarter of 1982 and the first quarter of 1983 was about "65 percent higher than bankers considered normal." And as would be expected, loan delinquencies were rising as well. A point when further extension of credit would no longer be in the best interests of the borrower was becoming evident.[77]

A comparable situation prevailed within the Farm Credit System itself. Loan losses in the Production Credit Association, for example, for the previous three years exceeded the combined losses for the preceding seventeen years. The estimated $240–$250 million in losses sustained by this association represented in one year approximately 40 percent of all losses throughout its fifty-year existence as part of the Farm Credit System. The institutions comprising the system were urged to stay with troubled borrowers as long as they had any prospect for recovery. Nevertheless, the governor of the system expected refinancing, repayment, and loan servicing problems to increase. By the spring of 1984, as this situation was becoming increasingly evident, "one of the most perplexing, frustrating and enduring problems of the farm debt crisis was the seeming indifference with which official Washington approached the problem"—a problem that both Bellmon and Boren had called to the attention of the Reagan administration, which claimed it had a handle on the situation. If it did not ignore proposals coming out of Congress, it did not endorse any seeking to cope with the mounting debt crisis. It did, however, seek to improve trade relations. In this area, Oklahoma wheat producers, as previously noted, benefited. Not so cattlemen. Oklahoma in 1984 had more beef animals per square mile than any other state in the nation. And with prevailing low cattle prices, beef cattle production, the biggest agricultural industry in the state, again faced bleak prospects.[78]

In 1984, while endorsing Reagan's reelection, Oklahoma voters, recognizing Boren's continuous efforts on their behalf, reelected him overwhelmingly. He carried all but 5 of the state's 2,354 precincts. Humbling though this victory was to Boren, it also put increasing pressure on him to prod an indifferent administration to meet the crisis head on. By the summer of 1985, the administration, according to press reports, was shifting its thinking on agricultural issues, searching for a new approach to the increasing problems of farmers and their bankers. Boren, no doubt, was prompting the administration to consider changing its approach, when in February he dramatically brought the farm crisis to national attention and in so doing projected himself to the forefront in garnering public attention.[79]

Soon after returning to Washington following his reelection, Boren announced that he would begin a vigil, consisting of a daily Senate speech calling attention to the "massive economic crisis in agriculture." His purpose was to initiate spadework for a new farm bill. President Reagan, in sending forth the name of Edwin Meese to be his attorney general, helped transform the vigil into a filibuster. While neither Boren nor the handful of senators from both parties who agreed with him opposed Meese, they intended to stall the vote until the administration took cognizance of the crisis overwhelming the American heartland. Their remarks now received increased attention. Most media coverage focused on Boren, who led the group seeking emergency credit legislation.[80]

While Boren sought action by the administration, the filibuster drew irate comments from the president, the secretary of agriculture, and Senator Robert Dole, chair of the Agriculture Committee. An emergency farm credit package negotiated with Republicans by Boren and J. James Exon of Nebraska was rejected by their Democratic colleagues after more than two hours of closed-door discussion. Failure meant the filibuster would continue, with William French Smith, who wanted to retire, remaining on until Meese, a close friend and ally of the president, could gain Senate approval. Finally, after four days, on February 23, 1985, the filibuster ended, paving the way for Meese's confirmation. The compromise, negotiated after acrimonious floor debate, allowed both sides to add farm aid amendments to an Ethiopian famine relief bill.[81]

Boren, the chief agitator of the filibuster and of the compromise, "seemed the most relieved player in the game." He claimed that the filibuster forced the administration to make "significant improvements in farm programs," but he offered no specifics. A Republican colleague offered his own evaluation: "David Boren did a great thing in getting the farm credit crisis on the front burner, but the fire got a little hot." Nevertheless, Boren came out of the filibuster with enhanced prestige and the respect of his colleagues, plus a lot of newspaper coverage and television time.[82]

In the House of Representatives, Glenn English and Wes Watkins got closer to the heart of the matter, calling upon the president to fire the budget director, David Stockman, and Secretary of Agriculture John Block for fostering austere legislation they claimed would eliminate the American family farm. Stockman was quoted as saying there is an "over-investment" in agriculture and that some farmers must get out of the business to achieve a market-oriented production system not dependent on price supports. In response, English noted that already up to 300,000 farmers in the past three to four years had already been wiped out and that problems such as shrinking foreign markets were not their doing. Further, his colleague Mike Synar noted that regardless of what Congress did, farmers would go out of business at a rate unprecedented since the Great Depression. Most would file for bankruptcy in an attempt to reorganize their debt and keep their land. Changes in the Bankruptcy Code,

Synar argued, would allow them to reorganize their debts and keep their land, a change the administration was not yet willing to consider.[83]

Following the approval of Meese's nomination, Boren played an active role in crafting emergency farm credit legislation. He was outraged when the president vetoed the measure. Reagan had asked Congress to spend $20 billion on foreign aid, while turning down $100–$200 million to assist farmers in coping with the economic collapse of agriculture. To explain the filibuster, his role, and what he sought to accomplish, Boren, in a lengthy letter published in the *Daily Oklahoman*, surveyed the dimensions of the situation, noting the meager concessions the filibuster had achieved as an indication of the administration's indifference to the concerns of Oklahoma farmers.[84]

While official Washington dickered and debated, a USDA report acknowledged that 93,000 mid-size farms, holding $47 billion in debt, were technically insolvent or on the verge of going broke, an increase of 45 percent over earlier figures. In many ways 1985 marked the height of the farm crisis. It was the year hotlines appeared, support groups were organized, and stress counseling got under way. It was also the year in which lenders generally realized that many loans were not going to be repaid, as farmers missed interest and principal payment deadlines. In Oklahoma, the bank commissioner listed the number of failed banks in his annual report: six in 1984; nine in 1985; sixteen in 1986, and twenty in 1987. In 1988 an additional sixteen banks failed; "however, total assets were reduced only slightly due to improved economic conditions." Though another sixteen banks were closed in 1989, five new charters were granted and twenty-seven branch banks were granted approval to purchase the failed banks' assets and assume the deposit liability.[85]

To help meet the impact of these failures by February of 1985, hotlines were functioning in Oklahoma and at least ten other states. Funded through churches, rural advocacy groups, contributions, and even public money, the lines were part of a network informing farmers where they could turn for help, or if there was any hope of help. Besides offering a voice over the phone, some staff members made "house calls" to counsel desperate farmers whose notes were coming due. As rural banks tightened their access to credit, even solvent farmers would fail. And the trauma of losing a farm that had been in a family for generations had devastating consequences: estranged children, marital breakup, alcoholism, physical abuse, depression, and at times suicide.[86]

In the first half of 1985, a total of 178 Oklahoma farmers in 53 counties lost their farms in foreclosures by the Federal Land Bank. While debt was at the essence of the crisis, concern about income was central to producers' outlook. Prices received by farmers in 1985 were 20 to 25 percent lower than the previous year and were predicted to continue falling. A report by agricultural economists at Oklahoma State University observed that one of every five farmers in the state was deep enough in debt to face financial failure.[87]

A study by an Oklahoma Conference of Churches task force resulted in a plea for churches to get involved with the state's farm and ranch families facing significant changes in their way of life. Dr. Max E. Glenn, the conference executive officer, expressed a "concern for thousands of persons who are suffering loss of income, loss of credit, humiliating loss of self-confidence, and even loss of ownership of the family farm." The conference report called for "understanding, compassion, justice and action" in addressing the situation in rural Oklahoma, where their study showed that more than 50 percent of the value of non–real estate productive farm assets was owed to creditors.[88]

The interfaith task force, after reviewing the situation, recommended community based farm crisis forums to plan local action, creation of an aid packet providing a listing of resources and agencies, and other items that could be of assistance. Glenn noted that the task force would develop a statewide network of individuals who would volunteer their expertise. This report marked the introduction of the faith community into the crisis, offering care and counseling for people in distress. Along with these efforts, there was widespread understanding that if the crisis would be abated, positive action from Washington was necessary. And thus far, despite valiant efforts by the Oklahoma delegation, the intensity of the crisis only increased.[89]

Though the filibuster failed to bring significant change, Boren, increasing his efforts, announced that the Senate Agriculture Committee, of which he was a member, had approved his amendment to extend the Farmers Home Administration loan program. He also wrote the secretary of agriculture, expressing concern about declining agricultural exports and complaining that "we are rapidly losing our export markets." Then, several days later, he announced that he would hold hearings in Oklahoma City on the financial crisis in the Farm Credit System. Officials of the system had recently called for federal help. Boren hoped the problem could be addressed by raising farm income, which would thereby enable farmers to meet their obligations at FCS and at commercial banks. The 1985 farm bill, with Boren's amendment and concerns reflected in it, to become law required Reagan's approval. And that was the problem.[90]

Earlier a panel of agricultural economists had blasted a proposal suggested by the president to wean agriculture from its dependence on subsidies. Even worse, as far as farmers were concerned, were Reagan's remarks at the annual dinner of the Gridiron Club, sponsored by members of the Washington press corps and attended by top government figures. Speaking supposedly off the record, Reagan quipped, "I think we should keep the grain and export the farmers." There were groans in the audience. Then, at breakfast with reporters the following Monday, Reagan was asked if "in retrospect" he regretted the remark. His reply: "Yes, because it didn't get a laugh," words that were given wide circulation and indicated the high hurdle that Boren and his colleagues faced in securing his support for the farm bill.[91]

Despite the roadblock posed by the administration, Boren continued to speak out and sponsor amendments before Congress shut down for a five-week summer break. Later in the year he accepted an invitation from Prince Philip to participate in a conference at Windsor Castle on world agricultural problems, at which he informed leaders of British agriculture that American farmers could no longer afford to bear the cost of a stable world agricultural policy by themselves.[92]

In Oklahoma some farmers began to denounce the president's failure to address the economic problems facing family farms. In addition, the Oklahoma Conference of Churches at year's end was busily recruiting more people to man the hotline and to counsel farmers. One attorney told the conference director that half the farmers coming to him for bankruptcy "wind up in divorce." On another level, Willie Nelson assisted Oklahoma farmers with $40,000 from his second farm concert. Checks totaling $15,000 were for food, the remaining $25,000 to be used for the hotline.[93]

While Nelson's gift was helping some Oklahoma farmers, Boren in the Senate was cosponsoring an amendment to bail out the Farm Credit System. The amendment was incorporated in a rescue package that centralized the system's loosely linked finances, tightened federal regulations, and offered standby financial help. But when the 1985 farm bill emerged from the Conference Committee, Boren was no longer optimistic, stating, "Overall, the bill fails to adequately address the income problems of farmers or to provide an aggressive program to increase exports." Its passage would do very little to reduce the crisis in rural America. And indeed, his unstinting efforts came to naught in the final version of the bill.[94]

Early in the new year, Boren again cosponsored a measure providing comprehensive farm credit legislation aimed at stopping farm loan foreclosures. It would specifically require the Farm Credit System, holding about a third of the nation's farm loans, to lower interest rates on restructured debt, thereby avoiding farm loan foreclosures. The bill also allowed farmers to write off up to 30 percent of the principal of an agricultural loan over a ten-year period and receive federally generated certificates to prevent sudden capital drains. With a new secretary of agriculture, with the departure of budget director David Stockman, and with Reagan devoting his energies primarily to confronting the "Evil Empire" and ending the Cold War, Boren had reason for some optimism that government could change its outlook and consider the farm crisis.[95]

Optimism manifested itself in the increasing number of press releases flowing from his office, delineating whirlwind activities on behalf of embattled farmers to restructure farm debt; to have the Commodity Credit Corporation advance funds to eligible farmers; to implement a "buy down" program offered by the Farmers Home Administration. In April Boren announced that the Farmers Home Administration would receive an additional $2.5 million for direct operating loans. At the same time Oklahoma clergymen were becoming better informed and were now aware that the crisis was a moral one, with spiritual and religious overtones as well. Clergymen and rural bankers could both provide counsel and assistance to individuals, while their delegates in Washington strove mightily to secure legislation from an administration becoming less rigid in its outlook.[96]

It was the increasing number of rural bank failures throughout the heartland, along with the collapse of major banks in some of its cities, that attracted national attention. In the first four months of 1986, the Federal Deposit Insurance Corporation reported 37 bank failures. During 1985 it had reported a total of 120 bank failures. In Oklahoma, major banks in Tulsa, Enid, and Oklahoma City failed or were seriously impaired because falling oil prices were wreaking further havoc on the failing economy.[97]

Nevertheless, there were definite signs that the times were changing. The Farm Credit System initiated loan restructuring policies and a more competitive method of pricing interest. The president of Professional Farmers of America told seven hundred wheat farmers in Enid that "the fabric has changed from negative to positive," that farmers with "the deepest problems have work-out plans." In addition, the legal coordinator for the Family Farm Defense Fund told farmers in Enid that her organization would provide full support to assist Oklahoma farmers being foreclosed by private corporations or federal agencies. Their work was facilitated by a measure enacted by the state legislature that placed a one-year moratorium on any Federal Land Bank Association seeking foreclosure action in a state court. By the spring of 1986 the nadir had been reached. T. S. Eliot called April the cruelest month; in Oklahoma it marked the beginning of the end of the farm crisis.[98]

But it was far from over. Before leaving for Austin, Texas, to attend Willie Nelson's Farm Aid II concert, the director of the Oklahoma Council for Churches observed that, according to projections, "25 percent of 17,500 farm and ranch families will lose their farms and ranches in the next 12 to 15 months." More disturbing, he said, were the kinds of calls received on the hotlines, ranging from financial distress to contemplating suicide. He cited eight suicides directly related to the farm crisis and mentioned other "accidents" that could not be authenticated. What the Reagan ddministration called "the realignment of rural areas and the rural economy," some in Oklahoma called genocide. In Austin the director hoped to secure funds to replenish their empty coffers and be of assistance to beleaguered farm families.[99]

In Washington, Boren along with his farm-state colleagues did not let up in their efforts to keep farmers in business by restructuring their debt and by providing advance deficiency payments for crops, and they were pleased when the administration sought a major grain sale to the Soviets. While these legislators were supporting measures to save the family farm, eighty Oklahoma farmers attended the National Farm Congress at St. Louis. The congress, an offshoot of the Willie Nelson Farm Aid efforts, discussed proposals for legislation that would do what Boren and his associates also sought to do, namely to stop the downward slide of the farm family.[100]

By year's end signs mounted, despite a difficult year, that the long, painful recession was bottoming out, that the downward slide was beginning to abate. Most encouraging was an evident slowdown in the decline of farmland values. Significant pieces of legislation played a key role. Changes in bankruptcy legislation called for enforced debt restructuring throughout rural America, while amendments to the Farm Credit Act bolstered the ailing Farm Credit System and the Food Security Act of 1985 reduced loan rates to assist farmers in becoming more competitive internationally. A year-end survey in the *Economic Review* was entitled "U.S. Agriculture on the Mend." In Oklahoma, with its wave of bank failures and its high rate of delinquency on agricultural loans, farm communities continued to suffer, as the farm structure slowly started to stabilize with fewer family farms than in previous years. And by the spring of 1987, prospects for recovery were evident as crop prices improved, inflation fears abated, and there was renewed Soviet interest in purchasing grain. A decline in the value of the dollar against other currencies contributed to a modest rise in the volume of farm exports.[101]

While the hotlines continued to ring in 1987 with tales of foreclosures, bankruptcies, and suicides, these were considerably fewer. While Willie Nelson's Farm Aid organization had distributed almost $6.5 million to various crisis groups throughout rural America the heartland was on the mend. Recovery was evident in record farm earnings, shared across crop and livestock operations, along with a stabilizing farm land market. As the farm financial crisis faded, agriculture's long awaited recovery was becoming abundantly evident.[102]

What conclusions or observations can be offered about the farm crisis that engulfed Oklahoma for about two decades? To begin, it was the policies pursued by the Nixon, Ford, Carter, and Reagan presidencies that caused and determined the dimensions of the crisis, not the hazards imposed by nature that farmers and ranchers encountered. And it was only the collapse of the Farm Credit System and the failures of increasing numbers of rural banks that allowed David Boren, the right person in the right place, to bring the crisis forcefully to the forefront of public attention. The other factor was a shift in the outlook of the Reagan administration. In Reagan's second term John Block and David Stockman, both hostile to rural concerns, were no longer in government service, and Reagan himself was heavily involved in foreign policy matters and seeking an end to the Cold War. But it should be emphasized that it was financial collapse, and not agricultural distress, that brought about the changes that resolved the crisis.

If the collapse of the credit structure in rural regions was central to ending the crisis, what then brought it on? Here we must return to developments launched in the Nixon years. With the decision to conduct the war in Vietnam without raising taxes, a policy that became a trademark of the conservative era that followed brought with it slowly mounting inflation. In addition, the Nixon administration, casting aside the New Deal outlook of seeking to keep supply and demand in balance, went all out in urging full-scale agricultural production. Since the bulk of Oklahoma grain and beef was consumed abroad, Oklahoma producers, in competition with producers elsewhere, found they were not competing on an even playing field. And as prices increased for the cost of everything necessary to continue operating, they soon found themselves in an ever-tightening cost-price freeze. To continue functioning and making ends meet, more and more producers borrowed money, using segments of their farm as security. Little of meaning was accomplished to resolve this situation until the banks failed. Oklahoma producers and their legislators could not muster enough support in an increasingly urban and corporate nation to hold on and pursue a meaningful way of life until the rural banking structure broke down.

Today there are few in Oklahoma who remember the farm crisis, and there are many who venerate Reagan as a leading figure of the conservative era that flowered during the years of the crisis.

Notes

1. *Statistical Abstract of Oklahoma: 1975* (Center For Economic and Management Research, University of Oklahoma) Section 3.00 Agriculture.

2. Carl Albert Remarks to Committee on Agriculture, June 18, 1974. Carl Albert Collection Legislative Box 233 Folder 23. Carl Albert Center Archives, University of Oklahoma. Hereafter, unless otherwise noted, all collections cited are in the Carl Albert Center. And instead of utilizing "box" and "folder," only numbers will be cited, box number first, as 233/23 referring to the above citation.

3. Carl Albert Remarks to Committee on Agriculture, June 18, 1974, Albert Legislative, 233/23.

4. Ibid.

5. David Hall to Richard M. Nixon, April 16, 1974. See too Hall to Dewey Bartlett, May 16, 1974. Both items in Bartlett Clippings 63/2.

6. *Daily Oklahoman*, May 24, 1974, story "Bellmon, Bartlett Urge Reduced Beef Imports."

7. *Waurika News-Democrat* June 13, 1974, Bartlett 41/19.

8. Ibid.

9. Bartlett: Draft Statement Before Agriculture Committee . . . , June 17, 1974. Bartlett 41/19; *Tulsa World*, June 18, 1974, "Cattlemen Face Financial Ruin, Senators Told." The purchase of $100 million worth of beef and pork by the government would have almost no effect on the sagging cattle industry, said a spokesman for the Oklahoma cattlemen. See story in *Tulsa World* by Mike Flanagan on June 19, 1974. Both clippings in Bartlett 63/17.

10. *Tulsa World*, June 24, 1974, "Ranchers' Petition Urges Import Curb," Bartlett Clippings 64/8. Stories re livestock in *Tulsa Tribune*, June 18 and June 25, 1974, and *Tulsa World*, June 18, 1974. All items in Bartlett Clippings 63/17.

11. *Daily Oklahoman*, October 6, 1974, "State Ranchers Plan Support of Slaughter." See too October 13, 1974, "Ranchers to Eye Slaughter." Albert Clippings 1/9 for both items.

12. *Daily Oklahoman*, October 10, 1974, "Biting Bullet . . . No Easier for State Cattleman," Albert Clippings 1/9.

13. *Sunday Oklahoman*, "Ranchers to Eye Slaughter" and "State Beef Consumers Not Getting Benefit of Cattlemen's Falling Prices," October 13, 1974. Albert Clippings 1/9 for both stories.

14. *Daily Oklahoman*, October 6, 1974, "Bellmon Calls Grain Sale Curbs Hasty, Ill Conceived," Albert Clippings 1/14; unidentified clipping August 11, 1974, Bartlett Clippings 7/30.

15. *Daily Oklahoman*, October 8, 1974, "Gowdy Slaps Wheat Action," Albert Clippings 1/14.

16. For the plight of one Oklahoma rancher, see the letter by Alice Hicks to the Editor of the *Oklahoma Farmer-Stockman* on p. 16 of the January 1975 issue. For Earl Butz's views, see "Crusader Butz," a 1975 article in the *Wall Street Journal*, n.d., in Bartlett Clipping file 7/30.

17. Lloyd Jones to Albert, January 17, 1975, and Albert to Jones, January 21, 1975, Albert Legislative 192/9. Jones's letter is typical of hordes of letters that poured into the offices of the Oklahoma congressional delegation. For an example of legislation that provided minimal relief, see the discussion of the Emergency Livestock Credit Act of 1974 in a memo from Tom Thornbrugh to Bartlett, January 30, 1975, Bartlett 42/27. For Bartlett's legislative efforts to aid cattlemen, see his newsletter,"An OKIE in Washington," n.d. [February 1975], and *Sunday Oklahoman*, February 9, 1975. Bartlett Clippings 63/2 for both items. See too his press release on February 6, 1975, in Bartlett 7/30, and Albert to Tom Foley January 27, 1975, Albert 192/15, for "state of near panic." For the delegation going to Washington, see Allan Cromley to OPubCo, January 29, 1975, Allan Cromley Papers, 9/1.

18. Glenn English to Dear Colleague, January 30, 1975, Tom Steed Legislative 71/5, Tom Steed Papers, Carl Albert Center. Leaflet, "Are Wheat Prices Going the Way Cattle Prices Did?," Albert Legislative 192/9. For the article "Price Perspective for Agriculture," see *Oklahoma Farmer-Stockman*, February 1975, p. 38.

19. Jesse Berryhill to Albert, February 11, 1975, Albert Legislative 192/9; unidentified clippings, February 11 and 12, 1975, in Bartlett Clippings 63/17. Albert to Carl Russell Richman, Albert Legislative 192/23.

20. For Boren's views, see *Tulsa Tribune*, "Wheat Sales Push Due?," February 19, 1975, Albert Clippings 1/14.

21. Carl Albert to Arvil Mauldin, February 26, 1975, Albert Legislative 192/23.

22. Statement of the National Farm Coalition, March 10, 1975, Steed Legislative 7/18; John W. Scott to Albert, March 14, 1975, Albert Legislative 192/15. Albert Statement in Support of Agriculture Bill, March 11, 1975, Steed Legislative 71/5.

23. Bartlett to Gerald Ford, April 23, 1975, Bartlett 7/30. Bartlett urged the President to reconsider his views. For further Oklahoma legislators' efforts to block the veto, see *Daily Oklahoman*, April 24, 1975, Albert Clippings 1/8. The House sustained the veto by a vote of 245 to 182, 40 short of the two-thirds necessary to override. See too *Daily Oklahoman*, May 3, 1975, Albert Clippings 1/8.

24. *Tulsa World*, July 17, 1975, "Soviets Buying Wheat," Bartlett Clippings 63/17; Albert to P. E. Winfrey, July 22, 1975, Albert Legislative 192/32.

25. Plain English by Glenn English, week of September 22, 1975, Cromley 9/1; William Woodward to Albert, August 7, 1975, Albert Legislative 192/32; AFL-CIO Executive Council Statement on Russian Grain Purchases: July 31, 1975, Albert Legislative 192/32; Bartlett press release, August 13, 1975, and September 7, 1975, Bartlett 7/30; telegram, Hinton, Okla., Kiwanis Club to Albert, September 5, 1975, and Bill Pope to Albert, September 11, 1975; Albert to Paul Kohler, September 24, 1975, all in Albert Legislative 192/32. See too the unsigned letter to Steed on September 17, 1975, in Steed Legislative 71/10. All items pertain to the Soviet grain sales.

26. *Oklahoma Journal*, October 23, 1975, "Cattlemen Voice Complaints," Albert Clippings 1/9.

27. Mary Hamblin, "Bank Lending to Agriculture: An Overview," *Economic Review* 60, no. 9: 13.

28. O. A. Meyer to Albert, January 20, 1976, Albert Legislative 192/32; *Daily Oklahoman*, January 25, 1976 story by Allan Cromley in Albert Clippings 1/8.

29. Glenn English Press Release: September 12, 1976, Cromley 9/2; Ed King to Bartlett, September 23, 1976 Bartlett 42/27; *Holdenville Daily News*, September 28, 1976, story by Harry Culver, Albert Clippings 1/9; *Oklahoma Journal* October 7, 1976, "Rep. English Joins Wheat Loan Move," Albert Clippings 1/14.

30. David L. Boren Statement, October 21, 1976, Albert Departmental 135/24.

31. David Nemechek to Steed, January 8, 1977, and Karen Sandini to Steed, February 18, 1977, both in Steed Legislative 83/5. *Oklahoma Farmer-Stockman*, February 1977, p. 3. Plain English by Glenn English, March 2, 1977, Cromley 9/3. Senator Bellmon introduced a bill to pay wheat farmers to take part of their acreage out of production and use it for grazing.

32. *Oklahoma Farmer-Stockman*, March 1977, p. 22, "Small Packer Worried Over Meat Imports."

33. Don Johnson to Steed, March 30, 1977, Steed Legislative 83/9. Johnson was president of the Washita County Farmers Union. See too "Sooner Summary" by Ernest Shiner in *Oklahoma Farmer-Stockman*, April 1977, p. 8.

34. See story in *Oklahoma Farmer-Stockman*, April 1977, pp. 40–41, 50.

35. Jenny Legg to Steed, April 18, 1977; Adrian Vincent to Steed, n.d. [1977]; Howard & Genevieve Nicholson to Steed, April 22, 1977; W. S. Merch to Steed, April 24, 1977 All in Steed Legislative 83/3. Similar letters can be found in other Oklahoma congressional collections.

36. See for example Mike Cordes to Steed, April 25, 1977, Clark N. Garfield to all Government Officials, n.d.; Roy and Donna Roth to Dear Sir, n.d.; Frank Kucera to Dear Sir, April 26, 1977. All items in Steed Legislative 83/3. Mary Ida Morrison to Steed May 1, 1977, Steed Legislative 83/1. *Oklahoma Farmer-Stockman* May 1977, p. 7, for wheat stories.

37. *Oklahoma Farmer-Stockman* June 1977, p. 6, 24, July 1977 p. 3 a letter from Mrs. Sallie Fisher to Dear Editor. *Daily Oklahoman* July 8, 1977, clipping in Steed Legislative 83/1; Cromley to *The Oklahoman*, July 8, 1977, Cromley 4/16, and Boren to Dear President Carter July 8, 1977, Cromley 4/16.

38. A copy of the chart prepared by the National Farmers Union is in Steed Legislative 83/1.

39. English to Steed, July 8 and July 15, 1977, Steed Legislative 83/3 for both items. Joe Neal Hampton to Steed, July 11, 1977, and Charley and Vala Duffy to Steed, July 14, 1977, Steed Legislative 83/9 for both items.

40. Press Release, n.d., "English Anti-Embargo Amendment Included in Final Version of Farm Bill," and Consumer Federation of America: Press Release, July 20, 1977, Cromley 9/3 for both items; English to Steed July 25, 1977, Steed Legislative 83/9; *Oklahoma Farmer-Stockman*, August 1977, "Sooner Summary," p. 8.

41. Henry Bellmon News, September 1, 1977, and Vahlberg to OPUBCO, September 1, 1977, Cromley 4/1 for both items. Shortly thereafter Bartlett joined Bellmon in criticizing the set-aside program. Bartlett News Release, October 14, 1977, Bartlett 46/2.

42. Bartlett Statement, September 20, 1977, Bartlett 44/29; See too the comprehensive statement of the National Cattlemen's Association, September 20, 1977, Steed Legislative 83/4.

43. Bellmon to Bob Bergland, October 31, 1977, Bellmon 4/1; Steed to Monty Morrow, October 31, 1977, and Morrow to Steed October 24, 1977, Steed Legislative 83/5 for both items. For the failure to sell wheat to China, see Vivian Vahlberg to Oklahoma Publishing Company, November 4, 1977, Cromley 4/1.

44. Morrow to Steed, October 24, 1977, Steed Legislative 83/5.

45. Steed: Attention November 1, 1977 (unsigned letter), and Lois Scott to Steed November 3, 1977, Steed Legislative 83/9 for both items; J. A. Carrick to Chief, Cooperative Staff, PSL Division, USDA, November 3, 1977, Steed Legislative 83/9. Carrick critiqued the 1977 farm bill. See too Washington Bureau to Oklahoma Publishing Company, November 4, 1977, Cromley 4/1. The set-aside provision re grazing was later modified.

46. *Daily Oklahoman*, December 23 and 24, 1977, stories by Jim Young and Ed Kelley, in Cromley 4/16.

47. *Daily Oklahoman*, December 24, 1977, story by Ed Kelley, in Cromley 4/16.

48. Steed to Mrs. D. H. Shumaker, December 30, 1977, Steed Legislative 83/9. See too *National Journal*, December 17, 1977, p. 1974. There were tractors in the national capital and thirty state capitals seeking to bring attention to the farm crisis.

49. John D. Scott to Bellmon, January 2, 1978, Steed Legislative 96/1; Jack Robinson to Honorable Senator, January 4, 1978, and Bartlett to Ted Wagoner,

January 10, 1978, Bartlett 10/27 for both items. The *Muskogee Phoenix* on January 6, 1978, in a story by Steve Ray Liman, covered a meeting where an organizer discussed American agriculture at the Trade Winds Motor Inn, Bartlett Clippings 63/17.

50. In January 1978 Steed received several hundred letters scattered throughout Folders 1 through 8 in Box 90. Bartlett received similar letters but not as many. See Bartlett 10/27.

51. *Oklahoma Farmer-Stockman*, January 4, 1978, p. 4; *Daily Oklahoman*, January 20, 1978, Steed Legislative 90/1, and *Daily Oklahoman*, March 17, 1978, story by Ed Montgomery, Bartlett clippings 63/17. The story in the *Oklahoma Times* of January 22, 1978, claimed that about six hundred Oklahoma farmers were in Washington, Bartlett Clippings 63/7. Later, at a governors' meeting in St. Paul, Boren observed that if OPEC could control oil prices, why couldn't the four nations, including the United States, which sold 85 perent of the wheat in the world, do more to improve wheat and grain prices? See Summary: 1-31-78, in Cromley 4/16.

52. *Dewey City Record*, January 26, 1978, Bartlett Clippings 63/17; *National Journal*, January 28, 1978, p. 162. See Lloyd Goodwin and C. W. Hathaway to Steed, January 30, 1978, Steed Legislative 90/1. Gardner and Hathaway of the Cherokee Hills Resource Conservation and Development Project called for halting the importation of all beef, live and frozen, until cattle prices reached parity.

53. See for example the flyer prepared by the farmers of the American Agricultural Movement of Duke (Okla.) and the story in *Frederick Press*, February 2, 1978, "Farmers Plan Strike Office." Both items in Steed Legislative 90/1, as an official policy statement of the American Agriculture Movement.

54. Bellmon to Bob Bergland, February 23, 1978, Cromley 4/2. Measures to provide greater flexibility were introduced in Congress by Keith Sebelius and Jack Hightower. See Sebelius to Dear Colleague, February 13, 1978, and Hightower to Dear Colleague, February 14, 1978, Steed Legislative 90/1.

55. Plain English, February 8, 1978, "A Report to the People of the Sixth District" by Glenn English, Cromley 9/4; *Oklahoma Journal* February 12, 1978, "Farmers to Mark Time Awhile," clipping in Steed Legislative 90/1.

56. News: U. S. Sen. Henry Bellmon: March 1, 1978, Cromley 4/2; *Oklahoma Farmer-Stockman*, March 1978, p. 3.

57. *Enid Morning News*, March 3, 1978; *Ponca City News*, March 2, 1978; *Enid Daily Eagle*, March 3, 1978; *Daily Oklahoman*, March 3, 1978.

58. *Oklahoma Farmer-Stockman*, March 1978, p. 11.

59. *Wall Street Journal*, March 22, 1978. James P. Gannon reviewed the situation in Congress, Cromley 4/2. *Oklahoma Farmer-Stockman*, April 1978, p. 11, discusses the views of President Carter.

60. *Tulsa Tribune*, March 29, 1978, "Oklahoma's Wheat Farmers Just Trying to Hold On," story by Ralph Marsh, Steed Legislative 9/10.

61. Memo: tr to Steed April 4, 1978, Steed Legislative 90/2; News: U.S. Sen. Henry Bellmon April 10, 1978, Cromley 4/2; *Enid Morning News*, April 12, 1978. and *Kiowa City Star*, April 13, 1978, for both items see Bartlett clippings 63/17. The *Kiowa Star* story related the favorable response of farmers to the farm bill, and the Duke American Agriculture Movement to Steed, April 17, 1978, expressed the pride of its members in the support the measure received from the congressional delegation.

62. Carol Woods to Dear Sir, April 25, 1978, Steed Legislative 90/2. At the same time the president signed into law far-reaching farm credit legislation, enabling farmers to refinance debts incurred during years of low farm prices. See undated story [May 1978?] in Cromley 9/5.

63. *Oklahoma Farmer-Stockman*, May 1978, pp. 6, 7, and 28. *Muskogee Phoenix*, May 7, 1978, story by David Egner, Bartlett Clippings 63/17.

64. *New York Times*, May 21, 1978, p. 25, Bartlett 46/2. See *Oklahoma Farmer-Stockman*, June 1978, p. 15, and July 1978, p. 20, for stories about the improving wheat outlook. The September 1978 issue (p. 5) offered a positive outlook for both cattle and wheat.

65. Bellmon statement to Mr. President, n.d. (October 1978?), Cromley 4/5. Bellmon did not give up. During the congressional recess he traveled to the Soviet Union, the People's Republic of China, and to Switzerland to discuss ways of improving the foreign market for American grain. He also went to Canada to work out an agreement that would put a floor under the price of wheat from both countries sold for export. See News: U. S. Sen. Henry Bellmon, October 13, 1978, and Bellmon to Bergland, November 1, 1978, Cromley 4/5 for both items. In December Bellmon announced that the People's Republic of China would purchase at least 21 million tons of grain from the United States over a four-year period. See News: U.S. Sen. Henry Bellmon, December 7, 1978, Cromley 4/5.

66. George W. Stone to President, January 10, 1980. Stone was president of the Oklahoma Farmers Union. Marvin Scherler et. al. to Bergland, January 9, 1980. Scherler and others were members of the Stillwater office of the Agricultural Stabilization and Conservation Service. See Steed Legislative 104/12 for both items. *National Journal*, March 8, 1980, pp. 384–88 for an extended discuss of the political implications of the embargo.

67. News: U.S. Sen. Henry Bellmon, April 25, 1980, Cromley 4/8. *National Journal*, September 6, 1980, pp. 1480–83, and July 19, 1980, p. 1197. The Soviets purchased grain from other suppliers, some of whom then turned to the United States for the grain reserve; see editorials in *New York Times*, August 4, 1980, *Des Moines Register*, February 19, 1980, and *Lincoln Journal*, September 24, 1980.

68. News from U.S. Sen. David L. Boren, March 24, 1981, Cromley 5/5. *National Journal*, May 23, 1981, pp. 916–19, analyzes the "no frills" approach of the Reagan administration.

69. *National Journal*, October 31, 1981, p. 1932 for support prices. *Daily Oklahoman*, February 13, 1982, and March 2, 1982, both items in Cromley 5/6.

70. Henry Bellmon testimony, March 8, 1982, Cromley 4/8.

71. For an excellent discussion of the Farm Credit System, see the article by Kerry Webb in the June 1980 *Economic Review*, pp. 16–30. The journal is a publication of the Federal Reserve Bank of Kansas City. See too News from U.S. Sen. David L. Boren, July 22, 1982, Cromley 5/6. *Daily Oklahoman*, September 17, 1982, p. 155, for a story "Smaller Farms Hurt Most."

72. News from U.S. Sen. David L. Boren, September 28, 1982. See too Senator David Boren's Agricultural Update, 1982 Fair Edition. Both items in Cromley 5/6.

73. News from U.S. Sen. David L. Boren, January 26, 1983, Cromley 5/7.

74. News from U.S. Sen. David L. Boren February 24, 1983, and Boren to John Block April 8, 1983, Cromley 5/7 for all items.

75. Wichita Farm Credit Banks: Directors Report, September 1983, 1/6 of the David McCurdy Papers.

76. Oklahoma Wheat Commission News: Immediate Release [1983]. Boren to Mr. Secretary, September 2, 1983, discusses the impact of the drought on Oklahoma agriculture, Cromley 5/7. On September 21, 1983, Secretary of Agriculture John R. Block told the House Agriculture Committee that drought-stricken farmers could not expect much new help from Washington. *Congressional Quarterly*, September 24, 1983, 1990.

77. Marvin Duncan, "Financing Agriculture in the 1980s," *Economic Review*, July–August 1983, 3–6. See too Duncan and Mark Drabenstott, "Better Times Ahead for Agriculture," pp. 22–23, in the December 1983 *Economic Review*, the publication of the Federal Reserve Bank of Kansas City.

78. Donald E. Wilkinson to Members of Congress [1984], excerpt in McCurdy 1/6. Wilkinson was the governor of the Farm Credit Association. Neil Harl, *The Farm Debt Crisis of the 1980s* (Ames: Iowa State University Press, 1990), p. 161, for quote re indifference in Washington and passim. Harl's excellent monograph focuses largely on the crisis in the Corn Belt. See Glenn English Press Release, January 31, 1984, McCurdy 1/6. English introduced a bill calling for foreclosure protection. See too Minnick et. al. to McCurdy, April 16, 1984, in McCurdy 1/19. The members of the Oklahoma Wheat Commission thanked McCurdy for his efforts to expand markets for agricultural products. Boren also sought to improve trade by introducing a resolution to modify the trade agreement with the Soviet Union. See *Congressional Record*, 98th Cong., 2nd sess., September 11, 1984, S10943–44. For the cattle industry see *Sunday Oklahoman*, April 29, 1984, clipping in McCurdy 1/12.

79. News from U.S. Sen. David L. Boren, November 28, 1984, Cromley 5/8; Harl, *Farm Debt Crisis*, p. 263, for press reports.

80. News from U.S. Sen. David L. Boren, January 28, 1985, copy in Cromley 5/9. The filibuster can be followed in stories filed by Cromley that appeared in the *Daily Oklahoman* on February 16, 19, 20, 21, 22, and 24, 1985. All are available in Mickey Edwards Papers 59/10.

81. Ibid.

82. *Tulsa World*, February 24, 1985, story by Ralph Marler puffing Boren and one by Cromley in the *Daily Oklahoman*, February 24, 1985, Edwards 59/10 for both items. See too *Tulsa Tribune*, February 25, 1985, story by Marilyn Duck, Edwards 59/10.

83. *Daily Oklahoman*, February 15, 1985, for story on firing Stockman and Block, Edwards 59/10. Mike Synar to Dear Colleague February 28, 1985, McCurdy 1/6.

84. News from U.S. Sen. David L. Boren, March 16, 1985, Cromley 5/9. *Daily Oklahoman*, March 6, 1985, Boren to the Editor, p. 7, Edwards 59/11.

85. *Daily Oklahoman*, March 11, 1985 p. 13; Harl, *Farm Debt Crisis*, p.189, re 1985 as height of the crisis; Reports of the Bank Commissioner of the State of Oklahoma from 1985 through 1989. The commissioner's survey introduces each annual report.

86. *Daily Oklahoman*, February 10, 1985 p. 238.

87. Ibid., July 11, 1985, p. 52, August 9, 1985, p. 27, and November 1, 1985, p. 29.

88. Ibid., July 6, 1985 p. 26.

89. Ibid.

90. News from U.S. Sen. David L. Boren, September 13 and 20, 1985, and Boren to Block, September 16, 1985, Cromley 5/9 for all items.

91. *Daily Oklahoman/Times*, March 15, 1985, p. 18; *Daily Oklahoman*, March 26, 1985, p. 33, for Reagan's quips.

92. News from U.S. Sen. David L. Boren, July 16, July 23 (two items), November 1 and November 9, 1985. *Daily Oklahoman/Times*, April 19, 1985. Cromley 5/9 for all items.

93. *Daily Oklahoman*, April 20, 1985, p. 14, and November 12, 1985 p. 13.

94. Boren: Farm Credit Amendment, November 14, 1985, Cromley 5/9. *Daily Oklahoman*, December 4, 1985, p. 3. News from U.S. Sen. David L. Boren, December 16, 1985, Cromley 5/9.

95. News from U.S. Sen. David L. Boren, March 11, 1986, Cromley 5/10.

96. News from U.S. Sen. David L. Boren, March 5, April 9, April 10, 1986, Cromley 5/10 for all items. *Daily Oklahoman*, April 27, 1986, p. 23. At the same time Boren was introducing bills, so too, for example, were Glenn English, Mike Synar, Jim Jones, and David McCurdy. Only Boren attracted wide attention and was best able to secure legislative assistance.

97. Congressional Rural Caucus, "Bank Failures at FDIC Insured Institution . . ." April 30, 1986, and *New York Times*, April 29, 1986, story, "Ailing Bank Jolts Oklahoma," McCurdy 1/23 for both items. For the failure of the First National Bank in Enid, see the *Journal Record*, November 7, 1986, p. 1, McCurdy 1/23.

98. Farm Credit Services News Release May 1986, McCurdy 1/6. *Daily Oklahoman*, May 8 (p. 33) and May 18 (p. 33), 1986. For efforts by the state to aid struggling farmers, see ibid., July 13, 1986 p. 7.

99. *Daily Oklahoman*, July 4, 1986 p. 38. For a story about one farm suicide, see ibid., July 11, 1986, p. 23.

100. News from U.S. Sen. David L. Boren, June 19, July 16, July 31, Aug. 1 (2 items), Cromley 5/11 for all items. For proposals by other legislators, see Mickey Edwards Press Release, August 4, 1986, and *AAM Reporter*, March 1987, Edwards 72/64 for both items. See too story on the National Farm Congress in *Daily Oklahoman*, September 28, 1986. p. 17. Mark Drabenstott and Alan Barkema, "U.S. Agriculture on the Mend," *Economic Review*, December 1987, 28–29. Harl, *Farm Debt Crisis*, p. 141.

101. *Daily Oklahoman*, March 15 (p. 4), March 26 (p. 17), May 24 (p. 31) and May 31 (p. 29) 1987.

102. Ibid., July 30 (p. 1), August 3 (p. 63), November 25 (p. 27), 1987, and *Economic Review*, December 1987, 41.

« 10 »

The Enigma of Mike Monroney

One afternoon in 1969, Julius Duscha visited Mike Monroney in his corner suite on the top floor of the New (Hart) Senate Office Building with its commanding view from the Capitol down the Mall to the Washington Monument. Monroney at sixty-six was a tall, friendly man with ruddy cheeks, iron-gray hair, and a folksy, down-home manner. He had served in Congress since 1939, first in the House to 1950 and then in the Senate. Defeated in his bid for a fourth term, Monroney was preparing to leave office when Duscha visited him. When asked about the pictures and plaques that adorned the walls of his office, Monroney replied, "I am going to save my Presidents (Roosevelt through Johnson) and those of my friends, and I guess I'll just throw the rest away." He did more than that. At his insistence he ordered that his papers be burned.[1]

Earlier in the year, lunching with a former staff member, then a Washington lawyer, Monroney was reminded that a gift of his papers to his alma mater, the University of Oklahoma, where he had earned a Phi Beta Kappa key, would be tax deductible. Monroney supposedly replied, "No, I'm not going to do it. Those letters and papers aren't mine. They were produced on government time, at government expense," adding that he did not think the papers were worth very much to anybody. In 1979 the Senate Historical Office informed the archivist at the Carl Albert Center that the General Services Administration in 1973 had burned, at Monroney's request, 248 boxes of his papers. The Carl Albert Center possesses only 98 cubic feet of papers, consisting largely of public records, published material, formal speeches, newsletters, and the like, but almost no political correspondence files and none pertaining to Monroney's House career.[2]

How then can one explain the enigma of Almer Stillwell "Mike" Monroney, who by any standard made significant legislative contributions that added to his luster and were of considerable value to the people of his state and the United States? It is the contention of this author that Monroney was a level-headed moderate, fearful for his political career as voters in Oklahoma, increasingly conservative in their outlook, moved after 1964 into the Republican Party in every presidential election since then through 2012. For example, Monroney was a close friend of Adlai Stevenson and worked hard on his behalf. Yet there is not a single piece of correspondence between the two men in the available Monroney papers. They do contain several lists of names pertaining to the 1960 campaign, wherein Monroney and Eleanor Roosevelt played prominent roles seeking to secure Stevenson a third presidential nomination. Even more strange is the fact that the eight-volume set of Stevenson papers contains not a single item of correspondence between the two men. Yet in 1969, after he left office, Monroney consented to be interviewed for the Adlai Stevenson Oral History Project. A file comprising 128 pages, principally of reminiscences, is available at Columbia University.[3]

In a September 1951 issue of the *Saturday Evening Post* entitled "Oklahoma's Mighty Mike," Milton MacKaye reviewed Monroney's congressional career and recounted his strenuous campaign to unseat Elmer Thomas in the 1950 primary election. He noted that businessmen in Oklahoma were bitter about Thomas's support of New Deal and Fair Deal measures. Fully aware of this sentiment, Monroney sought to stick to the middle of the road and avoid involving himself with issues too liberal or too controversial for Oklahoma voters. For example, while Truman expressed delight in his election to the Senate, Monroney opposed such measures as the Brannan Plan, the FEPC, repeal of the Taft-Hartley Act, and the so-called National Health Plan, all of which Truman endorsed. He supported the Marshall Plan and the Atlantic Pact and believed the farm price support program prevented a financial collapse in 1949, measures that could antagonize few of his constituents and helped indicate that their views and his were in harmony.[4]

But were they? For one thing, Monroney was born in Oklahoma City, while most Oklahomans had more rural roots. He was an Episcopalian;

most Oklahomans accepted a more evangelical, even fundamentalist, faith. Monroney was active in the affairs of the National Cathedral in Washington as was his wife, Mary Ellen Monroney, who was also born and raised in Oklahoma City. She was part of the wealthy Pittsburgh Mellon family and was active during his tenure on the Washington social scene, hosting lively dinner parties with ranking public officials, diplomats and other luminaries at their home in fashionable Northwest Washington. While she returned to Oklahoma to assist her husband's campaigns, she preferred to accompany him on his numerous trips abroad on official business. In brief, the Monroneys lived their life in the nation's capital on a level that was out of touch and out of reach with most of the constituents to whom he portrayed his native roots: his years in the family furniture business, as a reporter covering stories in Oklahoma City and elsewhere in the state, as an outstanding student leader at the University of Oklahoma. But like his life in Washington, there were other matters he wished to shield from his constituents.[5]

Early in his Senate career, as the antics of one of his colleagues, Joseph McCarthy, helped launch a second Red Scare (the first followed the First World War), Monroney, like many others, did not wish to tangle with him. Not a year into his tenure as a United States senator, Monroney chaired a special committee of the Subcommittee on Privileges and Elections, investigating the disputed Maryland election in which long-term incumbent Millard Tydings was defeated by John Marshal Butler in a sordid campaign with a handful of "dirty tricks," including a doctored picture of Earl Browder, the head of the Communist Party in the United States, with Tydings. Butler was charged with being responsible for the printing and distribution of this fake picture while he cast aspersions on Monroney and others involved with the investigation, which revealed how various individuals were seeking to discredit Tydings as a communist sympathizer. Through this investigation, which Monroney conducted in a calm and judicious manner, the Senate sought to affirm its constitutionally established right to judge the qualifications of its own members. At the same time, the state of Maryland began investigating alleged violations of its laws. Both investigations quickly unearthed duplicitous actions by McCarthy staff members. Meanwhile, the *Washington Times-Herald*, edited by Mrs. Ruth McCormick Miller, who was closely allied with McCarthy, noted that Monroney's 1950 campaign was the target of an "ugly rumor" about irregular practices in the circulation of literature "devoted to promoting the election of Fair Deal candidates," including himself. While there was no evidence to substantiate the "ugly rumor," the die was cast labeling Monroney a Fair Deal liberal, though, as already noted, he voted against much of Truman's domestic program.[6]

As Monroney's probing continued, and as McCarthy's endeavors to discredit the proceedings gained momentum in Congress and throughout the country, committee and staff members began to withdraw or secure other assignments. Margaret Chase Smith (R-ME), a member of the subcommittee, informed Monroney in April 1951 that decisions had to be made without delay to terminate the hearings. She listed eight points to be considered "without further discussion and delay." Monroney scratched "OK" beside three of them and indicated necessary action on others. There are a handful of incoming letters to Monroney in his papers, not one by him commenting on the hearing. What his available papers contain are copies of the hearings, press clippings, a copy of Margaret Chase Smith's conclusions and recommendations, and, most interesting, a copy of a press release from the office of Senator Joe McCarthy, concluding that "as long as penny politicians try to encourage other penny politicians to ignore or whitewash Communist influences in our government, America will remain in grave danger." Monroney no doubt concluded that McCarthy's charging the committee report a whitewash could create problems for him among his constituents.[7]

On September 8, 1951, Monroney submitted to the attorney general a copy of the report on the 1950 Maryland senatorial election. Refuting McCarthy and the smear tactics used to discredit Millard Tydings in his reelection bid, the report concluded, "Are future Senate actions as good and loyal Americans to be tarred with the same old pro-commie brush simply because it does not fit into the thinking of the opposing groups?" Yet, despite this tepid reprimand, after a lengthy investigation Monroney's subcommittee concluded that Butler could replace Tydings, despite corrupt practices and all sorts of outside money. Charming, likable Monroney was off to a most inauspicious start as a United States senator. But his actions merited no opprobrium in Oklahoma. A prominent journalist said of the report that it "suffered from the timidity of political compromise and the anemia of senators' investigations of a colleague." In short, Monroney's efforts suggested a pattern of behavior evident in his senatorial career: namely, avoid controversial issues and seek the middle ground or, better still, champion topics that were in accord with the views of voters in Oklahoma.[8] In one instance, however, Monroney berated McCarthy, not for his actions in the Maryland campaign, but for his seeking an investigation of the CIA, at that time considered an almost sacrosanct agency. While his remarks received press attention, no senator seconded Monroney or defended McCarthy. A handful of members congratulated Monroney, and McCarthy shortly thereafter dropped his call for an investigation of the CIA.[9]

There was one further issue surfacing at the outset of his senatorial career that Monroney left little evidence of in his files. It involved his close friend and colleague, William Benton of Connecticut, who presented the Senate with an indictment centering on a series of McCarthy lies and financial irregularities. The indictment was sent to a subcommittee chaired by Guy Gillette of Iowa. McCarthy refused to read or respond to the indictment, challenged the role of the committee, and denigrated some of its members. Most members, including Monroney, found reason to resign. Yet Benton's biographer, Sidney Hyman, asserts that fearful of the climate of fear engendered by McCarthy, Monroney was one of Benton's ardent but covert supporters, presumably working behind the scenes on his behalf. He told Benton that his files would be searched, his phone tapped, and his mail read and claimed the same was true in his case as a member of the Gillette Committee. His papers contain letters from Benton seeking support of his resolution to expel McCarthy from the Senate, and while other Benton letters detail his actions with regard to censuring McCarthy, nowhere in Monroney's papers is a response to be found to any Benton letter, though Hyman insists that Monroney never wavered in his support of Benton. Yet as the Senate was seeking to resolve the matter, Monroney was not available. He was on vacation in Europe.[10]

If he was not available to assist Benton, Monroney found a new cause and a new candidate to support by agreeing to head the Speakers Bureau during Adlai Stevenson's 1952 campaign for the White House. While there are letters from Benton in his papers, there are none from Stevenson, and the only item relating to Stevenson is found among the papers of one of Monroney's staff: copies of a speech Monroney delivered on behalf of Stevenson. Obviously, files of correspondence and other materials pertaining to McCarthy, Benton, and Stevenson went up in flames on Monroney's orders. All of this material pertained to Monroney's first two years in the Senate, when he was seeking to establish a firm base with his Oklahoma constituents and sustain a posture as a silent supporter of liberal causes.[11]

However, with Benton's defeat, McCarthy's demise, and Stevenson not a factor in his legislative role, Monroney no longer had need or inclination to be regarded as liberal. In a story filed in 1962 by Allan Cromley of the *Daily Oklahoman*, Monroney affirmed that he would maintain his reputation as a "switch hitter," that he would turn neither left nor right and would not become identified with any particular Senate faction. Nor would he involve himself in deals of any kind, unlike his colleague Robert S. Kerr, who as a "horse trader" accumulated chits and gained great influence among his colleagues. Senate liberals, like Albert Gore of Tennessee and Joseph Clark of Pennsylvania, often courted Monroney, only to find that he usually located himself on what they considered the conservative side of the issue. In short, Monroney was regarded as a "question mark on many an advance tally sheet until his name was reached on the roll call." Yet within these parameters Monroney established himself as a significant senator who furthered causes and measures that brought him national attention and won him three terms in the United States Senate.[12]

A further insight into the enigma of Mike Monroney is evident in an extensive 1959 interview with a *Kansas City Times* reporter. In the course of his remarks, Monroney made it clear that he detested labels. But if one had to choose, he preferred "a presidential scale" stating "I'm a Democrat—closer to Wilsonian democracy than to F.D.R.'s. To me, that means a practical progressive." Elected to Congress in 1939, envisioning Wilson's New Freedom and not F.D.R.'s New Deal as his guide, Monroney had trouble endorsing government playing an active role in providing relief, seeking recovery, and endeavoring to stride toward a more just society.

Thus Monroney could not endorse much of Truman's Fair Deal and Lyndon Johnson's Great Society. Deficit spending would be abhorrent to him, and he would not be lacking in sympathy for the states-rights views of many in Oklahoma. These concerns applied to domestic policy. When it came to foreign affairs Monroney was a true Wilsonian. And in this area he launched an important and successful battle, for which he received little lasting recognition, to create the International Development Association, a little World Bank.[13]

In December 1956, just back from a 25,000-mile world tour with half a dozen stop-offs in Asia, Monroney called upon the Senate Banking and Currency Committee to consider the feasibility of a program to finance more foreign aid projects under a new type of World Bank loan. At that time the ten-year-old Marshall plan, with its emphasis on unilateral grants in aid, had already achieved a large measure of success. Monroney called for beginning the transition to multilateral aid in the form of long-term loans, through the World Bank, to some Asiatic nations. He wanted the committee to explore the possibility of creating what he called "Class B" stock in the World Bank to finance these loans, with interest and amortization suspended for the first five years. Funds for this program could be made available to the World Bank from funds accruing to United States credit the world over as a result of American foreign aid outlays. Further, Monroney suggested that funds from the sale of surplus agricultural commodities abroad be made available to the bank to bolster the "Class B" capital available for this type of aid. Eventually, he believed, other countries might contribute to the reusable funds, making it a truly multilateral operation.

Monroney first floated the idea in a speech he made to the Inter-Parliamentary Union meeting in Bangkok, Thailand. (As a delegate to this organization, Monroney made numerous trips abroad.) Response to the speech was so favorable that Monroney discussed the concept with the president of the World Bank, Eugene R. Black, and with the chair of the Senate Banking Committee, J. W. Fulbright, before following through, once they approved, with a resolution for the inquiry. Within a year Monroney was championing the cause of the International Development Association, dubbed the "poor man's World Bank." Soon the idea attracted the attention of Treasury secretary Robert Anderson, and interest was expressed in several European capitals as a program that could be of great assistance to underdeveloped countries in Asia and Africa that preferred loans to direct foreign aid.[14]

In 1958 Monroney introduced a resolution calling on the administration to examine his proposal for the International Development Association. The Senate, the Eisenhower administration, and a national advisory council all responded favorably. The following year, governors of the World Bank approved the concept and requested the executive directors to prepare a draft of such an association for submission to the bank's member governments. In February 1960 President Eisenhower submitted the proposal to Congress authorizing United States membership, and on June 30 he signed a bill authorizing subscription funds to get it started. Finally, in September, the IDA came into being with an announcement at the annual World Bank meeting that over 65 percent of its $1 billion capital had already been subscribed by fifteen nations. This was a tremendous accomplishment that promised great dividends. Monroney merits commendation for defining a way to assist foreign countries without the unilateral grants and loans that had been the basis of U.S. economic aid since the Marshall Plan.

Monroney's proposal also countered the Soviet Union's long-term, low-interest loans to newly independent nations long on manpower and natural resources but short on hard currencies. As a member of the Senate Banking Committee, he held hearings on the proposal, lobbied extensively for it, and gained widespread press attention. He regarded the IDA with the fervor of a crusader and showed what one senator armed with knowledge, patience, and fortitude could accomplish. All discomfort pertaining to his unhappy behavior during the McCarthy era was behind him; thanks to his Bangkok speech, Monroney emerged as a statesman with a broad vision.[15]

If Monroney's battle for the creation of the IDA brought him wide favorable attention and called for minimal federal funding, his longstanding crusade for legislative reform raised him to the stature of a statesman, and favorable press coverage kept his name and his fight for a more efficient functioning of the legislative apparatus before the American public. Monroney's efforts called for no legislation and no expenditure of federal funds. The question thus arises, why did he not succeed?

By the mid-1960s some astute observers were calling attention to the fact that Congress was the weak branch of the American government. Richard L. Strout in the *Christian Science Monitor* pronounced it "inefficient, self-righteous, and verbose." For over three decades it had constantly lost power to the president, complained about it, and failed to take remedial action. It had been beset with scandals involving Bobby Baker, Lyndon Johnson's secretary when he was majority leader of the Senate, Adam Clayton Powell in the House, and Thomas J. Dodd in the Senate. More than corruption was the growing diminution of congressional influence and regard. How could the Congress compete with the Warren Court, which in key decisions was changing the contours of American life?[16]

In 1946, while serving in the House of Representatives, Monroney cosponsored with Senator Robert La Follette a joint Senate-House study, the first major overhaul of Congress in sixty years. The legislation reduced the number of standing committees from eighty-one to thirty-four, established committee jurisdictions, and provided for a permanent professional staff. The 1946 measure also improved appropriations procedures, gave statutory recognition to the Legislative Reference Service, and required the registration of lobbyists. Despite the failure of some of its provisions, the violation of others, and the fact that about 25 percent of the recommendations were not enacted, Monroney insisted that the act had "a profound influence" on the effectiveness with which Congress conducted its business for two decades.[17]

To enable Congress to better meet its responsibilities, Monroney on January 6, 1965, introduced a concurrent resolution establishing a twelve-member committee, six from each chamber equally divided by party. The president of the Senate and the Speaker would select the members to represent their chamber. The proposal quickly won bipartisan support in the Senate, and House members assured Monroney a similar resolution would be approved in their chamber. The question thus arises why Monroney called for legislative reforms at this time. Following the death of Robert S. Kerr two years previously, Monroney was seeking an issue to establish himself, as Kerr had done with water resources, which as an issue had commanded national attention and an Oklahoma constituency that took pride in his statesmanlike endeavor. After several false starts, Monroney was confident he now had such an issue, one that called for neither the expenditure of federal funds nor presidential approval.[18]

It was not that Monroney had little to do. He was among the busiest senators on Capitol Hill. Indeed, shortly after introducing the concurrent resolution, Monroney was hospitalized with a severe case of laryngitis, ordered off cigarettes, and told to get some rest. He chaired a full committee and four subcommittees, cochaired the Joint Committee on Legislative Reforms and served on several other subcommittees. With the death of Olin Johnston, he was thrust into the chairmanship of the Post Office and Civil Service Committee. He already had a heavy schedule as chair of the Aviation Subcommittee that conducted hearings on a wide range of issues and was a member of the Communications Subcommittee. In addition, he chaired the Appropriations Subcommittee that paid congressional salaries and provided money for necessary repairs and new construction. He was also a member of four or five other appropriations subcommittees. His work with aviation necessitated much traveling about the country. And he tried to attend the annual meetings of the Inter-Parliamentary Union, which in 1965 met in Rome. It was within this context that he took the lead in urging congressional reorganization, the issue that would enhance his stature and make him appear a worthy successor to Robert S. Kerr as Oklahoma's senior United States senator.[19]

In his lengthy remarks on January 6, Monroney mentioned numerous topics that the joint committee, once created, might consider, such as that committee chairs be selected by secret ballot rather than by seniority and that their terms be limited. With his own assignments in mind, he suggested that the thirteen separate appropriations bills offered for consideration each session be consolidated into one and provide funds for two years, thereby allowing Congress to concentrate on other matters every other year. These of course were suggestions. Nothing would happen until after the resolution was approved, the committee selected, and hearings held.[20]

Monroney lobbied hard, acquired in short order fifty-five cosponsors in the Senate, received national press attention, and was delighted when the Subcommittee on Standing Rules of the Senate Rules Committee promptly agreed to review the proposal. After winning committee approval, he called upon the full Senate to follow suit and approve the resolution. The Joint Committee thus would be authorized to carefully study the organization and operation of Congress, such as consolidating and reorganizing committees, and then recommend improvements, enabling it better to meet its responsibilities under the Constitution. But the committee would not be authorized to make recommendations with respect to the rules, procedures, and precedents of either chamber.[21]

The Reorganization Resolution passed the Senate unanimously on March 9, 1965 and the House unanimously two days later. Monroney and Representative Ray Madden were elected cochairs of the bipartisan twelve-member committee, equally divided between Democrats and Republicans. Monroney was elected as presiding chair, with authority to make decisions not considered necessary to be referred to the whole committee. In addition, he would handle all administrative matters. Congratulated on his victory, Monroney remarked that the time for that would come when Congress approved necessary reforms to give itself the tools needed "for action in a modern world."[22]

On April 13, in the Old Supreme Court Chamber in the Capitol, the Joint Committee announced that it would commence public hearings on May 10, and that members of Congress would be invited to testify during the first two weeks of hearings. The Library of Congress agreed to prepare a daily digest of the hearings, which, when duplicated, would be made available to all interested parties. As an interested party, the press gave Monroney and the hearings much attention. Early on, Senator Joseph Clark of Pennsylvania proposed twenty-four specific changes in Senate rules as well as overall congressional methods. Other members also offered suggestions, as Congress began to take a look at itself with the goal of updating and streamlining the way it did business. Some members called for overhauling the way committees functioned, others called for improved staffing. Representative Morris Udall of Arizona was one who challenged the seniority system, arguing that "it ignores all factors other than experience—including leadership qualities, intelligence and ability." Clark in his testimony told the committee that Congress did not truly represent "the majority of the American people as expressed in national elections." Most witnesses, some more specific than others, saw the legislative branch fast declining in influence and outstripped, as previously noted, by its constitutional rivals, the executive and judicial branches. Moreover, since the committee's mandate stipulated that it could not suggest changes in congressional rules, practices, procedures, or precedents, Monroney sought the opportunity to seek more services and staff for members as well as to suggest minimal changes in the regular routines of Congress. Thus Monroney, steering a path between members on the left and right, seemed assured of majority support and the opportunity to achieve at best minimal change. Indeed, it did not escape notice that two lawmakers noticeably identified as calling for changes in congressional rules, Senator Clark and Congressman Richard Bolling of Missouri, were not members of the Joint Committee. And *Congressional Quarterly*, which carefully monitored the legislative branch, contained a headline in a June issue that "Broad Changes in Congress' Operations Not Likely."[23]

Meanwhile, the Joint Committee continued its deliberations until July of the following year. If approved, the reorganization would be the first in two decades and only the second in the entire history of Congress. Among its recommendations was one giving a majority of a committee the authority to call meetings and permit it to require a chair to act on legislation the chair might oppose. It would also eliminate proxy voting. While it did not eradicate the seniority system, the proposal somewhat ameliorated it. Other recommendations were even more moderate, such as calling for hearings being broadcast or televised "to the maximum extent possible," and for no August session except in time of war. Another suggested that congressional business be conducted on a five-day work week rather than the usual Tuesday to Thursday schedule. The committee also called for curtailing patronage, recommending that members cease making appointments to the capitol police force and divest themselves of responsibilities for selecting postmasters. More important, the committee offered suggestions for increasing surveillance of lobbyists. In all, more than a hundred recommendations were approved by the Joint Committee. Monroney, hopeful that most of the recommendations would be favorably received, was anxious that they be voted on before the current session of Congress ended.[24]

To arrive at their recommendations the committee received the views of 199 witnesses over a five-month period commencing in May 1965. The testimony, together with documents and submissions, was contained in fifteen printed volumes totaling 2,322 pages. The committee and its staff further evaluated all the relevant scholarly literature, and its final report was filed on July 28, 1966. To assure its prompt approval, a Senate resolution was prepared by the six Senate members of the Joint Committee, calling for them to function as a special committee, the Special Committee on the Organization of Congress, to report on the reorganization bill, a procedure followed decades earlier when the Senate considered the Legislative Reorganization Act of 1946. This procedure would avoid referring the measure to standing committees, eliminate the need for a massive duplication of hearings, and allow members to take advantage of the expertise acquired by the senators serving on the Joint Committee.[25]

On September 21, on behalf of the Special Committee on the Organization of Congress, Monroney introduced the Legislative Reorganization Act of 1966. He called for a favorable vote at the earliest possible date so that the bill could be sent to the House for action prior to adjournment. Monroney lobbied hard but failed in his endeavor. He took some comfort when informed by the Democratic Policy Committee, which considered scheduling, that the Legislative Reorganization Act of 1966 would be one of the first orders of business when the new (90th) Congress convened in January.[26]

Once the new Congress convened, calls for congressional reform thrust Monroney to the national stage when, on January 16, 1967, he introduced the Legislative Reorganization Act of 1967 along with the Report of the Special Committee calling for favorable Senate action. He expressed confidence that the measure would soon be decided. As did the press. The story in the *Daily Oklahoman* proclaimed "Monroney Shatters Tradition." The *Washington Post* editorialized on "The Monroney Reforms." The *Christian Science Monitor* conducted an interview with "A

Congressional Reformer." Other newspapers, while not headlining Monroney, favorably commented in their stories and editorials. When Senate debate got underway on January 25, Monroney launched the discussion, calling the bill "an impressive step toward providing more of the organization capability needed by Congress in this complex and turbulent world."[27]

He also served as floor manager while colleagues discussed the urge to modernize from varying perspectives, with reporters keeping careful tabs on the proceedings. Early in February the Monroney measure survived a major test when supporters beat back (70 to 18) a move to send the bill back to committee. By late February some twenty-three modifications had been made, while thirty-three amendments had either been rejected or withdrawn. Monroney, unlike Kerr, had no political clout and could only rely on reason, logic, and legislative skills to keep the measure's supporters from accepting too many concessions and getting together on all the fine points. On Monday, March 6, Monroney informed his colleagues in a form letter of a vote on a critical amendment and perhaps the vote on final passage of the bill itself. The amendment pertained to strengthening federal regulation of lobbying by requiring individuals and organizations to register.[28]

On March 6 the Senate approved by a vote of 74 to 9 its first housecleaning move in twenty years by accepting more than seventy proposals making both major and minor changes in the way Congress conducted its business. Before the final vote the Senate defeated (55 to 30) an effort to eliminate tougher controls over lobbyists. Once again Monroney received national press attention. A *Washington Post* editorial paved the way with a "Salute to Monroney." His picture, of course, accompanied some press accounts. The *Oklahoma Journal*, in an editorial, proclaimed "Victory for Mike's Bill," stating, "Oklahoma's senior Senator is in line for heartiest congratulations on the whopping victory his bill gained in the Senate Tuesday." The *Norman Transcript* followed suit, asserting "Monroney Gains Reform Prestige." But there was a catch. For the measure to be effective, the House had to act as well. While Monroney thought the House would approve fewer provisions than the Senate, he still expected rapid approval.[29]

But, alas, it was not to be. Ray Madden of Indiana, cochair of the committee, ardently supported the joint resolution, as did numerous House members of both parties. Some revisions were made to gain support of the Rules Committee, whose approval was needed before legislative reform could be voted upon. But the Speaker, John W. McCormack, with his control of the Committee on Committees, refused to move on the measure, leaving it to face a slow death. The *Washington Post* insisted that "Mr. McCormack seems to regard it as a dangerously newfangled assault upon the congressional traditionalisms and inefficiency with which he is so closely identified." As House members of the Joint Committee sought futilely to compromise and make concessions to gain the approval of the Rules Committee, there was little Monroney could do except to ask the Senate Committee on Rules and Administration to extend the tenure of the Joint Committee so that if the House acted a final reform package could be cobbled together. The *Congressional Quarterly*, in a careful analysis of the situation headlined its account "House Outlook Dim for Legislative Reorganization Bill." And that's the way the effort to seek the second major effort at legislative reform ended—not with a bang but a whimper.[30]

As it was becoming apparent that legislative reform would not be achieved, Monroney, seemingly in frustration, lashed out at the behavior of a colleague, Thomas J. Dodd of Connecticut, who "because of conduct contrary to accepted morals, which derogates from the public trust expected of a Senator" merited the censure measure leveled against him. As a member of the select committee viewing Dodd's indiscretions, Monroney remarked, virtuously, "When an occasion does arise that requires us to examine our values and decide what our standards shall be, we should not hesitate to do so, because our whole system of government is in jeopardy." Given his tepid performance during the McCarthy era, Monroney's criticism of Dodd's use of campaign funds for personal use as tending to bring the Senate "into dishonor and disrepute," while favorably noted in Oklahoma, suggested frustration at failure to achieve legislative reform.[31]

If Monroney failed to achieve success in achieving legislative reform, his championing the cause of aviation was an unmitigated triumph. It kept him in the public eye and brought him into contact with businessmen and others prominent in the industry. In addition, as an advocate of air power he worked in close contact with Air Force leaders and colleagues to further the cause of aviation. Furthering the cause of air power fell within his parameter of not expending federal funds to effectuate social change. Authorizing funds for air power meant improved security, government contracts, and jobs that could benefit citizens of Oklahoma, who would have good reason to ensure his continued service in Washington in furthering the cause of aviation. As carriers were undergoing rapid improvements in speed, distance, capacity, and safety, amid mounting demand for additions and improvements of the links between places, Monroney played a major role in adding to the institutional apparatus of the United States through the creation in 1958 of the Federal Aviation Agency. Agencies such as the FAA were created to define guidelines and acceptable modes of behavior; Monroney, however, saw his legislative role as one of furthering the cause of aviation in American life, championing both military and commercial interests. When he first ran for the Senate, Monroney dubbed himself the "world's most enthusiastic air passenger." Thereafter he was the recipient of numerous aviation awards, including the 1961 Wright Brothers Memorial Trophy, one of the highest aviation honors. The trophy committee cited "his continuous emphasis on air safety, his pressure for further advancement in the act of air navigation and traffic control, his leadership in the field of air cargo development, and the foresight which put him in the vanguard of airport development throughout the country for over a decade."[32]

In 1955 Monroney established his leadership posture as the author of the Federal Airport Act. This was followed by his sponsoring and supporting further measures certifying feeder airlines, aiding supplemental air carriers, and promoting air safety, including scientific aids to aviation such as weather reporting. In 1956 he introduced the bill that severed the Civil Aeronautics Administration from the Commerce Department and led to the establishment of the independent Federal Aviation Agency, which soon located a center in Oklahoma City.

In 1958 Monroney, who for three years had been urging the removal of aviation from the Commerce Department, introduced the measure creating this agency, which called for control of air traffic and air space for both civil and military aviation. Following an April crash of two airliners in Las Vegas, Monroney announced that the time for further study of air safety was over and that he would submit a bill for an organizational setup that might eventually prevent such tragedies. And so, in his position as chair of the Senate Aviation Subcommittee, on May 21, the day after a military-commercial crash in Maryland, he did introduce such a measure.[33]

Earlier, as a member of the House, Monroney had promoted the establishment of Tinker Air Force Base in Oklahoma City and the Douglas and American airline plants in Tulsa, endeavors that helped make aviation the state's third major industry, behind agriculture and oil. Now, through his Senate subcommittee, he had the ability to bring aviation concerns to the fore and to fruition. He became a leading spokesman for the industry, introduced numerous bills on its behalf, and was quick to note the millions of dollars flowing into Oklahoma from its vast military aviation complex and civilian aviation activities. While the state drew its wealth from the ground, aviation added to it with funds from federal coffers and corporate allocations. Aviation, in brief, was an ideal instrument for injecting huge sums into the economy without reforming and or effecting social change. It allowed Monroney to establish cordial relations with corporate leaders and military brass, and it established his appeal to constituents as he carved out a role to define himself while emerging from the shadow of the state's former senior senator, the mantle Monroney assumed in 1961 following Kerr's death. A favorable editorial succinctly concluded with "The junior Senator from Oklahoma has come up with a unique combination—more defense punch without injuring the American economy.[34]

Oklahoma was home to three major air force bases: Tinker, Clinton-Sherman, and Altus, where the operation and upkeep of bombers was big business. The nurture and care of these installations was a primary concern to Monroney, who opposed efforts to reduce their funding. By 1963 Tinker Air Force Base was the largest single employer in the state, and the Federal Aeronautical Center in Oklahoma City employed nearly four thousand permanent personnel and was readying a new civil aeromedical center. While his efforts received widespread favorable attention, however, not everyone was impressed. Such was the case of the editor of the *Durant Daily Democrat*, who pointed out that the people in Bryan County had very little interest in aviation and that aeromedical research was something most people did not know the government was engaged in. "We're rural, Mike—we're self-centered. . . . We worry about our peanuts and our cattle and getting industry . . . not about airplanes and foreign aid and an urban affairs cabinet member." And what no doubt most distressed Monroney was the editor's comments "that as far as news goes, it's Bob Kerr this and Bob Kerr that; Carl Albert this and Carl Albert that. Rarely anything about Mike Monroney."[35]

By the mid-sixties aerospace contributions to Oklahoma's economy were on the rise. New space, research, and communications firms were entering the state and growing rapidly. Such firms in 1964 claimed 3,700 employees, whereas in 1960 there had been none. Not only was aviation a boon to Oklahoma, it had achieved "a position of unquestioned world leadership," although Monroney in 1964 was "rather apprehensive about our long-range prospects." Some aircraft needed to be upgraded or even replaced, and new markets for short-haul aircraft in developing nations were necessary to move commodities to markets in these countries. Moreover, the Cold War with the Soviet Union made the government's contribution to research and development of great significance. In short, Monroney's tenure as chair of the Senate Aviation Subcommittee brought him both state and national attention and added eminently to his stature as a distinguished public servant.[36]

With the war in Vietnam Monroney faced a new challenge. Secretary of Defense Robert McNamara, while announcing projected cutbacks in the Strategic Air Command's long-range bomber force, indicated that American strategic power would be focused more emphatically on long-range missiles. Monroney called the proposal "utter folly and false economy," especially since Clinton-Sherman Air Force Base was one scheduled for closure by 1970. He endorsed the wave of protests from the communities connected economically with the base. On the other hand, Governor Henry Bellmon disagreed strongly with Monroney and worked out a plan with the Defense Department to replace the facility with another economic base during the phase-out period. Bellmon recognized that "the Nation's defense requirements must be constantly re-evaluated and that Oklahomans had no choice but to express confidence in those charged with 'keeping our defenses strong and current.'" The governor's strong disagreement with Monroney marked the first serious challenge to his views on aviation matters. And Bellmon did not merely challenge Monroney's remarks; he worked out with the deputy secretary of defense a viable and constructive option.[37]

Monroney did not pursue the matter but continued his advocacy of federal assistance to aeronautical issues, both military and civilian. He went further in December 1967 when he urged air force leaders to reconsider the adoption of the C-141 military cargo jet aircraft as a manned bomber to replace the aging B-52s heavily committed in Vietnam. Toward the end of his tenure he devoted much of his effort to calls for modernizing the nation's airport and airways systems.[38]

Besides aviation, the other interest of Monroney that left an enduring imprint on Oklahoma was his tenure on the Post Office and Civil Service Committee, which began when he entered the Senate in 1951. As a member he worked hard to improve benefits available to postal employees, and when he became chair of the committee in 1965, upon the death of Olin D. Johnston, he took a strong interest in the problems of government and postal employees. Besides improving benefits, Monroney sought to expedite the speed of mail deliveries by the most efficient methods possible. Like Johnston, Monroney established close relations with government employees and postal unions and began to concern himself with patronage as a means of enhancing his political influence. In 1966 his committee sponsored legislation liberalizing mailing privileges to servicemen overseas. This legislation also benefited airlines because overseas mail would be priced at regular surface rates.[39]

Most important for Oklahoma was the announcement in 1966 that a contract between the Post Office Department and the University of Oklahoma to conduct training sessions for Postal Service employees from every section of the country. The program was designed to assist them in more effectively processing and moving the mail through the nation's 552 mail-processing sectional centers. At the outset thirty Postal

Service officers and trainees attended each session conducted by qualified university faculty. In addition, in the following year Monroney was able to announce that overnight postal service for first-class letters would result from a network of air routes in Oklahoma. Private contractors serving eight routes would fly mail to Oklahoma City and then distribute it to the state's sectional-center post offices.[40]

In the midst of his 1968 campaign for reelection, Monroney introduced a bill to create an authority with power to sell bonds to finance "a multi-billion dollar program" to construct modern postal facilities. His measure would provide "effective financial planning to serve the American people in the postal service." And it would not involve the allocation of federal funds. The proposal came at a time when the Postal Service faced hard times, with increasing costs, declining revenues, archaic facilities, and outmoded ways of processing mail. Severe cutbacks were threatened that Monroney, as chair of both the Post Office and Civil Service Committee and the relevant Appropriations Subcommittee, was able to curb.[41]

Another topic on which Monroney's views were in accord, as were those of the entire Oklahoma delegation, was in exempting natural gas from federal regulation and imposing mandatory controls on oil imports. In a 1961 address he summed up his views, stating, "We must seek maximum development of our domestic reserves, regardless of comparative cost," and "must never be dependent on others for our most vital resource for this nation's defense." His approach to natural gas production was to exempt producers from public regulation and to require the Federal Power Commission to regulate prices on the basis of a reasonable market price.[42]

Both industries were critically important to Oklahoma with oil or natural gas available in 70 of 77 counties, with 47 percent of the state's total land area either in production or under lease. Up to 1961, Oklahoma produced over $14 billion worth of crude oil and natural gas. Over 42,000 people were employed directly in their production with many times that number dependent indirectly on them. Indispensable to these efforts was the maintenance of the 27.5 percent depletion allowance. Like all members of the Oklahoma delegation, Monroney fought valiantly to maintain the allowance and to limit oil imports. No member of Congress, like most Oklahomans and indeed most Americans, showed much interest in the impact of these industries on the environment.

Throughout his 1962 reelection campaign and thereafter, Monroney defended the depletion allowance, attacked its critics, and showed how it benefited the nation, noting that "in 1926 a gallon of gasoline cost 20.9 cents. For the worker, one hour's work bought 2.6 gallons in 1926; today [1962] it buys ten gallons, exclusive of tax." For Monroney the wise application of the depletion allowance helped keep the cost of gasoline down.[43]

On other issues that came to the fore, Monroney's approach is less consistent and at times more revealing. In 1958, for example, he sought to arouse public indignation on the subject of the selling on Sunday of general merchandise in the District of Columbia. At a press conference, he called on business, civic religious groups, and newspapers to marshal public opinion "against the practice of desecrating our national holidays and Sundays by making a 'Baghdad on the Potomac' of our nation's Capital." If voluntary efforts failed, Monroney considered legislation as a last resort.[44]

While his plea received little attention, it revealed a conservative side of Monroney that led some to see him as a switch-hitter, a senator who shifted his views from issue to issue. When he entered the Senate, he had been regarded as a New Deal–Fair Deal liberal. But, as already noted, he voted against key aspects of Truman's legislative program. During the Kennedy administration, Allan Cromley, who covered Washington for the *Daily Oklahoman*, noted that in 1961 Monroney had lost his "liberal fraternity pin" in leading a fight against a minimum-wage bill provision for government regulation of retail stores. He had further opposed a proposal to provide forty-year housing loans for moderate-income families and successfully led opposition to an Administration proposal which he said would endanger existing school assistance programs. He had voted reluctantly for the Peace Corps, and in 1962 he had advocated the creation of a joint committee on the budget "which can effectively check and audit agency requests for additional personnel and funds." These were not major issues, and they did not receive widespread attention in Oklahoma, where they could have been well received, given that Richard Nixon carried the state in 1960.[45]

In 1960, however, Monroney still wore his "liberal fraternity pin." Early in the year he had participated in a losing Senate battle to strip Lyndon Johnson, the majority leader, of some of his almost unlimited authority. And later in the year he wore the pin very proudly when he made a pitch for Adlai E. Stevenson to be the Democratic presidential candidate for the third time. In April, before either of the national conventions, he asserted that Stevenson could defeat Richard Nixon, and soon thereafter he made political safaris to several cities and phone calls to others to drum up support for Stevenson as a compromise candidate in the event of a deadlocked convention. In June, Monroney and Eleanor Roosevelt announced the opening of the National Stevenson Campaign Headquarters in Los Angeles. Indeed, after an analysis of delegate voting strength, Monroney predicted a switch to Stevenson by the sixth ballot as the second choice of everyone. During the convention, he rushed from delegation to delegation, seeking support for Stevenson as a viable alternative to either Kennedy or Johnson.[46]

After the campaign Monroney literally removed his "liberal fraternity pin" and reverted to a conservative stance. The American Communications Association, a radical organization, gave Monroney a zero rating on such issues as tax reduction, civil rights, debt limit, local transit subsidies, house subsidies, and medical care, but it was the last issue that brought Monroney to national attention. Medicare for the aged was one of Kennedy's major measures before the Congress in 1962. Monroney voted against it, while endorsing the Kerr-Mills bill introduced by his colleague as providing care for the aged of low income without encouraging socialized medicine and not calling for an increase in Social Security taxes to pay for the services. Two years later, as Oklahoma's senior senator, and with Johnson now in the White House, Monroney withheld his vote until the last possible moment before voting aye, allowing Medicare to pass by a 49 to 44 vote. He had been listed as "doubtful" by Johnson staff people monitoring the measure. His vote, a prime example of Monroney as a switch-hitter, had been noticed. The Oklahoma State Medical Association strongly criticized him for changing sides.[47]

His position with regard to civil rights could also be regarded as doubtful. In June 1963 Cromley reported that Monroney had been conducting a quiet campaign seeking equal opportunities for Negroes in federal jobs and federally financed construction. Cromley considered his position a reversal of his "actions, if not attitudes in the civil rights field." But in the civil rights bill introduced in the Kennedy administration, Monroney had reservations. He could not accept desegregation of public accommodations and was concerned about a provision requiring government to withhold financial assistance to any program in which racial discrimination occurred. Earlier in the Kennedy Administration, Monroney had expressed doubts about Kennedy's program to expand Social Security to include medical care for the aged. He was not against the Social Security financing principle but thought the legislation did not make sufficient use of private insurance companies. And he was more assertive in his opposition to increasing the minimum wage across the board from $1.00 to $1.25. Regarding the president's program, Monroney said, "I don't mind being known as a switch-hitter." And he made it clear that he was not among the band of "liberal" senators seeking revision of Senate rules.[48]

On one topic he was consistent. He was opposed to repealing Section 14b of the Taft-Hartley Act. At the outset of his tenure in the Senate, it will be recalled, he had voted for the act. But in 1965 after carefully reviewing the issue, Monroney concluded that it was "primarily a question of states' rights for voters in Oklahoma to decide." Since his view did not prevail, he voted for the measure to the chagrin of President Johnson, who, like Truman before him, was calling for the repeal of the provision allowing a state to establish right-to-work laws prohibiting union shop contracts between employers and employees. While his colleague Fred Harris favored repeal, Monroney's position, whether based on principle or expediency, was viewed favorably by most editors in Oklahoma.[49]

So too was his "very unusual" decision to go to Vietnam. With legislative reform bogged down in the House, Monroney sought to view the conflict for himself and reassure the American public of the validity of the president's posture in pursuing the war. At the same time, now that Hubert Humphrey had to yield the position of majority whip to become vice president, Monroney quickly entered the race for the post. Seeking long overdue legislative reforms, a brief trip to secure a personal insight in a costly conflict, followed by selection as majority whip, would thrust Monroney to the fore as a major legislative leader and allow him to come out from under the shadow of Robert S. Kerr. In making the decisions to go to Vietnam and seek the post of majority whip, Monroney threw caution to the wind. No longer a careful "switch-hitter," he soon exhibited an exuberant confidence that contained within itself the seeds of his ultimate downfall. In late November 1964, with Johnson now firmly ensconced in the White House as president in his own right, and with a new Congress set to convene in January, Monroney, accompanied by his wife, embarked on a twenty-six-day Far Eastern tour.[50]

Despite traveling overseas, Monroney was confident he could become Senate whip because he felt neither of the two other contenders, Russell Long of Louisiana and John Pastore of Rhode Island, could gain a majority, one from the South, the other from the North, leaving his colleagues to turn to him as the moderate compromise candidate. He said several times that he was the "swing man" in the contest. While questions were raised about the wisdom of Monroney's action in seeking the post, he was confident of his chances, and upon his return, would reinforce them before the Democratic caucus convened in January 1965.[51]

In Japan, the first stop on his tour, Monroney inspected three military installations and announced he was "pleased to learn of the high state of readiness of both U.S. and Japanese military forces to meet any threat of Communist aggression in this part of the world." These remarks can serve as the theme of his trip: everything he saw assured him of the ability of American forces to repel Communist aggression. And everywhere he went, long-distance phone calls provided reassurance that he was still in the race for the majority whip post.[52]

Ambassador Maxwell Taylor hosted the Monroneys in Saigon. They lunched at the home of General and Mrs. William Westmoreland with eight officers from Oklahoma. He was briefed by top amy and air force commanders. A helicopter flew him to Bien Hoa airfield, northeast of

Saigon. Everywhere he went he was briefed and met officers from Oklahoma. And he uttered positive remarks in commenting on what he had seen and been told. "The war," he said, "is turning our way." Then he visited Quemoy, the disputed island off the coast of China, and found it an "almost impregnable fortress" that Chinese Communist forces could invade only at their great peril. After visiting Okinawa, he flew to Korea, where he conferred with President Park Chung Heeand and visited American troops on the truce line and in the village of Panmunjom. He stopped off in Formosa and Hawaii en route back to Washington. At each stop his reports were increasingly exuberant: "The war in South Viet Nam is now nothing more than a mopping up operation." "The war is turning our way. We are winning it." One point that he picked up on after his return was the day-to-day reporting of events in Vietnam. They tended to give a "somewhat distorted picture of the situation there." By Christmas the Monroneys were home in Washington, refreshed by a few days' rest in Hawaii.[53]

Back home, Monroney complained that the American public was being poorly served by second-rate reporters and poor cooperation from the "people on the ground." Too many reporters, he complained, were "sitting in Saigon and sucking stories out of their thumbs." On *Face the Nation*, a CBS radio and television show, Monroney insisted that the Vietcong held their areas by "fear and terrorism" and concluded that if the U.S. and Vietnamese forces had the patience, "We're going to win." To reinforce his views, he invited a selected group of big-name editors, reporters, and commentators in Washington and New York to a luncheon at a private club to brief them on the three days he had spent in Vietnam and to urge them to have "their very best reporters" in that war-ravaged country. To ensure the widest coverage of his views, Monroney sent a form letter to Oklahoma publishers and "other friends" delineating his views on Vietnam.[54]

At the same time that he was garnering public attention with his perceptions on Vietnam, he was deeply involved in a tight race for the post of Democratic Senate whip. Russell Long at the outset claimed he had 25 to 30 solid votes, with John Pastore close behind. While Long considered himself the front runner, Monroney loomed as the compromise choice, the role he had envisioned for himself before his trip to the Far East. Needed to win, if all sixty-eight Democratic senators in the Eighty-ninth Congress voted, were 35 votes. Pastore had too many negative aspects: his height (five feet, four inches), his caustic debating technique combined with loyalty to the Senate's traditional rules and customs that at times alienated liberal colleagues—and then there was the matter of his religion. Since both the Senate and House majority leaders were Catholics and Pastore was a Catholic, some supporters could reconsider their decision. Monroney further recognized that Long's triumph would greatly increase southern power in the Senate. But in the two previous sessions of Congress, Long had supported the president on only 57 percent of the votes cast. Thus Monroney had good reason to envision himself as the compromise candidate. Also in his favor were two strong points: namely, his support of the president was 84 percent during the previous (Eighty-eighth) Congress, surpassing Pastore's 70 percent, and his legislative voting record appeared favorably to all sections of the country and to liberal-conservative middle-road senators.[55]

But a problem quickly arose. Senate majority leader Mike Mansfield announced that he favored balloting on a "low man out basis." If adopted, Monroney as everybody's second choice would be quickly eliminated. Monroney, on the other hand, wanted the vote taken under the rules of the Democratic National Committee, the rules applied in national conventions. These called for the balloting to continue until one candidate received a 35-vote majority. The matter would be decided by the senators at the caucus when Congress convened in January 1965.[56]

When the votes were tallied, it was quickly evident that Monroney had lost his first election in a political career covering twenty-six years in Congress. He lost out on the first ballot when Long received 34 votes; Pastore 20 and Monroney 14. On the second ballot Long receive 41 votes while Pastore got 25. By accepting Mansfield's view of "low man out," Monroney's strategy collapsed. He later said he thought he had 27 "hard core" votes and had gone into the caucus confident of winning. His defeat now would give him more time to devote to enacting legislation reorganizing Congress. He took consolation in the hope that congressional reorganization in the long run would be of greater significance than "who 'in the hell' was whip."[57]

The three-week jaunt in Asia and the battle to become majority whip, designed to enhance his career, had actually sowed seeds for its demise. The new role Monroney sought for himself was seriously flawed, and no one recognized what had occurred more cogently than Allan Cromley, who followed Monroney as part of his beat covering Congress for the *Daily Oklahoman.* He asserted to associates, "Mike is on a jag of exhilaration that is hard to figure out although in the last few days he has shown signs that he's not impervious to criticism. His seemingly continuous ebullience goes beyond that of anyone I ever knew, at least it did while he was on the senate whip binge. He ran around talking like a guy who had had four quick martinis on an empty stomach, except that he was sober, kind of running off at the mouth." Cromley thought others had noticed Monroney's behavior, which he believed "slowed down a little" following the whip election.[58]

Cromley went further and explained that Monroney "has gone clear off his rocker on this Viet-Nam kick." While in Monroney's office several "big-time commentators and reporters returned phone calls, were greeted effusively and invited to a luncheon at a private club of which Mike is apparently a member." Among those invited, according to Cromley, were Scotty Reston, David Brinkley, Walter Cronkite, Chalmers Roberts, and William Lawrence, the elite of the Washington press corps. Monroney explained that "he wanted to tell them about his trip and about his conclusions that we are winning the war, which is not being accurately reported." Somewhat put out that he was not invited, Cromley passed it off, claiming, "He's just off in the blue yonder."[59]

When reflecting on the whip race, Cromley wrote that Monroney "was pitifully inept in counting noses." He counted on 27 votes, received only 14, leading Cromley to ask "what kind of a whip would he have been if he can't assess Senate sentiment any better than that." Later at a Capitol reception, talking with Monroney's wife, Cromley learned that before the 1962 election "Mike was offered a $75,000 a year job, which he seriously considered taking." He turned it down but, according to his wife, "seemed to regret not taking it because of his feeling that he was not providing her with a high enough standard of living." Cromley also related that after the 1964 election "Mike seemed to feel that he now was indeed the senior senator."[60]

This revealing letter, besides providing insight into Monroney's personal concerns, indicates that he was no longer a "switch-hitter" who sought to maintain a political posture as close to the center as possible, that he had thrown caution to the winds, that he was indeed the senior senator. He could sustain the premise because of his continuing role in seeking legislative reform, but he now was subject to mounting criticism, based on his support of the war in Vietnam. Letters appearing in the Friday Forum of the *Oklahoma City Times* dubbed Monroney a poor war reporter and noted that his remarks could more appropriately be made on April Fools' Day. An editorial in the *McAlester Democrat*, entitled "Monroney in Wonderland," suggested mounting sentiment against the war and was critical of his stance. Monroney gambled every time he insisted the war was going well because he was overly extending himself on a political limb from which it would be difficult to back off. And by 1966 observers were indicating that Monroney would be in a tough race for reelection two years hence. His most likely opponent, Governor Henry Bellmon, was already commenting critically on Monroney's forecasting an early end to the Vietnam conflict.[61]

Monroney persisted in his optimistic outlook. After General Maxwell Taylor, the former ambassador who had hosted Monroney in Saigon and was now a presidential adviser, testified before the Senate Foreign Relations Committee, the Monroneys entertained General and Mrs. Taylor and other high officials at a dinner party. Monroney thereafter issued a press release stressing his call for new funding of combat operations in Vietnam. While earlier in his congressional career Monroney might have been a favorite of moderates of both parties, he was now considered a hawk who would go all the way with LBJ when it came to the war in Vietnam. He was pleased to bring to the attention of his colleagues a 1967 student newspaper survey showing support of U.S. policies in Southeast Asia on the part of University of Oklahoma students. Later in the year he reiterated, in reflective comments on war, presidential responsibility and dissent, his view on the conflict. Dissent, to Monroney, was misguided and not reflective of the outlook of a majority of his constituents.[62]

In 1964 Monroney was a key person, the best campaigner, keeping a previously divided Democratic party united and relentlessly attacking Barry Goldwater more than most Democrats cared to. He was at the apex of his popularity as a political figure in Oklahoma, but such was not the case four years later when he sought a fourth term in the Senate. While his ongoing battle for legislative reform still commanded respect in Oklahoma and throughout the nation, by 1968 its fate, as already noted, was locked in the Rules Committee of the House of Representatives. And his hawkish views were not entertained by all members of his own party, a point exploited by his opponent, the state's first Republican governor and now seeking to become its second Republican senator.

In the course of the campaign Monroney and Bellmon engaged in two debates. In the first, Bellmon recalled, "Monroney blistered me." In the second, the now carefully prepared Bellmon was ready for their encounter on statewide television, and as Bellmon wrote later, Monroney "had had his fill." He never accepted another joint appearance, and Bellmon claimed that the race against Monroney was the easiest of all the statewide races he had made. He won the election by 50,000 votes. To be sure, 1968 was a Republican year, and the party was assisted by largely Democratic defections to George Wallace's American Independence Party. In Oklahoma the combined vote of these two parties far surpassed the Republican vote for Nixon. In the Senate race Bellmon's total exceeded that of his two opponents. He garnered close to 52 percent of the votes, while Monroney secured 46 percent. His defeat concluded a remarkable thirty-two-year congressional career, consisting of seven terms in the House and three in the Senate.[63]

Recognizing his inability to personally thank all the Oklahomans to whom thanks were due, Monroney issued a press release graciously thanking the people of Oklahoma for their support and friendship. He did not return to Oklahoma but maintained his residence in fashionable northwest Washington, and he was pleased that interest in congressional reorganization was still an active concern of many members in both chambers. When Congress approved the Legislative Reorganization

Act of 1970, Monroney took satisfaction in knowing that thanks to his efforts committee procedures would be more efficient and more democratic. Members would be better informed during floor consideration and better staffed to render judgments on public policy issues. And younger members would have more opportunity to participate in the legislative process. As one of his former staff members concluded, "None of this would have been possible unless you had been willing—twice during the past 25 years—to interrupt your other responsibilities and shepherd this effort." And in the Senate Lee Metcalf, who had taken up the cudgels when Monroney retired, gave him ample credit and recognition in his remarks on the chamber floor. In addition, Carl Albert, as House majority leader in 1970, played a leading role in getting legislative reorganization out of the Rules Committee, thereby assuring its passage, the Senate already having approved it. But two years after Monroney's defeat, few were the people in Oklahoma who showed an interest. His star was on the wane. By January 1971 Carl Albert had succeeded John McCormack as Speaker of the House of Representatives.[64]

In retirement, Monroney continued his involvement in the Washington social circuit, entertaining prominent guests at small dinner parties. In March 1969, less than two months after leaving office, Monroney signed on as a consultant and adviser to the Aviation Progress Committee to work with industry members in improving and expanding the growth of air transportation. Of course, given his work as "Mr. Aviation" in Congress, Monroney made an ideal lobbyist. Later in the year, Monroney went to work for Braniff Airlines as its principal representative in the capital. By this time he was already serving as Washington representative of several other firms, not all associated with aviation, including membership on the board of the $3 billion Anchor Fund, one of the largest and third oldest mutual fund.[65]

Several years later, Monroney at age seventy-six learned that the name of Oklahoma City's Federal Aviation Administration facility would henceforth be known as the Mike Monroney Aeronautical Center. In the following year, 1978, a portion of Monroney's ashes was released from the fuselage of a small plane above the runway apron of the center, while his widow and a group of family and friends were gathered below—a fitting end to Monroney's long love affair with manned flight. Previously a portion of Monroney's ashes had been interred at the National Cathedral in Washington, where a memorial service had been conducted. Another memorial service, prior to the disposal of his ashes over the Aeronautical Center, occurred at St. Paul's Episcopal Cathedral in downtown Oklahoma City, where his gentleness and warmth of character were recalled by family and friends for the prominent dignitaries in attendance.[66]

And finally, in 1982 a program of seminars, lectures, and conferences on ethics in public policy, in memory of Monroney, was established at the Washington National Cathedral. He had dedicated twenty years to service in the Cathedral Chapter, the guiding force for the institution. The Ethics in Public Policy program was intended to assist members of Congress in reflecting on the moral and ethical dimensions of their calling. It would help burnish the memory of Mike Monroney as a notable public servant.[67]

That Monroney was a notable public servant there can be no doubt. Two institutions that he was instrumental in bringing to Oklahoma—the Postal Training Center in Norman and the Aeronautical Center in Oklahoma City—are flourishing decades after their establishment. His proposal for the International Development Association was a brilliant suggestion that he helped to bring to fruition. While he did not bring his great effort to achieve legislative reforms to fruition, it was achieved shortly thereafter, and the creaky Congress began in earnest to modernize its procedures. His notable achievements only make the enigma of Mike Monroney more intriguing. Why did he order his papers burned when they could easily have been packed and shipped to the destination of his choice, a service available to all members of Congress? The small collection that did survive contains little on the topics discussed in this article. His reluctance to commit himself, unlike his friend and colleague William Benton, in opposing the Senate antics of Joseph McCarthy, was not unusual. Other senators did not speak out, nor did Dwight Eisenhower during the 1952 campaign. Yet in the available Monroney papers there are numerous letters from Benton indicating that he was in accord with

Benton's battle against McCarthy. And though Monroney chaired the committee examining the disputed 1948 Maryland election, there are only a handful of perfunctory letters on the subject available in his papers, nor is there any correspondence with Adlai Stevenson, another close friend who Monroney supported in all his campaigns.

What emerges from available evidence is that Monroney was not a liberal, neither a New Deal, Fair Deal or Great Society liberal willing to utilize the power of government in furthering the general welfare by tackling the pressing economic and social concerns besetting his constituents and the American people. When asked by a reporter, he called himself a Wilsonian Democrat, suggesting a broad international outlook. But he preferred the term "switch-hitter," indicating that he would consider each vote carefully and not tilt to either side of the political spectrum, rarely willing to fully commit himself. He abandoned fiscal conservatism only in support of aviation in its civilian and military aspects. And he could demonstrate how this support benefited his constituents in Oklahoma, while gaining him the acquaintance and friendship of prominent business and military leaders. Finally, he was more at home in Washington society than among his constituents in Oklahoma.

In all, there was nothing unusual or out of the ordinary in his behavior as a member of Congress. His long tenure indicates a measure of support few Oklahoma politicians could match. Truth to tell, he probably was his own worst enemy, as his trip to Vietnam and his campaign to secure the post of majority whip suggest. But none of these observations seeking to define Monroney offer an insight as to why he had his papers burned and thereby forestalled the opportunity to do justice to the long career of a prominent Oklahoma political figure whose tenure could rival that of his colleague Robert S. Kerr.

Notes

1. Julius Duscha, "Sen. Mike Monroney Remembers his Washington," *Washington Post Potomac*, January 12, 1969.

2. Story draft by Allan Cromley for the *Daily Oklahoman* (Oklahoma City), scheduled for publication on July 2, 1974. Box 14, Folder 95 (cited hereafter as box

number/folder number). Allan Cromley Papers, Carl Albert Center, University of Oklahoma.

3. *The Papers of Adlai E. Stevenson*, ed. Walter Johnson, 8 vols. (Boston: Little, Brown [1972–1979]) In the *Daily Oklahoman* of July 15, 1965, Monroney reviewed his efforts on behalf of Stevenson while recognizing that not many Democrats in Oklahoma shared Stevenson's views. Story in Cromley 14/4.

4. Milton MacKaye, "Oklahoma's Mighty Mike," *Saturday Evening Post*, September 22, 1951. Reprint available in Cromley 14/2.

5. For an insight on the Monroneys in Washington, I have relied on a draft by Allan Cromley of an obituary notice of Mary Ellen Monroney, who died in May 1994, available in Cromley 14/21.

6. *Washington Times-Herald*, March 8, 1951, editorial entitled "Sen. Monroney's Problem."

7. All of this material can be found in Box 3 of the Mike Monroney Papers in the Carl Albert Center.

8. A copy of the subcommittee report is available in Monroney 3/20. For the quote, see Jack Anderson with James Boyd, *Confessions of a Muckraker* (New York: Random House, 1979) p. 260.

9. Fred J. Cook, *The Nightmare Decade: The Life and Times of Senator Joe McCarthy.* (New York: Random House, 1971), p. 434; Thomas Lately, *When Even Angels Wept: The Senator Joseph McCarthy Affair—A Story Without a Hero* (New York: William Morrow, 1973) pp. 339–340.

10. Letters from William Benton to Monroney can be found in Monroney 3/3. See too Sidney Hyman, *The Lives of William Benton* (Chicago: University of Chicago Press, 1969), pp. 464, 467, 486. The lone letter from Monroney to Benton (July 12, 1952) is merely perfunctory, acknowledging receipt of two letters. It can be found in Monroney 3/3. See too Benton to Thomas C. Hennings, November 7, 1952, wherein Benton notes Monroney is leaving for Europe and that there "may be little likelihood of committee action in the near future." Copy in Monroney 3/3.

11. Press Release, August 26, 1952. A speech to a Maryland Democratic rally at Baltimore. Copy in Beth Campbell Short Papers 1/14. Carl Albert Center. Short, an Oklahoma native and the widow of Truman's first press secretary, came to work for Monroney in 1952 after serving as publicity director of the Democratic Senatorial Campaign Committee.

12. Story by Allan Cromley [December 26, 1962], Cromley 14/8. This is a file copy sent to the *Daily Oklahoman.*

13. W. W. Baker, "Monroney and the Little World Bank," *Kansas City Times*, May 7, 1959, copy in Short 3/16.

14. *Washington Post*, December 18, 1956. Story by Robert Albright. Copy in Short 3/16.

15. Short 3/11 contains a file of press stories regarding Monroney and IDA. In the file is a press release from Monroney's office of "Dates Associated with I.D.A," plus a report of the Committee on Banking and Currency dated July 12, 1958, and a draft of a speech by Monroney on IDA.

16. Richard Strout's article appeared in the *Christian Science Monitor*, August 16, 1958, copy in Monroney 1/12. See too the article by Roscoe Drummond in the same paper for August 1, 1966, copy in Monroney 1/4.

17. Monroney Press Release, September 28, 1966, Senate Statement. See too story in *Congressional News Service*, August 11, 1966. Monroney 1/4 for both items.

18. Monroney Press Releases: January 4, 1965, Short 5/6, and January 6, 1965, Cromley 14/11.

19. Allan Cromley, "Mike's Got More Irons in the Fire Than Wrangler," *Sunday Oklahoman*, May 2, 1965, p. 26. Copy in Cromley 14/4.

20. *Congressional Record*, 89th Cong., 1st sess., January 6, 1965, 165–69. *Daily Oklahoman*, January 7, 1965, copy in Cromley 14/11.

21. See a February 24, 1965, press release, in which Monroney listed newspapers that in editorials and articles endorsed his proposal. See too Monroney to the Editor, *Washington Post*, February 27, 1965, and the draft of a Senate speech Monroney delivered on March 8, 1965. All items in Monroney 1/6.

22. Monroney Press Releases, March 12, 1965, and n.d., in Monroney 1/3.

23. Monroney Papers: 1/3, 1/4, and 1/6 are crammed with clippings, press releases, and other items pertaining to legislative reform. See too Cromley 14/11 for stories filed by Cromley for the *Daily Oklahoman; Congressional Quarterly*, June 25, 1965, 1239–40.

24. Press clippings in Monroney 1/4 and 1/6. On August 12, 1966, on the Senate floor Monroney submitted a sheaf of editorials endorsing the work of the Joint Committee while urging approval of the report. *Congressional Record*, 89th Cong., 2nd sess., August 12, 1968, 18354–56.

25. Monroney Statement, August 17, 1966, Monroney 1/8.

26. Monroney Statement, September 28, 1966, Monroney 1/4; Monroney Memorandums to Members of Joint Committee, September 30, 1966, Monroney 1/8.

27. Press stories can be found in Monroney 1/11. Monroney Press Release, January 25, 1967 in Monroney 1/9.

28. Press stories in Monroney 1/11. One of the more perceptive accounts by Allan Cromley appeared in the *Daily Oklahoman* on February 5, 1967; Monroney to Senator, United States Senate, March 3, 1967, Monroney 1/9.

29. Press stories in Monroney 1/11 and 1/9. Monroney Press Release, March 12, 1967, in Monroney 1/19. This release quotes laudatory comments by his Senate colleagues.

30. Ray J. Madden to Monroney, May 8, 1967, and June 19, 1967, both items in Monroney 1/9. *Washington Post* editorial, "Shabby 'Ho-Dog,'" May 13, 1967, copy in Monroney 1/11. Madden Press Release, May 18, 1967, in Monroney 1/10; Monroney to B. Everett Jordan June 6, 1967, Monroney 1/9, and December 22, 1967, Monroney 1/10. *Congressional Quarterly*, June 9, 1967, 975–78. Richard Bolling of Missouri was a member of the Rules Committee who favored legislative reform. See his discussion of the Committee on Rules and the road to reform in *House Out of Order* (New York: E. P. Dutton, 1965).

31. Monroney Press Release, June 14, 1967, in Cromley 14/19; *Oklahoma City Times*, June 19, 1967, in Cromley 9/5; and "Dirksen Challenge Jolts Dodd's Case," *Daily Oklahoman*, June 20, 1967.

32. *Congressional Quarterly*, December 14, 1964, 4.

33. Monroney to L. F. Bellatti, July 16, 1958, Short 1/18.

34. *Stillwater* (Okla.) *NewsPress*, November 28, 1961, clipping in Short 2/15. Monroney Press Release, May 11, 1961, Cromley 14/7. A five-page file in Cromley 14/4 discusses Monroney's aviation activities from 1958 to 1961. For an example of Monroney's work with commercial and military groups, see "New Policy for MATS," in *Time*, February 22, 1960, p. 96, and Monroney Press Release, January 11, 1960, Short 1/15 for both items. Editorial, "Senator Mike's Airlift," *Tulsa Tribune*, October 21, 1959, copy in Short 1/19.

35. *Daily Oklahoman*, May 27, 1963, in Cromley 14/11, story entitled "Monroney Pushes for More Planes"; Monroney Press Release, September 4, 1962, copy in Short 1/8; Robert Peterson to Monroney, February 3, 1962, Short 2/13.

36. Monroney Press Release, 1964, in Short 1/18; "Monroney Interviews," *General Electric Forums*, 4, o. 4, (October-December 1964), copy in Short 3/9. *Air Transport World*, May 1965. Joseph Murphy, "What the Senator Thinks About Ten Big Industry Topics," pp. 13–14, copy in Short 5/2. See too Monroney Speech, "The SST—A Bird for All Nations," January 27, 1965, to Aero Club, Washington, D.C., draft in Short 3/18.

37. *Daily Oklahoman*, December 9, 1965; clipping *Herald Tribune Service*, "Missiles Get Bigger Role," December 9, 1965; *Tulsa Tribune*, December 10, 1965. Short 4/4 for all items.

38. Monroney Press Releases, December 31, 1967, Cromley 14/13; December 29, 1967, Cromley 14/19; and February 27, 1968, Cromley 14/20.

39. Monroney to Dear Friend, July 22, 1957, Short 4/4; *Federation News Service:* Bulletin 17, April 29, 1965, copy in Short 4/6; Monroney, *Washington Report*, November 1966, p. 4, copy in Cromley 14/12; Monroney Press Release, September 15, 1966, Cromley 14/18.

40. Press Release from the Offices of Monroney, Senator Fred Harris, and Representative John Jarman, June 15, 1966, copy in Short 4/6; Monroney, *Washington Report*, August 1967, p. 2, copy in Cromley 14/19.

41. To *Oklahoman* from Coffey, July 9, July 26, and August 1, 1968, Cromley 14/14 for all items.

42. Information in this and the following paragraphs can be found in *Mike Monroney's Record on Oil and Gas*, a 1962 campaign leaflet, copy in Short 4/2. The impact of the depletion allowance on the state economy is fully explicated in an article in the *Frederick* (Okla.) *Daily Leader*, April 23, 1962, copy in Short 2/15.

43. *Oklahoma City Times*, August 9, 1962, "Why Oil Depletion Allowance Helps Nation," from a speech by Monroney. *Daily Oklahoman*, August 12, 1962, copies in Short 2/15; *Oklahoma City Times*, February 7, 1963, copy in Cromley 14/9.

44. Monroney to Victor Schinnerer, December 23, 1958, Monroney 9/3.

45. Cromley, *Legislation*, p. 2, rough draft of comments on Monroney's record, Cromley 14/15.

46. *Oklahoma City Times*, January 14, 1960, Cromley 14/6; *Tulsa World*, April 17, 1960; *Lawton* (Okla.) *Constitution*, April 14, 1960; *Daily Oklahoman*, July 8 and July 14, 1960; *To All Illinois Delegates and Alternates* [July 1960], copy in Monroney 5/4. This statement is one of the very few items pertaining to Stevenson available in the Monroney papers.

47. Cromley, *Legislation*, p. 3, Cromley 14/15. *Purcell* (Okla.) *Register*, July 19, 1962. Short 2/15; *Oklahoma City Times*, September 9, 1964, Cromley 14/10, and September 3, 1964, Cromley 14/9.

48. "Doctors Rap Mike," *Daily Oklahoman*, September 3, 1963, Cromley 14/9.

49. *Daily Oklahoman*, October 9, 1965, Cromley 14/11; *McAlester* (Okla.) *News Capital*, October 13, 1965; *Tulsa World*, October 27, 1963; *Oklahoma Journal*, October 20, 1965; *Sapulpa* (Okla.) *Daily Herald*, October 12, 1965. Short 3/2 for all items.

50. *Daily Oklahoman*, November 28, 1964, Cromley 14/10.

51. *Pryor* (Okla.) *Daily Times*, "Oklahoma Reports," December 11, 1964, and *Daily Oklahoman*, December 20, 1964. Short 3/2 for both items.

52. *Oklahoma Journal*, December 11, 1964, and *Daily Oklahoman*, December 14, 1967. Short 3/16 for both items.

53. *Tulsa World*, December 23, 1964; *Daily Oklahoman*, December 23, 1964; *Tulsa Tribune*, December 21, 1964; *Oklahoma City Times*, December 18, 1964. Short 3/16 for all items.

54. *Daily Oklahoman*, December 28, 1964, two stories on this date. Short 3/16 for both items. *Daily Oklahoman*, December 29, 1964, Cromley 14/10; *Oklahoma Journal*, December 30, 1964, in Short 3/16; *Daily Oklahoman* editorial, "Who Mops Whom," January 3, 1965, Short 3/2; Monroney to Dear Friend, January 1965, copy in Cromley 14/11.

55. *Okmulgee* (Okla.) *Daily Times*, December 24, 1964, Short 3/16.

56. *Tulsa Tribune*, December 29, 1964, and *Washington Post*, January 4, 1965. Short 3/16 for both items. The story by Jack Anderson in the *Washington Post* was critical of Monroney, calling him "Too Gentle a Senator."

57. *Bartlesville* (Okla.) *Examiner Enterprise*, January 4, 1965; *Tulsa World*, January 9, 1965. Quotes are from the story by Malvina Stephenson. Short 3/16 for both items.

58. Cromley to Charlie Bennett and Ralph Sewell, n.d., [January 5, 1963], Cromley 14/11.

59. Ibid.

60. Ibid.

61. *Oklahoma City Times*, January 1, 1965. Cromley 14/10; *McAlester* (Okla.) *Democrat*, February 11, 1965, Short 3/2; *Daily Oklahoman*, January 16, 1966, Cromley 14/12.

62. *Oklahoma City Times*, "Monroney Backs Johnson's War Policy," undated clipping [1967], Cromley 14/13; Monroney Press Release, February 24, 1966, Cromley 14/18; Press Release, May 9, 1967, Cromley 14/19; *Oklahoma City Times*, May 27, 1966, Cromley 14/12; *Congressional Record*, 90th Cong., 1st sess., December 8, 1967, copy in Cromley 14/13.

63. Henry Bellmon, *The Life and Times of Henry Bellmon* (Tulsa: Council Oak Books, 1992), pp. 243–45; *Oklahoma Elections: Statehood to Present*, vol. 1 (Oklahoma City: Oklahoma State Election Board, January 1994), C-495 for the official vote.

64. Monroney Press Release [November 1968], Cromley 14/14; Monroney to Michael Mansfield, May 6, 1970, Monroney 1/13; W. Devier Pearson to Monroney, October 9, 1970, Monroney 1/3. *Congressional Record*, 91st Cong. 1st sess., August 5, 1969, E6640; ibid., 91st Cong. 2nd sess., October 7, 1970, S17323–24. Remarks by B. F. Sisk in the House and Lee Metcalf in the Senate, 91st Cong. 2nd sess., October 7, 1970, S17323–24. Monroney to Metcalf, March 26, 1971, Monroney 1/14. Carl Albert with Danney Goble, *Little Giant* (Norman: University of Oklahoma Press, 1990), 308–12. For the Legislative Reorganization Act of 1970, see *Congress and the Nation, 1969–1972*, vol. 3 (Washington, D.C.: Congressional Quarterly, 1973), 382–96.

65. Aviation Progress Committee Press Release, March 21, 1969, and Cromley to the *Daily Oklahoman*, October 2, 1969. Cromley 14/15 for both items.

66. *Daily Oklahoman*, June 6, 1978, February 14 and 29, 1980, and latter stories by Kevin Donovan. Cromley 14/15 for both items.

67. *Daily Oklahoman*, March 12, 1982, Cromley 14/21.

« 11 »

Oklahoma's Mike Synar Confronts the Western Grazing Question, 1987–2000

For more than a decade in the last years of the last century, there occurred a bitter war in the West and in Washington. It started over the fees charged ranchers who graze their cattle on public lands and soon became part of a deeper conflict over the use of the public domain. It involved colorful personalities and provoked animosities that quickly came to the fore in the West, and more slowly to national attention. This article focuses on two key figures: Congressman Mike Synar of Oklahoma, who started the fight, and Secretary of the Interior Bruce Babbitt, who broadened its parameters and witnessed its conclusion in a decision of the Supreme Court of the United States.

Elected in 1987, at the age of twenty-seven and a year out of law school, to represent the Second Congressional District in Oklahoma, Mike Synar quickly compiled a record as a strong advocate of good government. At the outset of his tenure he asserted, "I want to be a U.S. Congressman from Oklahoma, not an Oklahoma Congressman."[1] As chairman of the Government Operations Subcommittee on Environment, Energy, and Natural Resources, he was able to roam over a wide-ranging landscape in selecting issues that merited further investigation.

Throughout his career, Synar, genuinely concerned about making what he considered good public policy, called himself a maverick, a reformer, an outsider. As such he aroused the ire of powerful special interests: tobacco, oil, insurance companies, and the gun lobby, among others. To his work Synar brought a certain irreverence and a gift for phrases with an Oklahoma twang. His committee assignments allowed him to become deeply involved in some of the largest questions before

Congress, such as campaign-finance reform and national energy policy. In 1985 Synar strongly opposed the Gramm-Rudman deficit-reduction plan. He initiated a legal challenge that resulted in a pivotal section of the Balanced Budget Act being declared unconstitutional, while editorial writers and other critics castigated him for standing in the way of fiscal restraint.

Then, on June 14, 1987, Synar introduced a measure that soon made him a public enemy throughout most of the West. He said, "Mr. Speaker, today I am introducing legislation to increase the fee charged for grazing livestock on public rangeland managed by the Bureau of Land Management and the Forest Service." The current fee was $1.35 per animal unit month (AUM), which Synar said was far below the average appraised 1983 market value of $6.53 per AUM for all federal grazing land. The measure was a declaration of war on the ranching West, a war that outlasted Synar's tenure in Congress.[2]

Grazing fees on public lands was not a new subject. Since 1906 the Forest Service had been charging for grazing on National Forest Lands. Fees for grazing on public lands managed by the Bureau of Land Management dated back to 1934 with the passage of the Taylor Grazing Act. Synar's immersion in the problem came about in 1985 and 1986 as a result of hearings and a study prepared by the Subcommittee on Environment, Energy, and Natural Resources, which he chaired.

The Taylor Grazing Act, which closed the public domain, sought to prevent overgrazing and soil deterioration. It authorized the secretary of the interior to divide the public rangelands into grazing districts, to determine the amount of grazing permitted in each district, to issue permits to graze livestock, and to charge reasonable fees for the use of the land. To administer the grazing districts, the secretary created advisory boards made up of local ranchers. These boards soon became the governing body of each grazing district. But as Synar observed in a meeting of his subcommittee, "Those who graze livestock on public lands often have very different views about the use of the land than do other members of the public."[3]

The Federal Land Policy and Management Act of 1976 introduced the concept of multiple land-use planning and of public participation in that process. The introduction of multiple use (taking into account subjects such as watershed, minerals, fish and wildlife, scenic and scientific values, historical usage, and sustained yield) meant that ranchers would soon have to consider far more than grazing fees. Meanwhile, section 401 of the act froze fees for the 1977 grazing year pending further study. With the completion of the study, Congress imposed a further moratorium, signed by President Jimmy Carter in July 1978. And in October 1978 the Public Rangelands Improvement Act established, for a seven-year period, a formula to use in setting grazing fees. But with the pending termination of this period, fifty years after the passage of the Taylor Grazing Act, Synar said that "much of the public's land has been overgrazed by livestock."[4]

Together the Bureau of Land Management (BLM) and the Forest Service administered a range of about 307 million acres within the sixteen western states covered by the Public Rangelands Improvement Act. These rangelands were divided into more than 30,000 allotments, ranging in size from fewer than 40 acres to more than 1 million acres. Both agencies required that permittees pursue cooperatively developed plans specifying the number of animals to be grazed and the time frame during which grazing would occur. Grazing permits or leases were for a one-year period and were subject to renewal, with current holders having priority. They covered a significant portion of total grazing in some western states. In Idaho 88 percent, in Wyoming 64 percent, and in Arizona 63 percent of the cattle grazed during at least part of 1984 on public rangelands.[5]

In 1985, Synar claimed that only 2 percent of the 1.6 million of the nation's ranchers grazed cattle on BLM and Forest Service lands. For this privilege they then paid a fee of $1.35 per AUM, which contrasted with fees ranging as high as $14 per AUM, on state lands, private lands, and other federal lands. With Congress being lobbied to extend the current formula for setting the fee, and President Ronald Reagan pressuring Congress to cut spending without touching defense budgets and without raising taxes, a difficult situation, Synar observed, was created for a program whose 1984 costs exceeded receipts from grazing fees by more than $33 million. With the current fee scheduled to expire on December 31,

1985, and with no recommendations forthcoming from the administrative agencies, Synar wanted his subcommittee to inquire as to what the agencies' recommendations were and what they were doing to establish a fee based "on a formula reflecting annual changes in the costs of production." In particular he hoped to learn more about subleasing, wherein permittees allowed someone else to graze animals on their leased land for payment greater than the AUM rate, with this revenue becoming a windfall profit to the original permittee.[6]

This preliminary hearing led to an extended 1986 report based on a study of Synar's subcommittee and published as a House Report entitled *Federal Grazing Program: All Is Not Well on the Range.* Neither the hearing nor the report was intended for public dissemination, but they provided Synar with ample expertise, so that when he introduced his 1987 bill he was fully versed on the matter of grazing fees. Among other things the report noted that among the 27,000 permittees grazing livestock on public lands and paying $1.35 per AUM were "oil companies, agribusinesses, land speculators, doctors and lawyers." It added that the average 1983 appraised market value for grazing fees was $6.53 per AUM for all federal lands and $6.87 for nonfederal lands. Although the $1.35 based on the formula presented in the Public Rangelands Improvement Act expired at the end of 1985, President Reagan by executive order extended its use annually.

The report probed grazing fees, the profits garnered by permittees who subleased their grazing privileges, BLM regulations that were narrower than the statutory language, inadequate enforcement of trespass and other unauthorized use regulations, and practices pertaining to poor billing. In addition, it examined how the BLM was yielding some of its regulatory authority and its policy of allowing private parties to claim water rights on public lands without compensation to the United States Treasury. The fact that the BLM was unable to provide an accurate inventory of range improvements provoked questions as to how it spent its funds.

Thus, more than fifty years after the enactment of the Taylor Grazing Act, Synar recognized that overgrazing on public land continued to be a problem. Moreover, opportunities for fraud, waste, and abuse were evident in the failure of the BLM to properly account for range improvements. Another point also evident was that actual grazing on the public range was declining dramatically and steadily.[7]

Subsequently Synar testified before the House Subcommittee on National Parks and Public Lands of the Committee on Interior and Insular Affairs. The committee was considering three bills dealing with fees to be charged for grazing on lands managed by the BLM and the Forest Service, one of which he had introduced. It had no cosponsors, but it was similar to another bill before the subcommittee. Since the previous Congress had failed to consider Synar's bill, he explained the work of his subcommittee in concluding that all was not well on the range. The fundamental question, as he saw it, was "whether or not we should continue to subsidize the 23,000 permittees who graze their livestock on this BLM and Forest Service land." These permittees accounted for less than 2 percent of the total livestock industry and only 7 percent of western producers. They paid $1.35 per AUM on land appraised from $4.05 to $8.55 per AUM. To Synar the answer was an emphatic no, because taxpayers, "including livestock producers all over the country," would pay the difference. They included his family, "now going on three generations deep in ranching in Oklahoma."

Synar knew that many of the witnesses would argue that raising gazing fees would cast an undue economic burden on federal permittees. He urged committee members to keep two things in mind as they listened to these witnesses. One was that grazing permittees did not have a monopoly on hard times. All livestock producers had to cover their production costs, including higher rates for grazing lands, which in Oklahoma consisted of school lands and Corps of Engineers lands. And the other consideration was that some federal permittees could clearly withstand the effect of an increase. He mentioned Union Oil, Getty Oil, and Texaco, as well as land investment partnerships operating in areas near Aspen, Colorado, and weekend ranchers like lawyers and doctors. He again mentioned permittees transferring or subleasing their grazing privileges to individuals who paid them more than the $1.35 per AUM, with the government unable to collect the windfall profit that the permittees garnered from these transactions. Obviously, he concluded, "the market will bear a higher fee," thereby allowing the public, "which owns these ranchlands," to benefit. His bill provided that the fee be calculated on a regional basis, thereby establishing "a fee that closely resembles the value of the land" and creating a system that could be administered with relative ease, and also earmarked money to improve riparian habitat important not only to cattle but also to a wide variety of wildlife. Riparian areas, Synar claimed, were in unsatisfactory condition and were "particularly vulnerable to overuse by cattle." Indicating a parochial interest, Synar said that Oklahoma hunters, fishermen, and bird watchers "went to states like Colorado to pursue these interests.[8]

In 1989, with no grazing-fee legislation seriously considered on the floor of either branch, Synar was struggling to get national attention for grazing fees over the opposition of western delegations and the Reagan administration. In April 1989 he again appeared before the Subcommittee on National Parks and Public Lands. The committee was once more considering three bills, two of which looked at grazing fees and the third authorized funding for the BLM. Synar's remarks were brief because he was not associated with any of the measures. Reforming the grazing system, he said, involved "not just questions of fiscal responsibility" but also "basic issues of fairness": "Should the U.S. taxpayers, and 98 percent of the U.S. livestock industry who don't benefit from subsidized federal grazing, pay for the 2 percent who do?" Synar expressed the hope that, given the prevailing budget deficit, the committee would close some of the deficits and get taxpayers a better deal by raising grazing fees to a level that represented "a good deal for the use of these public resources."[9]

Now that he was secure in his views, grounded with facts garnered through extensive committee hearings, Synar began to speak out in more public arenas. For example, when Robert Burford resigned in June 1989 after more than eight years of managing the public range as director of the BLM, Synar's message was "Goodbye, good riddance, don't come back." Burford, he explained, served his personal interests by not fully divesting himself of grazing permits on public land and by providing ranchers subsidies in the form of cheap grazing and water. In so doing, Synar said, he "discriminated against the other 98 percent of ranchers."[10]

With the advent of the George H. W. Bush administration, Synar became more outspoken in his criticisms of federal grazing policy, but open hostility had not yet fully developed in the West. In July 1990 Synar said that "grazing on public lands is producing an ecological and fiscal disaster." In a letter to the chairman of the House Subcommittee on Interior Appropriations, Synar suggested that the fee be raised from the then prevailing $1.81. per animal to $8.70 per animal. The current fee, he noted, was 80 percent of the rate for grazing cattle on private land.[11]

On October 4, 1990, Synar and George "Buddy" Darden, a Georgia Democrat, introduced a bill calling for grazing fees reflecting the fair market value of forage on public rangelands. This measure, which was to gain more attention than Synar's earlier efforts, called for a graduated fee structure beginning at $4.35 per AUM in fiscal 1991 and increasing until in fiscal 1995 the grazing fee would reach $8.70 per AUM or fair market value, whichever was higher. Within two weeks the House had approved the proposal as an amendment to the Interior Appropriations Bill. Besides saving taxpayers $100 million a year, Synar insisted, it would help preserve the ecology of the nation's rangelands. After three years of pleading with the Rules Committee for permission to bypass the committee considering interior appropriations, Synar finally got a vote.[12]

By a vote of 251 to 155 the House agreed to increase fees on ranchers who grazed their cattle on public lands. But the Senate, where the public lands states were effectively represented, struck the proposal from its version of the appropriations bill. The issue now would be considered in conference, where western members predominated. It had no chance of gaining approval. But Synar's proposal hit several raw nerves and aroused emotional responses from western members, while gaining support from the conservative American Taxpayers Union on the one hand and major environmental groups on the other. Members from both urban and nonwestern rural areas found little to oppose in the proposal. The arguments, both pro and con, heard in various committee hearings had moved to the chambers of Congress, where they would grow in intensity and help make Synar a public enemy on western rangelands.[13]

Several weeks later, at the outset of the new Congress, the 102nd, a similar bill was introduced, this time by Darden, for himself and Synar. To widen its appeal, and with the addition of a third sponsor, Chester Atkins of Massachusetts, a revised measure was introduced that specifically mentioned Forest Service and BLM grazing lands. This revision allowed the bill to be referred jointly to both the Agriculture and Interior and Insular Affairs committees. The fee structure remained the same as in the 1990 measure, reaching, for fiscal year 1995, the $8.70 per AUM or the fair-market-value rate, whichever was higher. Synar in his remarks explained that for eight years as chairman of the House Government Operations Subcommittee on Environment, Energy, and Natural Resumes, he was charged with oversight responsibilities to determine whether natural resource programs were working and whether they were fair. His oversight led him to conclude that livestock grazing was "a valid and valuable use of suitable public lands" when managed by "resource professionals," that proper livestock grazing could benefit "both wildlife and livestock," and that a healthy livestock industry was an important element in maintaining western open space.[14]

But at the same time, Synar acknowledged that "an unreasonably large proportion of our public rangelands are in unsatisfactory condition," that "inadequate funding and staffing for professional resource managers and their programs" were impairing rangeland productivity and health. To remedy this situation necessitated raising grazing fees. He noted that in1990 grazers utilizing 250 million acres of federal rangelands paid a fee of $1.81 per AUM, far below the market rate. He added that, "ironically," the Department of Agriculture set the commercial value of forage on its lands at $8.70 and the BLM charged the same rate for trespassing on public land. But unless Congress changed the law, the federal government would continue to charge below market rates for legal access to public rangelands and the taxpayer would pay the difference.[15]

In his carefully constructed remarks, Synar made much of the fact that the domestic livestock industry had long prided itself on its independence. Indeed, "animal agriculture stands alone as being that element of the American farm economy that is most removed from federal intervention in the market place." When he spoke, there were "no commodity programs and no marketing orders, no laws, no insurance, no grants, and no federal interference." Nevertheless, a small segment of the industry, the holders of federal grazing permits, was "chewing through millions of dollars each year." Thus the purpose of his bill was to put federal grazing programs on a "pay as you go" basis, phasing out the grazing subsidy and using the savings to fund range improvement activities. Unless such action was taken, unless grazing fees were increased, Synar said that the government would "continue to encourage overgrazing," the costs of the program would continue to exceed receipts, and taxpayers would continue to subsidize 2 percent of the country's total meat production.[16]

Logical and persuasive as Synar's presentation was, the proposal faced serious challenges in Congress. To begin with, Synar's subcommittee, which focused on natural resources, energy, and the environment, was involved with a multitude of other concerns and could not devote serious attention to this specific matter. He needed to work through subcommittees of both Departments of the Interior and Agriculture where members from grazing-land states were well represented. This was not a problem in the House, where most committee members endorsed Synar's views and a large proportion of the full membership agreed with his call for reasonable rates that would benefit both taxpayers and the environment. Such was not the case in the Senate, where the key committees were heavily populated with members from public-lands states and where powerful senators were anything but favorably inclined. And now that his views were attracting public attention in the West, Synar was gaining in notoriety as well.

In addition, Synar was doing something more fundamental. He was in the process of breaking one of the strongest iron triangles in the West, one that had been forged with the passage of the Taylor Grazing Act. It allowed ranchers on public lands to work closely with the grazing boards, on which they were usually well represented, to develop policies, programs, and fees that were in accord with or met the approval of appropriate officials in the Forest Service and the Bureau of Land Management and of powerful members of the relevant congressional subcommittees. Furthermore, on a more subtle level, he challenged the rugged-individualist, macho image of the ranchers who utilized federal rangelands by suggesting that, by allowing taxpayers to make up the difference between their fees and the commercial value of forage on other grazing lands, they had feet of clay.

In March, five weeks after Synar spoke on behalf of fair-market grazing, the Subcommittee on National Parks and Public Lands met to consider the reauthorization of the BLM and its grazing fees in formulating the fiscal 1992 Interior Appropriations Bill. In his remarks, Synar, utilizing data from the Government Accounting Office and the Agricultural Research Service, claimed that "the ability to pay by our western ranchers has increased by 258 percent since 1882, while grazing fees had been lowered in 7 of the 9 years since 1982." A more reasonable fee, he thought, would be "somewhere in the neighborhood of 5 to 8 dollars," and he asked the subcommittee to request the Economic Research Service of the Department of Agriculture to validate those numbers. The simple truth, he concluded, was "that a few federal grazing permit holders are feeding off the Federal Treasury." Moreover, much of the public rangeland, five decades after the passage of the Taylor Grazing Act, was still in unsatisfactory condition. To change this situation, to improve the management of 250 million acres of federal rangelands, and to "make the taxpayers more than $325 million over the next five fiscal years," Synar called for the approval of the 1991 Fair Market Grazing for Public Rangelands Act.[17]

As would be expected, most of the people testifying before the subcommittee spoke in opposition to the measure Synar was endorsing. Opponents claimed it would end cattle grazing on public lands, would devastate the economies of western communities, and allow misrepresentation and emotion to determine range policy. But Synar was not to be deterred. In addition to the grazing-fee measure, he introduced two further bills, one to stop charging below-cost fees to private businesses at national parks, the other to do the same with regard to timber sales in national forests. Under Synar's plan, the government would report the fair market value of national assets and the fees charged for their use in the annual budget report.[18]

That Synar's proposals were not winning friends became evident that spring when the Wyoming Public Lands Council banned from 4 million acres of their private land those hunters and other outdoorsmen who lived in the congressional districts of Synar and the two cosponsors of the Fair Market Grazing for Public Rangelands Act. The secretary-treasurer of the lands council reported that ranchers in Utah, Nebraska, and Colorado were joining those in Wyoming in the access ban. The president of the lands council said a feeling among ranchers that their rights were being trampled had prompted the ban. Shortly thereafter, an official of the Idaho Cattle Association attacked Synar and his cosponsors for promoting legislation that was a political ploy to control land used in the West "and a cheap move at that," because it overlooked $700 million in cash receipts for cattle and calves largely grazed on public land in Idaho. The grazing act, sponsored by members from states with "virtually no federal land," allowed its sponsors to ignore the stewardship of western rangelands by livestock producers whose livelihood depended on the availability of both quality grazing and environmental quality.[19]

Responding to some of the criticism leveled against him, Synar said, "I don't know if you can describe the typical guy." But he did profile some gentlemen operators such as George Gillett of Vail, Colorado, who, besides owning a ski lodge, radio and television stations, a publishing company, and a meat-packing plant, had three federal grazing leases covering 277,000 acres of public land, and David Packard, a founder of the Hewlett-Packard Corporation, whose Idaho ranch had two leases covering 97,947 acres. Feeding their cattle at "the public trough" at rock-bottom prices aroused Synar's indignation. He claimed that small operators were the exception; that "10 percent control 90 percent of the land." Moreover, he noted that in 1991 some 20,000 ranchers grazed cattle on 274 million acres of Forest Service and BLM lands in eleven western states for a bargain price, by then $1.97 per AUM, clearly a losing proposition for the government. His bill to raise fees was seconded by the Government Accounting Office, the investigative agency of Congress, which said that taxpayers lost about eighty cents of every dollar spent on the grazing program.[20]

Synar's views were only strengthened after a five-day trip to Cortez, Colorado, where, at the behest of his Democratic colleague, Ben Nighthorse Campbell, he met with ranchers. The ranchers tried to prove to Synar that grazing on federal lands entailed myriad costs that did not encumber other ranchers, such as fencing, waterholes, irrigation, and the wages of cowboys to watch over cattle. To Synar these were not unique costs. He asserted, "I didn't see one cost . . . that I don't have to incur on my own operation." But to Campbell, whose district was loaded with ranchers, the prevailing $1.92 per AUM was "just fine," and he introduced legislation to keep it that way. Synar's bill, according to Campbell, would put ranchers out of work, wreck the economy of many western communities, and drive up the price of beef. In response to the critics who foresaw these dire consequences, Synar claimed that he was seeking to run government like a business and to avoid giving 20,000 ranchers a "virtual free ride."[21]

Ranchers throughout the West, vowing to fight Synar's proposals, were readying for another conflict over a question that was literally as old as the American West, namely, who owned the land and who should control its use. Meanwhile, the House of Representatives prepared to vote on the bill cosponsored by Synar, an amendment to an Interior Department appropriations measure that raised the grazing fee to $8.70 by 1995. It passed the House on June 25 by a vote of 232 to 192, but the language was dropped in conference with the Senate, which did not act on the measure, and met the same fate as Synar's 1990 amendment. As was the case in the West, there was on the House floor a bitter debate, with Donald Young, an Alaska Republican, labeling the amendment "the biggest bunch of whatever a cow leaves behind on public lands."[22]

The debate over Synar's proposal soon transcended being a regional controversy. The National Audubon Society aired a television special entitled *The New Range Wars.* It attacked the livestock industry for overgrazing cattle on fragile grasslands, destroying endangered species, and having too much influence with federal agencies. Western ranchers and cattlemen branded the special as unfair, and the Ford Motor Company, in withdrawing its advertising, agreed. A Ford spokesman cited segments that suggested that ranchers were "indiscriminate killers" of wildlife and that they were on "the public dole." Synar's proposal was backed by the National Audubon Society, the Sierra Club, the Wilderness Society, and the League of Conservation Voters, among others.[23]

But the fight was far from over. The House in June reconsidered BLM authorization for the fiscal years 1992 through 1995 because the Senate in the previous Congress had taken no action. Thus Synar, twenty-nine days after the House last approved his amendment, reintroduced his proposal, which now competed with an amendment offered by Ralph Regula, Republican from Ohio. Regula was in agreement that grazing fees should be increased, but only at a rate not to exceed 33 percent in any one year. Synar in his remarks commended Regula "for his excellent work in improving on what has been a mission between the gentleman from Georgia (Darden), the gentleman from Massachusetts (Atkins), and I to get fair market value for natural resources, not only for this generation, but for future generations." Fair market value to Synar meant charging everyone for the use of public lands, "whether it be for recreation, for minerals, or for grazing." Passage of either amendment, according to officials in both the BLM and Forest Service, would not involve the loss of a single lessee. What Synar was calling for, then, was the approval of the Regula amendment as a substitute for the amendment he was offering. It carried by a vote of 254 to 165. However, since the bill was opposed by the administration and the Senate, the measure again came to a political dead end. The BLM would rely, as it had since 1982, on an appropriation. The battle over grazing fees and reauthorization would continue, this time on a more intense level.[24]

Several days later wanted posters sprang up around Wyoming depicting the scowling faces of Synar, Atkins, and Darden, the "Hole-in-the Head Gang," "wanted for destruction of the West's social and economic structure and other acts against the peace and dignity of western states." The posters were signed by the Wyoming Stock Growers' Association, the Wyoming Wool Growers' Association, and the Wyoming Public Lands Council. The owner of the Muddy Gap Three Forks Service Station proudly hung one of the posters on the wall next to handwritten notes offering horses, hay, and trailers for sale. While the "gang" members were unpopular with western ranchers, officials with the Wyoming Farm Bureau said they knew of no organized effort to unseat the men in their 1992 election bids.[25]

However, within a month angry western ranchers began writing checks in multiples of $8.70, the goal of Synar's grazing-fee proposal, to support his potential primary opponent. "I don't care who the other guy is. We want to get rid of Synar," said Ed McNew, a livestock buyer in

Montrose, a western Colorado ranching town. McNew came across the funding solicitation at a sale barn in Montrose and quickly made copies to distribute. Unsigned notices were soon cropping up on bulletin boards at livestock sale barns in Wyoming and Montana as well. Colorado Congressman Ben Nighthorse Campbell thought that if 13,000 people holding federal grazing permits and paying the prevailing $1.97 per AUM contributed $10 each, the $130,000 would be most effective in an Oklahoma congressional campaign. Synar's press secretary responded that if ranchers could afford $10, they certainly could pay $8.70 for their grazing permits.[26]

Synar viewed his critics as harming both the land and most taxpayers, while huge operators, grazing thousands of acres of public lands, were in no way threatened by an increase in grazing fees. Among those he mentioned were the Metropolitan Life Insurance Company, Koch Industries of Wichita, the John Hancock Mutual Life Insurance Company, the Mormon Church, and the Utah Power and Light Corporation. These were not small mom-and-pop outfits seeking to preserve the family ranch. He soon dubbed these operators "welfare cowboys," who enjoyed a government subsidy that cost "140 million each year."[27] While Synar remained a public enemy throughout the ranching West and the Senate remained hostile to any increase in grazing fees, by the summer of 1991 it became evident that public-land policy was shifting, with preservation and recreation groups threatening mandates long enjoyed by ranchers, miners, and loggers. An increasing demand to utilize public lands for recreation promised to generate significant federal reserves and billions more in state tourism funds, overshadowing the amount of money secured from the more traditional industries that plied federal lands. In addition, demographic changes evident in the 1990 census showed that the West was almost as urban as the Northeast, with 83 percent of its residents residing in cities. With people living closer to federal lands, tensions arose among its varied users. And the political makeup of the House Interior Committee, which consistently supported Synar's efforts, included in 1991 only nine western members among its twenty-six Democrats, and three of them came from urban areas: Oakland, Los Angeles, and Salt Lake City.[28]

The Senate in September made it abundantly clear that the war was far from over. Westerners mustered a 60 to 38 vote to effectively kill the House measure that raised the current $1.97 monthly fee to $5.13 by 1996. Senator Pete Domenici of New Mexico called it a major victory after seven years of often emotional debate. But Synar, not discouraged, claimed that the grazing-fee hike "got 40 percent support in the Senate," indicating hope for the future. In an op-ed letter to the *Tulsa World*, Synar explained that ranchers in Oklahoma encountered the same problems as ranchers on public lands and at the same time were subsidizing 2 percent of America's cattlemen. He insisted that they "should not pick up the bill for operating the federal grazing program."[29]

Synar's views received a tremendous boost in November, when the General Accounting Office issued a report on rangeland management. It focused on the grazing program in the nation's so-called hot deserts—the Mojave, the Sonoran, and the Chihuahuan, located in Arizona, California, Nevada, New Mexico, and Utah. Among its conclusions were points Synar had previously noted: that livestock grazing on BLM allotments risked long-term environmental damage, that grazing-fee revenues were not sufficient to provide for adequate management, and that livestock grazing adversely impacted several wildlife species. All of these points led the General Accounting Office to conclude that "the BLM's current level of spending is insufficient to perform all necessary range management tasks."[30]

But the report went further and challenged the premises of Synar's critics. It concluded that "the economic benefits derived from livestock grazing on BLM lands in the hot desert areas are minimal," that BLM documents indicated that local economies did not depend on public lands ranching for survival, and that the primary economic benefits accrued to about a thousand operators holding grazing permits. The report also indicated that "many of those operators generate little net income from ranching the public lands." While the ranchers claimed an important benefit they received was the ability to maintain and enjoy a traditional ranching lifestyle, other public-land users valued the desert lands for recreation and environmental protection. Though the Government Accounting Office report reviewed rangeland management in only five states, Synar found support for his views in its conclusions.[31]

Meanwhile, Synar continued to arouse the anger of cattlemen. In November it was the president-elect of the National Cattlemen's Association, Jimmie Wilson, and in December Arizona rancher Alan Day, brother of Supreme Court Justice Sandra Day O'Connor, entered the fray. Both men sought to prevent Congress from raising grazing fees. But Day went further by trying to raise $500,000 to help defeat Synar in his 1992 primary race. Day insisted, "I'm not prompted by anybody in any organization. Nobody owns me. I'm a rancher that can see I can't exist if Mike Synar has his way." Synar responded in an equally blunt fashion: "I'd be upset too, if I were about to lose my sweetheart deal that I'm getting at the expense of other taxpayers." Day planned to contribute the funds he raised to Muskogee district attorney Drew Edmondson, Synar's expected opponent. But he admitted in December that he was not close to his $500,000 goal. Pam Neal, director of public lands for the National Cattlemen's Association, agreed with Day that people tended to forget that ranchers acted as caretakers of the public range. Day admitted to owning about 1,800 cattle, paying the government about $40,000 a year, or 3.5 cents an acre per month. He added that 30 percent of the ranch's grazing land was held by the Day family. It comprised more than 100,000 acres in southeastern Arizona and southwestern New Mexico; the other 70 percent was leased public land.[32]

The War in the West gained increased momentum in 1992, a presidential election year, as public land ranchers threatened to dispose of Synar by supporting his opponent in the Democratic primary. While these ranchers were battling to preserve their way of life, the myth of the West was growing among urban dwellers with extraordinary appetites for rural and western symbols. It was fueled by country singer Garth Brooks, who sold more albums in 1991 than any other musician in any category. Movies such as *City Slickers* were blockbusters, and western tourism shattered records. Cowboy hats and boots were finding acceptance among occupants of urban office towers, while no more than 3 percent of ranchers ran cattle on public lands. And to hear them tell it, Mike Synar, in seeking to raise grazing fees from $1.89 per AUM to more than $8.00, threatened their very existence. Western myth and reality were working at cross-purposes.[33]

The Bush administration, in an election year, finally recognized reality in Synar's criticisms. In March, the secretary of the interior, Manuel Lujan, called for an increase in grazing fees on public land and expressed confidence after talking with grazers that a regional average for what the private sector charged for leasing could be balanced by giving credit to the rancher for the improvements made on the public rangelands. While Lujan believed his proposal would be approved by the administration, he was not at all certain it would result in a bill before Congress. The proposal was a clear indication of the need for a more realistic set of grazing fees.[34]

But this need was not felt by Wyoming senator Alan Simpson, who debated Synar before a standing-room audience on Simpson's home turf in Jackson, Wyoming. Synar challenged Simpson to show him "one shred of evidence" that higher fees would harm western ranchers. Simpson retorted that in Washington "you can find a fact to support any argument." He insisted that raising fees would devastate the livestock industry, acknowledging at the same time that some federal land was damaged by overgrazing. But, he said, penalizing all ranchers would cause the downfall of many small towns, and if ranchers' fees were increased, then recreational land users, such as hikers and hunters, should also pay increased fees. "The people of this state would never take that medicine," Simpson told Synar, eliciting some catcalls, directed at Synar, from the capacity crowd. Synar's comments focused on below-market fees charged for the exploitation of natural resources on federal lands.[35]

Synar's outlook was sharply reinforced when a report prepared by the Departments of the Interior and Agriculture found that over the previous decade ranchers had paid less than 25 percent of the fair market value for forage on 250 million acres of public land, and that the government in 1991 spent $73.8 million to manage rangeland, with only $7.9 million in cash receipts deposited in the United States Treasury. Synar, who made it clear that he would use the report to promote his amendment that raised fees, found further ammunition in a May hearing of the House

Committee on Interior and Insular Affairs. While Synar did not testify, much of the testimony was grist to his mill, as was a feature story from the August 5, 1991, *New York Times*, entitled "A Range War of Words on Grazing in the West" which was included in the report. It suggested that public-lands ranchers were the most vocal and militant lobby against both fees and environmental protection.[36]

By the spring of 1992, the war was becoming more intense as Synar's primary campaign brought outside money into the coffers of his challenger, Drew Edmondson. Ranchers contributed $16,815 to Edmondson, and of that sum $15,515 was from ranchers out of state. Another $3,500 came from PACs representing ranchers. Later in the spring four prominent Idaho ranchers who supported Edmondson announced that they hoped to raise a nationwide $500,000 chest for him. And several Idaho cattlemen sent checks for $8.70, the level to which Synar was working to raise grazing fees.[37]

At this same time an Associated Press story reiterated Synar's view that grazing permits were not limited to ranchers. Fewer than five hundred corporations and wealthy individuals controlled nearly half—47 percent—of the 163 million acres leased by the BLM, according to congressional and Government Accounting Office researchers. Among them were Daniel H. Russell and his son, who had permits to graze cattle on 516 million acres in three states, and the ZX Land and Cattle Co. of Paisley, Oregon, a Metropolitan Life Insurance Company subsidiary with permits for 695,850 acres. This information helped Synar document his argument "that these are not bread and butter cowboys" grazing cattle on public lands. He reported that the five hundred largest permit holders controlled about 152,000 acres each.[38]

In July Synar's views were further reinforced when a House subcommittee asserted that "grazing is clearly not a benign use of our public lands," that reform proponents were "left with only blown out rangelands, degraded riparian areas and water quality, and uncharacteristic fauna such as the quail, pronghorn, and southwest willow fly-catcher." Clearly, the current fee system based on the 1978 Public Rangelands Improvement Act, which expired after the 1985 grazing year but which was continued by an executive order, was flexible and provided for annual adjustments reflecting changing economic conditions. Nevertheless, the subcommittee strongly advocated a change in the formula to one reflecting fair market value—more than $10 per AUM, higher than five times the current fee.[39]

By adopting a more equitable fee structure, along with other needed reforms, including the abolition of grazing advisory boards, the report concluded that Congress could make giant strides "towards relieving the taxpayer of the burden of supporting the destructive use of the public domain." It could also "generate increased revenues for the federal treasury," "put grazing on a more level playing field with other public land uses," and alleviate some of the funding shortfalls that hampered the BLM's ability to properly administer the lands. This report in its conclusions echoed Synar's views and set the agenda for the new administration installed in January 1993. Every Republican member of the House subcommittee was from the West, but the Democrats who chaired both the full committee and the subcommittee were southerners with no direct connection to western ranchers.[40]

To further boost Synar's hopes, the House on July 22, 1992, by a vote of 245 to 164, agreed to increase grazing fees by 33 percent, from $1.92 to $2.56 per AUM. In brief remarks Synar noted that for seven years, ever since the debate began, "as a Member who comes from a ranching family four generations deep, who is a two-time national 4-H winner," he had implored colleagues who opposed raising fees "to bring me the facts that would support their position." Not a single fact that supporters of fee increases presented in seven years, Synar asserted, "has ever been refuted by the Members who would argue that these grazing fees should not be raised." In the measures considered previously, the House had said that it was time to protect the taxpayers; now, Synar said, it is time to protect the environment. And as his time expired, he asked his colleagues "to do something which is long overdue, which is to give these Western whining welfare cowboys a good dose of free enterprise." Although Secretary Lujan said he would support changes in the fee structure, the Senate Appropriations Committee turned aside the issue and directed the Interior Committee to prepare a study on "new grazing fee concepts" by March 1, 1993. In September the House-Senate conferees killed Synar's proposal to raise grazing fees on public lands.[41]

At a hearing in Casper early in September, Senator Alan Simpson recalled his debate with Synar in Jackson. He claimed to have received "some rather fascinating mail," wherein "some folks evidently thought that I should have grabbed old Mike by the nape of the neck and ripped his collar button off and pitched him off the top deck of the Snow King Inn into the swimming pool which was frozen at the time." Simpson, of course, would not go that far, recognizing that Synar "is a very spirited person, rough and ornery," like Wyoming people, "sometimes." He also recognized that Synar in his reelection bid had been forced into a runoff in which 57 percent of the voters in his district had already voted for somebody else, and that "he might not make it back," Simpson adding that "hardly a tear will trickle down the cheeks of Wyoming folk at that time." As a realist, he recognized that even if Synar failed to return, there would be others "who will come and take up the cause, and the battle will continue."[42]

For several weeks in September the battle focused on Oklahoma's Second Congressional District, where Synar, one of only eight House members who did not accept contributions from political action committees, was locked in combat with Drew Edmondson. Synar had a long record to defend, while Edmondson, scion of a prominent political family, was seeking his first public office. Without a voting record to defend, he devoted his campaign to attacking Synar's. He attracted funds from powerful interests that Synar had managed to offend, and, as already noted, from western ranchers. Alan Day, with ranches in Arizona, New Mexico, and South Dakota, spearheaded the campaign. He reported that "I woke up one day and I wanted to do something for my industry that would have the most impact." It occurred to him that getting "Mike Synar selling shoes or flipping hamburgers" and getting him out of Congress would be worth the effort. These funds helped force Synar into a runoff with Edmondson, but in September Synar squeaked out a victory and assured himself an eighth term in Congress.[43]

Forthcoming change was evident after the election when the Bush administration, soon to be replaced, circulated a plan dramatically raising fees for ranchers who did not improve public ranges and wetlands. Synar proclaimed the plan "admits that the reformers have been right all along." The proposal surfaced after an audit by the Interior Department's inspector general revealed that 1,800 landowners could be making an estimated $5.2 million a year by subleasing their grazing rights. The plan would be tested in three western states, with the results submitted to Congress in March for the new administration, under President Bill Clinton, to review them. This proposal represented a victory for views Synar had expounded since 1983. As the fight to raise grazing fees now brought the War in the West closer to the center of national attention, Synar's central role in the controversy was to be diminished as the new secretary of the interior, Bruce Babbitt, a former Arizona governor and a policy wonk as well, began to push an aggressive agenda to raise grazing fees on public lands.[44]

No sooner was the new administration in office and the 103rd Congress under way than Synar introduced a bill to raise fees, commencing on March 1, 1993. His measure also called for the replacement of grazing advisory boards by "appropriate councils," with the federal share of grazing-fee receipts utilized "for restoration and improved management of riparian areas, and for implementation and enforcement of applicable land management plans, allotment plans, and regulations regarding the use of such lands for domestic live-stock grazing." In his remarks Synar made much of the fact that the measure could save taxpayers $325 million over the next five fiscal years. He expressed confidence that savings could be used "to fully fund federal range improvement activities on a 'pay as you go' basis." By no longer focusing exclusively on grazing, Synar was suggesting the approach Bruce Babbitt would emphasize in seeking range reform.[45]

His standing improved considerably when early in the new administration he was elected to chair the Democratic Study Group. Synar stated that congressional reform would be his main focus. And he was pleased when the Interior Department early in March announced that the secretary, Bruce Babbitt, would hold a series of meetings throughout the West on the government's plan to increase grazing fees as part of the Clinton administration's 1993 budget. Ranchers now signaled a willingness to consider the matter, a marked change from their vigorous opposition to past congressional efforts to change the fee structure. With the Clinton administration on record as backing an increase, the ranching industry appeared ready to deal, or, as Synar said, "to accept the inevitable." A spokesman for the National Cattlemen's Association suggested why ranchers had shifted their outlook: They would rather get in on Babbitt's deliberations than battle congressional efforts to increase their fees each year. Ranchers would be at the table for the meetings Babbitt scheduled in Montana, in Denver, and in Albuquerque in the spring, and all indications were that a plan would emanate from these meetings. "If you're a western rancher," Synar remarked, "your fees for grazing on federal lands will be more equal to those paid by Oklahoma ranchers, an increment that presumably would be passed on to consumers in the form of higher beef prices."[46]

While ranchers were willing to accept the inevitable, western senators lined up in opposition to a proposed 33 percent annual increase in grazing fees over a five-year period. Clinton's public-lands package also included increased fees or royalties for the production of hard-rock minerals, for recreational use, and for water irrigation. So intense was Senate opposition that by April there were signs that the administration would back down on aspects of its western land-use proposals. To firm up the wavering administration in its commitment to raising fees, Synar, as chairman of the Environment, Energy, and Natural Resources Subcommittee of the Government Operations Committee, threatened to stall action on a bill to elevate the Environmental Protection Agency to Cabinet status by claiming that his subcommittee was too busy to consider the legislation.[47]

And his strategy worked. Synar was assured by the White House that the president remained committed to raising grazing fees. "My enthusiasm is enhanced," he exclaimed, "as we come to closure on the important fee increases necessary to reduce the budget, to save the taxpayers money, and to improve the environment." A Synar aide said that Clinton had sent assurances of his commitment to fee increases about an hour after the controversy erupted.[48]

Thus the process started anew, with a House subcommittee holding hearings on grazing-management reform and increasing fees. The measure was introduced, as in the previous bill, by Synar and Regula. Again it called for abolishing grazing boards and for using the grazing-fee receipts to enhance the environment on the public rangelands. Synar and Regula were the lead-off witnesses for the Interior subcommittee that had actively considered these measures for the previous six years. The House in the previous two years had voted three times to revise grazing fees and to make other changes in law and policy that were again included in the bill now under consideration. In his statement Synar asserted that both he and Regula understood that a healthy livestock industry was an important element in maintaining "the western open space and western economy." But they did not believe that retaining "low cost grazing rights for 23,000 public rangeland livestock producers" was essential in sustaining western values. He issued one more report, similar to those he had presented over the previous eight years, insisting that none of the facts had ever been challenged. The BLM was irresponsible, its program demonstrating a lax attitude toward its expenditures and the condition of the lands it administered. Establishing reasonable rates for leasing publicly owned assets, Synar proclaimed, was both fair and just.[49]

Bruce Babbitt soon overshadowed Synar in arguing that federal grazing lands were overused and underpriced. In May he started touring the West, insisting that the Clinton administration was committed to raising fees in order to more closely reflect the market value of forage. But Babbitt, seeking consensus and "sensitive to families living on that land," told audiences that proposals would be drafted only after public meetings were held, adding that "then we're going to come back and do it all over again." Synar, delighted with Babbitt's remarks, commended the secretary as an ally in the fight against the unwarranted subsidies afforded individuals and corporations grazing livestock on federal lands. In doing so, he continued to chip away at the rugged individualism of western myth by dramatizing the ranchers' reliance on generous federal subsidies.[50]

But the fact that the administration, buffeted by pressure from western senators, scuttled its budget package raising grazing fees meant that Babbitt's search for another route to reform would foment further hostility in the West. The administration's sudden reversal angered those lawmakers and environmentalists who saw the budget process as the best way for resolving the situation. Babbitt, seeking to reform policy through administrative action, in part by reconciling contending groups, recognized that fundamental changes would be impossible to achieve through legislative action. Since he was seeking more than grazing reform on public lands, his efforts would meet more intense opposition than Synar's. Babbitt's approach through public meetings meant that western senators would have more time to consider compromises. While he indicated early on that "the question is not if these changes will occur, but how they will occur," the deeper question was whether the administration would seek to change some procedures or reform the entire system.[51]

How serious Babbitt was, and how intense the War in the West had become, was evident in a news item reporting that the Department of the Interior was considering revoking privately held water rights on government land. It proposed to do this by dramatically changing the management of western grazing lands, by making the BLM the sole owner of water rights. Lawmakers fought back in July, when the House dropped from the Interior Appropriations Bill a provision that increased grazing fees to market value, calling it a policy question inserted in a spending bill. Synar announced during the debate that once again he would push separate legislation to raise federal grazing fees up to market value.[52]

Babbitt meanwhile was developing a proposal to accomplish the same thing, using his authority. He was seeking a fee schedule assuring a fair value for taxpayers that could relate to land management reform. In brief, Babbitt was seeking grazing-policy options for overseeing public lands. At a press conference President Clinton explained that "what we had hoped to do is to turn that whole issue into an environmental one, that is, to give ranchers incentives to continually restore the ranch land as a way of avoiding higher fees and also to make sure that any fees that were imposed were not economically crippling to the people involved." He acknowledged that Babbitt was traveling throughout the West, visiting with ranchers and cattlemen, to discuss what could be done to ensure that "we're being environmentally responsible with this federal land and how we can use the grazing fee structure in a way that would encourage that."[53]

While Babbitt, armed with administrative authority to change policy, was conferring throughout the West, lawmakers appeared more willing to reach a legislative compromise in the summer of 1993 than ever before.

For the first time, western senators endorsed a measure (S. 1326) that would increase grazing fees 25 percent. And the House of Representatives again approved the grazing-fee proposal of Synar and Regula that would raise grazing fees 33 percent until fair market value was reached. Its supporters claimed the proposal would add weight to Babbitt's final recommendations. Exuberant about these developments, Synar thought the battle had been won "to get these whining welfare cowboys off the subsidy." Though either the secretary of the interior or that of agriculture could change grazing policy without legislation, Synar and others, including environmentalists and some industry representatives, favored legislation in order to avoid further changes and economic uncertainty under another administration.[54]

But the Clinton administration, on August 9, acted before Congress approved a bill. It proposed to more than double grazing fees. The increase would be phased in over three years to avoid harming ranchers. The changes envisioned greater involvement by local officials and environmentalists in formulating policy, including a provision allowing them to block permits for ranchers who poorly managed their public lands. Again Synar was delighted, exclaiming that the decision put the fee issue "out to pasture." The administration's proposal "was sound and practical," Synar said, "because it realizes that only the market place can allocate federal rangeland policies." Not everyone accepted Synar's evaluation. Environmental groups saw the reforms as a good start; ranchers and western members of Congress blasted them as misguided and draconian, claiming they would drive ranchers off public lands and harm the West's economy, their standard argument against change.[55]

The grazing rules, which applied to 270 million federal acres, were not expected to go into effect until late 1994, leaving ample time for lengthy public comment. Environmentalists and others were pleased that the new regulations would impose a steep surcharge on ranchers who leased federal lands and then rented them out, thereby unfairly profiting at taxpayer expense. Babbitt made it clear that decisions to issue grazing permits and their durations would take into account how ranchers managed the federal lands they utilized. In addition, the government would take over ownership of improvements made on the land as well as all claims for water rights, including ownership of any irrigation improvements.[56]

No sooner had Babbitt presented his proposal to overhaul public land policy than the western senators dealt him a serious setback in the form of an amendment to the fiscal 1994 Interior Appropriations Bill, which stopped the government from funding new policies to boost grazing fees and stricter environmental controls on federal rangelands. Environmentalists, the White House, and House members, Synar in the lead, planned to fight the moratorium in the form of a motion directing members to reject the Senate amendment. Failure to do so posed a serious threat to the administration's hope for overhauling western public lands. But it also placed the operation and upkeep of these lands in the home states of many senators in jeopardy. This was the argument Synar made when he suggested that "they may have shot themselves in the foot." At a news conference he added that the Senate's proposal was "a recipe for gridlock."[57]

In brief floor remarks in late September, Synar reviewed his arguments in favor of raising fees to encourage defeat of the Senate amendment. He noted that the secretaries of the interior and agriculture "went out to five public meetings and heard from literally thousands of citizens," and then discussed their views. Synar recognized that for those who supported the Senate moratorium there would never "be a right time to increase the grazing fee and there is never going to be an increase that is acceptable." This was most unfortunate because, Synar said, "this administration under the leadership of Bruce Babbitt, has given us a wise and workable solution to a long standing dispute that very frankly we in Congress simply cannot resolve." By an overwhelming vote of 314 to 109, the House instructed its conferees to insist on disagreement with the Senate amendment that placed a moratorium on efforts to reform government policy for livestock grazing on public lands. The stage was now set for a conference-committee showdown to determine if the gridlock could be broken.[58]

The gridlock was quickly broken because the Clinton administration agreed to a compromise with key Democratic members of Congress.

Accepting a more modest fee increase kept intact most of the reform package for public lands that Babbitt had proposed earlier. The compromise was struck among Senator Harry Reid of Nevada, several House Democrats, including Synar, and Interior Department officials. Reid announced the plan to the conferees. If the conference committee approved the compromise, it still needed congressional approval to reduce proposed rates from $4.28 per AUM, phased in over three years, to $3.45. This compromise gained the support of Democrats on the conference committee and thereby broke the logjam stalling the fiscal 1994 Interior Appropriations Bill. The compromise called for a relatively modest increment, though western Republicans in the Senate vowed to fight it. Senators Pete Domenici of New Mexico and Malcolm Wallop of Wyoming threatened a filibuster. Looming behind this maneuvering and war of words was the recognition that Babbitt had the authority to increase grazing fees administratively. Indeed, as noted above, the Senate had earlier sidetracked a Babbitt proposal to raise fees by barring for one year the expenditure of funds to implement any fee increase. This time, leaving nothing to chance, Babbitt sat outside the room where the negotiators were working on a grazing-fee compromise agreement.[59]

Whether Babbitt's positioning himself outside the conference room influenced the discussion is unknown, but he had to be pleased with the outcome, which Mike Synar, who was in the room, said would force ranchers to pay fair prices for their public-land leases. Synar announced that grazing fees would increase from $2.39 per AUM in 1994 to $3.45 two years later, when they would be hooked into the market value. "Finally," Synar remarked, "we are managing the government like a business"—and launching a new era of cooperation between House and Senate members. The amendment marked the first time that House and Senate negotiators had agreed to boost grazing fees. Western senators, however, vowed to stage a filibuster to kill the amendment. They sought fairness for ranchers whose livelihood, they argued, would be threatened by higher grazing fees. In addition, opponents were angry about the overhaul of rangeland policies included in the amendment crafted by Senator Reid in accord with Babbitt's views. It called for the abolition of grazing advisory boards, terminating the practice of granting ranchers ownership of stock ponds and other facilities they developed on federal land, and tying the length of a rancher's lease to environmental stewardship. As Babbitt raised the stakes by seeking to overhaul government policies on public lands, the War in the West would reach new levels of intensity.[60]

The House, several days later, on October 20, 1993, approved the Interior Appropriations Bill, with the compromise amendment, by a substantial majority, 317 to 106. Synar concluded the debate by admitting to "a little bit of melancholy" regarding what he thought would be the last debate "on this issue of grazing in the career of most of us." First he thanked colleagues who had played a prominent role in the fight. Then he addressed "the two very serious assertions and complaints" against the conference report. The first was that it constituted an attack on private property rights. Synar dismissed the charge by stating that it "was a complaint that the grazers made as early as 1906 . . . when we first imposed fees on federal lands." He noted that the Supreme Court in 1911 ruled "that grazing permits do not confer any private property rights."[61]

More immediate was the second objection, that the conference report changed the relationship between the federal government and the West "without adequate public input and without one single public hearing." Synar said the charge was "completely false," in that the Department of the Interior "under the leadership of Bruce Babbitt" held five public hearings throughout the West and that the administration had received "over 30,000 comments on the Range Reform bill of 1994 and they have been 2 to 1 in favor of that report." Moreover, he asserted, the reforms were not new. They merely "return us to the management of the BLM lands the way they were before Secretary James Watt unilaterally changed the grazing management in the 1980's." And he reminded his colleagues that his subcommittee in 1985 documented the grazing problem. From that conference report, he asserted, "the Range Reform Act of 1994 was written." The issue had been studied "almost to a point of ad nauseum." It had been debated on the House floor every year since 1976, with two "simple facts that have been undisputed." The first was that "the taxpayers of this country have lost more than a billion dollars during the decade of the 1980's subsidizing 2 percent of the cattle industry." And the second undeniable fact was that "as much as 60 percent of the public rangelands throughout our country will continue to be in fair or poor condition well into the next century." Synar urged his colleagues to stay the course "as we turn the page of history, ending an era of gridlock and opening a new age of bipartisan cooperation for public land and for budget reform." While the measure still needed Senate approval, Synar understood that even if the Senate defeated the bill, Babbitt would be free to increase fees administratively in 1994.[62]

The Senate, however, did not go gentle into that good night. A filibuster got under way, and three efforts to cut off debate, to secure the sixty votes necessary for cloture, were not successful. Infuriated and frustrated, Secretary Babbitt announced on October 28 that he would move to raise grazing fees and implement further rangeland management requirements, stating that "as long as gridlock persists, the department cannot stand idly by, waiting interminably for reform that never seems to happen." While western Republican senators filibustered, the two sides were closer to agreement than many observers realized. The senators were willing to accept increased grazing fees, but they vehemently objected to Babbitt's insistence on changes in public-land management policies. However, with almost every newspaper in the West endorsing the compromise, Babbitt was emerging as the federal marshal seeking to establish law and order in a region dominated by ranchers well able to pay higher grazing fees and to treat public lands with greater care. In short, Babbitt sought to bypass the Senate filibuster with written regulations not requiring legislative approval.[63]

But persistent Senate opposition, led by Republican senator Pete Domenici of New Mexico, led the administration, then seeking approval of the North American Free Trade Agreement (NAFTA), to back away. Babbitt's reforms had backfired because they were perceived to single out small family ranchers. On November 9 Reid agreed to drop the grazing compromise from the Interior Appropriations Bill, whereupon Domenici agreed to stop stalling the bill. The Senate approved the conference report, as did the House. Synar bewailed the fact that while "democracy's breaking out in every part of the world . . . we can't get democracy practiced on the floor of the Senate. Unless they deal with the filibuster, we're kidding ourselves that we're going to have the kind of change we so desperately need."[64]

With Babbitt backing down, a wave of optimism became evident among ranchers who grazed cattle on public lands. The president of the Wyoming Farm Bureau Federation beamed, while observing that "the federal bureaucracy has looked at the region as a wonderful playground for its environmental friends" and that the media was more "concerned about introducing wolves into national parks than with the lives of the West's people." But in helping ranchers regain their self-esteem, western senators, with the exception of Harry Reid, infuriated environmentalists. As 1993 came to an end, Synar, the Clinton administration, and federal rangeland reformers suffered a severe setback. The 27,000 western ranchers, dubbed "welfare cowboys" by Synar, once again rode high in the saddle. But with the defeat of the grazing-fee compromise, Babbitt was still free to pursue his other proposals through administrative action. The War in the West had not yet ended.[65]

The Department of the Interior budget for 1995 called for increased grazing fees, using the very same proposal that Congress had previously turned down. The proposal was part of the Clinton administration's scaled-back plan to protect rangelands from excessive commercial grazing. The fee increases would be phased in over three years, and the measure would for the first time declare new improvements made by ranchers to be the property of the government. Grazing fees would increase from the current $1.96 per AUM to $2.75 for the first year, rising to $3.96 by the third year, a decline from the $4.28 per AUM Babbitt had suggested previously. For about three-fourths of the ranchers, the higher fees, Babbitt claimed, would mean an increase in costs of less than $1,000 a year, a figure that could be reduced if ranchers met certain land-protection standards. But a surcharge could be levied if a rancher subleased a grazing permit.[66]

In this proposal, grazing advisory boards would be replaced by local advisory councils made up of ranchers, business interests, and wildlife experts. The councils would play a role in developing rangeland policy, including the ability to appeal local BLM decisions to Washington. And now, for the first time, ranchers would have to meet specific standards and guidelines, with local and state officials exercising broad authority in developing the standards. Babbitt's focus called for "shifting more management decisions closer to the land," While environmentalists expressed concern that the advisory councils would be dominated by ranching interests, Brad Little, an official of the American Sheep Industry Association, declared that "Babbitt's original proposal killed Western ranching. The new proposal puts us in intensive care." Synar recognized that the proposal was an improvement, but he was far from satisfied, stating that "it simply doesn't represent the level of reform we've been working on for these many, many years."[67]

Differing opinions clearly indicated that the War in the West had not yet run its course. Ranchers and their allies in the Senate continued to stymie responsible change, while urban westerners and environmentalists called for greater control of public lands. New western residents were attracted to the weather, quality of life, entrepreneurial spirit, and the region's tax structure. Few were coming to ranch. They looked to the public lands for relaxation and recreation. Hunters, hikers, campers, fishermen, bikers, and off-road vehicle enthusiasts were increasing in numbers, and were calling for the protection of wild and scenic rivers and endangered species, while forests and national parks were gaining increased attention. In addition, western states were also recognizing the economic significance of tourism based on public-land resources.

Secretary Bruce Babbitt, through his "Proposed Rule for Rangeland Reform '94," enunciated in the *Federal Register* and elsewhere, sought a compromise through a series of round table discussions in which interested parties could help shape the Interior Department's grazing proposal. These new groups began to listen to each other and develop mutual confidence as they searched for areas of agreement. Governor Roy Romer of Colorado started the process by bringing together a group of ranchers and environmentalists around his conference table. Babbitt attended an early session, was encouraged, and agreed to return for weekly meetings. Soon he was traveling throughout the West, meeting with similar groups interested not in staking out obvious positions but in finding reasonable accommodation with the needs of their neighbors. As the weeks went by, Babbitt realized that these groups, as an integral part of land management, could set policy as well as deal with its implementation. Change could not occur unless it was supported with "communication and consensus building among all stakeholders, especially those who live in the West." It was Babbitt's fervent belief that "in the New West the stakeholders, in all their diversity, can come together and forge a new consensus for public land management."[68]

But he had no intention of yielding on grazing fees, and this was the sticking point as ranchers and their political allies geared up for the 1994 mid-term elections. In a set of Senate hearings in Washington and Albuquerque, members led by Wyoming's retiring senator, Malcolm Wallop, announced their opposition to the secretary's program. Babbitt was on hand at both meetings to explain his position and to facilitate discussion. The senators and most of the witnesses were hostile to Babbitt's proposals, insisting in some instances that the range was in good condition, that ranchers were good land managers, and that Babbitt's program would adversely affect their livelihoods and the communities that served them.[69]

Grazing fees remained a hot topic, one that held dire implications for congressional supporters of Babbitt's land-use policies as the mid-term elections neared. In Colorado, for example, Senator Hank Brown charged that his state needed to fight grazing reforms because they would price many ranchers out of business and lead to an "environmental catastrophe." On the other hand, Governor Roy Romer was undaunted by Brown's complaints and argued, as did Babbitt, that changes in the final plan would be made as views presented at the round table meetings, along with others sent to the secretary, were evaluated. This approach was appeasement to some environmentalists who argued that the administration's proposed rangeland reforms offered no protection to dozens of wildlife species headed for extinction because of livestock grazing on public land.[70]

As the War in the West raged on, Babbitt and his Senate critics were now the dominant players. With no grazing legislation under consideration, Synar was relegated to the sidelines. But when the House considered the California Desert Protection Act, he spoke in favor of allowing current holders of grazing permits in the Mojave National

Park to continue operating until their permits expired, but no longer. He observed that intensive grazing in the California desert was particularly harmful to these arid lands and would cost more to administer than the federal government could receive in permit fees. The amendment Synar endorsed was defeated by a vote of 190 ayes and 207 nays, one of the rare defeats his point of view experienced in the House of Representatives.[71]

During the summer months, as the public comment period on the Interior Department's grazing reform proposals came to an end, Babbitt toured the West answering questions, listening to criticisms, and explaining his proposals. In rural Utah, for example, at a field hearing of the Senate Energy and Natural Resources Committee, he sat in the audience for five hours listening to the remarks of more than eighty Utahans, almost all of whom expressed fear about what rangeland reform would mean for their families and their livelihoods. In response, the secretary reiterated that grazing was "an enduring, important, positive part of the western landscape," that "the right level of grazing increases the diversity of plants and wildlife on the lands." What was necessary, he insisted, was to sunder "this long culture and tradition of fighting and divisiveness, to break [the tension] between urban and rural, between environmental[ist] and rancher." But in Utah, as elsewhere, most people attending these meetings were in opposition, as were most of the local and state officials, including professors, who presented data that contradicted the premises that Babbitt, Synar, and other proponents of rangeland reform presented.[72]

Babbitt's proposal, the one that most aroused western interests, called for $3.96 per AUM to be reached in 1997. In 1994 ranchers who used state grazing lands paid anywhere from $8.71 per AUM in North Dakota to $3.50 in Wyoming. The base rates on private lands in the western states were even higher, as much as $20. To be sure, state and private leases came with fencing, water, and other advantages that holders of federal permits had to provide themselves. While these differences were real, as Synar and others, including the Government Accounting Office, admitted, they in no way accounted for the enormous gap between the prevailing fee of $1.96 per AUM and all other fees. According to the secretaries of interior and agriculture, the grazing program cost $73 million annually to administer; fees brought in only about $27 million, a portion of which went to the states, a portion to the advisory boards, and a larger portion to fund the BLM and the Forest Service for projects benefitting range resources. As George Miller, a colleague of Synar's, asserted, "Uncle Sam charges fees well below the market and less than half of what it costs to run the grazing program, they spend more than half of the pittance it takes in to build fences, water lines, and stock ponds and manipulate vegetation." Moreover, as Synar continually noted, while there were about 24,000 permittees on 250 million acres of Forest Service and BLM lands, a small number, about 5,000 of them, controlled about 88 percent of the AUMs in the BLM program. Instead of driving ranchers off the land, Babbitt's proposals represented a sensible attempt to achieve balance in a program that then overwhelmingly favored one special interest at the expense of the environment, the taxpayers, and the many multiple users of the federal range.[73]

Synar did not play a prominent role in Babbitt's campaign during the summer because he was involved in a stiff battle to retain his seat. In the August primary he won only 47 percent of the vote against two little-known opponents and was forced into a September runoff election. In addition, the Republican candidate was running advertisements tying Synar to President Clinton, as well as denouncing the stands he had taken on broad issues that aroused powerful interests such as the National Rifle Association, tobacco companies, and cattlemen. Even more telling was the anti-Washington sentiment on the rise in Oklahoma. While Synar never let the winds of public opinion make his decisions, he was always forthright in explaining them to his constituents. Nevertheless, after eight terms representing the Second Congressional District in Oklahoma, Synar, at age forty-four, was defeated in the September 20 primary by 1,200 votes. In turn, his seventy-one-year-old opponent was defeated in November by his Republican challenger.[74]

Synar's defeat was a stunning blow to his congressional colleagues who championed grazing reform. But now that Bruce Babbitt was leading the fight from the executive branch, Synar's defeat was not as devastating to the cause as it might have been. He had an opportunity to return to the fray when he was invited to replace the embattled Mike Espy as secretary of agriculture. Synar took himself out of the running, explaining, tongue in cheek, to a White House official that "my last legislative goal was to solve the health care crisis, not create new ones," adding, "I could not sleep at night knowing I was giving heart attacks to the grazing, pesticide and tobacco industries."[75]

But the shootout in the West continued. Synar was the most prominent casualty as Republican candidates throughout the West ran against the Clinton administration's efforts to tighten controls on the use of public lands. With the heart, soul, and future of the American West at stake, Republicans blamed the president and Babbitt as being the perpetrators of the War on the West. Rangeland reform found few friends among western voters in the off-term election, and the results were a severe rebuff to the administration. Clinton later admitted that "the Interior Department made a mistake. . . . They proposed as a negotiating strategy raising the grazing fees too high in 1993." The strategy was wrong, and it was dropped. In 1995 the administration, in Clinton's words, was trying "to develop a responsible way of managing the federally owned lands that permit people to continue to graze them in a responsible manner."[76]

While Clinton was seeking a responsible way, western ranchers, with a responsive Congress in place, were supporting the Livestock Grazing Act sponsored by Senator Pete Domenici, Republican of New Mexico, and Representative Wes Cooley, Republican of Oregon. It would bring decision-making power closer to the local communities that depended on access to federal lands, and in doing so it would completely eradicate the program Babbitt was trying to create. From the perspective of the reformers, the bill enshrined livestock grazing as the dominant use on millions of acres, grazing that Babbitt, Synar, and others had sought to balance with competing interests. One environmentalist dubbed the measure "cowboy socialism."[77]

The law proposed to raise grazing fees slightly and create locally appointed boards of ranchers to monitor rangeland activities, thereby obviating Babbitt's plan. While the legislative tussle was not resolved in1995, with Republicans in control of the Congress, the ranchers had pushed the public aside in the battle over the use of public lands. "It's over," said Dave Nelson, who managed the Idaho ranching operations for computer billionaires William Hewlett and David Packard. Their cattle grazed on nearly 100,000 acres of federal land that adjoined their 15,000-acre private ranch. "The environmentalists," Nelson added, "have lost, and all they can do now is take potshots." Ranchers would be free from heavy regulation, and Clinton would be reluctant, given the Republican resurgence in Congress, to take on the livestock industry again. To ensure his reluctance, western ranchers filed suit in federal court in Cheyenne, Wyoming, to block the Department of the Interior from implementing an overhaul of grazing regulations. Babbitt's new rules made no mention of higher grazing fees, setting minimum standards for the management of federal lands but also creating regional "resource advisory councils" on which environmentalists would be guaranteed a place and including provisions allowing the federal government to claim all land and water improvements made by ranchers. Meanwhile, in July, the Senate Energy and Natural Resources Committee approved the measure introduced by Domenici and Cooley, and the House Resources Subcommittee followed suit in September. The proposals were then incorporated into the fiscal 1996 Interior Appropriations Bill. The conferees, in approving the measure, agreed to postpone until later in the year the implementation of the Interior Department regulations scheduled to go into effect on August 21. However, the whole matter became bogged down by divisions among western conservatives more supportive of the prevailing system and "deficit hawks" and environmentalists who opposed the fee structure as a federal giveaway. No measure was approved in 1995 as the 103rd Congress came to an end.[78]

For the remaining years of Babbitt's tenure, Congress fruitlessly debated overhauling rangeland management. Although there was general dissatisfaction with the management of western lands, clashes of interest and ideology thwarted efforts to craft a measure that could gain congressional or White House approval. While ranchers and their supporters in Congress largely dominated the debate, they were now in competition with growing numbers of backpackers, mountain bikers, bird watchers, ecologists, and others. And their spokespersons in Congress, not as well organized as the ranching interests, played a role in stymieing grazing legislation. Gridlock prevailed in the Congress, as Babbitt's administrative rules, in effect since late 1995, left ranchers writhing in anger. Their chief spokesman in Congress, Senator Pete Domenici, tangled with Secretary

Babbitt, whose rules Domenici's supporters considered an assault on their interests, one that made the bureaucracy more onerous. On the other side, critics argued that Babbitt's regulations did not go far enough, claiming that by not significantly raising grazing fees they continued an unjustified federal subsidy. No one throughout the extended controversy called for ending public ownership of the rangelands; the issue was about how they should be managed.[79]

Mike Synar died from brain cancer on January 10, 1996, at age forty-five, at a time when no resolution of the controversy appeared forthcoming. And that was the way it remained at the end of the Clinton administration. However, in an opinion written by Justice Stephen Breyer, the Supreme Court's decision of May 25, 2000, upheld the regulations instituted by Bruce Babbitt, declaring "that the Secretary is free reasonably to determine just how, and the extent to which grazing privileges are to be safeguarded." It rejected the petitioner's claims that the 1995 regulations exceeded the secretary's authority under the Taylor Grazing Act. Among the groups filing briefs of amicus curiae in support of the Public Lands Council's opposition to Babbitt's regulations were the state of Wyoming, the Alameda Bookcliffs Ranch et al., the Association of Rangeland Consultants, and the Pacific Legal Foundation. There were only two briefs urging affirmance: the Natural Resources Defense Council and the Nature Conservancy. Justice Stephen Breyer, writing for the Court, presented a comprehensive review of grazing on public lands starting with the first successful long drive of cattle north from Texas in 1867, but he devoted most of his attention to the period following the enactment of the Taylor Grazing Act in 1934 through to the end of the twentieth century. There were no dissents. Justice Sandra Day O'Connor, possibly with her brother's bitter opposition to Synar's efforts to raise grazing fees in mind, wrote a brief concurring opinion in which Justice Clarence Thomas joined. O'Connor wished to confirm that permit holders who believed that the specific application of the 1995 regulations deprived them "to such an extent that the Secretary's conduct can be termed a failure to adequately safeguard such privileges" could challenge the secretary's action.[80]

With the decision by the Supreme Court in 2000 the War in the West came to an end. There were winners and losers. Among the losers was Mike Synar. He not only lost his life and his seat in Congress, but the fight he launched to raise grazing fees on federal rangelands to a level commensurate with market conditions, thereby eliminating subsidization of western ranchers, among them some of America's wealthiest individuals and corporations. Among the winners was Bruce Babbitt, whose 1995 rangeland reforms effectively destroyed one of the most powerful iron triangles wherein ranchers and local and regional BLM and Forest Service agents, tied in with pertinent officials in Washington, made any change in fee structure and prevailing range conditions almost impossible to achieve. By eliminating the grazing boards and creating public land councils, environmentalists and other users of the public lands would now serve alongside ranchers. Multiple-use advisory boards would seek multiple uses for the rangelands. Grazing-fee receipts would now be utilized to support range improvement rather than ventures directed toward increased benefits for ranchers. Politically speaking, the rangeland reforms helped make the cause of the Democratic Party most difficult in states such as Wyoming, Utah, New Mexico, Colorado, and Arizona, where powerful ranchers grazed livestock on public lands. On the other hand, the controversy revealed to large numbers of citizens that these powerful ranchers, all rugged individualists, staunch believers in free enterprise, many of them contemptuous of government officials, had feet of clay and were subsidized by grazing fees that were infinitesimal compared with fees charged to graze on state lands, private lands, or other government lands such as military installations. For a brief period, these western ranchers, subjects of public ridicule, bitterly resented the exposure that Synar and others brought to public attention. The sanctity of the wide open public range was destroyed. Thanks in good part to Synar's efforts in challenging the culture and mythology of the West, the image of ranchers perpetrated by Hollywood, the advertising industry, and writers of pulp fiction was briefly impaired. While ranchers still have political clout, today they are challenged by corporate interests with more clout seeking to tap into vast reserves of natural gas and minerals on public lands. The West in the twenty-first century, the post–Synar-Babbitt West, could see a new war in which ranchers, environmentalists, and others ally themselves to battle outside corporate interests that seek to intrude on their turf.[81]

Notes

1. *Daily Oklahoman* (Oklahoma City), July 26, 1987. The quotation appears in an article by Allan Cromley.

2. *Congressional Record*, 100th Cong., 2nd sess., June 4, 1987, 14801. The grazing fee is paid by animal unit month (AUM), the amount of monthly forage needed to sustain one animal unit (one cow and calf, one horse, or five sheep or goats). Half of the fees collected were returned to the agencies (Forest Service or Bureau of Land Management) and deposited in a range-betterment fund. Portions of the remaining 50 percent were allocated to the states and the United States Treasury.

3. Ibid.; *Management of Livestock Grazing* hearing.

4. *Congressional Record*, 100th Cong., 2nd sess., 4 June 1987, 14801.

5. *Grazing Fee Review and Evaluation: Final Report 1979–1985*. Report of the Secretaries of Agriculture and the Interior, February 1986 (Washington, D.C.), p. 3.

6. The information in the above paragraphs is based in part on Synar's opening remarks before a subcommittee of the Committee on Government Operations of the House of Representatives. *Management of Livestock Grazing on Federal Lands by the Bureau of Land Management and the Forest Service.* 99th Cong., 1st sess., December 13, 1985. The hearings were printed for the use of the Committee on Government Operations.

7. *Federal Grazing Program: All is Not Well on the Range*, 99th Congress, 2nd sess., May 8, 1986, H. Rep. 99-593, 1–2 and passim.

8. Grazing Fees and Public Rangeland Management: Hearing before the Subcommittee on National Parks and Public Lands of the Committee on Interior and Insular Affairs, House of Representatives, 100th Cong., 1st sess., September 22, 1987, 41–53. Synar's oral remarks appear on pp. 41–42. The remaining pages comprise his formal written statement and accompanying documents. These hearings allowed presenters five minutes for their oral presentations. Their formal statements were included as part of their remarks. Synar's reiteration of his concern about riparian areas appears in the *Congressional Record*, 100th Cong., 2nd sess., July 12, 1988, 17480.

9. Reauthorization of the BLM: Hearing before the Subcommittee on National Parks and Public Lands of the Committee on Interior and Insular Affairs, 101st Cong., 1st sess., April 11, 1989, 46–48. See also Synar's brief remarks during a House debate on a BLM funding bill. *Congressional Record*, 101st Cong., 1st sess., July 17, 1989, 14881–82.

10. "Retiring Land Use Manager Applauded, Criticized," *Tulsa World*, July 5 1989, p. 12A. In another tirade that caught public attention, Synar claimed the government was losing up to $10 billion a year "by leasing or selling natural resources at prices below market value" and cited as examples below-cost national forest timber sales and below-cost grazing fees. See also articles in the *Daily Oklahoman*, February 28, 1990, p. 6, and *Tulsa World*, February 28, 1990, p. A16.

11. *Tulsa World*, Jury 25, 1990, p. A2.

12. *Congressional Record*, 101st Cong., 2nd sess., October 3, 1990, 27416; *Tulsa World*, October 16, 1990, p. B6.

13. *Congressional Quarterly Almanac: 1999*, in vol. 46 (Washington, D.C.: Congressional Quarterly, 1991), 873–74.

14. *Congressional Record*, 102nd Cong., 1st sess., February 6, 1991, 3277–78.

15. Ibid.

16. Ibid.

17. BLM Reauthorization and Grazing Fees: Hearing before the Subcommittee on National Parks and Public Lands of the Committee on Interior and Insular Affairs, House of Representatives, 102nd Cong., 2nd sess. (hearing held in Washington, D.C., March 12, 1991). Synar's oral remarks are found on pp. 25–27; see pp. 28–35 for his written testimony supporting the Fair Market Grazing for Public Rangelands Act of 1991.

18. *BLM Reauthorization and Grazing Fees* (comments of many western witnesses.) See also *Tulsa World*, March 13, 1991, p. A2, and March 31, 1991, p. A10.

19. *Tulsa World*, May 16, 1991, p. A16, and May 22, 1991, p. A8; *Daily Oklahoman*, May 22, 1991, p. 20.

20. *Tulsa World*, May 28, 1991, p. C4.

21. Ibid. Rex Coffman, a small rancher near Vail, reiterated many of the points the ranchers in Cortez made to Synar but added that in his tourist-oriented area ranchers had to deal with bicyclists, backpackers, and hikers on public rangelands. Coffman predicted that if a rancher could not stay afloat, "he's going to sell to the sub-divider and there won't be any open space in these valleys." For a long story as to how the controversy played out in New Mexico, see the *Dallas Morning News*, June 23, 1991, p. A1. In New Mexico, opposition to the view of hostile ranchers surfaced with the appearance of the Public Lands Action Network, which was designed to organize opposition to public-land ranching.

22. *Daily Oklahoman*, June 25, 1992, p. 8, and June 26, 1991, p. 15; *Tulsa World*, June 25, 1991, p. 3A. The House approved a similar measure in 1990 by a vote of 251 to 155. Though the vote this time was lower, the 1991 measure attracted more public attention than in 1990. Aside from Synar, only one of the six-member Oklahoma delegation supported the bill.

23. *Daily Oklahoman*, June 24, 1991, p. 6, and June 25, 1991, p. 8.

24. *Congressional Record*, 102nd Cong., 1st sess., July 23, 1991. See H5703–5704 for the vote and H 5677–5703 for the extended debate. *Tulsa World*, July 24, 1991,

p. B2. Funding for the BLM since 1982 continued only because each annual appropriations bill was considered under a rule waiving the point of order that otherwise would be against this authorized spending.

25. *Tulsa World*, July 26, 1991, p. A12; *Daily Oklahoman*, July 27, 1991, p. 23.

26. *Tulsa World*, August 3, 1991.

27. Ibid. Other large-scale grazing operators mentioned by Synar and his cosponsors at one time or another included Texaco, Getty Oil, Zenchikur Livestock of Japan, leasing 41,000 acres, and one lessee in Nevada controlling grazing rights on 5.2 million acres, an area almost the size of Massachusetts. One rancher in Kansas paid the government $20,000 in grazing fees and then subleased his rights in Nevada for $120,000. These large-scale operations were cited by James J. Kilpatrick in his column (*Daily Oklahoman*, August 17, 1991, p. 10).

28. See *Tulsa World*, August 8, 1991, p. 15A, for an incisive story on shifting public-land policy. Indicative of the changing trend was a story by the conservative columnist James J. Kilpatrick entitled "No Welfare for Ranchers." Kilpatrick concluded that "unless these ranchers are to be viewed as objects of public welfare, it is hard to justify what clearly is a subsidy in some degree." For Kilpatrick's column, see *Tulsa World*, August 16, 1991, p. A8.

29. *Tulsa World*, September 18, 1991, p. 19A; ibid., September 19, 1991, p. 10B; ibid., September 27, 1991, p. 15A. Leading senators in opposition were Ohio Democrat Howard Metzenbaum and Vermont Republican James Jeffords. Incidentally, the conference committee left grazing fees unchanged, ensuring further debate in the next session of Congress.

30. *Rangeland Management: GAO Report to the Chairman Subcommittee on National Parks and Public Lands Committee on Interior and Insular Affairs*, House of Representatives, General Accounting Office, Washington, D.C., November 1991, pp. 2–5.

31. Ibid.

32. *Tulsa World*, November 16, 1991, p. C1; *Daily Oklahoman*, December 18, 1991, p. 34. See also the article by Tim Curran, "Once Again Synar Faces Stiff Primary Challenge," *Roll Call*, February 13, 1992, pp. 1–2.

33. *Tulsa World*, January 14, 1992, p. Al. This lengthy article examines the growing myth of the West, contrasting it with a declining cowboy lifestyle.

34. *Denver Post*, March 10, 1992, p. Al.

35. *Tulsa World*, April 26, 1992, p. A2.

36. *Tulsa World*, May 1, 1992, p. 15A; Grazing and Public Rangelands: Oversight Hearing before the Subcommittee on National Parks and Public Lands of the Committee on Interior and Insular Affairs, House of Representatives, 102nd Cong., 2nd sess., May 12, 1992. The story from the *New York Times* appears on page 13.

37. *Tulsa World*, May 20, 1992, p. 3A; ibid., June 16, 1992, p. 6A; *Daily Oklahoman*, June 16, 1992, p. 7.

38. *Tulsa World*, June 19, 1992, p. 11A. In another story (see p. 16A) on the same day, insurance companies, oil and utility companies, and others were listed as "corporate welfare cowboys utilizing 76 million acres, an acreage greater than the land areas of Oklahoma and Pennsylvania combined."

39. Bureau of Land Management Reauthorization: Hearing before the Subcommittee on Public Lands National Parks, and Forests of the Committee on Energy and Natural Resources, United States Senate, 100th Cong., 2nd sess., July 1, 1992, 257–58.

40. Ibid.

41. *Congressional Record*, 102nd Cong., 2nd sess., July 22, 1992, H6441–43; *Daily Oklahoman*, July 23, 1992, p. 14; *Congressional Quarterly*, August 1, 1992, 2266. Senator James M. Jeffords of Vermont led the fight to raise grazing fees, but the body shunned his effort. See also *Tulsa World*, September 24, 1992, p. 2A, and *Daily Oklahoman*, September 24, 1992, p. 15.

42. Grazing Management and Grazing Fee Issues: Hearing before the Subcommittee on Public Lands, National Parks, and Forests of the Committee on Energy and Natural Resources, United States Senate, 102nd Cong., 2nd sess. (Casper, Wyo.), September 3, 1992, 32–33.

43. *Tulsa World*, September 8, 1992, p. 2A, 5A, 2 stories; *Daily Oklahoman*, September 8, 1992, p. 7. The Day ranch area in Arizona and New Mexico, including federal land administered by the BLM, consisted of roughly 250 square miles, about 16 miles across and 15 miles long. About two thousand cows, their calves, a few bulls, and some horses grazed on these lands. See Sandra Day O'Connor and W. Alan Day, *Lazy B* (New York: Random House, 2002), p. 18. In addition to funds from ranchers seeking to oust Synar, Edmondson received funds from tobacco industry PACs and the National Rifle Association, all seeking Synar's defeat. In the September runoff, Synar received 53.1 percent (56,662) to Edmondson's 46.9 percent (50,084) of the vote. See also "Cattlemen Try Ballot Box," *National Journal*, October 3, 1992, 2261–62.

44. *Tulsa World*, November 13, 1992, p.15A; *Daily Oklahoman*, November 13, 1992, p. 22.

45. *Congressional Record*, 103rd Cong., 1st sess.; January 26, 1993, Extension of Remarks, E176–77. Synar introduced this bill with Ralph Regula, Republican from Ohio. Synar was also concerned about the federal government failing to obtain fair market value for taxpayer-owned assets: timber sales, oil and gas royalties, below-cost contracts for recreation, and other federal fees, He cosponsored a bill to mandate that the federal government operate under sound business practices. See *Congressional Record*, 103rd Cong., 1st sess., February 2, 1993, E218.

46. *Roll Call*, February 4, 1993, p. 9; *Daily Oklahoman*, March 5, 1993, p. 19; *Tulsa World*, March 6, 1993, p. 7A.

47. *National Journal*, April 3, 1993, 832; *Washington Post*, April 7, 1993, p. A25.

48. Tulsa World, April 8, 1993, p. B10; *Daily Oklahoman* April 10, 1993, p. 12 (editorial critical of Synar as a liberal wheeler-dealer).

49. Grazing Management Reform: Hearing before the Subcommittee on National Parks, Forests, and Public Lands of the Committee on Natural Resources, House of Representatives, 103d Cong., 1st sess., April 20, 1983, 26–33. Synar's written statement appears on pages 28–33. See also *Tulsa World*, April 21, 1993, p. A6.

50. *Daily Oklahoman* (1 May 1993), p. 27; article, "Home on the Range, At What Cost?," by Synar in *Roll Call* for May 3, 1993. In this article Synar expanded his approach to include all resource industries benefiting from low fees for the use of public lands.

51. See *National Journal*, May 22, 1993, 1232–35, for a detailed discussion of these turf wars.

52. *Daily Oklahoman*, July 15, 1993, p. 17.

53. Ibid.; *Public Papers of the Presidents: William J. Clinton, 1993* (Washington, D.C.: GPO, 1994), Book 1: 1231 (part of a July 29, 1993, interview with the Nevada media).

54. *Congressional Quarterly*, August 7, 1993, 2150–51 (article on public lands by Catalina Camia.)

55. *Daily Oklahoman*, August 10, 1993, p. 13.

56. *Tulsa World*, August 10, 1993, p. B6. For a concise summary of the controversy at this critical juncture, see *Congressional Quarterly*, September 4, 1993, 2316.

57. *Congressional Quarterly*, September 18, 1993, 2449–50, and September 25, 1993, 2546 (articles on appropriations by Catalina Camia); *Daily Oklahoman*, September 22, 1993, p. 6.

58. *Congressional Record*, 103rd Cong., 1st sess., September 29, 1993, H7193 for Synar's remarks and H7196 for the vote; *Tulsa World*, September 30, 1993, p. B6.

59. *Tulsa World*, October 5, 1993, p. N14; *Congressional Quarterly*, October 9, 1993, 2723–24 (article on appropriations by Catalina Camia).

60. *Tulsa World*, October 15, 1993, p. N11; *Congressional Quarterly*, October 16, 1993, 2802–2803 (article on appropriations by Catalina Camia).

61. *Congressional Record*, 103rd Cong., 1st sess., October 20, 1993, H8293–94. It was Senator Harry Reid of Nevada who played the high-profile side in mediating an end to the bitter annual fights over grazing fees and in doing so incurred the wrath of his western Republican colleagues.

62. Ibid.

63. *Congressional Quarterly*, October 30, 1993, 2957–58 (article on appropriations by Catalina Camia). See also Margaret Kriz, "Quick Draw," *National Journal*, November 13, 1993, 2711–16, examining Bruce Babbitt's efforts at public-land reform.

64. *Daily Oklahoman*, November 28, 1993, p. 1; ibid., November 29, 1993, p. 1.

65. *Tulsa World*, November 28, 1993, p. N4.

66. "New Grazing Plan Is Announced," *Associated Press News Service* (March 7, 1994), *Congressional Quarterly* (19 March 1994), 670.

67. See the *Federal Register* (25 March 1994), p. 14314, for reform proposal. See also the remarks of President Clinton in *Public Papers of the Presidents: William J. Clinton, 1994*, Book 1: 496–97.

68. See story, "Beyond Grazing Reform," by Bruce Babbitt in *Roll Call*, April 11, 1994. See too *Rangeland Reform '94. A Proposal to Improve Management of Rangeland Ecosystems and the Administration of Livestock Grazing on Public Lands.* USDI/BLM in cooperation with USDA/ FS, August 1993.

69. Grazing: Hearings Before the Committee on Energy and Natural Resources, United States Senate, 103rd Cong., 2nd sess., Washington, D.C., April 20, 1994, and Albuquerque, N.Mex., May 14, 1994.

70. *Denver Post*, June 2, 1994, p, B1; *Associated Press News Service*, "Rangeland Reforms under Fire," June 6, 1994.

71. *Congressional Record*, 103rd Cong., 2nd sess., July12, 1994, H5492; see H5495–96 for the vote. One of the permit holders was the Anheuser-Busch Corporation.

72. Robert Bennett, "The Effects of Rangeland Reform '94," *Roll Call*, July 25, 1994. Senator Bennett reviewed the field hearing in Utah.

73. George Miller, "The Grazing Fees Gravy Train," *Roll Call*, July 25, 1994. Representative Miller's article succinctly summarizes views Synar had been expounding for more than a decade.

74. *National Journal*, September 10, 1994, 2094; *Tulsa World*, September 12, 1994, p. N8; ibid., September 25, 1999; ibid., September 28, 1994, p. N13. *Tulsa World* endorsed Synar for reelection. For an appreciation of Synar's service, see the column by David Broder in the *Washington Post*, September 25, 1994, p. C7.

75. *Tulsa World*, October 7, 1994, p. N9; *Daily Oklahoman*, October 7, 1994, p. 20.

76. Margaret Kriz, "Shoot-out in the West," *National Journal*, October 15, 1994, 2388–92; *Public Papers of the Presidents: William J. Clinton, 1995*, Book 1 (May 31, 1995): 776. The president was responding to questions posed by Jim Gransberry of the *Billings Gazette* in Billings, Montana.

77. *Washington Post*, July 20, 1995, p. A25.

78. *New York Times*, July 21, 1995, p. 1 (article by Timothy Egan); *Washington Post*, July 28, 1995, p. A18; *Congressional Quarterly*, August 5, 1995, 2363; ibid., September 16, 1995, 2799; ibid., September 23, 1995, 2884; ibid., January 6, 1996, 37.

79. For general discussions of the ongoing grazing controversy, see Allan Freedman, "Clash of Interests and Ideology Threatens Grazing Overhaul," *Congressional Quarterly*, March 4, 1996, 609–12, and Allan Freedman, "Short Term Victory in Senate May Not Save Grazing Bill," *Congressional Quarterly*, March

1996, 793. See also *Congress and the Nation, 1993–1996*, vol. 9, pp. 455–56 (for 1996), and vol. 10, p. 357 (for 1997); Betsy A. Cody, "Grazing Fees: An Overview," *Congressional Research Service Report for Congress*, May 21, 1996.

80. *Public Lands Council et al. v. Babbitt, Secretary of the Interior et al.*, 529 U.S. 728 (2000). For the concurring opinion, see pp. 750–52.

81. For an indication of a developing new War in the West, see Robyn Morrison, "Land Plan Attracts an Anti-Grazing Gorilla," *High Country News*, August 5, 2002, 5, and the letters in the January 20, 2003, issue of the same journal (p. 6).

Index

CPSIA information can be obtained
at www.ICGtesting.com
Printed in the USA
FSOW01n0057190216
17108FS

9 780806 149103